WE HAVE A RELIGION

D1520533

Published in Association with The William P. Clements Center

for Southwest Studies, Southern Methodist University,

by The University of North Carolina Press, Chapel Hill

WE HAVE A RELIGION

❖

The 1920s Pueblo Indian Dance Controversy
and American Religious Freedom

TISA WENGER

© 2009 The University
of North Carolina Press
All rights reserved

Designed by Rebecca Evans
Set in Whitman with Seria
Sans and AT Sackers Gothic
by Keystone Typesetting, Inc.
Manufactured in the
United States of America

The paper in this book
meets the guidelines for
permanence and durability
of the Committee on
Production Guidelines
for Book Longevity of the
Council on Library Resources.

The University of North
Carolina Press has been a
member of the Green Press
Initiative since 2003.

Library of Congress Cataloging-in-Publication Data
Wenger, Tisa Joy, 1969–
We have a religion : the 1920s Pueblo Indian dance
controversy and American religious freedom / Tisa
Wenger.
p. cm.
Includes bibliographical references and index.
ISBN 978-0-8078-3262-2 (cloth : alk. paper)
ISBN 978-0-8078-5935-3 (pbk. : alk. paper)
1. Pueblo dance. 2. Pueblo Indians—Religion.
3. Pueblo Indians—Rites and ceremonies.
4. Christianity and culture—Southwest, New.
5. Christianity and other religions—Southwest,
New. 6. Racism—Religious aspects—Christianity.
7. Religious tolerance—Southwest, New. I. Title.
E99.P6W45 2009
299.7′84038—dc22   2008040651

cloth   13 12 11 10 09   5 4 3 2 1
paper   13 12 11 10 09   5 4 3 2 1

For my husband, Rod
and our children, Jordan, Sophia, and Dylan

What an irony! Because the American Indian has so much religion, most white missionaries and our white man's government think he has no religion at all.
JOHN COLLIER 1926

Religion, as it has been and is still practiced today on the reservation, permeates all aspects of tribal society. The language makes no distinction between religion, government, or law. Tribal customs and religious ordinances are synonymous. All aspects of life are tied in to one totality.
CHIEF OREN LYONS Onondaga Nation, 1979

Clearly delineated religions do not have these characteristics by "nature" but acquire [them] as the result of fierce historical struggle, in the course of which they suffer amputations and are forced to withdraw from their involvement in many other areas of culture.
BRUCE LINCOLN 2003

CONTENTS

ILLUSTRATIONS

PREFACE

For Native Americans, religious freedom has been an elusive goal. From the federal government's nineteenth-century bans on indigenous ceremonial practices to twenty-first century legal battles over Indian sacred lands, the United States has often acted as if the indigenous traditions of the continent were somehow not truly religious, not eligible for the constitutional protections of the First Amendment. Through the story of a public controversy over Pueblo Indian dances in the 1920s, this book shows how some Native Americans first began to make use of the legal argument for religious freedom and so to challenge dominant cultural conceptions about what counted as religion. For the first time, a critical mass of non-Indian reformers joined Native American leaders in their defense. Together they insisted that Indian dances were authentically religious and therefore could not legally be suppressed. By the end of the controversy, the virtual Christian establishment that had long dominated Indian affairs lost ground to these new reformers, who saw positive value in Indian traditions and worked to reorient federal Indian policy on more secular and scientific grounds. Although Native Americans continued to struggle for religious freedom in other respects, the federal government could never again take for granted its right to suppress ceremonies now seen by many Americans not as "savagery" but as a legitimate expression of Native religion.

The apparently secular foundations of the new Indian policy, however, continued to perpetuate Euro-American cultural forms and institutions. The very concept of "religion"—as something separable from other culturally designated spheres such as law, politics, art, and nature—grew out of particular European histories of internal conflict and colonial encounter and had no equivalent in Native American languages. As filtered through the Enlightenment and enshrined in the U.S. Constitution, the dominant society understood religion as a matter of individual conscience and belief. These priorities were quite different from the indigenous focus on communal responsibility for maintaining the balance of the earth. Identifying Pueblo ceremonies as "religion" rather than as a matter of community obligation opened the door for progressive tribal members, some of whom had come to see indigenous traditions as inconsistent with both civilization and Christianity, to demand the liberty not to participate. In the name of democracy and progress, government agents, missionaries, and most non-Indian reformers supported these progressives against traditional tribal leaders who wanted to maintain the communal quality of the ceremonies. For better or for worse, adopting the concept of religion forced subtle changes in Pueblo norms of ceremonial participation and began to conceptually separate the newly labeled "religion" from other aspects of Pueblo life.

Beyond the dance controversy, the final chapter of this book offers a brief survey of the implications of "religion" and related concepts for Indian religious freedom struggles into the twenty-first century. The process of cultural redefinition continues as Native Americans defend the places they call sacred, geographical sites that are central to tribal histories and traditions. The term "sacred" has its own genealogies in Euro-American intellectual and cultural history, where it implies a contrast with those things marked as "profane"—a conceptual dualism largely incompatible with the relationality of indigenous traditions. As in the Pueblo dance controversy, the adoption or imposition of such cultural categories may subtly change Indian ways of viewing their own traditions. Native Americans, however, do not simply accept these concepts as given but actively redefine them in day-to-day use. In the larger culture, Indian demands for religious freedom continue to challenge the limits of dominant notions about what counts as "religion" in American public discourse.

As a non-Indian historian of American religions, I began my research focused not on Pueblo Indian religious history as such, or even on Indian religious freedom more broadly, but with questions about the historical development and political consequences of "religion" as a cultural category. Writing this book has given me a deep appreciation of the immense challenges Native Americans have faced to maintain and regain their land rights, tribal sovereignty, and traditions; and of their resilience in facing what has often amounted to cultural if not physical genocide. I have also come to respect the importance to many indigenous people, particularly the Pueblos, of maintaining traditional standards of secrecy in religious and ceremonial matters—standards that in Pueblo experience have been crucial for maintaining tribal integrity and cultural survival. For these reasons, the book offers only minimal description of Pueblo ceremonies and religious traditions, topics that in any case are tangential to the primary concerns of the book. By documenting the Pueblos' resourcefulness in defending their ceremonies, it is my hope that this book will make some small contribution to ongoing Native American struggles for self-determination. At the very least, I will donate any royalties from this book to the Indian Law Resource Center (http://www.indianlaw.org/main), an organization that provides legal assistance to Indian nations for the protection of indigenous lands, resources, human rights, environment, and cultural heritage.

ACKNOWLEDGMENTS

This book could never have been completed without the assistance of the mentors, colleagues, and friends who have so generously supported my research and writing along the way. Ann Taves first inspired my interest in American religious history, provided critical feedback and encouragement on an early version of this manuscript, and has continued to serve as a mentor and inspiration for all my work. At Princeton University I benefited from the warm and collegial environment of the Department of Religion, where Leigh Eric Schmidt taught me how to be a historian of American religion and has continued to be an exceptional mentor ever since. Along with him, Albert J. Raboteau, Robert Wuthnow, Jeffrey Stout, David Carrasco, and R. Marie Griffith offered invaluable advice and support in the early stages of this project. Tom Bremer, Wendy Cadge, Leslie Callahan, and Jenny Wiley Legath have given me the gift of their friendship and encouragement as well as critical readings of this work at various stages in its development. Thanks also to Patricia Bogdziewicz, Lorraine Fuhrman, and Anita Kline, who smoothed the way for all my work at Princeton. Princeton's Center for the Study of Religion provided financial support along with the opportunity to discuss my research. I am indebted to the participants in CSR's Religion and Culture Workshop in 2001–2 and 2003–4 for their advice and support.

Friends and colleagues from around the country have helped me develop my thinking for this book. I will be forever grateful to the incomparable Katie Lofton, who offered incisive critiques on every chapter as I wrote and did more than anyone to bolster my spirits when I was most discouraged. I benefited immensely from the opportunity to present my research at annual meetings of the American Academy of Religion, the American Society of Church History, the Berkshire Women's History Conference, the Organization of American Historians, and the Society for the Anthropology of Religion. For their counsel at these and other forums I especially wish to thank David Daily, Pamela Klassen, Joel Martin, Michael McNally, L. G. Moses, and Inés Talamantez. As reviewers for the University of North Carolina

Press, Joel Martin and Eric Michael Mazur (both of whom were kind enough to reveal their identities to me) read two versions of this manuscript and each time provided incisive critiques and useful advice for revision.

Southern Methodist University's Clements Center for Southwest Studies granted me the luxury of a year to write through support of the Bill and Rita Clements Fellowship. There I found a warm community of scholars who helped orient me to the fields of western history and Native American studies. Thanks are due especially to Andrea Boardman, Flannery Burke, Ben Johnson, Alexis McCrossen, Michelle Nickerson, Colleen O'Neill, Sherry Smith, and David Weber. The Clements Center also provided a subvention to aid with the publication of this book, and facilitated a full-day workshop where Jill Sweet, Ann Taves, and L. G. Moses joined the Clements Center community to provide me with invaluable feedback on my manuscript.

I have been fortunate enough to spend the past four years on the faculty of the Department of Religious Studies at Arizona State University, where this book has finally taken shape. As department chair, Joel Gereboff made sure I had the time needed to finish the manuscript and gave of his own time to read and comment on several chapters. Linell Cady, Tracy Fessenden, Moses Moore, Ken Morrison, Tod Swanson, and Shahla Talebi have all offered me invaluable suggestions and helped create a collegial environment in which to work. Special thanks are due to Ken Morrison and Shahla Talebi for their constructive feedback on several chapters of the manuscript. Beyond the department, Karen Leong, Myla Vicenti-Carpio, Ayanna Thompson, and other members of the Racial Formations Reading Group gave me critical comments on two chapters and offered their support when I needed it the most. Meanwhile, Linda Wood read each chapter as I wrote and helped me develop my arguments along the way.

Thanks are also due to the Pueblo Indian scholars and leaders who supported my work, especially historian Joe Sando at the Pueblo Indian Cultural Center Archives in Albuquerque, who offered necessary criticisms and helped me correct interpretive mistakes at several stages in my writing. My visits to Zuni Pueblo, Taos Pueblo, San Juan Pueblo, and Acoma Pueblo gave me some exposure to and appreciation for the ceremonial traditions and the resilience of the Pueblo Indian people. I am deeply grateful to San Ildefonso Pueblo and Tesuque Pueblo for their permission to reprint photographs of their public dances taken in the early twentieth century. I thank them for their generosity and hope that they will find some value in my analysis of Pueblo Indian history and Native American struggles for religious freedom.

This book would not have been possible without help from librarians and archivists around the country. In Albuquerque, University of New Mexico librarians Mary Alice Tsosie and Nancy Brown-Martinez provided crucial reference assistance. In Santa Fe, thanks are due to Tomas Jaehn at the Fray Angelico Chavez Library, Diane Bird at the Laboratory of Anthropology, Marina Ochoa at the Archdiocese of Santa Fe, Lee Goodwin at the School of American Research, and the librarians at the New Mexico State Records Center and Archives. I thank archivist Mark Thiel at the University of Marquette for locating and sending the microfilm reels I needed from the records of the Bureau of Catholic Indian Missions. Librarians and archivists at the National Archives and Records Center in Washington, D.C., and Denver, Colorado; Yale University's Beinecke Library; the Historical Society of Pennsylvania; the American Philosophical Society; and the Presbyterian Historical Society also helped find what I needed in their collections. At Princeton University, Western Americana curator Alfred Bush and the staff of the Rare Books and Special Collections Department helped me locate numerous resources in the early stages of my research, and the interlibrary loan staff at Princeton University and Arizona State University worked hard to fulfill my endless requests.

Elaine Maisner, my editor at the University of North Carolina Press, deserves substantial credit for helping me frame and reshape this book; her critical acumen and faith in my project helped me rethink and reorganize the manuscript at a time I might otherwise have abandoned it. I could not have had a better editor, and I thank her along with Ron Maner and the rest of the editorial staff at the press. Funding for my research came along the way from the Center for the Study of Religion at Princeton University, the Princeton University Graduate School, the Clements Center for Southwest Studies at Southern Methodist University, and a Summer Stipend through the "We the People" Initiative of the National Endowment for the Humanities.

This book includes adapted material from three of my previously published essays: "Land, Culture, and Sovereignty in the Pueblo Dance Controversy," *Journal of the Southwest* 46, no. 2 (Summer 2004): 381–412; " 'We Are Guaranteed Freedom': Pueblo Indians and the Category of Religion in the 1920s," *History of Religions* 45, no. 2 (November 2005): 89–113; and "Modernists, Pueblo Indians, and the Politics of Primitivism," in *Race, Religion, Region: Landscapes of Encounter in the American West*, edited by Fay Botham and Sara M. Patterson (Tucson: University of Arizona Press, 2006), 101–14 (© 2006 The Arizona Board of Regents. Reprinted by permission of the University of Arizona Press). Thanks to the *Journal of the Southwest* and the University of Arizona Press for their permission to adapt my essays for this book and to the University of Chicago Press for an editorial policy that makes such permission unnecessary.

None of my work would be possible without my family. My parents, Harold and Christine Wenger, first inspired my interest in scholarship and in religion, and they remain among my best role models for my life and work. Thanks especially to Mom for all the help with proofreading. My brother Aaron Wenger took the time to read the entire manuscript, providing invaluable fresh perspective when I thought I had nearly finished writing. Harold and Mary Ellen Groff have welcomed me into their family, providing a second home where I have enjoyed needed breaks from my academic life over the past twelve years. Finally, I dedicate this book to my beloved husband and our three children. Rod Groff has been my best friend and my strongest supporter, making work possible and life pleasurable during all our years together. Our son Jordan, daughter Sophia, and son Dylan— born respectively at the beginning, middle, and end of my work on this book—have contributed new joy and meaning to our lives, and made it all worthwhile.

WE HAVE A RELIGION

"When the slanting rays of the sun play their last game of light and shade over the irregular pile of adobe rooms of the pueblo, Indian men, one hundred or more, come in long lines from their estufas. One group crosses the old bridge of squared logs down near the high yellow cottonwoods, hinting at the Midas wealth of Glorieta cañon just beyond. On they come to the beat of the drum and form in double lines in front of the church door. In their hands the dancers hold branches of green and yellow signifying the full season of growth as well as their thanks to the deity who made possible the harvest—the Sun, their visible God." Taos Pueblo, the northernmost of nineteen Pueblo Indian communities in New Mexico, celebrates its annual feast day every September in honor of patron San Geronimo. Artist and writer Blanche Grant, who wrote this admiring description of San Geronimo's Day in her 1925 book *Taos Today*, offered little hint of the intense controversy that had recently surrounded the Pueblo Indian dances. Instead she celebrated the ceremony as a powerful demonstration of human unity in religion. "The stranger who watches this age-old prayer without words," she wrote, "must be callous indeed if he does not join in thanksgiving, no matter what his conception of God may be. Hard lines of belief are swept away in a consciousness of a great unity, after all, in what one terms—religion." For Grant, Pueblo ceremonialism was not only legitimately religious but epitomized the "primitive" essence of religion.[1]

Like many of the artists and writers who had settled in Santa Fe and Taos after the turn of the century, Grant considered the Pueblo dances a picturesque blend of "primitive" religion and Catholic ritualism. This combination was evident in her description of the Catholic mass and procession held in celebration of San Geronimo's Day. "To the tolling of a bell a procession moves from the church to a high leafy outdoor shrine," she wrote, "where is placed an image of San Geronimo, the patron saint of the day with its white canopy folded near. . . . In a flash, one is back in the days of the Spaniard with his sword and the friar with his beads." Next came the annual relay race pitting the fastest runners from Taos's north and south sides—a ceremonial as well as physical division—in competition to honor the saint. "Below in front of the ladder which leads to the shrine, drums sound again and aspen branches rustle gently while runners form a semi-circle quite in the manner of those days of the friars," she wrote. "Yucca is tied to the ankles and feathers stick in the hair—feathers for speed. . . . Back and forth go the relay racers until finally the north or the south pueblo has won. Then in two long lines the Indians face each other and slowly step their way to the beat of the drums toward the eastern gateway in the old crumbling wall where the lines separate and the men make for their respective kivas." She offered equally romantic views of many other important ceremonies observed through-out the year at Taos Pueblo, including the Christmas Eve procession and Matachines dance, the deer and buffalo dances held on New Year's Day and King's Day (the Feast of the Epiphany on January 6), and the series of summertime corn dances.[2]

In contrast, Grant's description of the pueblo's summer ceremony at Blue Lake, high above Taos in the Sangre de Cristo Mountains, left a strikingly negative impression. This important ceremony was and continues to be closed to all but tribal members. In the early twentieth century, many neigh-boring whites assumed that such a secretive event must conceal something shocking, and they had long circulated rumors that it featured such outrages as "sex orgies," "cannibalism," and "the giving up of maids to sensual sacri-fices." Even the photographer Edward Curtis, then a well-respected authority on all things Indian, suggested that the Taos Indians practiced human sacri-fice at Blue Lake.[3] Grant's own allegations expressed primary concern for the rights of Indian women and girls, an issue that helped mobilize sentiment against Indian dances among many female reformers in the period. Claim-ing that "girls and childless women" were "forced to go to the mountain" for unspecified atrocities "imposed upon them by the older men," she con-cluded that this was "the one ceremony to which the so-called reformers have a right to object." Unlike many of those who believed Indian cere-monies immoral, Grant argued that even in this case "the white man" should not presume to interfere with Indian practices. Still, she was confident that the boys and girls of Taos's younger generation, who had more exposure than their predecessors to "the white man's world," would soon "demand justice" and "abolish the custom." These reservations echoed many reformers' con-cerns about the "secret" dances of the Pueblo Indians in general.[4]

Such allegations were completely unfounded. There is no evidence of sexual or coercive features in the Blue Lake ceremony, and anthropologist John Bodine has refuted Grant's charges by pointing out among other things that "sexual continence is the unstated rule" during all important Pueblo religious events. For Taos Indians, the secrecy surrounding Blue Lake did not imply anything sinister but was necessary to protect the integrity of the ceremony performed there. Like many Native Americans, Pueblo people traditionally consider certain ceremonial knowledge too sacred and powerful to be shared beyond the specialized religious societies that rightfully possess it. For this reason Taos has never permitted outsiders to attend the Blue Lake ceremony, and only initiated tribal members know the full details of this event.[5] However, the people of Taos have never been reticent to discuss the general significance of the lake or of the ceremony performed there. Blue Lake is the source of the stream that runs through and sustains the life of the pueblo, and in Taos tradition the Mothers and Fathers—the *kachinas* (ancestral spirits) who bring rain and other blessings—are said to live under this lake in a subaqueous *kiva* (ceremonial chamber). "All life comes from the mountain," as an elderly Taos man told one visitor in 1924. The rites at Blue Lake conclude the process of initiating novices into Taos's various kiva societies, an intensive training that, depending on the society, takes six, twelve, or eighteen months. The ceremony is therefore essential for the transmission of tribal tradition to each successive generation. The suspicions against such ceremonies had more to do with reformers' own cultural preoccupations than with the Pueblo ceremonies themselves. In this case, rumors about what went on at Blue Lake may have helped to justify President Theodore Roosevelt's decision to strip the lake and its environs from Taos and add it to the National Forest Reserve—an action that the tribe continued to fight until Congress finally returned the area to them in 1970.[6]

By the time Grant wrote *Taos Today*, the merits and the future of the Taos and other Pueblo Indian ceremonies had become the focus of intense controversy. In the immediate sense, the Pueblo dance controversy of the mid-1920s is a story about reformers and government officials, most of whom had the best of intentions, who battled over federal Indian policy with often tragic results. And it is the story of the Pueblo Indians' struggle for tribal sovereignty, land rights, and the freedom to practice indigenous ceremonies —a struggle against deliberate exploitation, against the indifference of a nation preoccupied with economic expansion, and most directly against government agencies and reformers convinced that Indians must abandon tribal and "pagan" traditions in order to succeed in the modern world.

This book takes a close look at the public controversy over the Pueblo Indian dances in order to illuminate a much larger story about the dilemmas Native Americans face in their quest for religious freedom. The controversy allows us to see how concepts of "religion" and "religious freedom" are defined and understood in American culture and the implications of these concepts for federal Indian policy and for Native American life.

The boundaries of what counts as "religion" are always contested and always changing. In the United States, that designation is generally desirable because it affords constitutional protection. In the dance controversy, Pueblo tribal leaders and allied reformers fought government restrictions on Indian ceremonies by insisting, against the preconceived notions of their opponents, that the Pueblo dances were authentically religious and must therefore be granted religious freedom. Despite mainstream America's tendency to associate dancing with sexuality and with secular entertainment, they made the case for the religious legitimacy of Indian ceremonies by identifying them with Christian practices of prayer and worship. The artists, writers, and anthropologists who supported the Pueblo Indians employed often patronizing concepts of "primitive religion" that sometimes contributed to the barriers facing the Indians' quest for tribal sovereignty. In the long run, though, their mutual success at identifying the ceremonies as "religion" helped end Christianity's monopoly on American conceptions of legitimate religion. If Indians already had their own religion, the government could not easily justify direct efforts to suppress its ceremonies.

The dance controversy, and the new views of religion it introduced, facilitated a major transition in the history of federal Indian policy. A virtual Christian establishment, composed of missionaries and reformers who considered Christian missions and the elimination of "paganism" integral to the goal of "civilizing" and "assimilating" the Indians, had long dominated decision making in Indian affairs. After the controversy, aided by their expanded definitions of "religion," cultural modernists would unseat the Christian establishment as the dominant voices in this arena—part of a much broader "secular revolution" waged by American intellectuals who sought to replace religious with secular authority in the major institutions of American public life.[7] The balance of power changed most definitively in 1933, when President Franklin Delano Roosevelt appointed John Collier to shape his administration's "New Deal for the Indians." Collier had begun working to reform federal Indian policy in the 1920s, when he joined in the fight for Pueblo land rights and religious freedom. One of his first acts as commissioner of Indian affairs was to retract policies restricting Indian religious life, which he replaced with new directives giving indigenous religious leaders equal standing with Protestant and Catholic missionaries on the reservations and in Indian schools. Although his policies did not give Indians equal decision-making powers and were not always successful even on their own terms, they were at least an attempt to support the continuing practice of Native American religious and cultural traditions.[8]

At another level, this book examines the practical consequences within indigenous communities of adopting and adapting the concept of "religion." Understood as a set of beliefs, practices, and institutions that can be separated from other spheres of life and compared with other distinct religions around the world, "religion" is a product of European cultural and colonial history that has no direct translation in Native American languages or other non-European tongues around the world.[9] Pueblo Indians began to use the Spanish word *religión* to refer to the Catholicism that most of them adopted under Spanish rule in the seventeenth and eighteenth centuries, speaking of their indigenous ceremonial traditions simply as *costumbres* (customs). This terminology did not change after Mexican independence in 1821, when the Territory of New Mexico became part of the United States at the close of the Mexican-American War in 1848, or when U.S. government officials and Protestant missionaries began their work among the Pueblos in the late nineteenth century. The same was true throughout Latin America, where indigenous people today continue to use *costumbre* for indigenous traditions and to reserve *religión* for Christianity. As with the early twentieth-century Pueblos, contemporary conflicts over "religion" in Latin America are therefore framed as disputes between Catholics and Protestants (whose numbers are growing rapidly in much of the region), even when indigenous practices are the primary issue.[10]

This book demonstrates that many Pueblo leaders began to regularly apply "religion" to their indigenous ceremonies as a result of the dance controversy—a redefinition that proved advantageous in the fight against government suppression but hard to reconcile with older cultural norms. Pueblo Indians had long understood their tribal ceremonies as a kind of community work, in the same category as maintaining the irrigation ditches and cleaning the public spaces—all of which provide mutual benefits and must therefore be shared in one way or another by all members of the tribe. This understanding of ceremonial participation clashed with Euro-American ideas of "religion" as a distinct sphere of life and with the Enlightenment ideal of a free individual conscience that had shaped the U.S. Constitution's provisions on religion. For this reason, Pueblo leaders who defended the ceremonies on religious freedom grounds opened the door for self-identified "progressives" among their people, some of whom had come to see these practices as inconsistent with tribal "progress" and with Christianity, to protest the tribe's expectation that they participate as a violation of their own individual religious liberties. The dance controversy ended with a compromise that promised religious freedom for both tribes and individuals: as long as Pueblo leaders agreed that they would not force anyone to dance, the Bureau of Indian Affairs (BIA) promised not to interfere with their ceremonies. This resolution certainly did not destroy the traditional norms of ceremonial participation, which remain operative in Pueblo life today. At least in public debate, though, the redefinition of the ceremonies as "religion" subtly undermined the communal and holistic ideals of that tradition. My point is not to argue that this was a wholly positive or negative development—surely it had its pros and cons—but simply to point out that it resulted from a discursive and conceptual shift. Language shapes perception, and a tribal requirement that seemed matter-of-fact as long as the ceremonies were understood in terms of community work became a violation of individual conscience when they were redefined as "religion."[11]

Another limitation of the Native American adoption of "religion" is that, while it provided a measure of protection for tribal dances, Indians have rarely been able to use it successfully to defend other aspects of indigenous tradition. As we will see, Pueblo efforts to protect tribal systems of governance as part of their religion clashed with the dominant culture's ideal of a clear separation between the spheres of religion and politics. Even though BIA officials actively endorsed and often worked closely with Christian missionaries, they criticized the Pueblos' traditional integration of "religion" and "government" as a contradiction of constitutional provisions against "religious establishment." Similarly, despite the final success of Taos's quest for Blue Lake, Indian efforts to regain or at least protect sacred lands have most often failed whether they have focused on religious freedom or on the historical violation of treaty guarantees. It has proved difficult to fit Indian ways of relating to the land within America's predominantly Christian assumptions about what counts as religion. Perhaps more important, collective land claims have often clashed with other (and, it seems, more treasured) mainstream American values such as private property and economic development. Separated and abstracted from other spheres of life, "religion" becomes the picturesque repository of tradition and sentiment, made irrelevant to what appear to be the more real-world concerns of land and government.

The Pueblo dance controversy began in reaction to two directives sent by Commissioner of Indian Affairs Charles Burke to his agents on Indian reservations around the country. "Circular No. 1665: Indian Dancing," written in 1921 in response to missionary complaints about alleged "immoralities" in the dances of the Hopi Indians in Arizona and the Pueblos in New Mexico, instructed BIA agents to use "educational processes" or, if necessary, "punitive measures" to stop dances that they judged to be "degrading." Two years later, following a set of recommendations from Protestant missionaries in South Dakota, the commissioner issued "Supplement to Circular 1665" to advise agents that—while taking local circumstances into account—they should consider measures such as forbidding some ceremonies outright, restricting the rest to once a month during daytime hours, and banning Indians younger than fifty from participating in any dances at all. The ensuing controversy focused on the Pueblos largely because they had become favorite subjects for so many artists and anthropologists, who had only just become active in the politics of Indian affairs. These new reformers, along with Pueblo Indian leaders themselves, attacked Burke's policies as a violation of religious liberty. Arrayed against them were a coalition of Christian reformers and missionary leaders, who dismissed the religious freedom argument as a cloak for immoral "pagan rites" that merited prosecution rather than protection. Although most government officials accepted assimilationist principles, they found themselves caught between competing political pressures and tried to appease both sides. Commissioner Burke backed down from the dance circular and supported the religious freedom compromise not because his personal views had changed but because the Pueblos and their advocates were able to force his hand.[12]

An embattled missionary establishment fighting to maintain its influence in Indian affairs led the push to enforce the dance circular. In the 1880s predominantly Protestant leaders, determined to "save" the Indians by "civilizing" them, forged a consensus program aimed at gradually assimilating Native Americans into mainstream American culture. Government officials and reformers alike believed Protestant missions vital to that goal, and by the turn of the century the Catholic Church—with a long history and strong missionary presence among many Indian tribes—had the political influence to insist that its missions be given equal standing in that effort. By 1920 this consensus had shattered. Critics on all sides pointed to the evident failures of the assimilationist program: despite missions, boarding schools, reservation day schools, and the various civilizing efforts of the typical BIA agency, the vast majority of Indians had simply refused to abandon their indigenous traditions. On one side, radical assimilationists accused the BIA and the reservation system of actually perpetuating tribal traditions and identities and argued that these must be abolished if the Indians were ever to assimilate. On the other, a growing number of policy makers influenced by scientific racism believed Indians incapable (either permanently or for many generations) of becoming truly civilized and insisted that assimilationist ambitions should be abandoned in favor of less expensive programs that would equip Indians for manual labor as part of America's (racialized) underclass. It was to refute these critics and defend the assimilationist program that Protestant and Catholic missionary leaders diagnosed a resurgence of "paganism" among power-hungry tribal leaders, encouraged by deluded "sentimentalists," who prevented educated young Indians from sticking with "civilized" ways.

Their primary opponents in the dance controversy were neither radical assimilationists nor scientific racists but a new group of reformers who were just emerging as an identifiable voice within the politics of Indian affairs. I identify this group as cultural modernists because so many of them were part of the varied modernist movements in early twentieth-century art, literature, and anthropology.[13] By the turn of the century artists and anthropologists seeking "primitives" untouched by "modern civilization" had discovered the Pueblo Indians, whose adobe towns and colorful ceremonial dances made them seem somehow more authentic than other Indians, apparently less affected by the centuries of Spanish and Anglo-American rule. Their defense of the Pueblo ceremonies as "religion" participated in the tendency among many intellectuals of the time to represent those labeled primitive as intrinsically communal, spiritually authentic, and holistic—in contrast to a "modern civilization" condemned as individualistic, spiritually sterile, and fragmented. In this way, primitivism provided more or less of a challenge to late Victorian certainties about the steady march of progress and the superiority of Christianity and European culture. In the context of federal Indian policy, the modernist fight against Burke's dance circular inaugurated an anti-assimilationist campaign that became a serious threat to what had already become a fragile missionary establishment.[14]

For Native Americans, modernist celebrations of the primitive were a double-edged sword. Primitivism tends to identify those designated "primitive" as unchanging and ahistorical, and their traditions as essentially incompatible with modern life. Like colonial subjects in the rest of the world, Native Americans were expected to remain perpetual primitives, a sort of living demonstration of human history and a source of inspiration for modern artists. Modernist images of the Pueblos were strikingly similar to Orientalist formulations of the supposedly mysterious and mystical East, which as postcolonial critics have revealed were deeply implicated in the unjust power relations of the colonial order. Too often, modernists minimized the reality of historical change in Indian life and denied the Pueblos' abilities to manage their own accommodations to white America. Their celebration of Pueblo religion certainly helped to defend indigenous ceremonies against government suppression, but to the extent that they identified "religion" as part of humanity's past, such praise also served to marginalize traditional ways of life. In some ways, modernist ways of defining "religion" and the "primitive" contributed to the cultural barriers that would prevent Indians from defending land and sovereignty on religious freedom grounds. At the same time, through their close relationships with Indian people, individual modernist reformers could sometimes transcend the limitations of their primitivism to embrace a more comprehensive support for Indian self-determination.[15]

As we have already seen, Pueblo Indians were themselves divided on questions of tradition and assimilation. Self-identified "progressives," a small minority in most Pueblo communities, were typically well educated and considered themselves the agents of modernization in their communities. Although they supported much of the assimilationist program, few progressives wanted to abandon Indian tribal identities or traditions, and many actively participated in tribal dances. They allied with assimilationist reformers because they hoped to gain leverage against conservative tribal leaders, and because they found a practical gospel of progress more compelling than the modernists' romanticized celebration of Indian culture. Arrayed against the progressives were Pueblo leaders who fought Burke's dance policies and identified themselves as the defenders of Pueblo tradition. Their "traditionalist" or "conservative" position should not be understood as a statement of unchanging tradition—surely a contradiction in terms—but as a newly articulated defense of indigenous ways of life in response to new circumstances. Assimilationist programs, economic pressures that forced tribal members away from home to find employment, and increasing contact with Anglo and Hispano neighbors added up to unprecedented threats against Pueblo life. Far from rejecting all aspects of Euro-American culture, Pueblo traditionalists cautiously affirmed the advantages of such things as U.S. government–supported education and health care for the future of their tribes. Their appeal to American standards of religious freedom represented another kind of adaptation, one step in an ongoing process of cultural change over centuries of encounter under Spanish, Mexican, and U.S. rule.

There are real dangers in overemphasizing changes in Native tradition. Although all living cultures change to meet contemporary needs, academic concepts of "invented tradition" can leave the impression that the culture under analysis is somehow inauthentic. Such work can appear to discount the validity of indigenous traditions and thereby render tribal rights vulnerable to attack. For example, opponents of indigenous land rights in Australia and the United States have used scholarship on invented traditions to argue that the group in question has no legitimate claim to tribal identity and thus no right to the land.[16] Rather than isolating certain traditions as "invented," we need to stress that all traditions are adapted and adaptable. This idea of always-adapting traditions fits very well with historian Peter Nabokov's suggestion, part of a larger scholarly move to privilege indigenous epistemologies, that American Indian ways of doing history assume the need for contemporary relevance and include multiple points of view.[17] In the Pueblo case, any shifts that resulted from the traditionalist deployment of the category of religion are best understood as a necessary adaptation to contemporary conditions, an adaptation that helped enable the ongoing development of Pueblo ways of life. Attempts to deny such changes would not only fly against observable historical realities but also reinforce primitivist images of Indians as permanently separate from modernity and historical change.[18]

This book joins recent debates in religious studies and related fields about the history of "religion" as a cultural concept, the political implications of this concept, and its usefulness for scholars as an analytical tool. In recent years, some critics have questioned the academic use of the term "religion" by arguing that the bias of its European origins is so strong as to make it unusable as a cross-cultural category of comparison. Early Christians in the Roman Empire adopted the Latin term *religio*, originally meaning the faithful practice of one's ancestral rites, and redefined it to signify the worship of "one true God." In so doing, they added the monotheistic implication of universal truth and, by defining other groups as superstitious "pagans," succeeded in gaining authority in Roman society. Over the centuries, as Christian leaders struggled to define the boundaries of the faith, they increasingly conceived of religion primarily in terms of personal faith or belief. That tendency only accelerated with the intellectual ferment of the Enlightenment, which emphasized rational thought along with the freedom of the individual. Emerging out of Europe's religious wars, this discourse reflected the intense anti-Catholicism of both Protestant and antireligious revolutionaries. Influential philosophers and historians of religion idealized Protestant doctrine as pure and rational religion, excoriating what they saw as Catholicism's corrupt and meaningless ritualism as a remnant of "paganism." As I have already noted, the U.S. Constitution's provisions on religion reflected the Enlightenment framework of the founding fathers, who instilled in that document their view of religion as a matter of individual conscience and belief.[19]

Not surprisingly, European assumptions about "religion" have been an uneasy fit with many of the traditions regularly described as such. In fact, it was only quite recently that many of the so-called world religions came to be identified in terms of religion at all. To take just one example, nineteenth-century European scholars and British colonialists seeking to understand and control the people of the Indian subcontinent identified "Hinduism" as the single religion of all Indians who were not Christians, Muslims, or Buddhists. Yet these Hindus, a term that originally referred simply to all who lived in the Indus River Valley, practiced a set of diverse and intersecting religious traditions. The academic study of this newly discovered religion of Hinduism focused heavily on philosophical doctrines and sacred texts such as the *Rig Vedas*, despite the fact that many Hindus were barely familiar with these texts. By all accounts, most people in the subcontinent defined themselves in terms of caste and local identities and did not think of themselves as members of any defined religion, let alone one called Hinduism and shared by all Indians. Even today, despite significant movements toward a unified Hinduism by Indians themselves, the variety of religious expression in India and its diaspora belies the concept of a single, clearly defined religion. It would be a revealing exercise to compare this development of Hinduism with the history of ideas about Native American religions, where for a variety of reasons the emphasis has been on ritual practice and the diversity of tribal traditions. These no doubt represent Native American traditions more accurately than would any construct of a single belief-based religion. Yet it seems to me that Hinduism's status as a world religion in university textbooks and courses, and the exclusion of Native American and other so-called primitive or tribal religions from that category, rest in part on the historical construction of the former as doctrinally unified and the latter as tribally diverse.[20]

Another frequent objection to the category of "religion" is that it provided ideological support for the centuries of European colonialism. As increasing exploration and trade around the world brought a new awareness of the vast differences among the world's peoples, European thinkers increasingly used "religion" as an analytical concept that made it possible to compare and evaluate the systems of belief and practice that they observed in every human society. Not surprisingly, the comparative assumptions implicit in their theories of religion seem inevitably to have supported the conclusion that Christianity—either Protestant or Catholic depending on the writer— was superior to all other traditions. Ever since Christopher Columbus famously asserted in 1492 that the Arawak Indians "do not hold any creed nor are they idolaters," Europeans typically considered indigenous traditions either inferior religion, false religion, or no religion at all. All of these positions reflected implicitly Christian assumptions about what counted as "religion" and served to justify the conquest and exploitation of so-called pagan or heathen peoples in the Americas and around the world.[21]

Other scholars argue that the concept of "religion," even if it can be defined broadly enough to shed its Christian assumptions and its colonialist past, is intrinsically biased toward the institutions and presuppositions of Western modernity. The common definition of religion as that part of every society having to do with "symbolic meanings" has been criticized as one that makes religion a wholly private affair and so serves the interests of the modern (Western) secular state by divorcing anything considered religious from political power.[22] At an even more basic level, identifying certain aspects of a culture as "religion" seems to conceptually isolate the newly defined religion from politics, economics, and other spheres of life. If religion is understood to be "either the special repository of traditional values or alternatively a private realm of individual, nonpolitical, otherworldly commitment," as Timothy Fitzgerald puts it, then non-Western ways of life are marginalized and modern secular institutions (themselves the historical constructs of Western culture) appear to be the only rational possibility. The Pueblos' experience is a case in point, because their adoption of the category of religion certainly brought with it pressure to privatize and depoliticize their ceremonial traditions. Faced with such complications, a few critics have concluded that the term is so analytically imprecise and carries such ideological baggage that it should be abandoned as a category of scholarly analysis.[23]

However, "religion" is also a first-order term given meaning by religious practitioners and by their observers and critics in the wider culture, and I believe that efforts to abandon it in scholarly discourse would further diminish the academy's relevance to that larger culture. The redefinition of religion is an ongoing process, taking place in multiple arenas including the courts, legal codes, popular literature and entertainment, the news media, world's fairs, museums, and political disputes such as the Pueblo dance controversy. These are the sites of intersecting discourses, continually re-creating contemporary ideas about what counts as good or bad religion, and what counts as religion at all. Rather than drawing its own boundaries around what counts as religion, this book focuses on its evolution and implications as understood and used by the people I study—joining a growing body of literature offering insights into the history of religion as a cultural concept.[24]

Still, I am convinced that "religion" also remains valid as a second-order analytical concept, useful for constructing comparisons across times and places. Many other categories—consider words like "culture," "art," "tradition," and "politics"—have similar convoluted and problematic histories, and eliminating any or all of them would diminish our analytical toolbox without solving the problems of bias or imprecision in language.[25] Hoping to overcome the historical bias of the term religion, religious studies scholars have recently redefined it using concepts such as intersection, connection, and boundary crossing. Like many that precede them, these definitions tend to create a relatively broad field for what counts as religion, and some will not like them for that reason. I am convinced that such definitional disputes, although frustrating at times, ultimately improve our critical and comparative insights and so are beneficial for the field. Most important, the recognition that religion is both a first- and second-order category, and that its cultural referents are constantly changing, gives scholars the humility to acknowledge that any such definition must be contingent, constructed for the purpose of analysis, and cannot pretend to discover any unchanging essence of a cross-culturally identifiable thing called religion.[26]

It is also crucial to recognize here that Europeans and Euro-Americans do not have a monopoly on defining religion, and that the political implications of such redefinitions are neither predetermined nor limited to Western dominance. Pueblo Indians did not simply adopt religion as a static concept; rather, they actively redefined it and made use of it for their own ends. Their identification of their ceremonial traditions in terms of religion had complex consequences but nevertheless proved successful in defending them against immediate suppression. It was therefore not simply an imposition of Western models but a step in the ongoing development of traditional ways of life. Much the same is true around the world. When British scholars first identified "Hinduism" as a religion, they did so in dialogue with Indian elites who had their own reasons for encouraging this development. The nascent nationalist movement immediately embraced the development of a unified religious identity as a way to further its own goal of uniting India against colonial control, and today—sometimes at the expense of Muslims and other religious minorities—Hinduism remains a rallying point for Indian nationalism and has helped preserve ethnic and cultural identities for diasporic communities around the world. In very different ways, Turkey, Iran, and Japan have all supported nation-building efforts by intentionally redefining religion and its role in public life.[27] Conservative evangelical Protestants in the United States, along with radical Islamicists in parts of Asia and the Middle East, are reacting against the modern separation of religion from public life in order to advocate a far more expansive view of religion as the all-encompassing allegiance. That some of these revolts against "modern" concepts of religion are associated with terrorist violence only underscores the importance of understanding the cultural processes that reinvent the category of religion. In short, scholars do not have the power to eliminate the concept of religion from general usage or to control the meanings associated with it. These complex political realities make research on its cultural and intellectual history doubly important.[28]

My attention to shifting and conflicting concepts of religion also contributes to current debates about secularization and the nature of the secular. As I use it, the concept of "secularization" refers not to a decline in religious belief or practice or commitment but to an increasing privatization of religion—the implicit goal of Enlightenment theorists who defined religion as a matter of individual conscience—and to the resulting decline in its public or institutional authority. Historians and sociologists in recent years have overthrown their predecessors' assumption that religion would inevitably disappear or even become less influential as a consequence of modernity, but most continue to find the concept of secularization useful when defined in more limited and historically contingent ways. In many respects, the theory of secularization was an attempt at a self-fulfilling prophecy by nineteenth- and twentieth-century intellectuals, making their efforts to diminish religion's influence seem natural and inevitable.[29] The cultural modernists of the dance controversy should be understood as part of this secularizing cadre of intellectuals, working intentionally and directly to replace religious with scientific and secular authority in American life. Redefining religion—in this case, expanding the concept of religion to include Indian dances—was one of the ways in which these intellectuals challenged the dominance of Christianity in American public life.

The new and apparently more "secular" principles governing Indian affairs were by no means value-neutral. A growing body of scholarship demonstrates the cultural particularity of supposedly universal "secularism." Talal Asad has shown that the secular is necessarily defined in opposition to the religious and that both spheres will therefore be configured quite differently in different times and places. In the United States, the "secular" carries with it strikingly Protestant assumptions and norms.[30] The Pueblo experience in the dance controversy suggested the ways in which the new "secular" Indian policy would be governed by Enlightenment ideals of the separation of church and state and the primacy of individual conscience—ideals that emerged out of distinctively Protestant theological debates. Although they have proved inspiring to nationalist and liberation movements around the world, these "secular" ideas about religion continue to reflect their Protestant origins and so have their limits for anyone seeking to articulate alternative visions of religion. Because they do not value communal and land-based traditions, for example, such concepts of religion have added to the ongoing barriers facing Native Americans who appeal on religious freedom grounds for the repatriation of lands, artifacts, and remains defined as sacred.[31]

This book is organized for the most part in chronological order. Chapter 1 introduces Pueblo Indian history and ceremonial traditions in the context of Spanish, Mexican, and U.S. rule, examines the development of a Protestant establishment in Indian affairs, and shows how the Catholic challenge to that establishment reinforced the exclusion of indigenous ceremonial traditions from American concepts of religion. The second chapter adds cultural modernists to the scene, highlighting their attitudes toward "religion" and "primitive religion" and locating them among the secularizing intellectuals of their day; the third chapter then brings the modernists into dialogue with Pueblo Indians struggling to defend land rights and tribal sovereignty and shows how these issues shaped the politics of Indian affairs in the period. Chapter 4 describes the development of the public controversy over Indian dances, placing it in the context of larger cultural disputes over the meanings of morality and religion. The fifth chapter describes the religious freedom compromise that ended the controversy and its consequences for Pueblo ceremonial life. Finally, chapter 6 reflects on the implications of the category of "religion" for the larger history of Native American religious freedom struggles into the twenty-first century.

ONE

Pueblos and Catholics in Protestant America

The high point of Zuni Pueblo's annual round of ceremonies is the Shalako festival, held each year in late November or early December. The powerful beings who give the festival its name appear as giant birds, sometimes called the "Messengers of the Gods," who carry the Zunis' prayers for rain to all the corners of the earth. Members of the Zuni order of *koyemshi*, sacred clowns who are often called "mudheads" for their clay-brown masks, signal the impending arrival of the Shalako with announcements in the plaza. Meanwhile, the prayers and ritual purifications that make up the first stages of the ceremony are performed in seclusion in the kivas. Before the public festival begins, those who are to personate the Shalako go to a shrine outside the pueblo to plant feathered prayer sticks. There they put on their costumes— ten-foot white frame structures adorned with colorful blankets and a spread of eagle feathers above a blue face mask—and then process into town to begin the public festival. Their walk symbolically retraces the path of the ancestors as they journeyed from their place of emergence into this world, all the way to the Zunis' home at the center of the earth. Eight houses are newly built or renovated each year for the festival. One is dedicated to each of the six Shalako, one to the *koyemshi*, and one to the "Council of the Gods," an honored group of the ancestral deities known to the Zuni as *koko*, who return each year with gifts of rain and other blessings. The personators spend the night in these houses, performing chanted prayers and dances that they have spent the past year rehearsing.[1]

Zuni tradition holds that the successful completion of this and other ceremonies each year is necessary to ensure the well-being not only of the tribe but of the entire world. In a recent autobiography, the former Zuni

The Shalako cross to south side of the river, Zuni Pueblo, 1897. Photo by Ben Wittick. Library of Congress, Washington, D.C., neg. no. LC-USZ62-115456.

tribal council member Virgil Wyaco provides a moving account of the Shalako festival and its contemporary significance. He describes how, after their all-night performances, the Shalako personators face the considerable physical and spiritual challenge of competing in foot races the next morning. They are so exhausted by this time, Wyaco explains, that "if a rule has been broken or their hearts are not ritually pure, they may fall. The old men think on these matters," he writes, "and sometimes say that a disaster elsewhere in the world was caused by a Shalako falling." According to traditional Zunis, the Shalako and other ceremonies literally maintain the balance of the earth and its seasons. As Wyaco puts it, "The dances must be every year if the Zuni world is to survive." If not, then "we Zuni believe that the outside world, too, would cease to exist."[2] In December 1922 Zuni's six chief priests defended their land and ceremonies against threats of disruption by articulating the same significance. These were the Pueblo's "constant prayers for rain," they explained, crucial for the life of the tribe and indeed for "all the people who exist in this world." As the sixth priest concluded, "We the *Principales* agree to this matter, that this precious religion should never suffer harm."[3]

When he referred to Zuni tribal ceremonies by the English-language term "religion," this priest—or his Zuni translator—was employing unusual terminology for Pueblo leaders in his or any previous era. During the Spanish colonial period, after initial suppression of Indian "paganism," Franciscan missionaries and Pueblo Indians developed a mutual accommodation that recognized Catholicism as the Indians' "religion" and minimized the appearance of conflict between Catholicism and indigenous practices. Shaped by that history, Pueblo leaders would initially contest American restrictions on their ceremonies by defining them not as religious practices but simply as a beneficial and integral part of Pueblo life. The Zunis may have been quicker to adopt the language of religion to describe and defend their indigenous ceremonies precisely because, unlike the other New Mexico Pueblos, they did not identify themselves as Catholics.

The Protestant reformers, missionaries, and government officials who dominated nineteenth-century U.S. Indian policy uniformly derided Indian traditions as "paganism." Protestant leaders merged Christian traditions of religious comparison with anthropological theory to construct a hierarchy of religions with Protestant Christianity at the top. For them Indian "religion," if it merited that designation at all, shared the same "degraded" qualities condemned in the Bible and shared by other "pagans" worldwide. True religion cultivated "civilized" standards of conduct and morality, understood in exclusively Anglo-Protestant terms, and made its adherents fit for American citizenship. In this sense, only Christianity—and often only Protestant Christianity—qualified. Indigenous traditions of any kind could be seen only as an impediment to the civilizing process. Convinced that civilization relied on the one true religion, Protestant leaders prescribed Christian missions as the most effective way to achieve the government's civilizing goals.

Until the 1920s Roman Catholics represented the most significant threat to this virtual Protestant establishment in Indian affairs. Catholics had a far more significant history of missions among the Pueblos and many other Indian tribes than their Protestant counterparts, but they struggled for equal influence in the anti-Catholic environment of nineteenth-century America. Like most Pueblo leaders, Catholic missionaries defended against Protestant incursions by insisting that the religion of these Indians was Catholic. Forced to negotiate Protestant-Catholic conflicts, early twentieth-century government officials tried to establish religious neutrality on the reservations and in Indian schools. In effect, "religious liberty" for Indians in this era meant the freedom to choose between Protestant and Catholic religion. In this way, Catholic challenges to the Protestant establishment only intensified the exclusion of American Indian traditions from the category of religion. In such a context, it only made sense for most Pueblo Indians to continue their longtime strategy of defending their ceremonies as "customs" that did not interfere with their Catholic "religion."

"Customs" and "Religion": Pueblo Identity under Spanish Rule

Pueblo Indian stories of origin like that reenacted in the Zuni Shalako relate how the first ancestors emerged into this world from a series of previous worlds underneath this one. With the guidance of the spirits, they moved around from place to place until they settled at the very center of the earth where their descendants continue to make their homes. Archaeological research suggests that the group of tribes now known as the Pueblos developed th   xtures of the ancient peoples of the area. Ancestral Puebloans   side dwellings whose ruins are still visible around the Four   n of New Mexico, Arizona, Utah, and Colorado. Between 900   constructed the monumental Great Houses of Chaco Can-   precisely aligned kivas and other architectural features to

s in Protestant America

mark important solar and lunar events. When drought or other factors forced them to move south and east, they joined with other groups to build new towns and traditions. Around the beginning of the fourteenth century, the kachina cult of the ancestors (known at Zuni as *koko*) spread north from Mexico to the tribes of the Rio Grande Valley and then westward to the Zuni and Hopi. Starting in this period, warfare with the growing numbers of Athabaskan Indians moving into the area from the north forced villages to move and consolidate frequently, shaping the development of modern tribal identities. Today's Pueblo Indians can be divided into six distinct linguistic-tribal groups: the Tiwa, Tewa, and Towa, all three in the Tanoan family; and the linguistically unrelated Keresan, Zuni, and Hopi (an Uto-Aztecan language). Each of the nineteen modern pueblos holds a distinctive annual round of ceremonies that include saint's day festivals, summertime corn and harvest dances, deer and buffalo dances, and masked or unmasked kachina dances.[4]

Like other Native Americans, the Pueblo tribes have endured a long history of colonial conquest and violence, including repeated attacks on their ceremonial traditions. The Spanish explorer Coronado, in search of the fabled "Seven Cities of Cibola" and their treasures of gold, first encountered the Zuni and then the tribes to their east in 1539. It was not until half a century later that Juan de Oñate led an army from Mexico City to lay claim to the area. Oñate and his successors forced the local Indians to recognize their authority under the Spanish crown and the Catholic Church, often punishing them harshly for failures to provide tribute or for other infringements. Acoma Indians resisted these impositions by throwing several of Oñate's men to their deaths from the top of the high mesa where their town (which vies for the title of the oldest continuously occupied settlement in North America) is situated. Oñate famously retaliated with an attack that killed many Acoma people and punished the survivors by amputating one foot from each adult man and sentencing the children to twenty years of enslavement. Over the next few years, Spanish soldiers forced the women and children of Acoma to carry stones and lumber long distances and up the steep trail to the mesatop to construct a mission church, which still stands as a landmark of Acoma's historic pueblo. In an effort to co-opt native religious devotion, Franciscan missionaries placed this and other mission churches on top of indigenous shrines and kivas and permitted some native dances to celebrate the saint's days. Pueblo people used this opening to

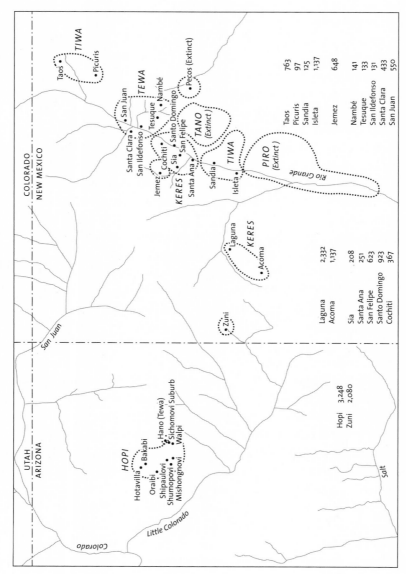

Map of the Pueblos, 1937 (with population figures). Adapted from Elsie Clews Parsons,

Pueblo Indian Religion, map 1. Courtesy University of Chicago Press.

Corn dance, San Ildefonso Pueblo, 1924. Photo by M. W. Wyeth. Courtesy San Ildefonso Pueblo and Palace of the Governors (MNM/DCA), Santa Fe, New Mexico, neg. no. 172888.

preserve indigenous tradition. Today tour guides at Acoma tell visitors how their ancestors built the mission church by dimensions of their own choosing, so that unbeknownst to the friars the numbers four, seven, and twelve (each with sacred significance in indigenous Keresan tradition) are repeated in every feature of the building.[5]

By the mid-seventeenth century, the Franciscans had grown increasingly frustrated at the persistence of indigenous religious practices and reacted against the indifference of a provincial governor in the 1650s who openly accepted Pueblo ceremonies as harmless entertainment. They now insisted that all native ceremonies must be classified as the mortal sin of idolatry— implying false religion—which civil authorities in New Spain were obliged to persecute. Although Indians were legally exempt from the Inquisition, mission discipline was less predictable and potentially worse. Those caught practicing indigenous ceremonies could be severely whipped, imprisoned, enslaved, or even hanged. In the 1660s, Franciscans raided kivas and destroyed ritual items including altars, prayer feathers, and more than sixteen hundred kachina masks. In 1675 a new governor accused forty-seven Pueblo people of "sorcery"; four were condemned to death by hanging, and the rest were given lashings or prison sentences. Angered by such treatment, the Indians staged a successful revolt in 1680, which killed many Spaniards and destroyed most tangible symbols of Spanish rule. They particularly targeted the Franciscan priests, the mission churches, and the material items of Catholic ceremonial life. But the Indians struggled with drought and dissension after the revolt, and starting in 1692 Spain reconquered all except the Hopis.[6]

The Indians' experiences under Spanish rule intensified their sense of common identity. In the colonial period, *pueblo de indios* (literally "Indian town") did not refer exclusively to any particular Indians but was an administrative category used for any settled indigenous community under Spanish civil and ecclesial control. Not until the early nineteenth century, when the first Anglos arriving in the region misunderstood the Spanish word, did the term "Pueblo" gain ethnic connotations as a unifying designator for this specific group of tribes.[7] By that time the Indians were ready to embrace this usage. Despite intermittent conflicts among the Pueblos, their history of joint resistance against Spanish oppression remained a unifying memory. By the late nineteenth century, the "Council of All the New Mexico Pueblos" met occasionally to address matters of common concern, and in 1922 this body—tracing its origins to the 1680 revolt—organized on a permanent basis to facilitate ongoing intertribal cooperation. (It has never included the Hopis, whose geographical distance and distinctive historical experiences have differentiated them from their counterparts in New Mexico.) Despite their many differences, the history and traditions shared by the Pueblos of New Mexico had in many respects forged them into a single people.[8]

After the reconquest of 1692, Catholicism increasingly became part of the identity and practice of most Pueblo tribes. Political turmoil, colonial oppression, and disease epidemics decimated Pueblo populations and resulted in new tribal consolidations. The Eastern Pueblos (the Tanoan and Keresan tribes of the Rio Grande Valley), especially those closest to the Spanish capital of Santa Fe, were forced to accommodate to the Spanish authorities and the religion they brought. Especially early in the eighteenth century, the open practice of indigenous ceremonies risked violent reprisals. Some of the more zealous Spanish governors sent soldiers to destroy kivas and ceremonial objects in the name of Christianity. Once again the people of these pueblos could not openly perform the masked kachina dances, which were condemned by the Spanish as demonic, but they continued to practice them without masks or in secret in the kivas. To compensate—or perhaps to create a public front for their own traditions—they gradually added Catholicism to their religious repertoire, reorienting their public ceremonial calendars around the Catholic holy days. Among most of the Eastern Pueblos, the Catholic patron saint's day became the most visible public religious festival, and Holy Week and Christmas also came to be celebrated with indigenous ceremonial dances. The deer dance, traditionally held to thank the deer for its gifts of life, now also honored the birth of the Christ child.[9]

Those pueblos located furthest from Santa Fe were generally least affected by the centuries of Spanish colonial rule. The Hopis, whose mesatop towns in the modern state of Arizona placed them farthest west, completely resisted the Spanish reconquest. Hopi tribal leaders were so opposed to any Spanish influence that in 1700 they attacked and destroyed Awatovi, the one Hopi village that had invited the return of the Franciscan missionaries. Much to the Spaniards' chagrin the Hopis gave refuge to other Pueblo people seeking escape from colonial oppression; a Tewa-speaking village founded by Indians who fled the Rio Grande region after the reconquest still thrives on one of the Hopi mesas. The Hopis and the Tewas they hosted never became even nominally Catholic, and their political and religious autonomy

Deer dance, San Ildefonso Pueblo. Courtesy San Ildefonso Pueblo and Palace of the Governors (MNM/DCA), Santa Fe, New Mexico, neg. no. 135305.

was not seriously challenged until the United States took over the region in the nineteenth century. Zuni Pueblo, although it was forced to accept the resumption of Spanish rule in 1692, was also located far to the west of Santa Fe and in practice remained largely self-governing. Zuni saw only occasional priestly visitors until the 1920s and remained minimally influenced by Catholicism until several decades later. For these reasons, Hopis and Zunis did not celebrate the patron saint's days that became so important among the eastern pueblos, and the masked *kachina* and *koko* dances remained the central organizing principle of their ceremonial life.[10]

Out of view of the Spaniards, the Eastern Pueblos also continued to practice far more of their indigenous traditions than their public festivals would suggest. To avoid the attention that might inspire repressive action, they barred outsiders from their environs for most ceremonies not linked to Catholic holy days. Such insistence on privacy for tribal ceremonies intensified and extended older patterns of secrecy in religious matters. In Pueblo tradition, specialized societies maintain the esoteric knowledge and ritual paraphernalia necessary to conduct the varied ceremonies; each society's initiates are the only ones with rightful knowledge of the ceremonies owned by that society. Over the centuries of colonial history, secrecy acquired additional urgency as a means of resisting suppression from the outside world.[11] Thus, nineteenth- and early twentieth-century government agents and schoolteachers reported indignantly that the Pueblo Indians would not allow them anywhere near their towns during certain "secret dances." This was especially true among the Eastern Pueblos, where closer surveillance meant that secrets had to be guarded more closely. Tony Lujan of Taos told anthropologist Elsie Clews Parsons in 1922 that he would never reveal sensitive information about Taos because "our ways would lose their power, if known." Lujan opined that the Zuni ways had already "lost their power" because the Zunis had been too quick to share them with outsiders.[12] By this time the Hopis and Zunis were also intensifying their traditions of ceremonial secrecy, a reaction against various intrusions by tourists, anthropologists, and government officials.[13]

Most eighteenth-century Franciscans were probably unaware of the extent to which the Pueblos continued their indigenous ceremonialism and gradually came to accept some of the dances as legitimate (or at least acceptable) Indian ways to celebrate the Christian holy days. Located as they were on the margins of an immense and turbulent empire, those Spanish authori-

vished to thoroughly suppress tribal practices lacked the institu-
ɩort to do so. Frustrated by the practical difficulties of enforcing
ɩinst Indian "idolatry," Franciscans throughout New Spain began
ɩigenous practices as *costumbres*. "Customs" did not necessarily
conflict with the Catholic "religion," and even when seen as problematic,
these were legally classified as venial rather than mortal sins, with less
serious repercussions. The eighteenth-century friars in New Mexico came to
see Pueblo customs as generally harmless, and believed that they were already disappearing anyway as the Pueblos became more committed Catholics. This new generation of Franciscans, as one historian has written, found
"feathers and face paint at mass as 'innocuous' as Spanish ribbons and
makeup." Thus, the priests tried to dissuade the civil authorities from directly suppressing the Pueblo ceremonies by minimizing any appearance of
conflict between Catholic and indigenous practices. This accommodation
was useful to the Pueblo Indians themselves, who kept their ceremonies free
from religious persecution by identifying them as "custom" rather than
"religion."[14]

When Mexico gained its independence from Spain in 1821, the new
nation devoted little attention to the Indians of its northernmost frontier. The Mexican government accelerated the process, already underway
under Spanish rule, of replacing Franciscan missionaries with secular priests
(those not affiliated with a religious order) from the Diocese of Durango.
Under Spain, provincial authorities had financially supported twenty-four
Franciscans in northern and central New Mexico, but the Mexican government was unable or unwilling to continue this arrangement. Further,
some of the Franciscans were forced to leave in the mid-1820s when Mexico
expelled most Spanish citizens from the country. No replacements could be
recruited, and the few who remained struggled to keep up the Pueblo missions. The bishop of Durango found himself unable to fill all the vacancies,
let alone to keep up with New Mexico's rapidly growing Hispano population.
For almost two decades, a total of only thirteen priests—including a dwin-
dling number of Franciscans until the last of them died in 1840—served
both the Pueblos and Hispanos of the region. Their number finally began
to increase again in the early 1840s, after the church made it possible for
young men from the area to attend the seminary in Durango and return
home as priests.[15]

In the absence of significant numbers of priests, the people of New

Mexico sustained their Catholicism on their own terms. Many Hispanos relied for spiritual leadership on lay confraternities that led community worship, catechism, and the celebration of Catholic feast days—especially the brotherhood of the *penitentes*, which became known for its public re-enactments of the Crucifixion during Holy Week.[16] Pueblos and Hispanos forged alliances against the Comanche, Apache, and Navajo tribes who raided their settled towns for livestock and other goods—experiences still memorialized in Hispano "Comanche" dances that illustrate the depth of New Mexico's cultural hybridity.[17] After the United States conquered the territory in 1846, the Catholics of New Mexico were transferred to the American branch of the church. Eager to claim religious priority in this historically Catholic region, the American Catholic church named the Frenchman Jean Baptiste Lamy as bishop of Santa Fe in 1851. Within fifteen years, the energetic Bishop Lamy had created several schools and placed fifty-one priests (many of them French) in his diocese. Lamy was eager to impose his view of Catholic orthodoxy and civilization on the region, but instead of targeting the Pueblos, he focused his efforts on the Hispano population, their controversial *penitente* brotherhoods, and the local priests whom he found hopelessly inadequate.[18]

Starting in the late nineteenth century, the Pueblo Indians would face new attacks on their indigenous traditions—this time from U.S. government officials and missionaries whose policies represented an overwhelmingly Protestant America. This virtual Protestant establishment in Indian affairs assumed very different concepts and hierarchies of religion, eventually forcing the Pueblos to adopt new strategies for the preservation of their indigenous ceremonies.

The Protestant Establishment and "Primitive Religion"

Daniel Dorchester, then superintendent of Indian schools for the U.S. Bureau of Indian Affairs (BIA), used his 1892 annual report to condemn "paganism" as the source for what he believed was a fundamental lack of morality in Pueblo society. Despite the Indians' "veneer" of Catholicism, he wrote, their "principal religion is the darkest of superstitions, a pagan fetishism which controls the whole life." In his view, this "religion assumes man's utter helplessness within the natural realm and excuses crime," leading to a "lack of truthfulness, consistency, and moral consciousness."[19] Dorchester saw

Catholicism in almost equally negative terms. At a high point of anti-Catholic sentiment in 1887, he had informed a gathering of Protestant leaders that the Roman Catholic Church was "inimical to the best progress of society . . . and in direct antagonism to the historic religion of the nation—the religion of the Holy Scriptures."[20] Such denigration of both "paganism" and Catholicism was typical among the Protestant missionaries, reformers, and government officials who dominated nineteenth-century Indian affairs. As a longtime Methodist minister and an influential historian of American religion, Dorchester serves as an apt representative of that establishment. In his eyes, only Protestant Christianity qualified as true religion and could instill the positive moral values necessary to the progress of American civilization. Such ideas helped justify anti-Catholic agitation along with the forcible suppression of Native American traditions.

When the United States took over the territory of New Mexico in 1846, federal Indian policy bore a more military than religious tone. Its primary goal, achieved through a combination of military campaigns and treaties, was to move Indians out of the way of white settlement. In the wake of America's increasing territorial ambitions, many tribes found themselves restricted to reservations that were distant from their homelands and unsuited for the agricultural pursuits that the government encouraged. Most Euro-Americans fully believed themselves and their way of life to be intrinsically superior and—as expressed in the doctrine of Manifest Destiny—justly destined to take over the continent. While some simply wanted Indians dead, those who were relatively sympathetic to Native American rights believed that Indians must assimilate into "civilized" society. As they saw it, the stereotypical "savage" Indian who roamed the land like an animal rather than farming and "improving" it must either become civilized or die out.[21]

Because the Pueblo Indians already lived in well-established agricultural villages and posed no obvious military threat, Americans initially viewed them in comparatively positive terms. The 1848 Treaty of Guadalupe Hidalgo stipulated that the United States would honor the Spanish colonial land grants to both Hispanos and Indians, and so unlike most tribes the Pueblos held legally recognized title to their land. The soldiers, surveyors, and other Americans who first encountered these Indians followed the precedent of both Spaniards and scientists by identifying them as "descendants of the Aztecs" and therefore already the most "civilized" Indians. Officers were far more concerned about the larger and seminomadic Athabaskan tribes in the area, the Apaches and Navajos, whose active resistance and military prowess posed a far greater threat to the consolidation of U.S. rule. In fact, the occasional praise bestowed on the "Aztec" Pueblos helped justify the military suppression of the supposedly "savage" Apaches and Navajos.[22]

In the years after the Civil War, facing the daunting task of meaningfully incorporating the vast western territories into the cultural and political life of a reunified nation, the government began to intensify its efforts to "civilize" the Indians. Most Americans assumed that this process required Christian missions. Galvanized by a series of tragic Indian wars in the 1860s, the congressionally appointed Doolittle Commission recommended education for all Indian children and more government support for missions as the best way to handle the "Indian problem." Quaker and Episcopal missionaries, frustrated with the notorious corruption of so many BIA agents, advocated for supervisory authority on the reservations where they were working. The newly elected president Ulysses S. Grant implemented their recommendations in his so-called Peace Policy of 1869. At the heart of the policy was the designation of responsibility for Indian reservations, including the right to name new BIA agents, to selected Christian denominations. The various churches were expected to restrict missionary activities to their assigned tribes, because more than one mission on a single reservation created denominational conflicts and was thought to confuse potential Indian converts. As Commissioner Francis Walker put it in 1872, the policy aimed to secure "harmony of feeling and concert of action between the agents of the Government and the missionaries . . . in the matter of the moral and religious advancement of the Indians."[23]

Although such arrangements strike most twenty-first-century Americans as a clear violation of the First Amendment, they were entirely consistent with long-standing nineteenth-century assumptions about the proper relationship between church and state. The vast majority of Americans did not understand the First Amendment's prohibition of religious establishment as anything resembling a "wall of separation"—except when this involved constraints on the Catholic Church—but as a simple restriction on the government's granting special status to any single denomination.[24] The Presbyterian clergyman Robert Baird, who authored the first major history of American religion, explained that the churches and the government were rightful co-workers "in the religious and moral instruction of the people."[25] Most Americans assumed that school prayers, Christian morality, and the

Bible were essential to the education of a civilized and moral citizenry. This was true for any race and doubly so for the "savage" Indians. In his 1882 report to the secretary of the interior, Commissioner Hiram Price called for increased government support for mission schools as the best way to civilize the Indians. As he put it, "In no other manner and by no other means, in my judgment, can our Indian population be so speedily and permanently reclaimed from barbarism, idolatry, and savage life, as by the educational and missionary operations of the Christian people of our country."[26] If American civilization relied on Christianity, then Christian missions were an essential ingredient in the government's efforts to Americanize the Indians.

The federal government, however, did not grant equal status to all Christian missions. In theory, under Grant's Peace Policy reservations were allocated to the church with the longest-established active mission. According to their own calculations, by this criterion the Catholics were entitled to seventy-five out of one hundred agencies. In reality, in the 1872 assignments all but seven—even some of those with centuries-old Catholic missions—were assigned to the leading Protestant denominations.[27] The designation of the Presbyterian Church to administer the Pueblo Indian agency in Santa Fe was a prime example. W. F. M. Arny, a former New Mexico territorial governor who was then the BIA agent in Santa Fe, saw the "two centuries" of Catholic missions as a complete failure in addressing the Pueblos' "ignorance" and "superstition," and he judged the contemporary Catholic Church to be incapable or unwilling to do any better. Thus, Arny eagerly invited Presbyterian missionaries to educate the Pueblos.[28] The Presbyterian Church soon established missions and schools at Laguna, Jemez, and Zuni and named a local Presbyterian elder as the next BIA agent in Santa Fe. On the national level, Grant's Peace Policy created the Board of Indian Commissioners, intended as an independent body of experts to oversee Indian affairs. This was an exclusively Protestant body until the appointment of the first Catholic in 1902, and for much of that time it met annually with representatives of Protestant missionary societies. No Catholics (and virtually no Indians) were present at these meetings.[29]

The Protestants' overwhelming influence in Indian affairs reflected their dominance throughout nineteenth-century American life. Most Americans with prominent positions in education, government, law, and other spheres were members of the leading Protestant denominations, and they understood Protestant Christianity as the foundation of American civilization. Baird argued in 1843 that Providence was guiding the great "evangelical" Protestant churches (whose basic unity transcended their minor differences) to triumph over the Catholics, Mormons, Jews, Spiritualists, and all other "non-evangelicals" whose "heathenism" belied their claims to true religion.[30] Half a century later, and a few years before his appointment to the Indian Service, Daniel Dorchester's voluminous *Christianity in the United States* paid tribute to Baird and expressed similar conviction that (with the aid of Providence) the vigor and religious truth of evangelical Protestantism was shaping the moral character of the nation. Dorchester was convinced that even the West, despite its plagues of "Romanism and infidelity," was destined to share in this Protestant unity.[31] Although bitterly divided along denominational and sectional lines, American Protestants forged a broad consensus in their hopes for the progress of a Christian civilization. As they saw it, true religion could be identified by its fruits of civilization and morality, and only Protestant Christianity fully qualified.[32]

Indeed, many Protestants feared "papism" as an allegiance to a foreign despot, making Catholics inherently undemocratic and anti-American, and thus a danger to America's religious and civic values.[33] In Indian affairs, most Protestant missionaries and reformers saw Catholics as an active impediment to the government's civilizing efforts. BIA agents who enthusiastically praised Protestant missions often ignored or even condemned the Catholic presence in the Pueblos. Edwin Dudley, superintendent in Santa Fe in 1874, accused the local Catholic priests of actively opposing the creation of government schools because they did not want the Indians to learn English or gain a meaningful education. He believed that the priests wanted to keep the Indians "ignorant" in order to preserve their own "close monopoly of missionary efforts." Dudley portrayed the Catholic missions as not only monopolistic but ineffective. The Pueblos still practiced "the same rites of a heathenish religion" as they always had, he wrote, "albeit slightly changed by the forms of the Romish Church."[34] Such "forms," Protestants believed, were useless in the project of civilizing the Indians. The pioneering Presbyterian missionary superintendent Sheldon Jackson (who established missions in Alaska as well as throughout the Rocky Mountain West) condemned the "Papist Church" in the Pueblo context as "a wisely constructed machine for extorting money out of the fears and superstitions of an ignorant people."[35]

In the eyes of the Protestant establishment, Catholicism was a religion of meaningless ritualism, superstition, and downright fraud, little better than the indigenous traditions.[36]

Protestant missionaries used anti-Catholic rhetoric to justify their presence among Indians such as the Pueblos where Catholics had long-established missions. Sheldon Jackson called for new missionaries to bring spiritual fulfillment for what he interpreted as the Pueblos' messianic hopes for the ancient Aztec king Montezuma: "As the Jews of old looked for a Messiah that should deliver them from Roman bondage and restore to them the kingdom, so do these Pueblos look for Montezuma to restore their kingdom. And as the Jews received a spiritual kingdom, so let these Pueblos receive the gospel at the hands of the 'white man from the east.' "[37] Jackson's implication here was not only that the Pueblos needed relief from their own "Roman bondage" to the Catholic Church but that Presbyterian missionaries could bring them spiritual succor without actually restoring their political sovereignty. One Presbyterian missionary advocate explained that the Pueblo Indians needed Protestant missionaries to bring both Christianity and civilization. "Rome never impressed their souls very deeply," she held, and did no better "in the direction of their temporal estate. . . . [The Indian] needs practical Americans to teach the rudiments of domestic economy, and an importation of soap and fine-tooth combs with missionaries to give them the truth."[38] These Protestant missionaries condemned the Catholic Church as an abject failure in conveying the intertwined blessings of civilization and true religion, and they were certain that they could do better.

The dominance of Protestants in Indian affairs long outlasted Grant's presidency. The Peace Policy itself—which exacerbated tensions between Catholics and Protestants, failed to solve the corruption in the BIA, and certainly did not end the military brutality against Indians—quietly faded in the mid-1870s. But even among the Catholic Pueblos, BIA agents throughout the decade typically acknowledged the Presbyterian day schools at Jemez, Laguna, and Zuni as de facto government schools, and the Presbyterian Church received the contract to operate the new BIA boarding school that opened in Albuquerque in the early 1880s.[39] In 1881, without even mentioning the extensive Catholic missions in his region, the Presbyterian-appointed agent Benjamin Thomas summed up the Pueblos' educational situation with gratitude to the Presbyterian Church and affiliated benefactors "for efficient co-operation and timely contributions in furtherance of the education of the Pueblos." Protestant missionaries worked closely with the BIA in other ways as well: at Zuni, too far west for effective administration from Santa Fe, Presbyterian and then Christian Reformed missionaries were officially recognized as deputy BIA agents for many years.[40] On many Indian reservations, Protestant missionaries and government agents continued their collaborations well into the twentieth century.[41]

In the 1880s, stimulated by new revelations about the nation's mistreatment of Indians, a new generation of reformers sought to transform Indian policy in order to immediately assimilate the Indians into mainstream American life. They found intellectual grounding in social evolutionary theories like those of the prominent American anthropologist Lewis Henry Morgan, who placed the so-called savage and barbarian races including all Indians (even the Pueblos) far behind in a supposedly common human advancement toward "civilization." By arguing for the shared origins and equal potential of all people, Morgan and other evolutionists hoped to counter the persistent idea that the human races were permanently unequal. In the context of U.S. and European imperial expansion around the world, however, their theories functioned to justify the conquest of "inferior" races as a natural part of human evolution in which the supposedly more advanced races were destined to dominate. Apologists claimed that the "superior" races even had a moral obligation to conquer (an idea later encapsulated in Rudyard Kipling's famous phrase, the "white man's burden") because European or American rule introduced colonized peoples to civilization. In Indian affairs, reformers demanded that the government honor what they saw as its moral obligation to bring civilization to people dispossessed by American expansion. They believed that Indians, forced to compete directly with "racially superior" Anglo-Saxons moving into Indian territory, could not survive much longer unless they were forced to adopt "civilized" ways. Morgan and other anthropologists opposed such proposals on scientific grounds, arguing that Indians must go through a natural process of evolution that could not be overly hastened and would take at least several generations. But advocates of assimilation were convinced that the Indians had to be civilized within a single generation and that the federal government must create the right environment to make this happen.[42]

Liberal Protestant leaders embraced evolutionary theory as a validation of their faith in progress and civilization. Of course, such a synthesis was always controversial. Many intellectuals were convinced that social evolution implied progress away from any religion toward scientific rationality. Christian conservatives, on the other hand, saw evolutionary theory as a serious threat to the biblical account of creation and to traditional Christian views of human nature. But liberals, who generally argued for the compatibility of religion and science, reinterpreted the creation story as a metaphorical account of God's guidance over the evolutionary process. Rejecting strictly Darwinian theories, which posited evolutionary change through random mutations and the process of natural selection, they embraced the neo-Lamarckian idea of evolution as linear progress toward higher forms of life. Interpreted this way, social evolutionary ideas supported the nineteenth-century Protestant enchantment with progress and civilization. In the politics of Indian affairs, this synthesis supported the conviction that Christian missions were essential to the civilizing process.

The leading organization in late nineteenth-century Indian reform was the Indian Rights Association (IRA), founded in 1882. Herbert Welsh, its cofounder and longtime president, would play a leading role in the dance controversy four decades later. Welsh was a scion of the Protestant establishment—member of a wealthy Philadelphia family, a committed Episcopalian, and the nephew of the Board of Indian Commissioners' first president. During his first trip for the new association, guided by the famous missionary Bishop William Hobart Hare, Welsh viewed the Episcopal converts among the Lakota Sioux as clear evidence that Indians were capable of assimilating if given adequate assistance.[43] Welsh and like-minded assimilationists aimed to finally bring justice to the Indians in the form of effective civilizing and Christianizing policies, and they defined themselves against those who viewed the Indians as racially inferior and irredeemably savage. They argued that Indians were human beings who, with the benefit of Christian missions and government aid, had the capacity to attain the highest levels of civilization. Only through Christianity, they believed, could the Indians achieve "rapid progress" toward the "higher things" of civilization and so be rescued "from the slow progress of the ages."[44] Welsh made his only personal visit to the Pueblo Indians in 1884, during the IRA's initial survey of Indian country. In keeping with his emphasis on positive Indian potential, he praised them as hardworking and successful farmers who were "entirely capable of civilization." With a good education and "the full privileges of citizenship," he was certain that they would soon achieve the few advancements that would make them fully civilized.[45]

Herbert Welsh. Courtesy
Historical Society of
Pennsylvania, Philadelphia.

The IRA and the other new organizations of the 1880s strengthened what was already a virtual Protestant establishment in Indian affairs. The Women's National Indian Association (WNIA), formed in 1879 to protest the violation of treaty guarantees to Native Americans, funded Protestant missions with the goal of bringing both Christianity and civilization to the Indians. The IRA regularly corresponded with Protestant missionaries in the field, lobbied the commissioner on their behalf, and worked closely with Protestant umbrella organizations such as the Home Missions Council and the Council of Women for Home Missions. The IRA wielded so much influence that its annual statements were typically included in the annual reports from the commissioner of Indian affairs to the secretary of the interior. Its Protestant bias was such that the renowned Franciscan missionary Anselm Weber called it "the greatest enemy we have."[46] In 1883 a member of the Board of Indian Commissioners initiated an annual conference of "Friends of the Indian" at a resort on New York's Lake Mohonk to bring together the many like-minded groups in Indian reform. This event, whose proceedings were included in the Board of Commissioners' annual reports for more than two decades, was a central institution in the formation of Indian policy. Like its member organizations, for most of its existence the Lake Mohonk Conference was an exclusively Protestant affair.[47]

Welsh's report on his trip to New Mexico outlined a set of proposals that summed up a virtual consensus of priorities among assimilationist reformers of the era and served as a guide for IRA advocacy well into the twentieth century. He called for the establishment of enough day schools and boarding schools to provide every Indian child with a good education; "the appointment of a high grade of Indian agents" to finally eliminate the corruption in the BIA; the right for each Indian to receive an individual allotment of the communally held reservation lands—a proposal grounded in Morgan's theory that privately owned family farms were a necessary stepping-stone in the evolution of a civilized race; the immediate application of federal and state laws on Indian reservations; "the right of suffrage" for all Indians; and "abolition of the reservations as soon as the work specified above shall have been thoroughly inaugurated and in some measure accomplished."[48] Taken together, these proposals were intended to expedite the "civilization" of Indians by granting them all the rights and responsibilities of American citizens. Although they could not quite come to a consensus on how soon the reservations could be eliminated, Welsh and other reformers of the 1880s agreed that this was the ultimate goal. It must happen sooner or later, they believed, because the very existence of the reservations reinforced tribal identities and traditions that must ultimately disappear if Indians were to adopt a "civilized" way of life.

Allotment, the only one of these proposals to find immediate political success, gained momentum in Congress partly because it coincided with the less benevolent interests of speculators and settlers eagerly eyeing Indian lands. The 1887 Dawes Allotment Act forced many Indians to accept small individual allotments of tribal reservation lands, making "excess" land available for sale to outsiders. Virtually all Indian tribes opposed this policy because they feared what the reformers advocated: that breaking up the remaining tribal lands would mean the end of tribal identities. The act did not seriously affect the Pueblos, who held legally recognized title to their land through the Treaty of Guadalupe Hidalgo and thus did not live on treaty-established reservations. For many other tribes, allotment resulted in a wholesale loss of land, often through extortion and other deceptive means. Some Indians, already impoverished, saw little option other than to sell their new allotments in order to survive. The resulting increase in Indian poverty and cultural dislocation would eventually help to shake the assimilationist consensus, but in the 1880s reformers overwhelmingly agreed that such policy changes could and would fully civilize the Indians within a single generation.[49]

In the 1880s assimilationists' concerns about Indian dancing focused not on the Pueblos but on the Plains Indians. In the "giveaway" ceremony common among many Plains tribes, a family celebrating an important occasion would sponsor a great feast where the festivities included generous gifts—sometimes including most of the family's possessions—to anyone in need. This ceremony epitomized the egalitarian and communal ethic of the Plains tribes and ensured the survival of their poorest members. Missionaries and assimilationists, however, condemned it as a deterrent to industriousness, claiming that it prevented Indians from adopting the concept of private property or any meaningful work ethic. The sun dance, another target of assimilationist ire, was performed among many Plains Indians to gain spiritual power for healing, warfare, or any difficult endeavor. This ceremony bestowed considerable prestige and sometimes powerful spiritual visions, but it could be an exhausting and painful ordeal for dancers. Among the Lakota, dancers who wished to sacrifice for a special cause would pierce their chest muscles with a thong, tie themselves to a central pole, and dance until they broke free. This, in the eyes of assimilationist campaigners, was a violent and bloody display of Indian savagery. Because it was sometimes performed as a prayer for success in war, government officials also condemned it as a "war dance" and feared that it might incite renewed Indian militancy. Thus, in 1883 the BIA implemented a "Religious Crimes Code" that specifically prohibited the sun dance and the giveaway, and authorized government agents to use force and imprisonment to stop any Indian religious practices that they believed to be immoral, subversive of government authority, or an impediment to the adoption of white civilization.[50]

Government restrictions on Indian dancing were coercive and sometimes violent. By the mid-1880s, the rapid disappearance of the buffalo and open plains had made it impossible to sustain the traditional Plains Indian way of life, let alone ongoing warfare with U.S. forces. The last holdouts among the Plains tribes were being forced onto reservations, where they found themselves impoverished, dispossessed, and enraged by the government's many broken promises. In 1889 a new religious movement spread rapidly among many western Indians as a beacon of hope. Wovoka, a Paiute

Indian prophet in Nevada, had a vision in which God instructed the people that if they would live in peace they would be reunited with their ancestors in a new world, where the buffalo ran freely on the plains and they could live according to the old ways once again. Wovoka described his vision to his fellow Paiutes and taught them a dance to perform in order to speed the arrival of the new world. Soon, Indians from far and wide were traveling to Nevada to hear Wovoka's revelations and learn the new dance. The Lakota were among those who embraced the new movement, which they began to call the "Ghost Dance" because they hoped to see their many lost relatives again. BIA officials on the Lakota reservation, along with other neighboring whites, misinterpreted the movement as a war dance and feared an Indian revolt. In late 1890 the government's efforts to suppress the Ghost Dance ended in tragedy when federal troops massacred several hundred Lakota in the misnamed "Battle of Wounded Knee."[51]

Long-standing Christian traditions of religious comparison helped to justify these policies. Nineteenth-century American encyclopedias of religion defined "heathen" and "pagan" synonymously with "idolatry," meaning "one who worships false gods."[52] As the encyclopedias' authors well knew, Christians had used concepts like paganism, heathenism, and idolatry to discredit their religious and political rivals ever since the days of the Roman Empire. This process had accelerated during the era of Europe's colonial conquests and continued to be found in the American treatment of indigenous traditions. Missionary advocates around the country portrayed Native American traditions as essentially equivalent with "heathenism" elsewhere in the world, and local missionaries among the Pueblos never hesitated to condemn their ceremonies in these terms. According to John Menaul, a Presbyterian missionary at Laguna Pueblo, "The heathen customs and worship of this people are much the same as that of any other sun worshippers . . ., and their degradation the same as the degradation brought on by polytheism and ignorance in any land."[53] Missionary advocates discredited this contemporary "heathenism" as identical, even historically continuous, with the idolatry condemned in the Bible. In Dorchester's words, the Pueblo Indians "still preserve some of the most ancient heathen rites, linking them with the old idolatrous Canaanites of earliest recorded history."[54] Such religious comparisons—not unlike those employed by the seventeenth-century Franciscan missionaries—defined Indian traditions as false religion that must, supposedly for the Indians' own good, be replaced by the true religion of Christianity and the civilization that accompanied it.

Early anthropological ideas about the origins and development of religion could easily be taken to support these conclusions. Seeking to explain the origins of religion, Enlightenment philosophers like David Hume had argued that polytheism was a "primitive" form of religion that had been gradually purified through reason and revelation into the more advanced religion of ethical monotheism. Motivated by the desire to discredit Catholicism as a devolution from Christian revelation, Hume identified Protestant Christianity as the rational religion par excellence. By the late nineteenth century, the nascent disciplines of anthropology, sociology, and the "science of religions" labored to ground their understanding of the development of religion through the study of "primitive" societies.[55] The early anthropologists working in the pueblos shared this mission. The self-taught ethnographer Frank Hamilton Cushing, who arrived at Zuni Pueblo in 1879 with the newly created Bureau of American Ethnology's inaugural expedition, wrote popular accounts of his experiences during four and a half years living in the pueblo—including his induction into one of Zuni's esoteric societies, the Priesthood of the Bow—and is now credited as a pioneer in participant-observer methods of ethnographic research. But Cushing's analysis of Zuni "religion" relied less on his often insightful observations of Zuni life than on his effort to elucidate what he called "primitive conception and polytheism." All Indians, he wrote, were "more or less devoted to their indigenous mythic and superstitious ideas."[56] Where missionaries diagnosed the false religion of "heathenism," anthropologists saw common elements of "superstition" and "polytheism" in "primitive" religion around the world. Both found Indian traditions clearly inferior.

Through the logic of social evolutionary theory, most anthropologists were convinced that "primitive" religion would inevitably be replaced by the "civilized" religion of Christianity, and a few actively supported missionary efforts toward that end. The well-known army ethnographer John Gregory Bourke, a close friend of Cushing's, described Hopi "religion" as a mixture of "all the devotional aberrations of which the human mind is capable." In his opinion, nothing could be more "repugnant and disgusting to the sentiments and judgment of people brought up in the schools of a Christian civilization." Although he had his share of conflicts with individual mission-aries in the field, Bourke clearly endorsed missionary intervention to civilize the Pueblos.[57] Even when anthropologists personally opposed aspects of the assimilationist program, government officials could easily use their work to demonstrate the need for civilizing efforts. Daniel Dorchester found evi-dence of the Pueblos' degradation not only in missionary accounts but also in the work of anthropologists including Bourke and the famed southwest-ern archaeologist Adolph Bandelier.[58] When he condemned the Pueblos' "pagan fetishism," Dorchester employed a term that European traders, colo-nial officials, and theorists of religion had used to justify the enslavement of Africans. Applied in the New World, the term served much the same pur-pose.[59] Christian and anthropological categories of comparison merged in support of the government's civilizing program.

The complexity of the anthropologists' position is evident in the career of Matilda Coxe Stevenson, another member of the Bureau of American Eth-nology's 1879 expedition. Stevenson's official role was "volunteer co-adjutor in ethnology," a sort of auxiliary to her husband Colonel James Stevenson, the self-taught geologist and ethnographer who led the expedition. While Cushing stayed in Zuni, the Stevensons went on to attempt a comparative survey of the pueblos; when the colonel died unexpectedly in 1888, his wife asked for a permanent paid position and became the bureau's first full-time female staff ethnologist. Although the bureau, in keeping with Victorian assumptions about "woman's sphere," expected Stevenson to specialize in women's and children's concerns, she was always more interested in cere-monial and religious matters, which in the pueblos were largely a male domain. She had a reputation for coercive research methods, including spurious threats that "Washington" would penalize the Indians if they did not permit her into kiva ceremonies. Like other ethnologists, she routinely collected ceremonial altars, masks, and other objects for museum display, even if that meant stimulating an illegal trade or stealing them directly from shrines. Convinced that Indian cultures were doomed to disappear, ethnolo-gists saw such "salvage ethnography" as the only way to preserve their memory. Ironically and tragically, their theft of indigenous artifacts became in itself a serious threat to Zuni ceremonial life.[60]

Their ethnocentric arrogance notwithstanding, anthropologists like Ste-venson represented a step toward a more positive appreciation of indigenous traditions. Although convinced that Indian traditions were inferior, Stevenson insisted on their scientific value and their legitimacy as religion. "While Zuni religion is based on non-scientific principles of animism and sun worship and is not as advanced intellectually as monotheism," she wrote in 1881, "it is a valid system of belief and can be used to show how religion developed."[61] Although she shared the civilizing goals of the missionary establishment, Stevenson saw the anthropologist's detailed knowledge of Zuni tradition as a far superior way to attain them. To illustrate the gulf between Indians and missionaries, she told the story of "Nina," a Zuni girl who attended a mission school and later renounced her "Christian" identity. Despite Nina's initial pride at the "marriage certificate given her by the minister," according to Stevenson she "had no real conception of Christianity" and later destroyed the certificate in order to "be rid of Christianity." The moral for the ethnologist was that missions were useless without deeper comprehension and communication. "The few who attend the Christian services," she wrote mournfully, "do so with no real understanding of what the services mean."[62]

Stevenson's civilizing agenda is especially evident in her campaign against witchcraft, the object of her greatest moral outrage, which she argued must be thoroughly "rooted out" before the Zunis could make any "great advance in civilization." When one missionary saved the life of an accused witch, calling in troops to arrest the bow priests who would have executed her, Stevenson judged the method ineffective because it was based on force rather than knowledge: "Primitive man must be approached according to his understanding; thus the prime requisite for improving the conditions of the Indian is familiarity with Indian thought and customs. . . . The Indian will never be driven." This insistence on sympathetic understanding, and on the validity of Indian traditions as religion, often led anthropologists like Stevenson and Cushing to criticize coercive civilizing tactics.[63]

Assimilationist reformers and government officials were far more committed to the goal of eliminating Indian ceremonies, but even they generally agreed that force was not the most effective way to do so. Many Native Americans had simply refused to obey the Religious Crimes Code of 1883, and some tribes continued to practice even the sun dance and other explicitly forbidden ceremonies in secret. The strength of this Native American resistance, along with the tragedy of Wounded Knee, convinced most officials that further force could backfire. Leo Crane, the author of several popular books on his experiences as a BIA superintendent for the Hopi and the New Mexico Pueblos, recalled that Commissioner Cato Sells had refused his request to send in troops to prevent the initiation of Hopi children during a snake dance in 1915. Crane complained that the "Washington office" had never given him enough support to restrict Indian dancing, and his books provided fodder for the opponents of Pueblo dances in the 1920s controversy. But even he acknowledged that the Indians' persistence made anything more than "a thin line of supervision and restraint" virtually impossible. Only after a younger generation had been educated in government schools, he wrote, would the Hopi dances "languish, and pass away entirely with the going of the elders from the mesa stage."[64]

Because they were convinced of the benefits of education, BIA agents exercised the most force in their efforts to get Indian children into school. In one notorious incident, Crane called in an army colonel to convince Chief Youkeoma of Hotevilla (the most conservative Hopi village) either to accept a government day school in the village or to send the tribe's children away to boarding school. "The Hopi had defied two former superintendents and for several years had done exactly as they pleased, in utter disregard of all admonitions emanating by mail from Washington," Crane wrote. "The example to about fifteen hundred other and disciplined Hopi and to several thousand unregulated and undisciplined Navajo, all in constant touch with these rebels, was not good." Youkeoma refused with a lengthy exposition on Hopi sacred history, concluding that unless they "cut off Youkeoma's head," he could not yield, "for then the Sea would swallow up the land, and all would perish." The colonel imprisoned Youkeoma, and his troops searched the village, collected sixty-nine children, and forcibly took them away to school—only one of many cases of enforced school attendance for Indian children.[65]

Assimilationists constantly struggled to strike the right balance between education and coercion. Mary Dissette, who would become a supporter of Burke's dance policy in the 1920s, came to Zuni as a Presbyterian missionary teacher in 1888 and nine years later became principal of what had become the government-operated day school in the pueblo.[66] In keeping with the women's missionary movement that shaped her identity, Dissette believed that "primitive" tradition was degrading to Indian women and girls: "Until [the Zunis] are compelled to treat their girls as other than female animals, but little progress in civilization will be made." She condemned the Zuni dances as "ruinous alike to health and morals," and as the source of the "male supremacy" that kept Zuni women in bondage. Nevertheless, she rejected the idea that they should be forcefully ended: "All the attempts aimed directly at the suppression of the dances will only arouse the bitterest hostility and a steady opposition to any scheme of education." Instead, she proposed an ambitious program of social engineering that she hoped would indirectly eliminate the ceremonies. Condemning the main Zuni town for its "unsanitary" conditions and its role as the tribe's ceremonial center, she advocated permanently moving all Zunis to the small farming villages where many of them already lived during the summer months. Children would attend a central day school and be assigned to live in cottages out in the villages where a staff "mother" could teach them "the refinement of family life." With such a system, she was certain that the dances would soon "die a natural death."[67]

Implementing such a program would of course require a fair amount of force, which Dissette justified as a necessary expedient for the Indians' own good. Her choice of metaphor reveals how closely she linked her assimilationist convictions with the health and sanitation reforms then advocated by progressive female reformers.[68] "The Indian is as full of fear of the results of inoculation with the virus of civilization as the white people were of vaccination when the first attempts to introduce it were made. Like them he too must be compelled to submit to the process until its good effects are apparent, when he will cease to resist. Without it, he is a walking pest house and a menace to the territory in which he lives." Dissette had come to believe that Indians would need to be forced to accept the first steps toward civilization until they could see its benefits for themselves. Like most advocates of assimilation, she believed that Christian evangelism and assimilation went hand in hand: "If I am ever permitted to see the inauguration of such a system, I will be ready to adopt with a modification, the sentiment of Simeon: 'Lord, let now thy servant depart (from Zuni) in peace, for mine eyes have seen Thy Salvation.'" Dissette's Christian commitments blended with her civilizing ideals so that the eventual elimination of the "pagan" dances, whether by education or by force, seemed absolutely essential.[69]

During the first two decades of the twentieth century, however, the leading organizations of the missionary establishment emphasized other concerns. Indian dancing was not even on the agenda at annual meetings of the Home

Missions Council of the Federal Council of Churches, the Indian Rights Association, and the annual Friends of the Indian conference at Lake Mohonk. These groups may have avoided the issue out of a fear that overly negative images would provide ammunition to those who saw Indians as permanently inferior. Plagued with disillusionment and dissention, the assimilationist consensus of previous decades had largely evaporated. Critics charged that Indians who had been given the benefit of private landownership under the Dawes Allotment Act had proved incapable of competing in the free market and that Indians educated at government expense were reverting to "pagan" traditions as soon as they returned to their reservations. On one side, radical assimilationists argued that the reservation system itself prevented Indians from adopting civilization and called for an immediate end to the BIA. On the other, policy makers influenced by developments in so-called race science concluded that the Indians were permanently inferior and called for scaled-down educational programs aimed at training Indians to accept a permanent position in America's racialized underclass. Many who refused this conclusion edged perilously close to it by adopting the "scientific" view that Indians would reach civilization only after a long process of racial evolution and until then must remain on the reservations under the BIA's careful guidance and protection.[70]

In the midst of these acrimonious debates, Welsh and the rest of the Christian establishment tried to maintain the classic assimilationist position as a middle ground, arguing that Indians could indeed become fully civilized in a relatively short time but still needed the BIA's guidance in the meantime. They blamed any apparent lack of progress not on Indians themselves but on government mismanagement and abuse. Some agents quite notoriously skimmed from the tribal funds they managed, received kickbacks from the sale of Indian land, or profited from illegal liquor sales to Indians, and the IRA focused much of its reform energies on removing agents who failed to set a "civilizing" example. To demonstrate the Indians' capacity for civilization, they offered examples of well-educated "progressive" and "Christian" Indians. Without a word against the "pagan dances" that would so preoccupy them a few years later, the IRA praised the "ability and earnestness" of the Santa Clara governor and tribal council that brought a litany of charges against Northern Pueblos superintendent C. J. Crandall. "The Santa Clara Pueblos are intelligent and industrious," wrote IRA secretary Matthew Sniffen in the association's 1920 annual report, while "the example set before them by Government officials is charged often to be degrading."[71]

Whether they prioritized education or forceful suppression, and whether they advocated gradual or immediate assimilation, those who directed Indian affairs were so certain of the necessity and superiority of Protestant Christianity that it rarely occurred to them that the principles of religious freedom might be applicable to Indian traditions. If Indian traditions were considered "religion" at all, they certainly were not the kind of religion that merited government protection. Instead, they were viewed as constituting an inferior and "primitive" religion that Christianity would sooner or later supersede, or—in classic missionary terms—simply as "heathenism," the degrading idolatry of pagans. In 1896 Congregationalist minister and Board of Indian Commissioners member Rev. Dunning summed up the prevailing views of his colleagues by noting, "if we press forward along the line of civilization, the Government taking care of the secular business, the churches imposing upon the civilization which the Government creates a loyalty to Jesus Christ, some of us will live long enough to see the name 'Indian' pass into history."[72] These leaders in federal Indian policy understood the government and the Protestant missions as essential co-workers in the ultimate goal of bringing Indians into the fold of a "Christian civilization" conceived in essentially Protestant terms.

"Their Religion Is Catholic": Challenging the Protestant Establishment

Despite their strength, Protestants never enjoyed absolute or uncontested dominance in Indian affairs. Both Indians and Catholics, sometimes in unison, challenged the Protestants' privileged position and their assumptions of religious superiority. At least a few BIA agents were sympathetic to their demands. As early as 1873, Nathaniel Pope, then agent in Santa Fe, reported "a general feeling of insecurity among [the Pueblo Indians] on account of alleged attempts at interference in their religious affairs, and . . . serious troubles at one of their villages on account of religious differences." According to Pope, he told the Indians that the U.S. Constitution "guaranteed the right to all to worship as they might select" and promised them "that no man or set of men would be permitted to dictate or interfere in their religious affairs."[73] The Pueblo leaders who met with Pope were evidently protesting against such outside interference, but the report gives no hint about whether they or the agent first interpreted the issue in terms of religious freedom, or about how the Indians themselves might have understood or applied this principle. As time went on, they used it to defend their traditions— most often on the basis of a *Catholic* religious identity—against Protestant incursions.

Pope himself seems to have considered religious freedom applicable to Catholics and Protestants but not to the indigenous Indian traditions. The main religious troubles he reported were at Laguna, where the influence of the Presbyterian Marmon brothers, a government teacher and a missionary who both married into the tribe, made Laguna the only pueblo with significant numbers of Protestants. As Pope reported, the Protestant group conflicted with "the Indians who still worship Montezuma, and insist that all others shall do the same." The agent clearly sympathized with the Protestant group and hoped that the Marmons would help to protect the tribe from "heathen" domination. In fact, he did not even deign the "followers of Montezuma" worthy of the term "religion." Except at Laguna, he wrote, "most of the Pueblos who profess any religion are Catholics." Unlike many of his fellow agents, Pope considered the Catholic Church a legitimate American religion and a valuable ally in the civilizing effort: "the Catholic Church has done an immense amount of good among them in years past," and "without aid or encouragement from the Government" had placed "teachers in most of the principal villages." Pope was so enthusiastic about the positive effects of the Catholic missions and schools that he asked Commissioner Francis Walker to "turn over the Pueblo school-fund" so that Bishop Lamy of Santa Fe could directly administer the Pueblos' education. Not surprisingly, both Walker and his successor Edward P. Smith, a former Congregationalist missionary, rejected this proposal. Nevertheless, Pope's report illustrates the potential for Catholic as well as Protestant involvement in the administration of Indian affairs.[74]

Catholics worked very hard to ensure that this potential would be realized. The BIA began to grant contracts to churches for the operation of Indian schools in the 1870s, and despite the ongoing Protestant bias in Indian affairs, the Catholic Church was well positioned to become the primary recipient of these funds. Divided and disillusioned by the difficulties of administering the reservations under the Peace Policy, most Protestant denominations were having trouble sustaining their missions to Indians. In the meantime, outraged at their exclusion under Grant's administration, Catholics had created a new Bureau of Catholic Indian Missions (BCIM)in Washington and were working to expand their presence on the reservations. These efforts gained support from heiress Kátherine Drexel and from the growing numbers of Catholic immigrants who joined religious orders, some of whom became missionaries. By 1886, mostly because they applied for a majority of the contracts, the Catholics operated thirty-eight out of the fifty mission schools that received government funding.[75] Serving the Pueblo Indians at that time were thirteen day schools—two government-operated, seven Catholic, and four Presbyterian—and three boarding schools, two of them Catholic (both with government contracts) and one, formerly under contract to the Presbyterians, which the BIA was now managing directly.[76] Catholic fortunes in the BIA would further improve under the Democratic administrations of President Grover Cleveland (1885–89 and 1893–97), when significant numbers of Catholics were appointed as Indian agents.

Protestant missionaries and reformers worked to combat this growing Catholic influence. In the 1880s the contract school system was the major point of contention. Herbert Welsh complained that "very significant favoritism is being shown the Roman Catholic church by the Indian Bureau." Welsh believed that this situation was not only unfair to Protestants but an active threat to American values. The "Romish Church," he informed the secretary of the interior in 1888, is "un-American" because "controlled by a power [the Pope] outside of our commonwealth." Lake Mohonk's "Friends of the Indian" immediately took up the cause. The contract schools, opined speakers at that year's conference, were "un-American" because they represented a "*quasi* union of Church and State." Many agreed with Rev. Lyman Abbott, the influential Congregationalist minister and social gospel exponent, who called for a universal, compulsory school system for Indians run completely by the federal government. The only solution, according to another Congregationalist minister, was "to have no aid to denominational schools afforded by the Government. This principle is as sound in Dakota as it is in Boston." With Catholic schools receiving most of the government contracts, Protestant leaders called for an end to the entire system.[77] These arguments echoed the previous year's campaign by Protestants in Boston (and earlier in New York) against public funding for Catholic parochial schools. Catholics, who disliked the Protestant character of the regular public schools, demanded equal rights in the form of government funds for their own schools. Protestants, who considered the public schools "nonsectarian" despite their decidedly Protestant prayers and Bible readings, angrily denounced such a proposal as a violation of the suddenly urgent constitutional principle of the separation of church and state.[78]

The same was true in Indian affairs. In 1889 the new Republican president Benjamin Harrison nominated two veterans of the Catholic school controversies to manage Indian affairs for his administration. For superintendent of Indian schools, he selected our friend Daniel Dorchester, whose book *Romanism vs. the Public School System* was written during the Boston controversy as a bitter polemic against Catholicism. His choice for commissioner of Indian affairs was Thomas Jefferson Morgan, a former Baptist minister and professor at the Baptist Union Theological Seminary in Chicago who had an equally anti-Catholic record. Morgan had long been an outspoken advocate for universal public schools as a way to create a moral citizenry, and now he applied these principles to the Indians. A good education, as he told the Lake Mohonk conference, would "convert [the Indians] into American citizens, [and] put within their reach the blessings which the rest of us enjoy"—including "the solace and stimulus afforded by a true religion."[79] Together, Morgan and Dorchester worked to eliminate the contract school system and bring all Indian schools under direct government control. As in the state public schools, anti-Catholicism motivated predominantly Protestant leaders to "secularize" the Indian schools.[80]

Catholics tried to defend the contract school system by arguing that their schools not only were of excellent quality but were the choice of the predominantly Catholic tribes they served. In 1891 Commissioner Morgan explained the need for a new government-operated boarding school for the Pueblos by attacking the educational standards at St. Catherine's, the Catholic boarding school in Santa Fe that had formerly received government contract funding. Morgan raised the familiar Protestant allegation that centuries of Catholic missions had failed to improve the Pueblos' conditions and accused the church of opposing the new government school in order to maintain a religious monopoly that failed to meet the Indians' needs: "Unless something is done, [the Indians] must continue, as they have long been, in a semilethargic condition, making little progress in civilization." Archbishop J. B. Salpointe of Santa Fe responded by arguing that he had never opposed the government school as such but only its Protestant bias. "We do not attack," he wrote; "we are the attacked in the war Mr. Morgan is waging against the religion of our Pueblo Indians." The new government boarding school, he explained, was teaching "religious principles" that were opposed to "the [Catholic] religion the Indians have professed for over two centuries and which they earnestly wish to be the religion of their children." Like so many others, Archbishop Salpointe identified the "religion" of the Pueblos as exclusively Catholic. From this perspective, religious liberty for the Pueblos meant the freedom to remain Catholics and to attend Catholic schools.[81]

Commissioner Morgan attempted to avoid overt discrimination against Catholics, insisting that the government schools did not and could not favor any "particular creed." However, he struggled to reconcile this legal requirement with his conception of Catholicism as a regressive influence. "If the work done in these public schools interferes with the faith of any of the pupils, whether Protestant or Catholic," he explained, "it is incidental and constitutes no part of the work of these institutions." In other words, if in their work of "preparing the children for citizenship" the schools turned students away from Catholicism, this should not be seen as religious discrimination but simply as a necessary corollary to the civilizing process. Like other members of the Protestant establishment, Morgan was convinced that only Protestant Christianity could positively contribute to the government's civilizing agenda. By protesting discrimination against Catholics, Archbishop Salpointe forced the BIA to at least officially acknowledge that Catholicism was a legitimate religion against which the government could not constitutionally discriminate. But the commissioner's continuing anti-Catholicism (and its policy implications for the BIA schools) suggests just how strong the Protestant establishment remained.[82]

As Salpointe suggested, most Pueblo Indians at the turn of the century expressed firm commitment to Catholicism. Dolores Romero, a triple rarity as a Hispanic, Catholic, and female BIA agent, had reported to the commissioner in 1885 that the Pueblo Indians wanted Catholic rather than Protestant schools. She pointedly criticized the Protestant missionary teachers for neglecting their students in favor of "missionary work" and called for government support for the Catholic schools: "The parents of the children told me that they, being Catholics, did not like and would not send their children to Protestant schools."[83] At Jemez Pueblo, the vast majority of the Indians cooperated with Father Barnabas Meyer's ongoing battle against the struggling Presbyterian mission. At Meyer's request, all but one of Jemez's *principales* agreed to sign a statement expressing their opposition to any "Protestant, non-Catholic or non-denominational" religious exercises or schools, and their firm desire "to remain true members of [the] Roman Catholic Church, and . . . to have our children instructed in said Roman Catholic Church."[84] Like the government schools, Catholic schools provided the Indians with instruction in English and other skills that they needed to negotiate in the outside world. Even when Catholic schools did restrict indigenous practices, the Pueblos often preferred them simply because Catholicism had been a part of Pueblo tradition for so long. Presenting themselves as good Catholics helped them to resist the incursions of Protestant missionaries who demanded far greater changes in Pueblo life.

While Catholic priests insisted on the Pueblos' commitment to the Catholic religion, they expressed growing ambivalence about the indigenous Pueblo ceremonies. On one hand, by representing these as legitimate Catholic practices, they could defend against the Protestant claim that the centuries of Catholic missions had achieved nothing. Starting in 1899, a few of these priests were once again Franciscans, who came at the request of the new Archbishop Pierre Bourgade to help revitalize the Pueblo missions.[85] Fridolin Schuster, a longtime Franciscan missionary to Laguna Pueblo who would later join the assimilationist crusade against Pueblo dances, wrote positively in the 1910s about dances held to "honor the Holy Child" and the Catholic saints. On one occasion he even affirmed "one of the very few secret dances still held by the Lagunas" as "entire proper."[86] Apparently such images had a broad appeal among American Catholics. The *Indian Sentinel*, which served as a fundraising tool for Catholic Indian missions, published similar pieces on such a regular basis over the years that its editors must have found them useful for reaching potential donors.[87] At times priests blamed Protestant influence rather than the indigenous traditions for any problems they saw among the Pueblos. At Isleta, Father Docher worried that the Indians in his care were now "in grasp of Protestantism" because the teachers at the local BIA day school were Protestants and refused to take them to mass. Because of this Protestant influence, he complained, these Catholic children were now "being raised like little animals, without fear of God or respect for their parents or even their priest."[88] In keeping with their early Franciscan predecessors, priests like Schuster and Docher most often considered the Pueblo indigenous ceremonies as a matter of "custom" and sometimes even as legitimate Catholic practice—certainly not as a competing "religion."

On the other hand, as the priests defended their work against Protestant criticisms, they increasingly condemned what they called the "immoral dances and practices of the Indians."[89] The Franciscan Anselm Weber, a pioneering missionary to the Navajo who also revived Catholic missions at Zuni, wondered if his church should continue to tolerate indigenous Pueblo ceremonies. Privately he wondered "whether the Catholic policy of tolerating paganism, while hoping and trying to unsnarl the pueblo religious dichotomy, half pagan, half Christian, would net any long-term results; or whether the Protestant approach in demanding of its converts a complete cultural rupture with pueblo life was not sounder policy."[90] Many priests were less hesitant, especially when it came to the mysterious "secret dances" that had never been linked to Catholic ritual and persisted as a nagging reminder of the Indians' "paganism." Applauding any government agent who would try to stop the Cochiti Indians' "secret and abominable customs," Father Jerome Hesse concluded that his "greatest desire" was "that something would be done to abolish [these] secret dances."[91] Such doubts seem to have grown stronger in the early decades of the twentieth century, at the very same time the Catholic missionaries were seeking full inclusion in the administration of Indian affairs. As Catholic missionaries fought the Protestant establishment, their need to prove themselves successful reinforced their categorization of indigenous ceremonies in terms of "custom," even as it intensified their opposition to any dances that could not easily fit within the rubric of Catholic practice.

Influenced by such missionary sentiments, the Bureau of Catholic Indian Missions in Washington occasionally lobbied for government intervention against Pueblo traditions. In 1915 BCIM director William Ketcham forwarded a series of letters from the sisters at St. Catherine's to the commissioner of Indian affairs to ask that he do something to stop the practices they reported. "Christian children returning from school" to Tesuque Pueblo, he claimed, "are forced back into revolting pagan practices against their will. The result is that the work that is being done for the children is undone in the pueblo."[92] Ketcham's concern reflects the same assimilationist priorities that shaped the IRA's support for returned students. At the same time, alongside the church's simultaneous discouragement of Hispano *penitente* rituals in New Mexico, the priests' growing concern about "pagan" ceremonies reflected a desire among Catholic leaders to prove that their church was fully compatible with American values. Catholics felt the sting of Protestant prejudices in the Southwest as well as against immigrant Catholics in the East. If Catholic missionaries could effectively Americanize Hispano and Native American populations, then perhaps they could finally prove that Catholicism was an all-American religion.[93]

As the priests' reservations hinted, no matter how committed the Pueblos were to their Catholic identity, they did not necessarily submit to the authority of the church. Like their counterparts in Protestant and BIA schools, Catholic administrators complained that the Pueblo Indians took their children out of school for the "Indian ceremonies" and sometimes did not want to enroll them at all.[94] Pueblo leaders made it quite clear that they and not the church controlled the religious life of their people. Santo Domingo's tribal council instructed its people to avoid confession, where tribal secrets might be revealed, and to avoid sending children to St. Catherine's, where they might be taught to despise Indian traditions. The pueblo's sacristan kept the church key and effectively controlled the building, allowing the priest to visit only to conduct baptisms and say mass. The priests assigned to Santo Domingo had little alternative but to accept this arrangement and did not insist on Catholic orthodoxy because they knew they did not have the power to do so. In the 1930s most of the pueblos resolutely resisted Archbishop Rudolph Gerken's efforts to demand greater conformity. Santo Domingo's council refused to allow a priest and several nuns to take up residence in the village and persisted even when the priest refused to provide any religious services until the council complied. Five years later, Santa Fe had a new archbishop more sympathetic to the Indians, and he sent a priest to say mass at Santo Domingo once again even though the tribe had not backed down on any of the disputed points. In the 1960s Isleta Pueblo expelled a priest who tried to stop the Isleta Indians from performing their dances in front of the church, and the pueblo was left with no priest at all for more than a decade. As long as the priests were willing to overlook the ceremonies as "harmless customs," there was little conflict. When they began to actively oppose the indigenous traditions, the Pueblos resisted.[95]

It was partly because Zuni's early twentieth-century leaders refused to define themselves as Catholic that they were among the first of the Pueblos to conceive of their ceremonies as a distinct "religion." The influence of so many anthropologists—attracted to Zuni partly because its resistance to Catholicism fit their criteria for "pristine" native cultures—also influenced the tribe's strategies of self-representation. When Anselm Weber secured the BIA's approval to reopen the Catholic mission at Zuni in 1907, tribal governor Quicko Chavez asked Matilda Coxe Stevenson whether Washington would be angry if the tribe refused to accept it. She told him that the Zunis were free to do as they wish, having "the right, as every citizen of the U.S. to worship as they please so long as they commit no offense against the law." Chavez informed the government agent that his people wanted "to please Washington in every way we can," but they also wished "to keep our religion and be let alone by other religions," and so did not want the Catholic mission.[96] The tribe did not allow a priest to take up residence until 1922, and then only through the intervention of a Catholic BIA agent; not until midcentury would the majority of the Zunis begin to consider themselves Catholics.[97] Zuni leaders adopted the language of religion and religious freedom as a way to defend against the civilizing missions of the government, the Catholics, and the Protestants alike. If assimilationists could use anthropology to support their agenda, the Zunis showed that Indians could do the same.

By the first decade of the twentieth century, Catholic challenges had forced the BIA to ensure scrupulous parity with Protestants in the growing network of Indian schools. In 1902 BIA superintendent C. J. Crandall reported that both Catholics and Protestants provided religious education for the Indian children at the Santa Fe Indian School. The children went "to church in the city on Sundays, care being taken to see that the Catholic children attended their own church and the Protestant pupils the churches to which they belong."[98] In 1907 the superintendent of the government boarding school in Albuquerque formed an agreement with the local Catholic priest, to be enforced by school officials, that not only permitted but required all Catholic students to attend Sunday School, confession, and mass.[99] These arrangements gave Catholic and Protestant missions equal status by actively endorsing both of them. That same year, the Bureau of Catholic Indian Missions won a Supreme Court case against the Indian Rights Association, ending yet another controversy with the ruling that Indian trust funds could be used to support mission schools. This was a major victory for the Catholics. Although their schools could no longer receive direct government funding as in the old contract system, they could now—with tribal permission—be partially supported by the funds that the BIA held in trust for the tribes. All these changes signaled the gradual dilution of the Protestant establishment's influence.[100]

BIA officials responded to ongoing Catholic-Protestant conflicts by appealing to the government's stated religious neutrality. In the 1910s Catholic priests often complained that the predominantly Protestant teachers in the government schools exerted undue influence on the "Catholic" Indians. Father Jerome Hesse went so far as to ask the BCIM to lobby against a new government school at Santo Domingo Pueblo because the teachers were unlikely to be Catholics: "No matter how favorably [non-Catholic teachers] may be disposed to our Church, as far as Religion is considered they can never replace good Catholic teachers."[101] A few years later, Father Fridolin Schuster at Isleta Pueblo appealed for day school teachers who would at least be sympathetic to the Pueblos' Catholicism: "A bigoted teacher can do much spiritual harm, especially if he or she works with the Presbyterian minister located at Laguna."[102] For the Catholic priests, the point was clear: the Pueblos were Catholic and should have teachers and agents who, if not Catholics themselves, would at least respect the Indians' Catholic religion. The BIA typically refused such requests on the grounds that so few Catholics were available and that, in any case, the government could not legally consider religion in employee placement.[103] Thus, requests for Catholic teachers were hampered by the very principles of religious neutrality that Catholics otherwise advocated.

Charges of religious bias worked both ways. In some places, the government took over what had been Catholic schools and continued to employ the nuns as teachers. When the same thing happened at Protestant mission schools, former missionary teachers easily blended into the cultural norms of the government schools. Catholic sisters, who continued to wear their religious garb, remained more visible. It did not take long for Protestants—including the interdenominational Home Missions Council and the Indian Rights Association—to complain that the nuns' obvious Catholic identity suggested government endorsement of Catholicism. In 1912 the Presbyterian missionary at Jemez Pueblo complained "that it was unconstitutional to permit the Sisters to teach a Government school," and once again the Presbyterian Board of Missions demanded that the BIA stop employing "garbed" teachers. Commissioner Valentine had responded to similar complaints the previous year by prohibiting teachers from wearing religious garb, but he had since resigned over other matters. The BIA inspector who came to Jemez determined that despite their garb the sisters were not teaching religion during school hours and so did not violate constitutional principles. In the end, the secretary of the interior shaped a compromise, ruling that those nuns already teaching had entered government service under special circumstances and must be allowed to continue as they were, but agreeing with the Protestants that new teachers in government schools should not be permitted to wear such identifiably religious attire.[104]

In the sense that the Indian schools were now government- rather than church-operated, these changes represented secularizing trends in the administration of Indian affairs. As in the nation's public schools, Protestant fears about Catholic influence had created a new expectation that church and state must be kept strictly separated. But by no means did the government stop endorsing Christianity. Instead, BIA officials now expressed their appreciation of both Catholic and Protestant missionaries as co-workers in the mission of civilizing the Indians. In 1921, when Commissioner Cato Sells expressed his ardent appreciation for "the constant labors of the Christian missionaries," he was careful to list both Protestant and Catholic examples: "Governmental administration must indeed count itself fortunate in having the assistance of men and women whose best powers, and often their lives, are freely given for the moral ideals of Christian citizenship."[105] Far from abandoning its view of the civilizing benefits of Christian missions, the BIA had simply expanded its horizons so that Catholic as well as Protestant Christianity could now be considered a legitimate American religion that could fully share in that responsibility. In this sense, what seemed to be secularization was simply the expansion of an exclusively Protestant to a more broadly Christian establishment.

The supposedly neutral government policies of this era effectively reinforced the exclusion of Native American traditions from consideration as legitimate religions. In 1910, in response to Catholic protests about the Protestant bias of the government schools, Commissioner Valentine had established new guidelines requiring parents to specify in writing which religious services and Sunday Schools their children should attend while they were enrolled in boarding schools. Missionaries and school principals were to arrange specific times for "religious instruction," either Protestant or Catholic. To ensure neutrality in school assemblies, Valentine instructed that "the religious part" of these gatherings should be led by government employees rather than missionaries, and that "Scriptural readings" should include only the four gospels and the Acts of the Apostles (texts supposedly free of denominational bias).[106] In effect, Indians were required to choose their religious affiliation from whichever Christian churches happened to have local missions. This policy, which remained in effect until John Collier became commissioner of Indian affairs in the 1930s, defined religious instruction, and by implication religion itself, as exclusively Christian. In this way, efforts to ensure parity between Catholics and Protestants excluded Native American traditions from what counted as "religion" in the Indian schools.

Not surprisingly, most Pueblo Indians did not yet attempt to define their traditions as "religion," preferring instead to continue their long-standing strategy of defending them as a part of a newly respectable Catholicism. When missionaries and government officials intensified their efforts against the Pueblo ceremonies in the early 1920s, it would only make sense for many of them to respond, at least initially, by claiming a solidly Catholic identity. By that time, an influx of cultural modernists in New Mexico had brought entirely new ways of thinking about Indian religion.

◆

TWO

Cultural Modernists and Indian Religion

Mabel Dodge Luhan, arts patron and former member of Greenwich Village's bohemian avant-garde, recounted in a four-volume autobiography her long quest for a place that would satisfy her inner hunger. "Only religion will fill me," she remembered thinking. "Someday, I will find God." Like a number of early twentieth-century artists and intellectuals, she eventually found this sense of fulfillment in New Mexico and especially in her encounters with the Pueblo Indians. She recalled that during her first excursion north from Santa Fe, one crisp winter day in December 1917, the earth itself had seemed to resonate with her inner sense of the divine. Watching "the hills, the canyons, the cottonwood trees," she wrote, "I heard the world singing in the same key in which my own life inside me had sometimes lifted and poured itself out . . . 'Holy! Holy! Holy!'" A few days later, at Santo Domingo Pueblo's Christmas Eve ceremony, Luhan concluded that the Pueblo Indians possessed the most powerful religion she had ever observed. She reacted vehemently against a comment by the artist Paul Burlin that the Pueblo dances were an "art form which should be known to the world, so people could enjoy it." Burlin was one of many in their circle who defined the Pueblo ceremonies primarily in terms of art or, more commonly, as a model of the "primitive" unity between art and religion. Although Luhan shared this general perspective, she disagreed with Burlin's emphasis. "This isn't an art form," she remembered telling him. "It's a living religion—it's alive like the Greek religion was alive before it became an art form and died out. . . . As soon as religion is commercialized it has turned into an art form!" Here Luhan rejected the term "art" because it suggested a commodified cultural product, something separate from the vibrant heart of communal life that she identified as "religion." This chapter examines the significance of her and other modernists' increasing use of the term "religion" to describe the Pueblo ceremonies, and of their growing conviction that this appellation offered the most promising way to protect Pueblo traditions.[1]

Luhan represented a familiar pattern of American cultural elites fascinated with Indian ways of life. In a romantic tradition derived partly from philosophers like Rousseau, idyllic descriptions of various peoples described as "primitives" were a recurrent theme in European and American history, serving as a foil for the assorted maladies that cultured critics diagnosed in "civilized" societies. Primitivist images of Indians could be found in almost any period of American history, but their prevalence and their dominant themes changed over time. In Enlightenment thought, Indians exemplified the "natural man" and, as such, were believed to reveal the original ethics, aesthetics, and social arrangements of the earliest human beings. Although this trope implied a human ideal against which the "civilized" could be found wanting, it also suggested a childlike simplicity that must (perhaps regrettably) be outgrown. Ultimately, the "natural man" must give up the innocence and poetics of childhood in order to advance to racial maturity. Even though it was more positive than the outright disparagement that typified frontier attitudes, or the missionary attacks on "heathenism," this "noble savage" ideal also helped make European conquest and then U.S. western expansion appear natural and therefore inevitable. Such relatively sympathetic depictions faded temporarily in the mid-nineteenth century through the controversy over slavery and the momentum of westward expansion. Overtly racist theories deeming Indians along with all nonwhites permanently inferior reached their peak of influence in the early twentieth century, a time of heightened racial discrimination against African Americans, Asians, and Native Americans. Meanwhile, middle- and upper-class intellectuals disillusioned with the inauthenticity they saw in late Victorian culture had grown more and more enthralled with medieval, Oriental, and so-called primitive societies—all of which seemed to offer communal and spiritual virtues that "modern" civilization lacked.[2]

This chapter charts the changing views of "religion" and the "primitive" among early twentieth-century artists, writers, and scientists and, in the process, introduces a number of people who would help to defend the Pueblo ceremonies in the dance controversy. The first to arrive in New Mexico, including anthropologists Frank Hamilton Cushing and Matilda

Coxe Stevenson, writer Charles Lummis, and artists like John Sloan, were often fascinated with Indian ways of life but did not share Luhan's romantic idealization of Indian "religion." Those who did not directly support Christian missions understood all religion—including Christianity and the Indian traditions—as a part of humanity's primitive past. Their occasional praise for the Pueblo ceremonies revealed as much about their desire to discredit Christianity as it did about any intrinsic interest in Indian religion, and they emerged in the early twentieth century as a new threat to the Christian establishment that had dominated federal Indian policy for so long. That challenge intensified as America's intellectual and cultural elites embraced artistic and literary modernism, depth psychology, and new anthropological theories of cultural relativism. Following the lead of European modernists like Picasso and Cezanne who looked to African, Oceanic, or other cultures that they labeled "primitive" for artistic inspiration, growing numbers of American artists hoped to revitalize their art by drawing on American Indian cultural and spiritual resources. Luhan and other members of the avant-garde embraced this movement, including its fascination with the primitive, as a part of their larger rebellion against late Victorian certainties and orthodoxies. The tragedies of World War I intensified many modernists' disillusionment with Euro-American civilization, and Luhan was among many who turned to art, nature, and religion—all of which they associated with the primitive—for answers. Luhan was not the only one who came to see the Pueblo dance ceremonies as the rites of the most authentic and vibrant religion still in existence, even as a potential source for the revitalization of modernity itself.

The political impact of this sort of primitivism has been the subject of intense scholarly debate. According to their critics then and now, early twentieth-century artists and writers were interested in Indians primarily to enrich themselves and titillate their spiritual and artistic desires. By perpetuating images of Indians living harmoniously in an "enchanted" landscape, apparently untouched by the corruptions of modernity, artists and writers throughout the period mystified and denied the increasing poverty, racial conflict, and economic exploitation experienced by both Hispanos and Indians in the region. In many ways, the modernist elevation of Indian "religion" only intensified these tendencies. Because modernists saw Indians as timeless primitives and, for the most part, wanted them to stay that way, they often had trouble viewing Indians as real people struggling to maintain tribal identities in difficult circumstances. Although their goals were very different from those of the assimilationist "friends of the Indian," they too believed they knew what was best for Indians and failed to understand the diversity of Indian perspectives.[3] Yet in very real ways modernists aided Indian efforts for cultural and political self-determination. Their primitivist fascinations sometimes brought them into relationships with actual Indian people, who offered them a more realistic understanding of the challenges Indians faced. In the long run, modernists and Pueblo leaders would develop the primitivist celebration of Indian "religion" into a political argument for religious freedom, land rights, and tribal sovereignty. Despite the modernists' mystifications and subtle coercions, their positive reevaluation of Indian "religion" opened up cultural spaces for the emergence of Indian voices into public debate and for the critiques of primitivism that followed.[4]

Secular Evolutionism: All Religion Is Primitive

In the nineteenth century, anthropological theories of evolution provided a primary foundation for secularist critiques of religion. Most evolutionists agreed with Protestant leaders that Christianity was the most highly evolved religion, but they differed from assimilationists like Herbert Welsh because in the end they relegated all religion to a "primitive" residue that the most civilized societies would soon leave behind. The pioneering British anthropologist E. B. Tylor, whose *Primitive Culture* (1871) had helped inaugurate social evolutionary theory, identified religion as a characteristically primitive mode of thought that became more sophisticated as civilization evolved. Using typical anti-Catholic polemics against "rites more naturally belonging to barbaric culture," he depicted Protestant Christianity as the most rational and therefore most advanced form of religion. But religion disappeared altogether in the highest stages of human development, when "religious authority is simply deposed and banished, and the throne of absolute reason is set up without a rival even in name."[5]

The same was true for Lewis Henry Morgan, whose *Ancient Society* (1877) mapped out the evolutionary "stages" of savage, barbaric, and civilized. Morgan did not devote much of his writing to what he called "primitive religions" because he found them uniformly "grotesque and to some extent unintelligible." His Christian premises were evident in framing comments that attributed the "marvelous fact" of civilization's emergence to the "good providence of God." This sort of intellectualized and almost deistic Protestant faith was common among nineteenth-century American scholars, a faith that made the divine so removed and so transcendent that it was largely irrelevant to the practical concerns of life. Morgan and Tylor both held their deepest faith in human progress, implicitly moving beyond Christianity altogether, and prioritized their version of scientific evidence over any religious truth claims. Theories of "human degradation" that attributed "savage" forms of religion to decline from an original monotheistic revelation, Morgan wrote, were merely "a corollary from the Mosaic cosmogony" and lacked any modern scientific foundation. Karl Marx, who saw religion not only as an "opiate" that facilitated oppression but as a stage to be outgrown as humanity moved toward the communist ideal, drew the social evolutionary foundations of his theory from Morgan. Colonel John Wesley Powell, the Civil War hero, self-taught geologist, and founding director of the Bureau of American Ethnology, was another disciple of Morgan's and an atheist who considered scientific theory a replacement for religious truth claims. All agreed that science rather than religion was the appropriate foundation for government policy.[6]

In short, the evolutionist framework shared by most late nineteenth-century scientists implicitly diminished religion's sphere in the modern world. This was the case even for Matilda Coxe Stevenson, who supported the government's civilizing agenda and enjoyed positive relationships with the Protestant missionaries at Zuni. Conversant with the scholarly debates over the origins of religion, Stevenson affirmed the theory that religion was a primitive way of explaining the world that became obsolete with the development of science. As she wrote in *Zuni Indians*, "Mythologic philosophy is the fruit of the search for the knowledge of causes. The reasoning of aboriginal peoples is by analogy, for at this stage of culture science is yet unborn. . . . The philosophy of primitive peoples is the progenitor of natural religion." Stevenson's reasoning reveals how such theory gave a far broader scope to "primitive" than to "civilized" religion. "Civilized man . . . understands natural phenomena through analysis and correlation," whereas "primitive man . . . accounts for them by analogy. Civilized man lives in a world of reality; primitive man in a world of mysticism and symbolism. He is deeply impressed by his natural environment; every object for him possesses a spiritual life." Stevenson's fascination with religious life among the Pueblo

Indians may have grown to some degree out of this sense that religion in her own society no longer held such significance or power.[7]

Such ideas help explain why some nineteenth-century anthropologists openly opposed the government's civilizing programs, grounded as they were in the Protestant establishment's synthesis of Christianity and progress. Scientists who had themselves largely left religion behind had little reason to value Christianity as a modernizing influence. In any case, their view of Indians as a "living laboratory" for the early history of all human societies meant that, if only for the sake of their research, most hoped to prolong the survival of Indian traditions for as long as possible. Ethnologist Stewart Culin, then working at Zuni, protested that BIA commissioner William Jones's 1902 order forbidding various Indian "customs," including long hair for men and face painting, was both cruel and unnecessary. "Left to themselves," he wrote, "the dances and other native customs will go too soon— alas, for the student of aboriginal customs and religion." Even though these anthropologists assumed that Indians would inevitably abandon tribal cultures and adopt "civilization," most believed that at least for the time being indigenous practices provided a sense of meaning and social cohesion for Indians and therefore, for the good of the Indians as well as for scientific research, should not be forcibly suppressed.[8]

By the end of the nineteenth century, a growing number of artists and writers were joining anthropologists to challenge the role of Christian missions in Indian affairs. One such critic was Charles Fletcher Lummis, a lifelong promoter of all things southwestern who would later join in the dance controversy in defense of Pueblo religious freedom. Neither a scholar nor a great literary talent, Lummis is still widely recognized as a pioneer who did more than anyone else to create the regional image of "the Southwest." Raised a Methodist, Lummis was religiously unobservant as an adult and ultimately considered all religion a relic of the "primitive" past. He serves in this chapter to illustrate the range and the impact of secular evolutionist ideas about "religion" and the "primitive."

As a young man, Lummis saw the West as a land of adventure and took the "civilizing" goals of the government for granted. Bored with his life as a Methodist minister's son in New England, he remembered his own childhood as overly regimented and even stifling and was drawn as a boy to travel narratives and novels of the "Wild West." When the flamboyant ethnologist

Charles Lummis, with singer
Tsianina Redfeather (Cherokee-
Creek) and Santiago Naranjo
(Santa Clara Pueblo), 1926.
From Turbese Lummis Fiske
and Keith Lummis, *Charles F.
Lummis: The Man and His West*,
courtesy University of
Oklahoma Press, Norman.

Frank Hamilton Cushing visited Cambridge with a delegation of Zuni Indians in 1882, Lummis was a student at Harvard and found Cushing's colorful tales of life at Zuni irresistible. Too restless to be a good student, he never
finished his degree at Harvard. Instead, he moved to Ohio near the family of
his new wife, a medical student named Dorothea Rhodes. Within a year he
managed to secure a job offer from the *Los Angeles Times* and soon set off for
his "tramp across the continent," a five-month walk all the way from Ohio to
Los Angeles that established his reputation and became the defining experience of his life. Lummis funded the trip through an occasional column
narrating his adventures, which appeared in his local Ohio paper and the
Times and was gradually picked up by other papers along the way.[9] His early
writings demonstrated deeply ambivalent views of Indians. Impressed by his
first encounters with the Pueblos, he praised the people of San Ildefonso for
their honesty, cleanliness, and moral virtue. "I wish they would send out
missionaries to their American brothers," he concluded. But he voiced racist
stereotypes against other tribes such as the Hualapais of Arizona, whom he
characterized as "unwashed, vile, and repulsive-faced . . . fallen into harm-
lessness and worthlessness." Convinced that even the most admirable In-

dians must embrace "civilization," he praised the "progress" of Indian students at Haskell Institute in Lawrence, Kansas, and even in reference to his favored Pueblos he opined that boarding schools were preferable to day schools because "the people do better when entirely removed from the home influence and customs."[10]

Lummis turned against the boarding school system after he saw its impact at Isleta Pueblo, where he lived for four years during his recovery from a stroke in 1888. His landlord at Isleta was Juan Rey Abeita, a member of the pueblo's most prominent family and a firm believer in the benefits of education who had enrolled his three sons in the Albuquerque Indian School. Thirty-six children from Isleta were at the school in 1891 when a new principal, convinced by General Pratt's methods at Carlisle Indian School that "civilizing" Indian children required strict separation from their "pagan" parents, forbade the students from visiting their homes even for summer vacation. At the pueblo's request, Lummis orchestrated a publicity campaign condemning the new policy as a serious injustice. "The fundamental objection would be the same," he wrote in the *Los Angeles Times*, "if a superior race (self-asserted) were to come from Mars, overrun the land and force us to send our children away from home to be rid of our silly superstitions, religion and customs, and instructed in the better ways of the people of Mars." With a hint of the cultural relativism that would later emerge in anthropological theory, Lummis asked white Americans—so certain of the superiority of their own "religion and customs"—to put themselves in the Indians' shoes and imagine an alien people forcibly imposing their own ways of life.[11]

More immediately useful for the Isleta families, he helped file a legal challenge in 1892 that eventually forced the superintendent to let their children return home. But children from other tribes remained virtual captives at the school. Alerted to their plight by Lummis's campaign, newspapers in Washington, New Mexico, and California maintained a stream of negative publicity against the "slavedriving principal" and the BIA administration that supported him. The key figures here were none other than BIA commissioner Thomas Morgan and Superintendent of Indian Schools Daniel Dorchester, whose diatribe against Pueblo "paganism" in his annual report that year was largely intended to refute Lummis's glowing portrayals of life at Isleta. Despite Dorchester's efforts, the U.S. Congress in its next session made forcible enrollment and confinement in Indian boarding schools illegal, and within two years Morgan, Dorchester, and the Albuquerque principal had all resigned. Day schools and boarding schools could and did continue to forbid students from practicing Indian religious and cultural traditions, but the BIA was at least forced to grant Indian parents access to their children. As the new BIA commissioner D. M. Browning put it, "Even ignorant and superstitious parents have rights, and their parental feelings are entitled to consideration." In this and in other instances, Lummis helped shape government policy toward at least a limited tolerance for indigenous practices.[12]

Nevertheless, Lummis's career revealed generally patronizing attitudes toward the Indians he wanted to help. Some years after he returned to Los Angeles, he became involved in the plight of the Warner's Ranch band of California's Mission Indians, who had just lost a Supreme Court case that gave a private landowner the right to evict them from their ancestral land. As a Harvard classmate and personal friend of President Theodore Roosevelt's, Lummis had influence with the administration and managed to obtain federal funding to purchase new land for the band. But he neglected to consult with the Indians themselves about their preferences and eventually found himself in the embarrassing situation of directing the forcible eviction he had tried to alleviate. During this crisis he founded the Sequoyah League to advocate for "fair play" for Indians, a task that he believed required the perspectives of tough-minded westerners, "Out-Door men" who knew the real conditions and needs of the Indians. Like other reformers of his day, Lummis assumed that only Anglos could set Indian policy, and the board of the Sequoyah League included no Indians except for the well-educated Omaha reformer Francis LaFlesche.[13]

Like so many of his contemporaries, Lummis assumed a racial hierarchy with white Americans at the top, and he placed New Mexico's Hispanos somewhat higher than Indians on measures of intelligence and sophistication. He expressed this preference in reference to both historical and contemporary questions. With enthusiasm for every bit of southwestern history, he celebrated the Spanish conquest as "the most romantic and gallant chapter in the history of America," casting the Franciscans and *conquistadores* as pioneers of modern civilization. Such unambiguous admiration for the Spaniards led Lummis to condemn even his favorite Pueblo Indians as "warlike savages" in their 1680 revolt against the "gentle missionaries."[14] He presented the Hispanos of his own day as a modern people with much to contribute to the nation's future and expected far more sophistication from them than from Indians. While unsurprised that the "aborigines" of America like the "pigmies of Africa" would hold to such "absurdities" as belief in witchcraft, he was frankly astounded to find that the majority of New Mexico's Hispanos—"voters just like you and I"—were also firm in this "article of faith." Lummis presented the "educated" segment of the Hispano population as peers and actually adopted an Hispano persona in language, dress, and life-style. In contrast, by dressing his children in Indian clothing, he revealed his identification of Indians with childlike and primitive innocence.[15]

Through all his writing and reform efforts, Lummis found his primary motivation in promoting the Southwest. To encourage tourism and development, he portrayed Indians as the raw material for the cultivation of an authentically American national identity, and this view set the tone for many artists and writers to follow. Indians appeared in much of his writing as part of an unincorporated frontier that brought world-class historical, natural, and cultural riches to the nation. He argued that Americans should learn to know the wonders of their own country before they traveled abroad. With "its strange landscapes, its noble ruins of a prehistoric past, and the astounding customs of its present aborigines, the wonderland of the Southwest" rivaled anything that could be seen around the world. Lummis argued that touring the Southwest had benefits beyond its intrinsic interest to those seeking the exotic. "If we would cease to depend so much upon other countries for our models of life and thought, we would have taken the first step toward the Americanism which should be, but is not, ours." The very strength and unity of the American nation relied on its citizens learning to know those regions that seemed most foreign. As an amateur ethnographer and archaeologist who befriended well-known scientists like Adolf Bandelier and John Gregory Bourke, Lummis considered anthropological research an invaluable tool for uncovering these hidden riches. His work made explicit one purpose for the artistic and anthropological fascination with Native Americans: to incorporate them into the mythological past of the expanding nation. In other words, even as he aided the cause of Indian self-determination in certain respects, his praise for the Indians' "customs" also helped on an ideological level to complete their conquest and subordination by the United States.[16]

Lummis's depictions of Pueblo ceremonial traditions reinforced the image of Indians as an artifact of the past. Hoping to attract visitors to view the exotica that could "still" be found "in the heart of the most civilized nation on earth," he wrote of the southwestern Indians generally as "savage peoples whose customs are stranger and more interesting than those of the Congo." He described the Hopi snake dance—already attracting growing numbers of tourists in the 1880s—as "one of the most astounding barbaric dances in the world" but made little effort to understand what he called its "superstitious aims." And he marveled at how the Pueblos somehow managed to be "as sincere a Catholic as pagan," revealing—despite his own lack of religious observance—a lingering Protestant distaste for even the most picturesque blending of religions. With "unhypocritical duplicity," these "quaint folk . . . contrived" in their saint's day celebrations "to do homage to the *santo* and to all the pagan Trues at one fell swoop."[17]

Even Lummis's most admiring portraits of Indian religion ultimately identified it as a historical relic incompatible with modern life. In 1903 the Sequoyah League mounted a campaign against Charles Burton, BIA superintendent for the Hopi and Navajo Indians, for conducting what Lummis called "a reign of terror" against the "gentle" Hopis. Burton's tactics reportedly included the use of whips, guns, and sheep shears to enforce Commissioner Jones's infamous "haircut order," and he was accused of requiring teachers to take schoolchildren "forcibly from their weeping mothers" and then beat them for using their own language at the school. Although Lummis continued to affirm the goal of educating Indians, he condemned Burton's methods as "the kind of 'education' which thinks it can Drag a Horse to the Water, and Kick his Ribs and Beat him over the head until he Thinks he is Thirsty." Such offenses were especially outrageous because they targeted the Hopis, whom Lummis praised as "the gentlest, most tractable and most inoffensive of American Indians," a "People of Peace" who possessed a "gentle dignity and self-respect, [and] a reverence for law and religion so profound that we worldlier folk can hardly comprehend." In Lummis's eyes, their "Quaker" religion made the Hopis pliable, passive, and amenable to instruction. By treating them kindly and showing them the benefits of civilization, Lummis believed, "anyone fit to teach these Indians (or any others) could lead [them] forward in civilization if there were not a gun nor a club in Arizona, nor a soldier left in America." Neither his opposition to coercive methods nor his praise for Hopi religion changed Lummis's basic view of Indians as childlike "primitives" who must eventually be civilized. Indeed, in his eyes these Indians' peaceful religion provided the ideal preparation for the civilization that must inevitably supersede it.[18]

Lummis and his opponents shared the evolutionists' certainty that Indian religion would fade in the face of modernity but offered opposing evaluations of Christianity's prospects. His nemesis Dorchester had identified the Pueblo Indians as "laggards" in a "world's march" away from the "darkness" of superstition: "Centuries of credulity have given place" in most of the world "to an age of clear-eyed men, unawed by phantoms." For him, Protestant Christianity was the true and rational religion that characterized European modernity and would necessarily be a part of the civilizing process for Indians as well.[19] In contrast, Lummis implicitly located Christianity too in humanity's primitive past. As exemplified by Superintendent Burton, Protestants in Lummis's view were fanatics opposed to reason. In his hands, Burton's reputation as a conscientious man became a liability. Just such "conscientious people" had conducted the Inquisition in Spain and "the flogging of Quakers and the hanging of witches" in New England—but "people whose mental Watches stopped 200 years ago" no longer deserved positions of public authority. "Any person fit to Go out Doors," Lummis concluded, "would rather trust his own business to a Reasonable Rascal than to a Sanctified Idiot." His rhetoric here reversed the standard characterizations of Protestant Christianity as the "good" religion instilling morality, tolerance, and other civic virtues and of other religions as disorderly and dangerous. Ultimately, he saw all religion—Hopi, Quaker, Methodist, and Catholic—as doomed to extinction. These views of religion were typical of turn-of-the-century secularist intellectuals who sought to challenge Protestant authority in American public life. Christianity, for him, was simply the European version of superstition. More than his occasional praise for Indian "religion," this secular evolutionist perspective was perhaps Lummis's most serious threat to the Christian establishment.[20]

Just as Lummis viewed Indians as the foundation for a national identity, the artists who gravitated to New Mexico in the late nineteenth and early twentieth centuries saw them as a "primitive" resource for an authentically American art. American artists often envied the historical and cultural riches of Europe, where most of them found it necessary to travel for training, inspiration, and artistic credibility. In what Helen Carr has called a "postcolonial" impulse, many hoped to develop a distinctively American tradition that did not rely on European precedents. The artist Joseph Sharp traveled around the country in the 1880s seeking resources for such a tradition and settled on Taos as his favorite destination. He returned in 1897 with artist friends Ernest Blumenschein and Bert Phillips, and these three became the founding members of the Taos art colony. They and others who followed were drawn to the natural grandeur they saw in the mountains of northern New Mexico and to the proximity of Taos Pueblo, whose multistory adobe architecture soon became a favorite subject for painters and photographers. Around the same time, another cluster of artists began to settle in Santa Fe, attracted by that city's tricultural character and to its Spanish colonial history and architecture. Whether they came to Taos or Santa Fe, artists found the "primitive" qualities they saw in local Indian and Hispano cultures especially appealing. The Pueblo Indians in particular, linked as they were to the ancient cliff dwellings and other ruins scattered around the Southwest, offered a rich cultural tradition deeply rooted in the American soil. As one artist put it, here Americans could "live down their national curse of new-ness" through the "fountainhead of a civilization older even than that of Europe." Like Lummis, they saw in the ancient ruins, the people, and the landscapes of New Mexico a kind of raw material for constructing an authen-tically American culture.[21]

Not surprisingly, paintings of Indians by these early New Mexico artists reveal typical primitivist tropes. E. Irving Couse, an established artist in New York who had already gained a reputation painting Indians in Michigan and Oregon, began spending summers in Taos in 1901. Among the most finan-cially successful of the Taos artists, he became the first president of the Taos Society of Artists in 1912. Like other artists working in New Mexico before the mid-1910s, Couse predated the modernist movement and worked in the romantic realist style then favored by the leading institutions of America's art world. He depicted stereotypically dressed Indians engaged in traditional activities, most often in idyllic natural settings and without a trace of Euro-pean impact or presence. Whether hunting, courting, or playing "the Indian flute," the Indians he painted almost always seemed to be in the woods, in the mountains, or gazing reverently at springs of water. Cumulatively, his work presented Indians as a timeless part of nature, romantic figures full of the nobility and spirituality lost to "modern" civilization.[22]

Couse's images of Pueblo Indian religious life reinforced these stereo-types. Often he focused on small groups of Indians engaged in rituals away from the village, such as planting prayer plumes or performing ceremonies at mountain shrines. When he did paint indoor ritual activity, such as making sand paintings or kachina dolls, he directed an intimate gaze on the individual ritual specialist and his work—leaving the interior details of the home so darkened that the Indian might almost have been outdoors.[23] With the notable exception of his famous painting of the Hopi snake dance, Couse very rarely painted the public ceremonial dances that later came to epitomize Pueblo culture. His focus on the individual Indian, depicted almost exclusively in natural rather than village settings, contrasts with the later modernist depictions of a deeply collective and communal Pueblo religion. What would not change was the importance of a supposedly "natural" spirituality in representations of the "primitive" Indian, who appeared entirely set apart from the transformations and corruptions of modern life.

From the beginning New Mexico's artists demonstrated an almost willful blindness to the power relations of their social environment. Their portrayals of Hispanos, who were overwhelmingly poor and made up the vast majority of the population, were almost as romanticized as those of the Indians. Where artists saw Indians as pure "primitives" and a part of nature, they painted Hispanos as "salt-of-the-earth" laborers and simple folk artists who practiced a picturesque and semiprimitive Catholicism. The systematic marginalization of Indians and Hispanos in New Mexico's economy, and the artists' own participation in that economy, remained invisible. Growing numbers of Anglo settlers were claiming what had previously been Indian and Hispano land and water. Such realities forced both Hispanos and Indians into wage labor that took them far from their homes. Many artists arriving in New Mexico bought land from financially strapped Hispano families, and in several cases the former owners became domestic servants for the artists, an aspect of provincial life not depicted in their paintings. A few Pueblo Indians worked regularly as artists' models, despite some reservations about the spiritual implications of such representations. In a 1908 interview with the *New York Herald*, Couse commented that he had first "found the Indians very superstitious about posing," but now they were so eager for this employment that he had "to send them away in processions." Indian perceptions of this relationship were not always so benign. The Taos Indian Joseph Sandoval, one of Couse's regular models, recalled years later that as a young boy he had run away from the artist's studio because he was frightened at the thought of the artist "catching" his image in paint. Couse's wife caught him and chained him to a chair, forcing him to model with the chain concealed by a blanket.[24]

For better or for worse, all of this artistic and anthropological attention to the Pueblo Indians helped create New Mexico's image as the "land of enchantment" and facilitated the growth of its tourist economy. The development of the Atchison, Topeka and Santa Fe Railroad in the 1880s had made Santa Fe easily accessible to leisure travelers from around the country. The railroad's advertising office and the Fred Harvey Company (which operated hotels and concessions along the route) hired ethnographers, artists, and writers to help market the region's healthful climate, dramatic landscapes, and exotic blend of cultures. Each year throughout the 1910s and 1920s, the railroad's annual calendar featured paintings of Indians, most of them by Couse. Local civic leaders intensified their promotional efforts after New Mexico and Arizona achieved statehood in 1912. Chief among them was the archaeologist Dr. Edgar Lee Hewett, who would later defend the Pueblo ceremonies against Commissioner Burke's policies by calling them an invaluable asset for the state's tourist economy. Hewett was an expert on the region's archaeological ruins with a doctorate from the University of Geneva, and in 1907 he founded the School of American Archaeology and the Museum of New Mexico in Santa Fe. In 1915 he served as director of exhibits for the Panama-California Exposition in San Diego, an event that brought many easterners to Santa Fe for the first time en route to California. Four years later, he spearheaded the revival of the Santa Fe Fiesta, a Spanish colonial festival commemorating the reconquest of the Pueblos in 1692—a symbol of Indian subjugation, though not openly recognized as such by Hewett and company. Relying heavily on exhibitions of Indian arts, crafts, and dances, the revived fiesta further accelerated the commodification of Pueblo culture. Lummis's dream was being realized: New Mexico and its Indians were definitely on the map for American travelers.[25]

Modernist Anthropology and the Advent of Cultural Relativism

By the early twentieth century, new theories of cultural difference were beginning to challenge anthropology's social evolutionary foundations in ways that would help to transform concepts of "religion" and the "primitive" among America's intellectual elites. Franz Boas (1858–1942), a German Jewish immigrant who became one of the leading figures in twentieth-century American anthropology, played a pivotal role in this critique. Boas had earned his doctorate in geography at the University of Kiel and shifted to anthropology after a research trip to Alaska in the early 1880s. He emigrated to the United States in 1887 and, after a series of temporary positions, joined the faculty at Columbia University. There he mentored several generations of graduate students, who became the dominant cohort in the professionalization of anthropology and reshaped the intellectual trajectory of the discipline.[26]

Boas intended his attack on social evolutionary theory to rebut ideas of racial inequality. As early as the 1880s his research among the Eskimo led him to ponder "what advantages our 'good society' possesses over that of the 'savages,'" and his letters from the field expressed harsh criticisms of missionaries and of any government interference with Indian ceremonies. His most sustained and explicit writings on racial issues, however, were directed at the "negro problem." His pivotal book, *The Mind of Primitive Man* (1911), amassed historical, cultural, and biological evidence to show that the differences between the "negro" and the "white" were far less than the variation within each group, concluding that social prejudices and antimiscegenation laws were tragically misguided. Boas deconstructed standard social evolutionary theory by demonstrating that different levels of cultural achievement could be explained as products of environment and historical experience rather than any universal evolutionary process. He also pointed out that racial classifications were difficult to determine with any precision because all people were racially mixed as a result of ongoing human migrations. Boas did not dispute the obvious point that human cultures evolved, but he denounced the idea that they did so in any linear or universal way, or that historical changes in culture could reveal anything about different levels of racial achievement.[27]

Boas and most of his students were thoroughly secular intellectuals from German immigrant families, giving them ethnic and cultural as well as theoretical distance from the American Protestant mainstream. As a secular Jew, Boas had felt the sting of anti-Semitism in Germany and emigrated partly because he hoped that America would provide freer opportunities for all—a background that motivated his critique of racism in the United States as well as abroad. His first doctoral student, Alfred Kroeber, described a childhood in New York where gentile and Jewish families mixed freely and everyone he knew "took it for granted that one did not believe in religion." Kroeber, whose parents had rejected their own families' Protestant and

Catholic faiths, remembered his mother's membership in the secular humanist Ethical Culture Society founded in New York by "an agnostic rabbi (and family friend)." As historian David Hollinger has shown, when significant numbers of Jewish scholars took positions in American universities they played a crucial role in challenging Christianity's privileged position in the academy. As a part of that process, Boas and his students intensified the secularization of a discipline whose evolutionist founders had already theorized religion's decline.[28]

Not surprisingly, Boas, along with evolutionary scientists, identified all religion as incompatible with the modern world. This view of religion relied on the long-standing dichotomy between "primitive" and "civilized" races. Boas argued that civilized societies had developed methods of rational interpretation that made them more adaptable, being more skeptical about and less tied to inherited traditions. He identified "totem" and "taboo," terms then used by a wide range of scholars to designate the earliest stages of religion, as the basis of the static traditionalism that characterized the primitive. Religion therefore appeared in his work as the central conservative force in primitive society, inhibiting the development of civilized rational thought. Primitive cultures could become civilized through a kind of evolution, though not in any universally predictable pattern, in which the ethical principles he treasured, "reason, freedom, and human fellowship," gradually replaced religion. "The number of thinkers who try to free themselves from the fetters of tradition increases as civilization advances." He sketched a kind of progression from "primitive mythology" to "medieval theology" to "modern philosophy," an implicit theory of secularization in which religion gave way to modern philosophy, science, and free thought. Where the primitive "has been taught to consider the heavenly orbs as animate beings, modern man has learned "to explain the whole range of phenomena as the result of matter and force alone." The consequential point for Boas was that the difference between primitive and civilized was not one of intelligence or biology but of cultural inheritance. Nevertheless, like other secularist intellectuals, he saw religion as a marker of the primitive, something to be respected but certainly not to be emulated.[29]

Although an independent and sometimes contentious bunch, the first generation of Boas's students largely shared these theoretical perspectives. Kroeber, who would speak out in defense of the Pueblo ceremonies in the 1920s, established a successful anthropology program at the University of

California at Berkeley and conducted research on many western tribes, including the Zuni. Kroeber saw the study of religion as a useful entrée into the historical development of human societies. In a direct rebuttal of social evolutionary theory, his influential *Anthropology* (1923) argued that even the most widespread "customs" could not be predicted as evolutionary stages but had spread through a process of "historical diffusion" involving migrations and cultural encounters. He identified four historical stages in the development of religion in America, moving from shamanism—which he believed represented "remnants of a once world-wide rudimentary form of religion"—to the uniquely American patterns of secret societies, the organized priesthood, and finally large-scale temples linked to the institution of human sacrifice. Because human sacrifice was associated exclusively with the Mayans and the Aztecs, the largest-scale urban centers of civilization in the Americas, Kroeber saw this "shocking custom" as the most advanced stage of Native American religion and suggested that it was only beginning to spread when the Spaniards arrived.[30]

Even though Kroeber intended his theory of historical diffusion to counter the idea of universal stages of evolution, he too placed the world's religions within a developmental hierarchy. Calling Native American traditions generally "lowly and backward," he located them "four to five thousand years" behind the religious developments of the Old World. "In a few thousand years more of undisturbed growth," he wrote, the custom of human sacrifice "would probably have been superseded" in the New World just as it had been in the Old. Like so many theorists of religion, Kroeber understood Christianity, Islam, and Buddhism as the world's most advanced religions. Although he praised Judaism for developing "the monotheistic idea" into the "cardinal, enduring element of a national civilization," he believed that Judaism and Hinduism both remained limited by their tribalism. In contrast to Hinduism, Buddhism "tried to be international instead of national, to overlie all cultures instead of identifying itself with only one," and both Christianity and Islam had managed to shape Judaism's monotheistic insight into "universal" religions. In what is by now a familiar move, the personally nonreligious Kroeber hinted that even these highly developed religions would ultimately fade away as science and rationality advanced. Thus, with Boas he maintained the social evolutionists' assumption that all human societies would eventually undergo the twin processes of modernization and secularization. The idea that religion would inevitably decline rested on an identification of religion with the "primitive," and no matter how much these anthropologists tried to give sympathetic and unbiased accounts of Native American culture, their theoretical presuppositions brought them back to the assumption that Indian religion could not and probably should not survive.[31]

One of the first anthropologists to question these ideas was Elsie Clews Parsons, another member of Boas's circle, who began to develop very different perspectives on Indian religions as sites of cultural resilience and resistance. Born into an upper-class New York family in 1874, Parsons was a lifelong rebel against the restrictive social conventions and hierarchies of Victorian high society. She was part of a generation of ambitious women who rejected the ideals of female domesticity and virtue that had been celebrated by the nineteenth-century women's movement. Instead, the new feminism insisted on full equality with men and on a woman's right to combine marriage and family life with public careers. Parsons lived out that ideal. The first woman to earn a Columbia University Ph.D. in sociology, she married Republican politician and progressive reformer Herbert Parsons and managed to build a successful career as a sociologist, folklorist, and anthropologist while raising four children. Her early work developed extended critiques of the social structures and conventions that blocked women's equality. In a sociology textbook, *The Family* (1906), she argued for dramatic transformations in sex relations including trial marriage and divorce by mutual consent. Parsons's writing was so virulently denounced from the pulpit and in popular magazines that she feared the fallout would rebound on her husband, who had been elected to Congress in 1905, and she tried to avoid more public controversy until after he lost his seat in 1910. But her lifelong ambition remained, as her contemporary Gertrude Stein put it, "to kill what was not dead, the nineteenth century which was so sure of evolution and prayers."[32]

Like so many intellectuals of the time, Parsons's early work presented religion in almost entirely negative terms and assumed that it would and should eventually disappear. In the early 1910s she joined forces with a group of Boas's students, led by Alexander Goldenweiser, Robert Lowie, and Paul Radin, then engaged in a wholesale attack on the shibboleths of nineteenth-century anthropology. Parsons used the comparative data of the ethnologists to challenge taken-for-granted social norms and, in a comment to Boas, to

Elsie Clews Parsons in New Mexico. Courtesy American
Philosophical Society, Philadelphia.

satirize the assumed dichotomy between "primitive" and "civilized" as "a remarkable, if unremarked, instance of folklore." Her writing was cutting-edge, incisive, and funny, making it hugely popular with the growing number of bohemian intellectuals gathering in Greenwich Village.[33] *The Old-Fashioned Woman* (1913) offered an ironic analysis of the special conventions associated with "woman," including the ways in which women were policed across cultures by the cultural invocation of supernatural forces and divine sanctions. She noted wryly that the advent of secularism had not yet ended such tactics, because even Nietzsche wrote "that a woman without piety would be 'something perfectly obnoxious or ludicrous to a profound and godless man.'"[34] These critiques of religion were aimed squarely at the Christian mores of Victorian society, but her comparative examples from around the world made it clear that she believed the same was true of all religion. Religion "fosters the state of mind which is intolerant of innovation and respectful of whatever is traditional or authoritative"—making it a major impediment to the social transformations she desired.[35] *Fear and Conventionality* (1914) concluded with a vision of Parsons's ideal "unconventional society," one where nobody would gain special privileges by virtue of their age or gender or social position, and where individual differences could be respected and celebrated rather than feared or forced into group classifications and hierarchies. Needless to say, this utopian vision did not include any mention of religion.[36]

For many of New York's intellectuals, the outbreak of war in Europe and the conservative backlash it inspired at home led to even deeper disillusionment with the prospects of Euro-American civilization. Appalled by the militarism and nativism of the war years, Parsons became dissatisfied with her role as social critic and increasingly focused on the detailed ethnographic research so characteristic of the Boasians. She and her colleagues built on Boas's work to develop the methodological stance known as cultural relativism, insisting that each culture had its own moral standards and values and that an individual's behavior could be understood or judged only in the context of that culture's norms. Still, they could not resist judging "civilization" against the positive values they found in the "primitive," and Parsons's own vision of the ideal society occasionally resurfaced in her ethnographic summaries. Praising the Pueblo Indian's "sense of town solidarity" and "his kindly live-and-let-live attitudes," she concluded, "Social responsibility combined with individual tolerance—here perhaps is an

American lead to that working substitute for the glorification of god or of State or of Mankind other Americans are seeking."[37] In search of a model for cultural adaptation, Parsons used her research on African American folklore and Pueblo Indian tradition as a way to investigate the processes of cultural encounter, adaptation, and change. Laguna Pueblo, neglected by most anthropologists because it was so Hispanicized and Americanized, was interesting for Parsons precisely because of its cultural hybridity as an ideal place to study "the problems of acculturation." She criticized those who avoided it for "a variant of the race snobbery which is ever seeking for pure races." Rather than viewing Indians as timeless and unchanging "primitives," she helped create a new interest in living Indian cultures and their creative adaptations to new circumstances.[38]

In her two-volume masterpiece, *Pueblo Indian Religion* (1939), Parsons struggled to reconcile her own emphasis on historical acculturation with the increasing tendency among many Boasians to interpret culture as personality writ large. Most famously, Ruth Benedict's *Patterns of Culture* (1934) characterized the Pueblo Indians as "Apollonians" for what she saw as a cultural emphasis on restraint, and contrasted them with the supposed abandon of the "Dionysian" Plains tribes. Reacting against the nativist and assimilationist climate of their day, Benedict and like-minded scholars tended to see any outside interference with "primitive" tribes as a polluting influence that would only create cultural hybrids inferior to "pure" specimens of either race. In this way, the new theories of cultural personality intensified the desire to study Indians only in their supposedly pristine state.[39] Parsons found some merit in the idea that cultures had distinctive personalities. Even as a "convinced historian," she did not shy away from identifying a "Pueblo genius" that "tends strongly toward group rather than individual experience" and had tried to honor the Pueblo Indians' own "feeling of cultural integrity" as well as the "various habits of life and of mind which others, if they like, may call the cultural core or configuration of the Pueblos." Yet she cautioned readers that, "without more knowledge of the occurrence of these traits in individuals," such generalizations were "highly speculative," and "that no trait is uniquely or even distinctively Pueblo merely because parallels in other Indian tribes are not mentioned, not to speak of culture at large." In this way, she rejected the idea that every Pueblo individual would necessarily share the traits that their culture generally valued or, for that matter, that cultures had clear boundaries or unique essences.[40]

This research trajectory subtly changed Parsons's view of religion. In keeping with the consensus view that both religion and the primitive would decline, she was capable of suggesting that indigenous traditions could not survive their encounter with American society. "It is likely," she wrote in 1922, "that the religious drama of Zuni is fated to go the way of the Greek tragedy or medieval mystery play." And at the beginning of *Pueblo Indian Religion*, she defined religion in terms similar to those of both Tylor and Boas as "a form of instrumentalism controlling the natural through the supernatural . . . less antithetical to science than it is science gone astray"—in other words, a way for people who had not yet developed modern science to understand and control their world. Yet, increasingly Parsons presented Pueblo religion as one way in which the Indians had adapted and survived throughout their history of colonial encounters. On the basis of her research at Zuni, she theorized that the kachina cult represented not "pure" native tradition—she found no evidence of such masked dances before the Spanish conquest—but a creative accommodation between indigenous ceremonialism and the Spanish Catholic cult of the saints. Both involved holy figures who had once lived among men, now lived in "mountaintops or springs or the sky," were accessible either through images or impersonators, conferred blessings on the faithful, and expected prayers and pilgrimages from their devotees. Like contemporary scholars of religion, she recognized the culturally constructed nature of the categories she used. "Obviously from both native and scientific points of view," she wrote, "the book should be concerned with the entire life of the Pueblos and not merely with the segment we are pleased to call their religion." In much of Parsons's anthropological writing, then, religion appeared not as a primitive stage to be left behind but as a crucial site of Pueblo cultural adaptation and resilience.[41]

Romantic Primitivism: Reenchanting the World?

For many of the modernist artists and writers who came to New Mexico after the war, the Pueblo ceremonies offered far more than simple artistic inspiration or ethnographic data. Rebels against the certainties of "Christian civilization," they identified among the Pueblos a "primitive" or "pagan" religion that they hoped could bring new vitality to their art—and perhaps even reenchant what seemed to them the barren wasteland of Euro-American civilization. Some saw in the Pueblo ceremonies not only a legitimate religion but quite possibly the most vibrant and compelling religion anywhere in the world.

Mabel Dodge Luhan did more than anyone else to bring artists and writers to Taos, and perhaps more than any of them she found inspiration in Pueblo religion for the revitalization of modern life. Like Parsons, Luhan came from a wealthy family and had waged a lifelong battle against social conventions and restrictions wherever she found them. Her first husband John Evans, the father of her only son, died in a hunting accident near their home in Buffalo, New York. On a trip to Europe, the young widow met her second husband, the architect Edwin Dodge, and moved with him to Italy where she socialized with expatriate American artists and became a patron of modern art. In 1913 the family moved to New York City, where Luhan (then Dodge) became famous for bringing artists, intellectuals, and political activists together for evenings of scintillating conversation in her Greenwich Village salon. During her first year in New York, she helped to organize the ground-breaking Armory Show, the modernist movement's first public challenge to New York's conservative art establishment. A year later she proposed and planned the famous Paterson Strike Pageant, a dramatic presentation intended to convince workers in New York to join workers in New Jersey on strike. After her marriage fell apart, she defied conventional sexual mores through open love affairs, first with her pageant co-organizer, the Marxist journalist John Reed, and later with the Russian-born artist Maurice Sterne, who became her third husband. In the words of her biographer, Luhan was "a rebel who had spent much of her adult life constructing a series of utopian domains that were intended to overturn 'the whole ghastly social structure' under which she felt the United States had been buried since the Victorian era."[42]

When the outbreak of war in Europe disturbed this freewheeling Greenwich Village subculture, Luhan was among those who grew disillusioned with radical politics. A conservative backlash against dissenters targeted anarchists and socialists in Luhan's circle, and in the conservative political climate modernist artists and writers found their work threatened by renewed censorship efforts. "With a world at war," Luhan later wrote, "one somehow ceased to war with systems and circumstances. Instinctively I turned once more to Nature and Art and tried to live in them." She retreated with many of her friends to the rural art colonies of Provincetown and then Croton-on-Hudson, where she married Sterne in 1916 in the hope that she could serve as his artistic muse.[43] Luhan also experimented during this time with alternative religious movements, meeting regularly with the famous New Thought healer Emma Curtis Hopkins. New Thought taught that the ultimate reality was spiritual and that the transformative power of "mind cure" could not only heal individual maladies but would eventually usher in a new age of spiritual enlightenment. Before the war, such hopes had meshed easily with the utopian ideals of socialists and revolutionaries. In the new climate, embracing religion seemed to require a rejection of politics. The renowned Freudian psychoanalyst Dr. A. A. Brill—an outright secularist who mocked New Thought along with all religion—tried to persuade Luhan to return to New York and the active life. Brill "called all my mysticism a fantasy life," she remembered, and "tried to remove every vestige of my belief in an inner power." Luhan recalled that she felt a palpable sense of relief when she made the decision to reject Brill's counsel and, at least for the time being, to end her psychoanalysis. The constellation of art, nature, and religion had triumphed over secular rationality and political action.[44]

Luhan would find her encounters with the Pueblo Indians—already stereotypically associated with just these qualities—deeply transformative. She originally went to New Mexico simply intending to visit Sterne, who had gone to the Santa Fe art colony in search of new inspiration. Appalled by "the stupidity and petty crimes" of the "Indian office," he told Luhan that here she could find a new "object in life." "Save the Indians, their art-culture," he wrote. "Reveal it to the world!" He could not have anticipated the intensity of her response.[45] Watching the dancers at that first Christmas Eve dance at Santo Domingo, she found a "magical power" in the "communal" expression of "the Tribe," in sharp contrast to her own society's "raging lust for individuality and separateness" that only led to "dismemberment." Luhan saw tragic consequences in the desacralization of her own society: "It has always been true that the hermetic religions preserved the life-forces of the people. Life itself depends upon its mystery for its enhancement and its enlivening stimulation, and if vision and wonder have forsaken our people it is because, cracking the nut we worshiped, we have found it apparently empty." Applying the psychoanalytic logic of repression, she explained that the Indians had retained their vitality because they had a "living religion" in which all of life remained sacred. "They had not any phrase about life in their language, like ours when we speak of the 'creation myth!' They were too healthy for words like that."[46] Against Sterne's wishes, she insisted on moving to Taos, a day's journey north of Santa Fe, and began to visit the nearby pueblo on a daily basis. Soon she struck up a friendship with the Taos Indian Tony Lujan, who became her guide to the region, helped her choose land for a new home just outside the town of Taos, and became her fourth husband in 1923 (she respelled his surname "Luhan" to correct her friends' mispronunciations).[47]

In her enthusiasm for the Pueblo Indians, Luhan revised but did not entirely upend the racial hierarchy that so many Euro-Americans felt compelled to construct. All "primitives" were certainly not created equal. Where the Indian had "a living religion that has its source in love," she wrote that "the African . . . is inspired by apprehension."[48] She saw the Hispanos of New Mexico as semiprimitive, more natural and authentic than non-Hispanic whites but without the natural purity and vibrant religion she attributed to Indians: "Mexicans seemed to fit into the land better than the Americans, their constant touch was with fire, water, and the earth." In contrast with Pueblo religion, though, she found Hispano Catholicism rather pathetic and even dysfunctional. Where she had insisted that the Indian ceremonies were pure "religion" rather than commercialized "art," she described the *santos*—saints' images painted on wooden retablos—as a picturesque "folk art" created as a substitute for real religious fulfillment. In patronizing terms, she wrote that the *santos* were "the only true primitive art America has ever had . . . pressed out of nowhere by inarticulate and untutored men in their extreme need for something to answer their religious needs."[49]

Hispano people appeared to Luhan as "pinched, discouraged, and baffled," and she theorized that "the resignation of defeat" lingered "in their blood along with the hatred and fear of the white American conqueror." She used the psychoanalytic concept of repression to interpret the *penitente* brotherhoods as the self-inflicted punishment of a defeated people. The *penitentes* "flayed themselves, unconsciously perhaps, to diminish the accumulated bitterness and despair that they could not pour out on us. Turned inwards upon themselves, they drew their own blood, identifying themselves with Jesus Christ, who died for them, and who is still dying for them, in their flesh." Here she analyzed Catholicism as a ritualized reinforcement of Hispano suffering: "Their Catholicism is violent and their violence is catholicized." If the "modern civilization" of white Americans seemed lifeless and devoid of spiritual meaning, the "primitive" for Luhan was suffused

Mabel Dodge Luhan and Tony Lujan in Taos, ca. 1924.
Courtesy Huntington Library, San Marino, California.

with an emotion and physicality that was not always positive. In these examples, religion appeared as an intrinsic racial characteristic, revealing the inner essence of a people.[50]

Luhan's desire to join the Indians remained in tension with these concepts of racial and religious difference. If race determined religion, then conversion to an alien religion would seem ultimately impossible. Perhaps it was for this reason that, although from her first sight of Taos she wanted nothing more than to belong there, she felt an "illimitable distance" from the Indians, "something powerful but quite undefined that shut us off from each other." Yet, like so many primitivists, she seemed to see herself, the white "modern," as mobile and changeable in a way that "primitives" could never be. United with Tony "I could leave the world I had been so false in. Oh, I thought, to leave it, leave it all, the whole world of it and not to be alone. To be with someone real at last, alive at last, unendingly true and untarnished." Tony appeared to her unchanging and reliable, the pure Indian "uninjured and unspoilt by the torture of combining in himself two opposing modes." Mabel believed that she would be changed by their union rather than Tony, and in 1922 she described their union as "a kind of symbol" of her "conversion" to the "Indian current."[51]

The reality of their life together was far more complex. Indians had their own reasons to set racial boundaries, and Mabel could not literally join in the ceremonial life at Taos. Tony Lujan refused to share the religious details that tribal law forbade him to reveal, and like any other outsider, she was permitted to attend only the public ceremonies. In fact, their marriage changed the day-to-day realities of Tony's life far more than it did hers. His decision to leave his first wife Candelaria for Mabel had offended many Taos people, and the wealthy life-style on Mabel's compound created both literal and symbolic distance from the pueblo. Tony's marriage to a white woman also resulted in his banishment from kiva ceremonies at Taos for more than a decade, a painful exclusion that intensified his separation from pueblo life. But he maintained close relationships in the pueblo, and in the mid-1930s he was granted the right to join in the kiva ceremonies once more. Tony was "often away during the day and a good many evenings," one of Mabel's friends reported, with "his own interests, his farming, his Indian and Mexican dances and parties, his many nephews." These dimensions of his life remained largely closed to Mabel.[52]

Although filtered through his wife's narrative, Tony Lujan's own analysis of racial and religious difference offers an instructive perspective. In his characteristically nonjudgmental fashion, Tony attributed the negative qualities he saw in white people to divine design. "God put all the little and big animals on the earth each in his own place and with his own way," he told Mabel once, and "they all stayed where he told them to stay." For this reason, only a "bad witch Indian" would try to change "one thing to another." In contrast, even "good white people" were always trying to change things "because God put it in them to do it." Here was the source of the problem. "Their religion is in machinery to change things, and now they come to want to change the Indians though God told them to stay Indian."[53] Another comparison highlighted the materialism that both Tony and Candelaria saw in white society. According to Mabel, Tony had told her early in their friendship that "Indian houses are empty because God said Indians cannot have things. White people have things, but God give the Indians just what grows on the mountain." Candelaria, who had accompanied them on this excursion, responded to this with "a silver, ringing laugh and said something that made Tony smile." Candelaria's reasons for resenting the presence of white people in Taos were already becoming very personal, and she neatly glossed the wealth of whites like Mabel to the Indians' advantage. Tony explained that Candelaria had pictured a "wheel turning" that would soon take the whites down with the weight of their possessions. "So many things carry the wheel down, with the white people underneath. Pretty soon Indians come up again. Indians' turn next." Candelaria was likely not the only Pueblo Indian to hope that, if they could just wait long enough, the whites would eventually bring on their own destruction.[54]

As critics then and now have argued, primitivist images like Luhan's have often led to the romanticization of Indian poverty and to the denial of agency to Indians who were struggling to manage very difficult and changing conditions. If Indians were timeless primitives, then they should not need to change. If the perfection of Indian religion rested on its primal and natural quality, then its authenticity must be protected. Luhan and other modernists often seemed to believe that they must prevent the intrusions of modernity that they feared would destroy the Indians. And while many Indians welcomed their help in fighting forced assimilation programs, problems developed when modernists believed they rather than Indians—who, of course, were internally divided on these questions—should set the boundaries for change. After World War II, when Luhan told returning Taos veterans not to agitate for modern conveniences because the old ways were better, one young Indian suggested that he would gladly trade houses with her so that she could try living without electricity and indoor plumbing. Indeed, despite Luhan's "conversion" and her claims that she no longer cared for material things, she never gave up any of the comforts of her life as the wealthiest person in Taos.[55]

According to recent critics, "going native" or "playing Indian" as Luhan did allowed Euro-Americans to renegotiate their own identities in relation to their violent colonial history, permitting them to legitimate themselves as the true inheritors of Indian land.[56] Whether or not Luhan's primitivism served this purpose, her intentions were certainly otherwise. In several different passages, she symbolically articulated the Indians' right to the land, and even—in response to Tony and Candelaria's critique—envisioned them retaking it. Luhan wrote that she had pictured "the huge wheel turning slowly, weighted down with all the accretions of our civilization . . . [and] on the other side of the wheel, rising bare limbed and free, heads up bound with green leaves, sheaves of corn and wheat across their shoulders, this dark race mounting. . . . The time to come is his, and he knows it." Elsewhere, rejecting anthropological theories of Indian origins, she wrote that she had "never believed they were Mongolian as the scientists insisted they were. Why should not the Indians have dwelt on this continent as long as the Orientals upon theirs?" The Indians' primal claim to the land, she suggested, portended its future destiny. "These miles of continent were permeated with the Indian psyche as the Far East is saturated with the Indian psyche. . . . [The Indians'] five hundred years of quiescence has been like a twilight sleep in which their forces accumulate in the great racial reservoir. They are sleeping while their brothers here in these mountains keep the true fire burning and alive till the morning of emergence." Whatever the ultimate truth of such prophecies, Luhan also cared about the more immediate and concrete problems of Pueblo land rights. When she eventually reentered the world of political activism, it would be for this cause.[57]

To her credit Luhan gradually accepted Taos Pueblo's ceremonial secrecy, taking pride that she was "not an anthropologist where Tony and his people are concerned" and would never "write a book about Indians." Instead, she intended her own life story as a parable of a soul-sick and dying civilization, with the Indians as the only hope for revitalization. On a trip to New York in 1918, an occultist told her that Taos was "the beating heart of the world," and that Luhan herself had been cosmically chosen to transmit the ancient secret that the Indians possessed. She wrote her autobiography in hopes of passing on this spiritual knowledge, of showing others how to bring the vitality and holism of the Indians into their own lives. "My reason for living is to show how life may be, must be, lived." Even though she could never truly be a part of it, Luhan was convinced that the Pueblo Indians had the true religion that would prove essential to humanity's future.[58] This appropriation of Indian culture can be read in very negative terms. White Americans have repeatedly attempted to appropriate Indian spiritual resources to revitalize their own society, strengthening themselves by stealing culture from the very people whose land they have already taken. In the process, they have been accused of threatening the integrity and even the survival of indigenous religious traditions. Yet Pueblo Indians would be able to use the modernist celebration of Indian "religion" as a way to defend their ceremonies from government suppression, and so to facilitate their ongoing development in Pueblo life.

Although Tony and Mabel's marriage was sometimes rockier than she wanted to admit, it endured because it had value for both of them. Tony seems to have believed that their marriage could benefit his people as well as hers. Mabel recalled that when they first considered becoming intimate, he predicted a life's work for both of them as cultural brokers. "Can you leave your people and can I really leave mine?" she remembered asking. "Perhaps we help more when we go back, leavin' for a little while," he replied. As a result of their marriage, Tony became an important translator between the Pueblos and the outside world, serving (among other things) as tour guide for countless cultural luminaries when they came to visit. More important in his own eyes, Tony pursued the goal of unifying the nineteen pueblos in New Mexico to defend their land and sovereignty. When one of Mabel's friends rather mean-spiritedly characterized him as "unmotivated," she tried to articulate his sense of mission and his hard work over the years to accomplish it. "He has been building up the solidarity between [the Pueblo tribes] for twenty years," she wrote in 1935, "for when he forfeited many of his Pueblo activities by coming with me, he turned outwards and began working in a larger circle. Lately he told me he thought God had brought us together, so he would be turned to the outside work for Indians." The leaders of Taos Pueblo apparently shared this assessment, because that same year they permitted Tony Lujan to resume his participation in the kiva ceremonies.[59]

Most of the era's artists and writers did not share Luhan's mystical identification with the Indians, seeing themselves as secular moderns who could no longer be religious even in unconventional ways. Robert Henri, a leading figure among New York's artistic rebels on the cusp of the modernist revolution, began to spend his summers in Santa Fe as early as 1916. Henri was a philosophical anarchist and an atheist who denounced institutionalized religion in Nietzchean terms, associating it with a loss of individual autonomy. The "regulations" and "restrictions" of religion, he believed, served only to "hide vice" and to "shut people up," preventing them from accomplishing anything worthwhile: "freedom alone bears morality."[60] John Sloan, one of Henri's former students, was a prominent modernist who joined the cohort of Santa Fe's summer residents a few years after Henri. Sloan never lost his love for the high-church ritual of his Episcopalian childhood, but he rejected the Christian faith as a young adult when he read evolutionary theory and the Enlightenment critiques of religion. Along with Henri, he associated religion with restriction on individual freedom. And like so many of his peers, Sloan lost his faith in political action during the war and resigned his membership in the socialist party because he feared the increasing totalitarianism he saw among European socialists. He was "opposed to socialism *as a religion*," he wrote, "the communist form that was taking a leaf out of the Roman Catholic book" by establishing a "religious system with saints and inquisitions." For these modernists, religion was a leftover from humanity's childhood that unfortunately maintained too much power, posing a persistent threat to the freedoms of the modern individual.[61]

It is therefore not surprising that most modernist artists defined Indians primarily in artistic rather than religious terms. Reflecting the continued concern for an authentic national artistic tradition, Sloan argued that Indian artifacts should not be assigned to museums as ancient curios but recognized as vibrant forms of art in their own right, indeed as "the only 100 percent American art produced in this country." Art colony pioneers like Couse had found inspiration in Indians as subjects to be painted, but for the modernists Indians provided stylistic inspiration as well. Prioritizing emotional impact over realistic scenes, modernists identified their own work with this "primitive art" as a way to denigrate the practiced techniques of academic realism. In a later essay, Sloan defined artistic modernism as a return to the primitive. "The academic point of view is really a very modern sickness," he wrote, "and the so-called modern movement is more nearly related to the ancient art spirit of mankind." Many of New Mexico's artists shared this idealization of the primitive as the best model for artistic vitality. By 1921 even Couse was describing the Indians as "natural cubists," and Blumenschein and Phillips indicted "the effort to standardize the Indian" because it would "eventually destroy their wonderful art."[62]

Many writers in New Mexico similarly identified Indian chants and songs with recent innovations in modern poetry. Anthropologists had been recording and translating these songs since the 1880s, but it was not until the twentieth century that they were redefined as "poetry" with the potential to affect Anglo-American writers. One influential figure in these developments was Natalie Curtis, a classically trained musician who traveled around the West starting in 1903 recording Native American songs and chants. *The*

Indians' Book (1907), which she hoped would help develop Indian pride in indigenous traditions, introduced both writers and popular audiences to the poetics of Indian music.[63] In the next decade a variety of modernist writers, convinced that their work expressed the same artistic impulses as "primitive poetry," began publishing their own interpretations of Indian verse. When the leading modernist journal *Poetry* featured their work in a special "aboriginal poetry issue" in 1917, Carl Sandburg commented wryly that one might suspect "that the red man and his children committed direct plagiarism on our modern imagists and vorticists." The Santa Fe writer Mary Austin interpreted this trend as a product of the natural environment in her book *The American Rhythm* (1923), which argued that the American landscape inevitably shaped poetic rhythms so that authentically American writing would naturally come to resemble indigenous styles. But like both "religion" and "art," the category of poetry is of course a product of European culture, and it implies a focus on individual genius and on the carefully composed text in ways that are largely incongruous with the performance of Native American chants and songs as a part of ceremonial life.[64]

Despite their alienation from religion as such, modernists found Indian art appealing largely because, like Luhan, they found in it a spiritual vitality that they believed had been suppressed by "modern civilization." Harriet Monroe, the founder and longtime editor of *Poetry* and a leading figure in Chicago's modernist circles, first traveled to Arizona in 1899 to recover from pneumonia and witnessed the Hopi snake dance two years later. Monroe had long admired Europe's great artistic heritage, much of it religious, and had worried that America's scientific and pragmatic spirit made it incapable of such "immaculate beauty." She saw the southwestern landscapes and peoples as a source not only for an authentically American identity but also for an artistic recovery of beauty and religious reverence. Like "a Homeric rite in Attica, or a serpent ceremony in old Egypt, the snake-dance at Walpi, or the corn-dance at Cochiti, are also revelations of primitive art, expressions of that original human impulse toward the creation of beauty which modern civilization does so much to defeat and destroy." In her eyes the Southwest was "a treasure-trove of romantic myth . . . guarded by ancient races practicing their ancient rites" and ripe for "modern poetry" to discover. The awesome grandeur of the Grand Canyon and the "primitive" beauty of indigenous ceremony gave poets access once again to the "abode of gods," the "mystery of omnipotence" that made truly beautiful artistic creation possible.[65] The modernist artist Marsden Hartley, who is best known for his paintings celebrating Maine and its rural folk culture, described the Pueblo dances in similarly exotic terms as "the solemn high mass of the Indian soul . . . a wholly bodily conception of a beautifully lofty spiritual idea." And despite his distaste for religion, even Henri would express admiration and outright envy for Indian "spirituality": "Materially they are a crushed out race, but even in the remnant there is a bright spark of spiritual life which we others with all our goods and material protections can envy. They have art as a part of each one's life," revealing "a certain spirituality we would like to comprehend."[66]

Modernists who rejected conventional religion—or any religion at all—saw in the Pueblo Indian ceremonies an original or primal unity of "art" and "religion" that they hoped to recreate in their own work. The Santa Fe poet Alice Corbin Henderson, formerly Monroe's assistant editor at *Poetry*, wrote of the Pueblo "dance-rituals" as "a living organism, a beautiful and vital art" that survived "in the face of discouragement and under the constant threat of suppression" largely because they were "ritualistic and religious . . . the incarnation of the Pueblo soul." For herself and other moderns, Henderson believed, art had taken the place of religion. "If I stress the aesthetic rather than the religious aspect of these dances," she wrote, "it is because that term has come to supplant the other, for us." She called for poets to "regain something of this older unity" in order to rejuvenate their own work, "which seems to suffer from this lack of any spiritual source or background."[67] If modernity had so disenchanted the world that most intellectuals could no longer be personally religious, it still seemed possible to reclaim the beauty and awe of religion through art—especially art inspired by "primitives" who had never distinguished these realms of life in the first place.

A parallel impulse drove many of the innovators in modern dance. Isadora Duncan, who had been a frequent guest at Luhan's Greenwich Village salons and was well known for her interest in religion, found primary inspiration in ancient Greece rather than among the Indians. But her admirers in New Mexico linked the emotional and spiritual intensity of her work to Indian dances. "The first time I saw the Santo Domingo Corn Dance," wrote Sloan, "I felt the same strong emotion from the rhythm of the drums and primitive intensity of that age-old dance ritual that I experienced when I saw Isadora Duncan fill the stage of the Metropolitan Opera House with her great personality." Within a few years, modern dancers like Ruth St.

Denis, Ted Shawn, and Martha Graham found inspiration in a variety of "exotic" cultures and dance traditions including those of ancient Egypt, Japan, China, and India. In the 1920s and 1930s, they would also turn to Pueblo and other Native American ceremonies to inspire the integration they desired between dance and religion.[68]

Full of admiration for the artistry and spirituality of Pueblo culture, the artists of Santa Fe and Taos initiated a number of efforts designed to ensure its survival. In the late 1910s Mary Austin and others began a movement to train and support Indian artists, and by stimulating markets for Indian pottery and other crafts they made possible careers like that of the famous San Ildefonso potter Maria Martinez. They also helped stimulate the development of painting as a new Indian art form. Austin remembered her amazement at the striking originality of "water-color paintings of the dance figures" done by Indians working as artists' models "who had during their rest hours made use of the materials at hand." Along with Sloan and Hewett she created the Indian Arts Fund to solicit support for this new genre of Indian art, and in 1920 they managed to organize exhibitions for several Pueblo artists at the Independent Art Show and at the American Museum of Natural History—where their classification as "art" was perhaps less clear.[69] By cultivating an interest in Indian art among an elite public, modernists hoped to inspire sympathy for Indian economic and political problems and also to provide a livelihood for at least some Indians that could help preserve rather than destroy indigenous culture. In 1931 the Exposition of Tribal Arts (with Sloan as its president) held a major exposition of Native American works in New York that netted $6,595, much of which went to the Native artists themselves. As Joel Pfister has put it, they saw "exploited, not vanishing Indians" and looked for effective ways to end that exploitation and to meet real-world Indian needs.[70]

Such efforts to support Indian arts and crafts could also be controlling and counterproductive, especially when modernists elevated themselves as the judges of which art was authentically "Indian." In the Museum of New Mexico journal *El Palacio*, one writer who praised San Ildefonso water-colorist Awa Tsireh offered the patronizing comment that the Indians "do interesting work as long as they stick to the hereditary primitive symbolism." Modernists who collected and marketed Indian pottery would take only bowls and pots decorated according to their stereotypical ideas of what Indian pottery should look like, refusing to accept more unconventional forms such as human and animal figurines, which they denigrated as "tourist junk." Barbara Babcock writes that the rejected styles "did not make for a vision of authenticity, of timeless, useful, and subjugated beauty" and so were largely marginalized, even though they drew on aspects of Pueblo tradition in far more innovative ways. Despite the modernists' goal of stimulating native arts and crafts, pottery production in several of the New Mexico Pueblos actually declined in the first half of the twentieth century. Because modernists would not exhibit or buy from Indian artists whose work they did not consider "primitive," in some respects their concern for authenticity limited the development of indigenous forms of art.[71]

When cultural modernists began to involve themselves more directly in the politics of Indian affairs—first to defend Pueblo land and then Pueblo religion—their efforts would have similarly complex results.

———◆———

THREE

Land, Sovereignty, and the
Modernist Deployment of "Religion"

In the early decades of the twentieth century, while modernists celebrated Indian religion, the Pueblos themselves were facing unprecedented threats to their land, sovereignty, and cultural traditions. As the Bureau of Indian Affairs (BIA) worked to educate and "civilize" Indians around the country, its officials asserted more and more control over Pueblo life. At boarding schools or at the local day schools that most Pueblo children now attended, missionary or government teachers tried to instill a "civilized" disdain for indigenous tradition. Government agents and state authorities assumed the right to overrule tribal governors on both criminal and civil disputes within the pueblos and did everything they could to discourage tribal ceremonial life. Perhaps most serious of all, New Mexico's growing population brought increased competition for the precious resources of land and water. These conflicts came to a head in the fall of 1922, when draft legislation known as the Bursum Bill would have legitimated the theft of Pueblo land and water rights and further restricted the Indians' tribal sovereignty. As they had done in past crises, the Council of All the New Mexico Pueblos met that November to forge a common protest: "We, the Pueblo Indians, have always been self-supporting and have not been a burden on the Government. We have lived at peace with our fellow-Americans even while we have watched the gradual taking away of our lands and waters. . . . We have kept our old customs and lived in harmony with ourselves and with our fellow-Americans. This bill will destroy our common life and will rob us of everything which we hold dear—our lands, our customs, our traditions. Are the American people willing to see this happen?" Like other Native Americans, the Pueblo Indians found their struggles for "lands, customs, and traditions" to be inextricably intertwined. But as this statement illustrates, most did not yet use "religion" as a major category for understanding or defending Pueblo ways of life.[1]

The Pueblos sought help in this fight from a broad coalition of reformers, prominent among them the cultural modernists who had become so enthralled with Pueblo traditions. Over the course of this campaign, modernists unleashed an unprecedented volley of publicity that used primitivist images of the Pueblos to demand extensive reforms in federal Indian policy. Briefly emboldened by the popularity of the cause, Mabel Dodge Luhan dared to believe that her hopes for a transformed America were coming true. "Is it possible that the little drop of Indian in every one awakened and answered the call? We want as a nation to value the Indian as we value our selves. We want to consciously love the wholeness and harmony of Indian life, and to consciously protect it." John Collier spearheaded the publicity campaign as his first foray into a long career in Indian affairs. In contrast to the anthropologists and cultural modernists introduced in the previous chapter, Collier was first and foremost a social reformer dedicated to political action. More than any other single person, he was responsible for deploying the modernist celebration of Pueblo "religion" as a way to defend the Pueblos' rights to their land and traditions. In short, the fight against the Bursum Bill propelled the modernist redefinition of Pueblo "religion" into the public eye and set the stage for the dance controversy, which would begin even before the land crisis was resolved.[2]

The Pueblos' Struggle for Land and Sovereignty

Long before the arrival of Spaniards, Mexicans, or Americans, the Pueblo Indians were building towns and cultivating fields along the banks of the Rio Grande and its tributaries. With the hubris of a colonial power, Spain had assumed the right to distribute ownership of this land and granted each pueblo title to its surrounding area. Mexico honored these Spanish land grants; and at the close of the Mexican-American War in 1848 the United States promised in the Treaty of Guadalupe Hidalgo to do so as well. That promise became more difficult to honor as the territory's population grew, creating heightened competition for the region's scarce water and irrigable land. More and more non-Indian settlers moved onto Pueblo lands, some of them purchasing land in good faith either from Indians—with or without tribal permission—or from descendants of early Spanish settlers, whose own colonial-era land grants overlapped with the Indians'. Others simply squatted, disregarding the Indians' claims. For decades the federal government had refused to intervene because of an 1876 U.S. Supreme Court ruling that the Pueblos were not wards of the government like other Native Americans but "civilized Indians" with clear title and the right to sell their land. The court reversed that precedent in the 1913 *Sandoval* case, ruling that the Pueblos were entitled to the same federal assistance granted to other tribes, including protections against their land being sold to or settled by non-Indians. Over the next ten years, a series of government-employed attorneys filed lawsuits intended to evict settlers who did not have legitimate title. Most of these cases went nowhere. Pueblo people repeatedly complained about settlers erecting fences around what was legally Indian land and appealed for boundary markers to prevent further encroachments. At times they resorted to tearing down such fences, resulting in occasionally violent confrontations.[3]

Pueblo leaders wanted the government to remove illegal settlers and definitively resolve the situation, but they found most BIA officials unwilling or unable to help. They protested that the BIA only made matters worse by transferring superintendents from one agency to another and that the most effective superintendents were often the first to be replaced. Settlers' groups were known to lobby the Interior Department to have their choice of candidates placed in these positions. At a meeting of the Northern Pueblos in 1921, Governor Ramos Archuleta of San Juan Pueblo told a visiting BIA inspector that the Indians wanted to keep their current superintendent and that a settlers' group had been responsible for the complaints about his performance that reached Washington. According to Archuleta, the candidate being pushed to replace the superintendent owned disputed land on both the Santa Clara and San Juan grants and so would certainly take the settlers' side. It seemed to Archuleta that any superintendent who actually tried to advance Indian interests would promptly be transferred. "In the past the Government has sent us superintendents," he said, "and when they try to help us then the Government removes them." Even aside from politically motivated transfers, the BIA typically moved superintendents around so often that even the most able and well-meaning people were in the job barely long enough to understand the local issues before they were sent elsewhere.[4]

To the dismay of the Indians, the federal government seemed far more interested in meddling with internal tribal affairs. BIA policies on tribal governance were unclear and inconsistent, and Pueblo governors protested that superintendents overruled or ignored tribal policies and decisions so regularly that they could no longer exercise meaningful authority. The Council of All the New Mexico Pueblos wrote a petition to "the President and Congress" in 1911 demanding that Pueblo governors' authority to maintain discipline be recognized—a necessity in order for their people to "live in cleanliness and decency." Specifically the council requested the "authority to enforce the public works which are most necessary in the pueblos . . . to work on the common ditch, to sweep the town; to repair the church and cemetery; to work on the public roads; and in some pueblos, to herd the horses." These tasks were essential for the welfare of the entire community and so were shared by all pueblo members under the supervision of the governor. Just as important, they asked for the right "to punish disorders, fights, and drunkenness in our pueblos." Because they knew that the BIA would want to guard against excessive punishments—and to retain control over the most serious offenses—the council promised that their governors would punish offenders only with fines or extra community work rather than whippings or other violent means. With a typical disregard for Indian ideas, though, nobody in Washington paid serious attention to this proposal.[5]

The Pueblos' internal affairs included their ceremonial life, and here the Indians wanted no government involvement at all. Traditions of ceremonial secrecy helped shape these concerns, as a story from Elsie Clews Parsons's fieldwork in Jemez Pueblo illustrates. In the summer of 1921, the BIA superintendent asked the farmer at Jemez (a BIA employee assigned to teach the Indians modern farming techniques) to arrest a man whose daughter had given birth to an illegitimate child. The farmer was told that the man was away, which as Parsons explained was "the common way of avoiding reference to a [ceremonial] retreat." He soon found out where the man was and demanded that he come out of the kiva and submit to his arrest immediately. The "Fathers or Old Men" of Jemez took this "disregard of their *costumbre*" very seriously (note here again the reference to "custom" rather than "religion"). According to Parsons, some months later they canceled a planned rain ceremony despite a severe drought "because the man taken from the *estufa* [kiva] was a member of the officiating society and had been rendered ceremonially unfit by the forced violating of his retreat the year preceding."

The Jemez did not tell the farmer anything about these consequences because "to let him know would be to enlighten him in regard to the ceremonial life, besides it might have no effect at all on his future conduct."[6]

Outside pressures on tribal sovereignty and tradition tended to exacerbate existing divisions within Pueblo communities. Whereas "conservatives" tried to resist change in the name of tradition, "progressives" argued that the future of their communities depended on adopting at least some aspects of American technology and culture. Most progressives had attended missionary or government boarding schools that, on the model of Carlisle Indian School, forbade the use of native languages or any indigenous traditions and tried to inspire students to return home with the goal of "civilizing" their people. Most Pueblo students, reacting in part against the discrimination that left few job opportunities for Indians off the reservation, rejected such indoctrination and were eager to participate in the ceremonial life when they returned home. However, a few were convinced that what their teachers called "paganism" was inconsistent with Christianity or with tribal progress, and by the early 1920s there were a few progressives who no longer wanted to participate in the tribal ceremonies at all.[7]

One of these was John Dixon, a Carlisle graduate and the leader of Cochiti Pueblo's progressive faction. A Keresan pueblo southwest of Santa Fe, Cochiti had a relatively large progressive faction as a result of many intermarriages and other close ties with neighboring Hispanos and Anglos. Dixon held the position of judge for Cochiti's "Indian Court," a system that the BIA created in 1883 with the goal of teaching Native Americans to follow the U.S. legal system. Because the Indian judges reported to the BIA superintendents who appointed them, these courts tended to undermine tribal sovereignty and created power struggles with existing tribal leaders. At Cochiti, Dixon characterized the tribe's conservative leaders as "centuries behind in habits and customs." The factional conflicts in the Pueblos, he told John Collier, centered on whether he and other progressives should once again become like the "savage" traditional faction and "howl like coyotes in savage dances, jump up and down like madmen, have feathers and fuzz sticking out from the hind end of our pants, sing dirty, nasty songs, do many other things too vile to describe, too obscene to be permissable [sic] in Dante's Inferno." Dixon's comments offer a negative caricature of Indian dances as the "savage" antithesis of the American respectability he desired for himself and his people. Disturbed and offended by his efforts, Cochiti's conservative governor and council did everything they could to limit Dixon's influence and refused him any role in tribal decision making or in the meetings of the All-Pueblo Council. Beyond Cochiti, Pueblo leaders found the work of the Indian judges so disruptive that a council of the Southern Pueblos petitioned the BIA in October 1922 "to have all Indian judges withdrawn from the Pueblo country."[8]

Progressives in Dixon's mold believed that the ceremonial traditions were a drain on resources and negatively affected tribal development. They drew on the rhetoric of assimilationist reformers, who had long criticized Indian dances for taking too much time and energy away from farm work and other productive labor. It was in this vein that Antonio Montoya, a recent graduate of Santa Fe Indian School and another member of Cochiti's progressive faction, complained in February 1923 that his people spent so much time dancing that they could not make any further "progress" toward civilization and so would not be able to become "good citizens." But Montoya moved beyond standard assimilationist tropes by protesting against what he saw as an unfair distribution of labor. Pueblo tradition understood ceremonial participation as another form of community work, along with maintaining the irrigation ditches, roads, and other public spaces. For this reason, those occupied with ceremonial activities could be temporarily exempted from other community work. "Each society takes a turn to be lock[ed] up for four days" to prepare for a ceremony, Montoya complained; "the men that don't dance don't like it, because there might be a ditch work to be done and only few of the men will be present"–namely, "the ones that don't take part in the secret dances or any kind of dance." "The rest," he claimed, "will have an easy time getting ready for dance." Here Montoya presented ceremonial preparation and participation as little more than an excuse to avoid the physical labor that he and other progressives were left to shoulder.[9]

In this context, religious freedom initially appeared to traditional Pueblo leaders as simply another avenue for the restriction of tribal sovereignty. Assimilationist reformers concerned about the Indians' lack of "progress" accused "reactionary" tribal governments of forcing returned students like Dixon and Montoya to resume the "pagan" tradition. Following this logic, BIA superintendents began to demand that tribal leaders stop requiring ceremonial participation and phrased this demand in terms of "religious freedom" for the progressives. In its 1911 petition, the All-Pueblo Council had promised that if the BIA would clearly recognize the authority of the

Pueblo governors, the governors would no longer "enforce ceremonies or religious customs." In 1921, when a Cochiti progressive named Pablo Quintana claimed that tribal officials were persecuting him because he refused to dance, Southern Pueblos superintendent Leo Crane reminded tribal leaders of his long-standing rule that "Pueblo officials . . . have no authority of law for seeking to compel anyone of the tribe to join in religious ceremonies that are distasteful to them." Through such policies, BIA agents redefined Pueblo ceremonies in terms of the English-language category of religion, which in keeping with American tradition they understood as a matter of individual conscience and therefore distinct from the sort of "public works" that the tribal government could require. Crane insisted that his policy was intended to guarantee religious freedom for all Indians. As he put it, "The order works both ways: to prevent disturbance of proper ceremonies by others and also to guarantee that the ceremonies will not affect Government business or the individual liberty of anyone." However, especially given the BIA's occasional interference (and regular threats to interfere) with any ceremonies the agents found improper, Pueblo leaders no doubt experienced this policy not as a guarantee of liberty but as a further limit on their authority.[10]

Indian resistance to such orders made them hard to enforce, and not all BIA superintendents shared Crane's fervor. H. P. Marble, who replaced Crane as Southern Pueblos superintendent in 1922, also held assimilationist goals but did not believe they could immediately be achieved. In response to Antonio Montoya's complaint, Marble wrote that it was impossible to stop the dances as long as participants were not breaking any laws. He counseled patience, encouraging Montoya to remember that the "older people" who were so committed to the dances had not had his opportunities for education. Marble also instructed Judge Dixon and Governor Alcario Montoya of Cochiti—in conflict once again over the dance question—that they must respect one another's roles in tribal government and work together "peaceably and quietly" to equip their people to become "a part of the citizenship of the state and nation." "Your people, if they are ever to achieve satisfactory self-government," he wrote, "must recognize and obey the will of the majority in civic or community matters just so long as that majority does not demand that laws, religious or personal convictions be violated." Aware that for the time being the majority of Cochiti's people supported the conservatives rather than the progressives, Marble believed it more important to respect the principle of democratic government than to interfere with ceremonial traditions. With the passage of time and generations, he was convinced that Cochiti's progressives would be able to bring about the changes they desired. On the definitional problem of whether those who refused to participate in the ceremonies were asserting their right to religious freedom, as Crane and the Cochiti progressives would have it, or whether they were simply violating tribal law, he offered no resolution.[11]

In 1921 New Mexico senator Holm Bursum proposed settling the disputes over Pueblo land with an original bill and then a revised version the following year that threatened to make things even worse for the Indians. The Pueblos and most of their supporters agreed that some non-Indian land claims merited consideration, particularly where they had claims in good faith that dated to before the *Sandoval* decision. Many "settlers" on Indian land were poor Hispanos who had been there for generations and had few other options. But the Bursum Bill would have awarded nearly all disputed land and water rights to the non-Indian claimants, even where they were recent and clearly illegal settlers or land speculators. New Mexican politicians favored the settlers—who had some effective political representatives in the state—over the nonvoting Indians. Bursum's proposed bill helped him win election to the Senate in 1921, and Interior Secretary Albert Fall (also from New Mexico) agreed to support the bill in exchange for other favors from Bursum. Fall appointed Colonel Ralph E. Twitchell, a lawyer in Santa Fe who was an expert in Spanish colonial history, to serve as special assistant to the U.S. attorney for Pueblo affairs, and Twitchell helped draft a revised bill that even more strongly favored the settlers. Commissioner Burke knew little about the Pueblos, and Fall convinced him to support this bill even though the BIA's own agents in New Mexico opposed it. According to its opponents, the Bursum Bill of 1922 would have stripped the pueblos collectively of sixty thousand acres of land, making some communities virtually impossible to sustain. The Indians fought it in every way they could.[12]

One of the key leaders in this struggle was Pablo Abeita (1871–1940), the head of Isleta Pueblo's "progressive" faction, who also illustrates some of the range of opinion among progressive Indians. A nephew of the man who had rented rooms to Charles Lummis, Pablo Abeita made his living through the general store established in the pueblo years earlier by his grandparents. Abeita had been educated at St. Michael's College, the Catholic boarding school in Santa Fe, and was fluent in Spanish and English as well as his native Tiwa. His efforts to modernize tribal politics, agriculture, and other practices made him a favorite of a series of BIA superintendents, one of whom appointed him as farmer for Isleta in 1904. As president of Isleta's progressive business council, which he cofounded in 1912, Abeita helped improve the tribe's finances and made it possible to repurchase a significant amount of Isleta's traditional land base. After the *Sandoval* decision in 1913, Abeita was optimistic that the way was finally clear for "the advancement towards civilization" that he desired. The first step was to "make real farmers of my people," he told Father Ketcham of the Bureau of Catholic Indian Missions, though "of course we will need help once in a while from Uncle Sam especially as regards implements and seeds." Within the year, a new BIA superintendent had named Abeita the Indian judge for Isleta. As at Cochiti, a power struggle developed between the progressive judge and a series of conservative Isleta governors. Eight years after Abeita's appointment, he complained to Ketcham that "the reactionaries who want to go back to the old times ways of fifty or sixty years ago [have] control of the Pueblo," and he could not implement the changes he wanted.[13]

Unlike Dixon, however, Abeita's progressive convictions did not lead him to do away with Indian "customs" entirely. Throughout his life he participated in Isleta's ceremonial life. "Every morning, with his corn pollen sack in hand," Pueblo historian Joe Sando has written, "[Abeita] would address the Great Spirit, thank Him for the many blessings, and beseech Him for peace and prosperity for all mankind in the world."[14] In 1928 Abeita would instruct a group that included many self-identified progressives to take care not to leave behind their "customs," which by then he had also come to identify in terms of religion. "Progressive is that a man can plow his ground better with a riding plow than with a hand plow," he told them. "Drifting away from Indian customs, I don't call that progress. . . . the Indian Office has told us time and again that they don't want to take away from us none of our religion or our ceremonies—time and again. Yet we find that most of us—not only among the younger people—but even the older are drifting away from being Indians, so that something must be done." To Abeita progress did not mean abandoning an Indian identity, and an Indian identity meant maintaining at least some aspects of traditional ceremonial life.[15]

Abeita insistently countered the patronizing attitudes of reformers and government agents who assumed Indians incapable of shaping the policies that affected them. Arguing that only an educated Indian like himself could

Pablo Abeita. Courtesy
National Anthropological
Archives, Smithsonian
Institution, Suitland,
Maryland, INV 06338400.

really understand Pueblo needs in the current situation, he criticized the
reliability of even the most well-meaning writers and reformers. He had read
most of what had been written "about Indian Customs, etc.," he told Father
Ketcham, and "[there is] no truth in their writing, none." He criticized
Charles Lummis's entry on the Pueblo Indians in F. W. Hodge's *Handbook of
American Indians* (1910) as mostly inaccurate guesswork. "Lummis says a lot
of us Isletas and can only say that his guesses are wrong; he probably heard
some talk and then wrote what he thought would be taken as so by the
Bureau. Not until I finish my book which will probably be in about ten or
twelve years more, then those living then will know the real and true tradition of the Pueblo Indians of New Mexico." Although Abeita never completed his book, he repeatedly advised BIA superintendents, attorneys, and
commissioners on how to manage Isleta and the Pueblos more generally. He
knew only too well that even the most well-meaning reformers and philan-
thropists could make things worse rather than better. While he was gratified

to learn that the philanthropist Rodman Wanamaker had some interest in his ideas, he worried that "such persons as Mr. Wanamaker" tended to "do things in large scales and . . . [this] may hurt the Indian . . . instead of [do] good to them." As an energetic advocate for his people, Abeita traveled to Washington so many times that he claimed to have shaken hands with every U.S. president from Grover Cleveland to Franklin Delano Roosevelt, with the exception of Calvin Coolidge.[16]

Although Abeita fought the Bursum Bill in his typically indefatigable style, the responses he received illustrate how easily U.S. officials dismissed Indian concerns. In October 1922 he wrote to ask for the support of Father William Hughes, who had replaced Ketcham as the director of the Bureau of Catholic Indian Missions. "From the first time I saw and read a copy of the Bill, I did not like it," he told Hughes, "and I at once started to write to those who I thought were my friends." Commissioner Burke had replied only that "the Bill was a good one, as it would do away with all the land troubles we the Pueblos were having with our neighbors, etc." Abeita received no response at all from the BIA attorney for the Pueblos, whom he had long since judged as unwilling to expend any effort on behalf of Indian needs. Colonel Twitchell—whose role in writing the Bursum Bill Abeita apparently had not known—first seemed to respond favorably. But when Abeita went to consult with him in Santa Fe, "all I got out of him was to call me names, and tell me that I was an ungrateful Indian, that I did not appreciate what he was doing for us Pueblos." Abeita told Twitchell "that if that was all he could do for us Pueblos, he could, as far as I was concerned could go straight to HELL." After that experience, Abeita changed tactics, traveling "from Pueblo to Pueblo [to tell] all those who would listen to me what is coming to us through the Bursum Bill." Now he hoped that a delegation of Pueblo Indians would be able to travel to Washington, and asked Hughes for whatever support he could offer. "I am called a pagan Indian but I hope to die as I live 'a Catholic.' But of course I am a persistent worker for my people, and I have succeeded in obtaining what I went in for. Just now we are in for a fight to a finish, and if we do not win this fight here will be trouble, lots of it."[17]

Hughes and other Catholics were already working against the bill, although political considerations ultimately muted their support. Among the most persistent advocates for Pueblo land rights was the Franciscan Fridolin Schuster, stationed at Laguna Pueblo. Three months before Abeita's letter, Schuster had informed Hughes that when he and a Laguna delegation met with Commissioner Burke to explain the land crisis, the latter cut their interview short by telling them that "the Secretary was preparing a bill which would put an end to all these land disputes." Schuster knew that the bill in question was designed to satisfy powerful interests rather than to rectify injustices, and he warned Hughes that the Indians would need to "put up a stiff fight" against what would amount to "nothing else but piracy and robbery." Hughes encouraged Catholic leaders around the country to do what they could to see that the bill was defeated. Presenting this effort as a good way to demonstrate Catholic allegiance to American values, he told members of the hierarchy in Los Angeles that they should publicly oppose the bill not only because the Pueblos were Catholic but more broadly "on the ground of American justice and right." But Hughes himself did not identify with the cause in public for political reasons, explaining that he did not want to destroy his bureau's close relationship with "a certain high official . . . [who] is, in a large degree, responsible for the Bill." Archbishop Daeger of Santa Fe, who had formerly worked as a priest among the Pueblos, also seems to have stayed out of the fray—perhaps to avoid offending the pre-dominantly Catholic settlers and their supporters in New Mexico. Con-cerned about preserving Catholicism's hard-won status both nationally and regionally, the Catholic hierarchy provided only ambivalent and inconsis-tent help in this fight.[18]

In the fall of 1922, a historic meeting of the Council of All the New Mexico Pueblos brought 120 delegates representing all nineteen pueblos together in protest against the Bursum Bill. At this meeting the council organized on a permanent basis and elected its first permanent officers. They chose Sotero Ortiz of San Juan as chairman, and Pablo Abeita—who had served at previous council meetings as a translator and delegate from Isleta—to be secretary. Along with their protest against the bill's impact on Pueblo "land, customs, and traditions," the delegates denounced their exclu-sion from the legislative process: "We were never given the chance of having anything to say or to do about this Bursum Bill. The pueblo officials have tried many times to obtain an explanation of this bill from officials of the Indian Office and especially from the attorneys of the government, and have always been put off and even insulted." Finally, the council determined to raise $3,500 to send a delegation to Washington that winter for the sched-uled congressional hearings on the bill.[19]

John Collier and the Modernist Crusade
for Pueblo Land Rights

In the end, the Pueblos probably could not have defeated the bill without the aid of a new coalition of reformers, primarily cultural modernists who entered the politics of Indian affairs through this struggle. "Just as I was about to give up my hopes," Abeita told Hughes, "here comes a big help, the General Federation of Women's Clubs and others who are interesting themselves for the good of the Pueblo Indians, who are at present working through a Mr. John Collier of California."[20] Collier (1884–1968) was a dedicated social reformer who had first encountered the Pueblo Indians in 1920 through his longtime friend Mabel Dodge Luhan, and just before the Bursum Bill crisis he began working as research associate for the Indian Welfare Committee of the General Federation of Women's Clubs. He combined Luhan's mystical and communal ideals with the skills and temperament of a political activist and helped to stimulate and shape the modernists' new involvement in Indian affairs.

Collier drew both his activism and his mysticism from early life experiences. His commitment to public service came from his father Charles Collier, a prominent Georgia banker and lawyer who became Atlanta's mayor in the late 1890s, while his mother Susie Rawson Collier gave him a profound love for nature and for literature. Tragedy struck the family in Collier's early teens, when a financial scandal discredited his father and his mother died of a laudanum overdose. Three years later, the devastated Charles Collier committed suicide. The bereaved son took solace in the poetry of Wordsworth and Whitman and then even more profoundly in what he later called the "terrible joy of the living earth." He took to hiking and camping for weeks at a time in the Appalachian Mountains, celebrating in "the quasi-hallucinatory experience when I looked down from a wooded hilltop on a whole forest engaged in a rejoicing dance." For the rest of his life he found solace and motivation in a vision he experienced at age eighteen, when he saw "a huge bird, silent and almost as fleet as light . . . [which] uttered, silently, a clear summons: 'Onward, into the struggle not lost and not won, and the immortal effort toward creation in which I, the bird, need you' "—a summons that he found "could not be forgotten or disobeyed through all my later and across my present years." Where Luhan had found it necessary to reject political

John Collier. Collier Papers,
Manuscripts and Archives,
Yale University Library,
New Haven, Connecticut.

activism in favor of nature and art, Collier's mystical experience of nature provided direct motivation for his calling as a reformer.[21]

Like so many other modernists, Collier rejected conventional religion but only after he had developed a deep love for the Catholic tradition. Catholicism represented not a rebellion against his family's "vigorous Methodist tradition" but the embrace of an ancient and vibrant spiritual tradition. One of his aunts, his mother's closest friend, was a convert to Catholicism, and he wrote that his own parents had been "strongly attracted to the Jewish and Catholic minorities." After his mother's death, the young Collier went to live and attend school at a Georgia convent, where he formed lifelong friendships with several nuns and with one of the priests. Collier's autobiography made it clear that he had only positive feelings about that time, an emphasis that also reflected the importance of Catholic alliances in his later career. "Within Catholicism, I experienced nothing except wisdom and great human kindness," he wrote. "I passed out from Catholicism with no inward struggle, with no pain, and with lifelong gratitude." He explained that he had left the faith only because he found "the theory of organic evolution . . . possessing my mind" and faith itself became an intellectual impossibility. "Removing myself from Catholicism was removing myself from the absolutist God of any creed, any philosophy." Still Collier maintained his mystical sense of communion with the natural world and never lost his attraction to spirituality and ritual.[22]

Collier's college years at Columbia University turned him into a committed social reformer with a strong grounding in philosophy and social theory. Alongside his coursework, the private tutor Lucy Graham Crozier mentored Collier free of charge and introduced him to a whole world of ideas, starting with her own passion for Nietzsche, a favorite among many of the cultural modernists. Collier took from Nietzsche the "concept of the 'beyond man' as the yet-unrealized potential within living man . . . and of the entire task of life as the ordering of society and of thought so as to invoke the beyond-man from present man." From the sociologist Lester Frank Ward— who, like the Boasians, was engaged in the deconstruction of social evolutionary theory—he gleaned the principle that "invention, deliberate innovation, and individual creativity" were the necessary ingredients for social transformation. Collier left Columbia in 1904 for his first organizing effort, an unsuccessful attempt to organize railroads and chambers of commerce "in a system of distributing unemployed immigrants onto the land in Georgia, the Carolinas, and Alabama." After this and a subsequent project failed, Collier worked for some time as a journalist in Georgia and then met his wife Lucy Wood on a trip to Europe. The young couple spent a year living in Paris, where they drew inspiration from "the cooperative and labor movements of France, Belgium, England, and Ireland." Throughout his career, Collier would see social cooperation as the prerequisite for optimal individual development.[23]

As a social worker with immigrants in New York, Collier developed the principles he would later apply to Native American policy reform. In 1907 he started working for the People's Institute, which hoped to unite intellectuals and the primarily immigrant working class through educational programs aimed at giving "knowledge, leadership and public voice to wage earning masses." Where most reformers in this era of growing nativist sentiment tried to "Americanize" immigrants by discouraging their native languages and traditions, Collier and his colleagues believed that traditional cultures should be celebrated and preserved as a resource for community development. In that spirit, he helped organize the 1914 Pageant and Festival of the Nations, a huge public drama involving hundreds of performers from each of the major immigrant groups. Exemplifying the coercive moralism so typical of Progressive Era reform, Collier also helped establish a National Board of Censorship in hopes of ensuring that the increasing cultural influence of the film industry would be used to stimulate positive community development rather than social decay. In all of these efforts he sought to implement scientific principles, turning to "experimental sociology" to create and nurture the communalism that he found so vital to human development. This passion for social reform and breadth of experience as an activist differentiated Collier from Luhan and most other cultural modernists.[24]

When Collier encountered the Pueblo Indians, he saw in them the living embodiment of his communal and spiritual ideas. During the mid-1910s he had been a regular participant in Luhan's Greenwich Village salons, and like so many of her circle found himself devastated by the First World War and its aftermath. "My own disillusionment toward the 'occidental ethos and genius' as being the hope of the world," he wrote years later, "was complete." His work with immigrants suffered from the wartime rise in nativist sentiment, and he moved his family to California in 1919 to take a position working with immigrants there. Forced to resign after a conservative business organization called him a communist, Collier finally accepted a long-standing invitation from Luhan to come and see the "magical and mystical Indians" of Taos.[25] He arrived just in time for the pueblo's Christmas Eve ceremony and the deer dance a few days later. The dances he witnessed that week were "the community itself consciously living in beauty," he wrote a few months later, "enormous ritual dramas of song and dance which engulf the whole tribe in their ecstasy." Collier praised the Pueblos for having developed an ideal way to shape a strong yet communally minded individual —his version of the Nietzschean "beyond-man." "Through travails, fastings, lonely marches and group-assemblages, the youth prepared himself that the spirit of the dead, the genius and consecration of the supernatural tribal ancestor, might enter him, convert him, empower him, command him. All that was deepest, most awful, most romantic, most energizing in his emotions, rose within this social setting and discharged itself toward social ends." As he wrote years later, he was beginning to think that the Indians alone "were still the possessors and users of the fundamental secret of human life—the secret of building great personality through the instrumentality of social institutions." Although he celebrated Pueblo "religion" from the start, he placed more emphasis on this question of the individual in community.[26]

Collier's burning question at the time was whether these intensely beautiful communities could survive in modern America. "I was still possessed with the prevailing anthropological view of those years," he recalled in his autobiography, "that all primitive and ancient cultures were doomed to be swallowed up by the white world." In 1921 he wrote rather mournfully, "Their religions and institutions, languages and arts, are proscribed. White encroachment has cut their farm lands to mere remnants, appropriated the waters from their ancient ditches, invaded even their plazas, built stores and dance halls alongside their immemorial kivas. They have retreated into their own spirit-eternity; on this social earth they are doomed. Modernity, America, Government, and unequal laws have doomed them." At least in these early years of his career in Indian reform, he shared the standard evolutionary assumptions that linked religion with the primitive, assuming both to be on the decline. "These tiny communities of the red man, archaic, steeped in a non-rational world-view of magic and animism and occult romanticism— it seems a wild if alluring fantasy that they might live on, that they might use the devices of modern economic life, and pragmatically take over the concepts of modern science, and yet might keep that strange past of theirs . . . so communal yet individually reckless, so human and so mystic." The Pueblos seemed to Collier to reveal the crux of the modern dilemma, and the stakes were high indeed. "Can races of different origins live side by side . . . enrich each other and correct each other, or must they only poison and devour each other?" he asked. "Unless that question is answered 'Yes,' then there is no hope of putting an end to wars and not much hope for the spiritual and esthetic future of this planet." To one steeped in Euro-American concepts of the disappearing primitive, this seemed an unlikely fantasy indeed.[27]

Back in California, Collier met Stella Atwood, a leading figure in California's women's clubs. Atwood had begun working for the cause of Indian citizenship when she learned about the discrimination experienced by returning Indian war veterans in the late 1910s. Under her leadership, the Southern California Federation of Women's Clubs created an Indian Welfare Committee in 1916, and five years later she convinced the General Federation to make the committee national with herself as its first chair. In the summer of 1922, a wealthy supporter offered to fund a new position for Collier as research associate for Atwood's committee, with an initial assignment to investigate Pueblo conditions. With a letter of introduction from Charles

Lummis, he began to tour the pueblos and learned of the proposed Bursum Bill from one of the local superintendents. Atwood found out around the same time that the Senate had already passed the bill without debate, which infuriated her because she had opposed the bill's first version and had been assured of its demise. Atwood immediately set to work to ensure its defeat in the House, mobilizing women's clubs across the country (representing a membership of some two million women) to write to Congress and the Department of the Interior in protest. Meanwhile, Collier traveled with Abeita and Schuster around the pueblos to make sure they all understood the stakes involved, and he helped organize the All-Pueblo Council meeting and protest that November. He also penned numerous essays and articles appealing for public support for the Pueblos' cause, using primitivist images of Indians in defense of their land rights.[28]

The network of writers, artists, and anthropologists in New Mexico and New York also joined in the campaign. Luhan and Parsons, both of whom had moved away from activist causes during the war, now found themselves returning to political action. Parsons helped rally professional organizations to the cause, including the American Museum of Natural History, the American Ethnological Society, and the Peabody Museum. Luhan was the driving force behind the nationally publicized "Protest of Artists and Writers against the Bursum Bill," signed by luminaries including Parsons, Mary Austin, Witter Bynner, Zane Grey, D. H. Lawrence, Harriet Monroe, Carl Sandburg, William Allen White, Vachel Lindsay, and Edgar Lee Masters. The writers in the group placed articles in popular magazines and inspired editorial opposition to the bill in local and national papers. Alice Corbin Henderson's essay calling for artists to recognize the Indians' spiritual value for modern art was intended as a call to arms. This was "the cause of every American artist, the cause of art itself," she wrote, "as against the materialistic tendency of the age and its lack of vision." The campaign created "widespread publicity on a scale unknown before in Indian affairs," Collier wrote. This was an "all-American and all-Indian movement" that began "with an effort to secure elementary justice and to lift artificial handicaps," which he predicted would end with "the winning of a future for a whole race." For better or for worse, cultural modernists in New Mexico, New York, and beyond were now fully engaged in the politics of Indian affairs.[29]

In the process, they created three new organizations that would be instrumental in the dance controversy and in the larger world of Indian reform for the rest of the twentieth century. Members of the Santa Fe art colony formed the New Mexico Association on Indian Affairs (NMAIA), whose guiding spirits included Bynner, Henderson, her husband William Penhallow Henderson, and the artist Gustave Baumann. The Santa Fe lawyer Francis Wilson, remembered by Pueblo Indians as one of the most effective BIA attorneys they had ever had, joined the NMAIA and helped make the legal case against the Bursum Bill. The Eastern Association on Indian Affairs (EAIA) was centered in New York and Boston and wielded considerable financial and political influence; its members included prominent anthropologists like Parsons, Warren Moorehead, F. W. Hodge, Pliny Goddard, and Stewart Culin. Collier brought together his networks from New York, California, and New Mexico to form the American Indian Defense Association (AIDA) in the spring of 1923, with himself as executive secretary. The AIDA's ambitious "Announcement of Purposes" called for cooperative efforts "to induce the Government" to meet "its treaty and contractual obligations" toward the Indians and to provide Indians with "the same rights to life, liberty, and property," including "religious freedom," that other Americans enjoyed. For more than a year, all three of these groups devoted the bulk of their resources to a favorable resolution of the Pueblo land crisis.[30]

Indians and Reformers on Pueblo Tradition

Along with the Bursum Bill's threat to Pueblo land, Pueblo Indians and modernist reformers feared its likely impact on Pueblo religious traditions. The Pueblos' loss of land had already imperiled aspects of their religious practice. Shrines and pilgrimage sites throughout the regional landscape, many of them marking important events in tribal stories of origin, were increasingly inaccessible or even destroyed. As settlers appropriated more and more agricultural land, growing numbers of Pueblo men could not make a living farming and had to find outside employment, making it difficult for them to return home for tribal ceremonies. The bill could only exacerbate these problems. More directly, the bill threatened tribal sovereignty and standards of ceremonial secrecy by placing internal Pueblo affairs under the jurisdiction of the notoriously unfriendly New Mexico state courts. As Collier put it, the bill "proposed to bring before a federal court all disputes or complaints concerning Pueblo office holders," men who were "also religious dignitaries and officers of secret societies." Its passage would therefore "have made it possible for any discontented individual to force the hierarchy into court where, under penalty of a jail sentence, they would have been required to disclose the most sacred secrets of the tribe." Pueblo Indians had good reason to fear the bill's impact on tribal governance and ceremonial traditions.[31]

Making matters worse, the Bursum Bill's supporters attacked Pueblo religious traditions as a way to justify the theft of Pueblo land. The struggle to define and judge Pueblo tradition reached a peak at the congressional hearings on the bill, held by the Senate Committee on Public Lands and Surveys in January 1923 and the next month by the House Committee on Indian Affairs. By that time, the bill had received so much negative publicity that it was no longer politically viable. Still, its supporters hoped to pass a minimally revised version, and toward that end they marshaled the accumulated years of missionary and assimilationist attacks on Pueblo tradition. Colonel Twitchell quoted a description of the Pueblos from the *Sandoval* case as "largely influenced by superstition and fetichism, and chiefly governed according to the crude customs inherited from their ancestors." Ironically, the Supreme Court had used this description in 1913 to paint the Pueblos as savages who required a government wardship that included the protection of their land. Now Twitchell and his colleagues argued that the "savage" Pueblos had no need for the land and claimed that the settlers who also desired it were more industrious. Assistant Commissioner Meritt told the committee that San Ildefonso Pueblo had far more agricultural land than necessary and that these Indians wasted so much time on the "execution of their pagan dances" that even if they had more land they would never increase the amount under cultivation. In truth, San Ildefonso and other pueblos had lost so much of their best land to settlers that they were cultivating less than ever before. Earlier that year, San Ildefonso had reported that it retained possession of only 248 of the 1,250 irrigable acres in its original 12,000-acre grant. Twitchell and Meritt illustrate how the rhetoric of "savagery" and "paganism" served to support attacks on Pueblo sovereignty and land rights.[32]

The Pueblo Indians were therefore forced to defend their ceremonies along with their land. Martin Vigil of Tesuque, a member of the delegation to Washington, was an emerging Pueblo leader who spoke English well as a result of his years at St. Catherine's boarding school in Santa Fe. An accomplished eagle dancer, Vigil spoke eloquently on behalf of the ceremonies he loved. As he remembered years later, on the way to Washington he told

Martin Vigil. Courtesy National Anthropological Archives, Smithsonian Institution, Suitland, Maryland, INV 06346700.

audiences in Chicago and New York that the dances were simply part of his people's "Catholic religion." He countered stereotypes against both Catholics and Indians by pointing out that the people of Tesuque did not "worship the image" of their patron San Diego but performed their saint's day ceremonies each November in his honor. Vigil denounced evaluations of Tesuque's dances as "wicked" or "pagan," defining them instead as acts of worship dedicated "to our Great Spirit and God." He recalled that Archbishop Patrick Hayes of New York had been so touched by this that he embraced Vigil and said, "You told the truth, son." As other Pueblo leaders had done before them, delegates like Vigil defended their ceremonies as a part of their Catholic practice or simply as their "custom," rather than as a distinct "religion."[33]

Other Pueblo leaders used tribal histories and prophecies to defend Pueblo land rights, denouncing Euro-American assumptions of superiority from the perspective of Pueblo tradition. Pablo Abeita protested against the

Eagle dance, Tesuque Pueblo, 1924. Photo by T. Harmon Parkhurst. Courtesy Tesuque Pueblo and Palace of the Governors (MNM/DCA), Santa Fe, New Mexico, neg. no. 4734.

many seizures of Pueblo lands, pointing out that despite the claim that Columbus had found "a new world, [t]his world was not lost, and may have been and may be as old if not older than the one Columbus came from." He refused to create a hierarchy of "primitive" and "civilized" religions, bringing indigenous and Christian sacred histories into dialogue on an equal footing. "Who knows if this country was destroyed by deluge during Noah's time?" he asked. "Our traditional history says that we are not descendants of Noah, but of another being more sacred and superior, so that who can tell?" A self-proclaimed Catholic, Abeita was not suggesting that the story of Noah and the flood was false but simply that Indians had their own sacred history that was more valid for this land because "the white people were not here then, but the Indians were." He went on to tell the committee that the "Great Spirit" had predicted the coming of "people from the East" who, although very greedy, were able to "see justice." He identified the Americans as the people from the East, and advised them to ally with the Indians against the prophesied "people from the West"—a people "deformed from the setting sun" who according to prophecy could destroy this world. Here, Abeita suggested that, despite their violations of justice, white Americans were capable of redemption and should make common cause with the Indians against a still more dangerous common enemy to come. He refused to see Pueblo religious tradition either as pagan savagery or as the romanticized "primitive religion" of the modernists but presented it as a living system framing the debate.[34]

The Pueblo delegates' testimonies to Congress presented the land crisis as a matter of life and death for their people. In a letter read to the Senate committee as their closing statement, the delegation asked, "Is it the wish of the American people that the last remnant of a once happy people perish untimely from the face of the earth?" They were not interested in theories of the supposed incompatibility of "primitive" traditions with "modernity," and they saw nothing inevitable about the destruction that now threatened them. Instead, they explained that the danger came from "a selfish few who curse and revile us," those who would confirm the theft of their land and water. "May God forbid that anyone refuse us the right to live. Land and water means the life of the Pueblo Indians; without these we can not survive."[35]

Meanwhile, Collier and other modernists were developing their primitivist ideals of Pueblo religion into a publicity tool aimed at the dismantling of assimilationist policies. They began by insisting that the Pueblo Indians had a legitimate religion that must be respected as such. In terms appealing to a predominantly Protestant America, they presented the Pueblos as a people of peace comparable to the best of the Christian tradition. At the Senate hearings, Stella Atwood borrowed Charles Lummis's comparison to the Quakers to make her own case for the existence and positive value of Pueblo religion, telling the committee that, despite centuries of oppression, the Pueblo Indians had kept "alive in their own spirits the kind of ideals which are best known as the ideals of the Quakers."[36] Modernists also appealed to liberal Protestant principles of tolerance and diversity. Ina Sizer Cassidy, a writer and longtime Unitarian married to the Santa Fe artist Gerald Cassidy, argued that no Christian should condemn Indians whose worship was sincere. "Is our God so great that he can have his creatures worship in no way but a certain prescribed formula? Or is he so great that He finds worship in the pure heart, and simple faith regardless of ritual?" With sincerity of worship and ethical principles to rival any Christian church, the legitimacy of Pueblo religion must surely be respected.[37]

Another strategy was to celebrate the indigenous tradition as an "old magical, pagan religion" distinct from and perhaps even superior to Christianity. "Superficially, most of [the Pueblos] are Roman Catholic," Collier wrote in the Survey Graphic, "but all of them are fundamentally pagan—an active, institutional paganism with ritual and creed exceedingly rich, dramatic and romantic." Collier believed that in both spiritual vibrancy and ethical results this Indian paganism surpassed even the much-touted heights of the Quakers. "The Quakers never faced such a temptation to hatred as these Indians have long faced. And the Quakers never loved life with the gay and fierce passion of these Indians, or maintained a community rich in life-giving institutions like theirs." If the Indians were "admittedly weaker" in material development, "on the human and spiritual side" Collier found them more impressive than anything the "White Man's civilization" had produced. "They are groups of men and women rich in beauty, rooted in an inconceivably rich social inheritance, and, after generations of complicated persecution, still faithful to their way of the spirit—a way which might lead us white men far if we wished or were constituted to travel it." Far from the "idolatrous savages" their enemies alleged, Collier argued that the Indians had developed and preserved a religious civilization that in crucial respects surpassed the best of the Christian tradition.[38]

In the fight against the Bursum Bill, Collier and other modernists articulated the broad scientific and human value they saw in Pueblo civilization. For Collier, these Indians represented the best of the Mesoamerican civilizations that had elsewhere been destroyed by Spain—the "northern outposts" and the "last survivors" of "that great cultural system of the Mayans and Aztecs." These were remnants miraculously preserved in the modern world, equivalent in value to "the last mountain peak of a sunken Continent of Atlantis." In a mild version of the Black Legend that Anglo-Americans had so often used to vilify the Spanish Empire, Collier suggested that the beneficence of the Franciscans could be sustained only because the Pueblos had so little of value to the gold-hungry Spaniards. While "goldseekers [had] devastated the Indian civilizations of Mexico," the Pueblos had managed to survive only because they "had no gold and [so] were spared." For those interested in the diversity and development of human cultures, the Pueblos' continuing survival seemed to offer invaluable insights into the world of ancient America. Surely they should not now be arbitrarily destroyed.[39]

If anyone doubted the intrinsic significance of that world, Collier compared the Pueblos to a still-flourishing medieval European society. "It is as though mediaeval Chartres with all its priests and astrologers, its folk and artisans, had survived unchanged into present-day France." Such comparisons tapped into a widespread romanticization of medieval life that had been present in the upper echelons of American culture for decades, part of the same reaction against the perceived sterility of modernity that also spawned this celebration of the Pueblos. Invoking one of the most widely admired legacies of medieval Europe, he praised the Pueblo ceremonial dances as "a great form of cooperative dramatic art . . . as noteworthy as the Gothic cathedral was in the middle ages." Collier's emphasis on the "cooperative" qualities of both dancing and cathedral building revealed his characteristic interest in community-building institutions. Whereas Gothic cathedrals still remained as the evidence of medieval European communal genius, though the civilization that created them was long gone, the Pueblos' cooperative ceremonies had survived unchanged from the ancient civilizations of the Americas, providing a possible model for modern community-building efforts.[40]

Collier also identified the Pueblos with the civilization of ancient Greece. "If the civilization of Crete had not perished at the beginning of the Homeric Age of Greece, but through a miracle had survived and were today blooming and vigorous on its mountain island; then we should have a perfect parallel of the Pueblos." Greece made a compelling comparison because, at least since the Enlightenment, Europeans had celebrated its culture as the foundation of Western civilization.[41] Just as if the ancient Greeks were still available for study, the Pueblos became a living demonstration of civilization's origins. Collier argued that in some ways the Indians even surpassed the cultural legacy bequeathed to Europe. The Pueblo Indians had "achieved democracy, the rule of love, a social ideal of beauty, at a date before Greek thought and Christianity had begun to civilize the Aryans of Europe." Once again he defended the Pueblos not by attacking the values of European civilization but by arguing that the Pueblos lived up to them far better than Europeans or their American descendants ever had.[42]

Having established the legitimacy and significance of Pueblo religion, Collier argued that the Bursum Bill threatened to violate the Indians' religious freedom in ways nobody would dare to impose on more familiar traditions. The Pueblos' "sacred secret knowledge . . . [is] just as holy as are the secrets given to Catholic priests in the confession," he told the committee, and the government should no more force their disclosure "than to legislate that the Catholic priests shall reveal the secrets of the confession, if we believe in religious liberty." Such action would threaten the very life of the Pueblo communities, a result that would surely be inconsistent with the principles of "Americanism." "If the Pueblo can gradually make its adjustment and can keep its really beautiful system of home life . . . its wonderful motives and legends, its great unwritten literature," he asked the committee, and "if those things do no harm and do not get in the way of other things, why object to or discard them?" When one congressman asked whether Collier himself adhered to the biblical commandment "Thou shalt worship the Lord thy God," he answered that whatever his own religion neither he nor the "American Government" had any right "to say to any citizen, 'Thou shalt worship the Presbyterian, or the Catholic, or any other God.' " Whether or not they worshiped the Christian God, he insisted that they had their own religion that must be granted the same freedoms guaranteed to any other religion in America.[43]

Although he clearly separated Pueblo "paganism" from Catholicism, Collier thought very highly of the historic Catholic presence among the Pueblos. Disregarding the historical fluctuations of Franciscan policy, he praised the friars of both colonial and modern times as the only Europeans who had not tried to destroy indigenous traditions. "The Franciscans had no wish to stamp out the beauties of the archaic life," he wrote in *Sunset Magazine*, "and it is these missionaries, and they alone, who showed statesmanship toward the Indians in the whole of America and through all the centuries to the present day." Hoping to build an alliance with the Bureau of Catholic Missions, Collier forwarded this essay to the new BCIM director Father William Hughes and told him that the church's impact on the Pueblos had been so positive that he believed the Catholics should be given "sponsorship" over "the entire range of their problem, not only religious and moral but equally [its] social and economic phases." Affirming the Franciscans for their tactics of colonial management, he argued elsewhere that the U.S. government should learn from the Franciscan success in contributing the positive aspects of "Christian creed and Christian morality" without undermining the Pueblos' indigenous traditions. Here—despite or perhaps because of his primitivist romanticization of Pueblo religion—Collier revealed a continuing assumption of Christian and Euro-American superiority in certain practical realms of life.[44]

All this praise for Pueblo "paganism" certainly helped make the case for Indian religious freedom, but it also continued the primitivist and Orientalist themes that had long painted Indians as incapable of managing the modern world. The civilization of the Pueblos was as old as China's but "more spiritually conscious than the Chinese," wrote Collier. "There is nothing in the Libyan Desert, or Turkestan, or the Caucasus more picturesque and wild, more throbbing with vitality than these unknown Pueblo communes."[45] Like the "oriental" peoples to whom they were being compared, these Indians appeared mysterious, communal, and deeply spiritual, in sharp contrast to an Anglo-American civilization imagined as materialistic, individualistic, and oriented toward practical goals.

It is no wonder that reformers who viewed Indians in this way often assumed their own right to make decisions for the Pueblos. This tendency surfaced during the planning for the Pueblo delegations to the East Coast and later to California for publicity and fundraising purposes. Mabel Dodge Luhan told Collier in the fall of 1922 that "we must select [the delegates] ourselves" because the Indians "always vote that their smart, short-haired Americanized ones should go: just the wrong ones." Planning another delegation a year later, Collier hoped for "representative Indian[s]," including "someone who can talk—simply as the typical Indians talk, not artificially the way Pablo Abeita talks," and delegates who could "sing together" and "dance together."[46] Primitivist discourse continued to identify Indians with the past, rather than with the modern world in which they actually lived, and placed them in the sort of passive role that Abeita and other Pueblo leaders had so firmly rejected. Abeita complained that this strategy had left educated Indians like himself "in the dark" and unable to take effective action. The "John Collier Company . . . just wanted the long-haired ones . . . for exhibition purposes," he wrote bitterly, "they would have nothing of the short-haired ones, anybody can guess the rest." Where modernists looked for delegates who would meet white expectations for Pueblo religious authenticity, the Indians wanted to send representatives who could communicate their practical needs to an American audience.[47]

Modernists and Moderates on the Pueblos' Future

The artists, writers, anthropologists, and reformers who opposed the Bursum Bill held widely varying opinions on the best course of action for the Pueblos' future. Some saw no future at all, employing the old trope of the "vanishing Indian" to mourn what they believed was the Indians' inevitable demise. An editorial criticizing the bill in *Current Opinion* introduced the Pueblos as "the relics of a cultural life which is passing but which still inspires," and quoted the famous British modernist writer D. H. Lawrence— then in New Mexico as a long-term guest of Mabel Dodge Luhan's—to chastise all reformers for interfering in what he argued could otherwise be a peaceful end. "For Heaven's sake keep these Indians out of the clutch of politics," wrote Lawrence. "Let us have the grace and dignity to shelter these ancient centers of life, so that, if die they must, they die a natural death." Lawrence wrote a biting letter to Luhan arguing that she and Collier would only "destroy the Indians" by setting "the claws of [their] own White egoistic *benevolent* volition into them." In his eyes, their efforts were no better than the interference of the missionaries. "Jesus, and The Good as you see it, are poison for the Indians," he wrote. For Lawrence it was the Indians' religion more than anything else that separated them from the modern world: The "Red Indian" was "a truly religious man, religious in perhaps the oldest sense, and deepest, of the word," with a civilization "much older than Greeks, or Hindus or any European or even Egyptians." In his eyes they preserved the "root meaning of religion," with "no conception of a god" but only the effort to establish "sheer naked contact, *without an intermediary or mediator . . .* with the elemental life of the cosmos." This was "the religion which precedes the god-concept, and is therefore greater and deeper than any god-concept." In classic secularist fashion Lawrence believed that religion was doomed in the modern world, and it was precisely because he saw the Pueblos as the purest expression of religion that he did not believe they could survive.[48]

In fact, Lawrence's primary concern was not with the Indians but with the crisis he diagnosed in white America. While the Indians had so far kept on "burning an eternal fire, the sacred fire of the old dark religion," and so remained the real Americans, "this great welter of whites" who were fated to replace them "is not yet a nation, not yet a people." On this basis he predicted "some fearful convulsion" in "the vast white America" when the Pueblos were gone. The only solution was for white Americans to "take up" the Indian vision "without forgetting we are ourselves." "For it is a new era we have to cross into. And our own electric light won't show us over the gulf. We have to feel our way by the dark thread of the old vision. Before it lapses, let us take it up." Lawrence's primitivism, far more than Luhan's, assumed the right of the "white American" to build a new national identity by appropriating Indian cultural and religious resources. In his vision, white America must drink of the Pueblos' "old dark religion," the only religion rooted authentically in the American continent, in order to become a truly unified and a truly American people.[49]

Other modernists argued that it might be possible for the Pueblos to survive with their cultural and religious traditions intact, but only if they could be kept completely separate from the outside world. In its editorial statement against the Bursum Bill, the *Nation* magazine argued that the Pueblos' land was the most important buffer against interference. "Opposition to the bill should be nation-wide and party-free unless America wishes to see the Pueblo civilization die within the next ten years," the editors wrote. "The tribes which are still primitively vigorous are those, like Santo Domingo, or Zuni (on its reservation), where there has been little or no encroachment; the tribes that are dead or dying, like Pojoaque, Picuris, Nambe, are those which have been unable to prevent non-Indian elements from creeping like a net about their communal villages." Eastern Association board member and legal counsel Roberts Walker, a New York attorney with personal and business connections in New Mexico, told the Senate committee that the Indians were not "ready to be entrusted with full citizenship," but that they had "a genius for form, for design, for pattern, and for various crafts, of basket making, pottery, and worship" and were "a precious and unusual thing that should be preserved in this country under as serene conditions as possibly could be granted to them." In typical primitivist fashion, these reformers assumed an essential incompatibility between the "modern" and the "primitive."[50]

Expanding on the long association of "primitive" Indians with nature, some reformers proposed saving the Indians by adopting the same strategies used to preserve America's scenic wonders. According to Judson King, an old friend of Collier's in New York who helped with publicity against the Bursum Bill, the Pueblo Indians were "as distinct an asset as Niagara or the Falls of the Yosemite and should be preserved in the same spirit."[51] Alice Corbin Henderson appealed to New Mexico's financial self-interest, arguing that the Pueblo Indians were "one of its greatest assets" and ought to be preserved as such. "Perhaps the best thing for the Pueblo Indians would be for the government to make their grants National Park areas, or monuments," she suggested, "and keep the Indians as vanishing specimens of an almost extinct species—like the Buffalo!"[52] For a time Collier too dreamed of "making Taos (and Zuni too) a national monument." Along with Stella Atwood, he explored this possibility with the National Park Service and considered a national publicity campaign along these lines, but never came close to realizing these ideas.[53] All these proposals defined the Indians as natural resources, valuable largely for the cultural and financial enrichment they offered to the nation. There is considerable irony here, because the National Park system had only recently expelled Indians from Yellowstone, Yosemite, Glacier, and other parks in order to keep them fully "natural," which in that case was taken to mean free from any human presence.[54] But if the Indians were irrevocably part of the natural American landscape, then their preservation required that they too be isolated and protected from the apparent corruptions of modernity.

This desire to protect the Indians' cultural purity merged with ideologies of racial difference. As we saw in Luhan's case, modernists tended to see religion as an intrinsic racial characteristic. As Collier put it, "the races of man" had "tribally yearned . . . and created those disciplines and forms of thought and of prayer through which there is realized the Communion of Souls"—and even though many Indians had "welcomed the Christian revelation," they had not "forgotten the path that leads to their original racial fountainhead." They could "cling to their coveted remnants of soil" and "resist the [Indian Bureau's] efforts to turn them into drifting social half-breeds," he wrote, only while they remained "united in this life of religion."[55] Such disgust for "half-breedism" and "mongrelism" revealed reformers' anxieties about the nation's multiple cultural and racial mixings. Anthropologist Frank Speck of the University of Pennsylvania, who joined in the protests against the Bursum Bill, disdained those "thoroughly deculturated" Indians who "lose their pride enough to mingle and marry with their social inferiors among certain classes of negroes or whites," and he opposed assimilationist policies because he believed that Indians should not be asked "to lower themselves socially to the status of our heterogeneous dark-skinned masses."[56] Once again, it is evident that reformers who idealized the Indians often shared contemporary convictions about the permanence of racial difference and maintained racist sentiments against other minorities in America. The modernists' primitivist conceptions of Pueblo culture created an obsession with the Indians' racial and religious purity, too often leading them to oppose virtually any change or adaptation in the Indians' way of life.

Many of the Bursum Bill's opponents were moderates who believed that Indians must eventually integrate into Euro-American civilization but should also maintain as much of their traditional culture as possible. In the spectrum of views on Indian culture, these reformers shared a primitivist admiration for the Pueblos but stopped short of Luhan's and Collier's heights of enthusiasm. At the Senate hearings on the Bursum Bill, the attorney Francis Wilson argued for the Pueblos' right to their land by quoting a former superintendent's description of them as "the last relics on this continent of the famous Aztecs and the descendants of the Montezumas . . . nearer to civilization than any of the Indian races." Echoing anthropological theories of evolution, Wilson saw the Pueblos as more advanced than other Indians but still not quite worthy of the label "civilization."[57] Moderates compared the Pueblos not to the heights of Greek civilization but to its beginnings, an invaluable resource for archaeologists and artists but surely not the equal of contemporary European culture. Elizabeth Shepley Sergeant argued that the Spanish conquest had halted the Pueblos' development by forcing them to devote their energies to self-preservation: "The Pueblo civilization was arrested—and save for minor 'progressions' remains today at just about the point where Greek culture began."[58] J. D. DeHuff, the superintendent of the Santa Fe Indian School during the 1920s, was another moderate who socialized with the city's artists and writers along with his wife Elizabeth DeHuff, herself an artist. DeHuff suggested that if Indians were permitted to continue their cultural development, they may in time create art as compelling as anything the Greeks had produced. "Who is here that would say that if the American Indian is permitted to remain an Indian, his ceremonials may not in time be sublimated and transmuted into the gold of something as worthwhile and world-compelling as the tragedies of Aeschylus?"[59]

Moderates placed themselves in a kind of shepherding role, hoping to gently introduce the Indians to the benefits of Euro-American civilization while encouraging the ongoing development of authentically Indian culture. Although the boards of the Eastern Association and the AIDA agreed in June 1923 that "the Indian should . . . be educated in the arts and sciences of today," they cautioned that "transformation in habits of life" should not be "so violent that they undermine basic virtues of filial respect and of loyalty to old friends." They counseled large-scale policy changes that would honor "the Indian genius in painting, sculpture, music and literature" as a necessary part of Indian self-respect and as "a genuine contribution to the sum total of Americanism."[60] DeHuff believed that "Indian education" must give the Indian "what he needs of our culture and civilization to enable him to stand up in the face of competition" but must also "foster and preserve the Indian's native culture," and he specifically defended the Pueblo ceremonies against charges of immorality. "Let the Zuni have his shalako dance, the Rio Grande pueblo his corn and harvest festivals, the Navajo his yebachai of thanksgiving and the Hopi his snake ceremonial. The dances, even if barbaric, are beautiful, and have not the slightest suggestion of an untoward or unbecoming nature. . . . They are as great in their way as the Grand Canyon or Niagara Falls." In keeping with that ideal, Elizabeth DeHuff established and directed an arts program at the Santa Fe Indian School, including theatrical productions that featured Indian dancing, and received considerable criticism from her husband's assimilationist-minded colleagues. The superintendent himself organized an Indian arts and crafts display for the annual Santa Fe Fiesta.[61] Neither advocating the active suppression of Indian traditions nor passively mourning their demise, these reformers believed that at least some aspects of Indian culture could provide the foundation for the Indians' entry into mainstream American life. Like the modernist effort to preserve Indian culture—and sometimes the two blended indistinguish-ably—such ideas led to patronizing and even destructive judgments about which works of art were "authentic." They too assumed that Indians did not really have the capacity to manage their own affairs. Yet, unlike some modernists, these reformers did not want to restrict Indians to the "primitive" past and saw positive value in the ongoing development of Indian tradition.

Although Collier sometimes expressed the desire for the Pueblos to remain untouched "primitives," his final proposals for Indian development expressed a great deal of optimism that they could develop and integrate into the larger society without compromising their cultural integrity. He argued quite perceptively that the destruction threatening these Indians was not an inevitable result of contact with contemporary America, but a product of unequal opportunities and of "that 'Americanization' which beats down and drives underground the community life." He concluded that if only the Indians were given fair treatment they could live on *as Indians* with their communal structures intact. "These marvelous little nations with their self-government, their world-old democracy, their institutions for causing the human spirit to bloom into love and splendor must be permitted to live their own lives, forward into their own future, not apart from the White man's world but cooperating with it." He envisioned an economic but not a cultural assimilation. "Assimilation, not into our culture but into modern life, and preservation and intensification of heritage are not hostile choices, excluding one another, but are interdependent through and through. It is the continuing social organism, thousands of years old and still consciously and unconsciously imbued with and consecrated to its ancient past, which must be helped to incorporate the new technologies." In this view, the Pueblos could incorporate the best of modern technologies and invest them with their own cooperative cultural genius—thereby serving as a model to the rest of the world.[62]

Despite this conviction that Indians must be involved in shaping these adaptations, Collier never abandoned a colonialist conception of the problem as one of managing "primitive" peoples. He pointed to Canada's treatment of its Indians and to Spanish, British, and Dutch colonial policies as models for the "indirect" rule of "a dependent or subject race." The same primitivist conceptions of the spiritual, communal, and ancient Indians that motivated Collier's activism left him with the assumption that the Indians were not quite capable of managing their own affairs. The Pueblos were in a "theological stage of thought . . ., inward looking rather than outward looking." "Social change or social invention," for that reason, "could be promoted only with considerable difficulty by a pueblo dweller, himself a pueblo creation." In keeping with his progressive emphasis on scientific management, he argued that such developments would require professional oversight. "With government indorsement, cooperative modern enterprise could be set in motion within the pueblos," and the resulting blend of tribal communalism and modern enterprise "would become educational in directions not only important to the Pueblo but to mankind." There is no record of whether Abeita or other Pueblo leaders read these essays; if so, they would no doubt have expressed concern about Collier's proposals as just one more threat to their sovereignty, another big idea that would likely do more harm than good.[63]

Although they had united in opposition to the Bursum Bill, the Pueblos' cultured admirers found that it was more difficult to agree on what legislation they wanted to promote. After the congressional hearings, Francis Wilson—then serving as legal representative for the General Federation of Women's Clubs as well as the New Mexico Association—helped forge a compromise bill known as the Lenroot Substitute. This bill proposed a three-man board to evaluate the competing land claims, subject to the decisions of the District Court of New Mexico and to appeal by either Indian or non-Indian claimants. It met with general approval from the Bursum Bill's supporters and the relevant congressional committees along with the Eastern and New Mexico Associations, and very nearly passed Congress in March 1923.[64] Collier missed these negotiations because he was raising funds for his soon-to-be-established AIDA and was infuriated that Wilson had approved the compromise. Because the Lenroot Bill accepted the legitimacy of many settlers' claims and provided for no compensation to the Indians, he considered it a "more polite, more conventional" method for benefiting the same "propertied interests" who had created the Bursum Bill. He accused Wilson of deliberately deceiving him and turning traitor to the Indians in order to benefit his own career in New Mexico.[65] Wilson insisted in response that he had every right to negotiate a compromise measure, that he shared Collier's desire for compensations and had been assured that these would be included in a separate appropriations bill, and that under the circumstances this measure represented the best possible outcome for the Indians. But the difference between the two men was fundamental. Collier was convinced that the 1913 *Sandoval* case meant that all non-Indian encroachments on Pueblo land had been illegal and that, although some settlers deserved compensation, any legislation must presume the Indians' basic right to the land. On the other hand, Wilson believed that those non-Indians who had purchased Indian land in good faith before the *Sandoval* decision had claims just as valid as those of the Pueblos.[66]

Collier and Wilson's ongoing dispute forced reformers to take sides between them, creating a permanent rift in the coalition that had defeated the Bursum Bill. Collier retained core groups of supporters in New York, California, Chicago, and New Mexico. But the Eastern Association on Indian Affairs and its counterpart in New Mexico supported Wilson, pointing out that they had never accepted Collier's rather arrogant claim to "leadership of the whole movement." Most of their members were moderates inclined to work with the BIA rather than alienate it, and some had already come to think that Collier's confrontational tactics caused more harm than good. Like Wilson, most sympathized with the plight of those "settlers" who had been on their land for generations and were generally very poor. These groups presented themselves as the moderate, balanced alternative to the unacceptable extremes of the settlers' advocates on one hand and Collier's AIDA on the other. As Roberts Walker put it, despite Collier's "ill-judged rhetorical outbursts," the only real solution was that "bona fide settlers should be confirmed, while the Indians should be protected from invalid claims." Fridolin Schuster, who came to think of Collier as a "nut" and a "radical man," also sided with Wilson. By the end of 1923, even Mabel Dodge Luhan had come to the conclusion that Collier's tactics were self-defeating, that an "atrocious fight will defeat its own ends, our ends," and had stopped providing financial or organizational support for his work. Once again, Luhan would retreat at least for a time from activist involvement.[67]

These conflicts over land legislation were closely related to the reformers' differences over Pueblo culture. The moderates of the Eastern and New Mexico Associations denounced what they considered Collier's romanticized and sentimental evaluations of Pueblo tradition. Walker mocked Collier's assertion "that the Eagle Dance was a 'Gregorian chant'" by commenting that "the lamented pope or Emperor Gregory would be slightly startled to get this information." He also made fun of a Santa Barbara speech in which "Collier likened the Indian civilization and culture to the Pan-Hellen days of ancient Greece and stated that in its way the Indian arts and fundamental accomplishments of the American Indian were just as great, as beautiful and worthy of preservation as the dramas, libraries and writings of Plato, of Alexandria and of Athens," concluding, "I wonder what the late Horace would have said of Collier's statement!"[68] Although Walker's differences with Collier on the land issues inspired much of this ridicule, he clearly could not stomach the suggestion that Pueblo civilization might be literally comparable to the undisputed heights of ancient Greece. In the end, he was convinced that the Euro-American civilization was superior and that the Indians would eventually need to assimilate: "Without proselytizing or openly 'Americanizing' them, by making our own civilization and beliefs so real and so inviting that they will in time—no hurry—gladly come over to us." Walker inaccurately accused Collier of wanting to preserve Indians as perpetual primitives. "Should we make museum exhibits of their homes and living, they would die off like captive animals."[69]

The modernists' evident admiration for Pueblo culture also inhibited their cooperation with assimilationist reformers on the land issues. The Indian Rights Association had immediately opposed the Bursum Bill as "obviously in aid of the trespassers and not the Indians," but it did not take a leading role in the fight. Partly this was a matter of tactics. The IRA had always preferred behind-the-scenes lobbying over the loud publicity campaigns so effectively employed by the new modernist reformers. In keeping with that approach, IRA staff appealed directly to Commissioner Burke, the Interior Department, and members of the relevant congressional committees for the bill's revision.[70] But Stella Atwood complained that the IRA had never responded to her requests for cooperation on this issue, a reticence that no doubt reflected their substantive differences regarding Indian culture.[71] Suspicious of the modernists' agenda, the IRA maintained formal opposition to the bill but largely stayed out of the fray. And over the next few years, IRA staff would focus its energies on questions of religion and morality rather than the ongoing negotiations over Pueblo lands.[72]

The IRA's approach also reflected its ties to assimilationists in New Mexico who supported the Bursum Bill. One of the association's longtime informants on Pueblo issues was Clara True, who would briefly work for the IRA during the dance controversy. True had first met Herbert Welsh when she was principal of the Lower Brule Boarding School in South Dakota in the 1890s. She first went to New Mexico to teach at the Santa Clara Pueblo day school in 1902 and then went to Southern California in 1907 to be one of the

BIA's few female superintendents. In 1910 she left the Indian Service and returned to New Mexico, where she became an informal mentor to Santa Clara's self-identified progressives—many of whom were her former students—and lobbied against BIA agents whom she believed guilty of mismanagement or corruption.[73] Those stung by True's crusades claimed that her efforts were motivated less by her concern for the Indians than by her own interests in Pueblo land.[74] She owned several ranches and a livestock business in the region, including holdings within both San Ildefonso and Santa Clara Pueblo's land grants—which according to tribal leaders had been fraudulently obtained—and was among the most vocal advocates for the settlers' cause.[75] She headed a committee of the "citizens of San Ildefonso Grant" and, in that capacity, had hired A. B. Renehan, coauthor of the Bursum Bill, as the settlers' attorney.[76] True saw no conflict between her advocacy for the settlers and for the progressive Indians. She believed that the Bursum Bill promised justice for both settlers and Indians and, by affirming the Pueblos' right to sell their land, would also support the long-standing assimilationist goal of individual landownership for Indians. True had therefore advised the IRA to moderate its opposition to the bill, the basis of a complaint by Alice Corbin Henderson that settlers' advocates in New Mexico had persuaded the IRA to "tacitly" endorse it.[77] There is little doubt that its agreement with True and Renehan on issues of assimilation inclined the IRA to trust these New Mexicans on land issues as well.[78]

In August 1923 representatives of every pueblo in New Mexico gathered for a meeting of the All-Pueblo Council to propose their own solution to the land crisis. Francis Wilson and Margaret McKittrick of the New Mexico Association asked the Indians to support the Lenroot Bill, warning them that Collier was deluding them with impossible dreams of regaining all their land and that they would be better served by more realistic proposals. But Collier, along with other AIDA representatives and Atwood from the General Federation, encouraged the council to affirm the basic principle of Indian ownership, recognizing the need to relinquish title in some cases as long as they received full compensation. The council's final statement acknowledged the claims of some good-faith settlers "to fair compensation" where government negligence had created their predicament and offered to cede "portions of their lands . . . [now] occupied by populous towns . . . in return for other lands or money." But it insisted that the "flagrant land seizures" of recent years "be dealt with drastically and at once" and that clear measures "be

Clara True with Santa Clara Pueblo boy, 1907. Courtesy National Anthropological Archives, Smithsonian Institution, Suitland, Maryland, INV 02337900.

taken to prevent further encroachments." Finally, the council authorized "the American Indian Defense Association and the Indian Welfare Committee of the General Federation of Women's Clubs," and these organizations only, "to take such steps as may be necessary and possible to protect the rights of the various Pueblos." Pueblo Indian leaders, as represented by the All-Pueblo Council, very clearly shared Collier's views about their best interests in the land crisis.[79]

After many more months of wrangling, Congress finally passed the Pueblo Lands Act in June 1924. The bill created a three-member Pueblo Lands Board to arbitrate all relevant disputes under specified guidelines and provided for compensation to both Indians and "good faith" settlers who lost their land. Much to the Pueblos' relief, the act took no action in matters of tribal governance, but the board's final decisions on the land questions proved a serious disappointment. The board initially determined that the Pueblos had collectively lost title to more than 40,000 acres of land, which its appraisers valued at nearly $1.9 million. The task of assigning compensation was delegated to board member H. J. Hagerman, a former territorial governor of New Mexico and a prominent businessman in the state. Hagerman was under considerable pressure from the Bureau of the Budget to limit expenses, and in the end he slashed the total amount awarded to the Pueblos to only $600,000, extinguished the Indians' title to more than 19,000 acres without any compensation at all, and failed to fulfill the act's promise of purchasing new property for them. When Collier became commissioner of Indian affairs in 1933, among his first actions was to push through legislation that tried to make up for the board's actions by appropriating $761,958 for the Pueblos and $232,068 for settlers whose compensations had been inadequate. These results were surely preferable to those the despised Bursum Bill would have produced, but still the Indians had been forced to accept the loss of thousands of acres of irrigated land.[80]

These land disputes provided the immediate political context for the dance controversy, which erupted more than a year before the passage of the Pueblo Lands Act. From the early days of their fight against the Bursum Bill, Collier and like-minded modernists had used their vision of Pueblo religion to argue for religious freedom as it intersected with Pueblo land rights. When Commissioner Burke released his dance circular supplement in March 1923, these ideals would come into direct conflict with the missionary establishment's growing concerns about Indian "paganism."

◆

FOUR

Dance Is (Not) Religion
The Struggle for Authority in Indian Affairs

Among the most outspoken critics of Indian dancing in the mid-1920s was William E. "Pussyfoot" Johnson, former chief special officer for the Bureau of Indian Affairs and a close associate of the Indian Rights Association. In a widely circulated article published in September 1924, Johnson called for the BIA to enforce its own policies against what he called "hidious, obscene and revolting" Indian dances. Singling out the "secret" Pueblo ceremonies for condemnation, he claimed that "boys and girls are stripped naked and herded together entirely nude and encouraged to do the very worst that vileness can suggest," and he quoted a claim by former missionary teacher Mary Dissette that at Zuni "little girls were debauched in these dances under the guise of 'religious liberty.'" According to Johnson, the Pueblo dances amounted to nothing less than "the survival of an ancient Phallic worship, much more degrading than the Phallic worship of the Ancient Greeks and Hindus." He argued that such ceremonies not only were morally degenerate but undermined educational and other "civilizing" programs that cost taxpayers "several millions of dollars annually," making them an economic drain on all Americans. In his eyes, they merited prosecution, certainly not protection.[1]

Allegations like Johnson's, which helped justify the BIA's efforts to suppress Indian dancing in the 1920s, met with direct rebuttals from modernist reformers and Pueblo Indians alike. The All-Pueblo Council did not learn the details of what was being said about the Pueblo ceremonies until two years after the dance controversy began, a delay that reflects its lack of direct involvement in much of the debate. The council's response was straightforward: "We solemnly state that [these statements] are false in every part and are slanderous and libelous, and we ask whether the American people will tolerate their continued circulation in an effort to destroy what we Pueblo Indians hold sacred."[2] In the meantime, artists and anthropologists had rightly condemned claims of "debauchery" and sexual violation in the Pueblo ceremonies as completely unfounded. As for "phallic worship," they argued that the sexual symbolism present in some Pueblo ceremonies had to be understood in cultural context as a sacred invocation of fertility and was not in any way "immoral."

Such debates revealed far less about the Indians than about the reformers who engaged in them. The charges of sexual immorality were part of a long tradition of Christian polemical rhetoric accusing so-called "heathens" and other religious rivals of sexual deviance. In the dance controversy, such charges took shape in the convictions of nineteenth- and early twentieth-century female missionaries like Dissette that "heathenism" was intrinsically degrading to women. As historian Margaret Jacobs has shown, these allegations also provided a place for reformers to address their quandaries over changing sexual mores and gender roles in the larger society. Nineteenth-century Victorian ideals of women as guardians of moral purity in the domestic sphere were crumbling, challenged on one hand by the liberated "New Woman," who insisted on her right to education, career, and personal freedoms, and on the other by the playful daring of the flapper girl. But these reformers could rarely do more than denounce the openly sexual popular dance styles of the "Roaring Twenties" and fought a losing battle to censor radical intellectuals like Elsie Clews Parsons, who advocated "free love" or other alternative sexual arrangements. Moral reformers involved in Indian affairs may have believed they could make more of a difference among Native Americans, who as a colonized people were legally government "wards" and therefore subject to the scrutiny and control of an Interior Department that believed itself duty-bound to "civilize" them. The fact that modernist feminists like Parsons and Luhan saw the Pueblo dances as the expression of a "natural" and healthy attitude toward sexuality and celebrated Pueblo society as a model for women's economic and sexual freedoms only added fuel to their fire.[3]

These tensions over sexual mores and gender roles intersected with an equally heated battle over the place of religion in American public life. Modernist critics of Commissioner Burke's dance policy—and increasingly the Pueblo Indians as well—argued that the ceremonies in question were both moral and legitimately religious and must therefore be granted the constitutional protections guaranteed to all religions in America. Their identification and legitimation of Pueblo religion served as a direct challenge to the Christian establishment in Indian affairs. Burke's circular on Indian dancing was motivated by missionary concerns about Indian dances, and most assimilationists applauded them as a necessary step in the civilizing project. As Johnson's reference to "phallic worship" illustrates, Christian missionaries and reformers imagined a worldwide "paganism" intrinsically opposed to the Victorian Protestant moral standards that they believed universally valid and necessary to civilization. In their eyes, Indian dances seen as immoral and degrading were by definition not legitimately religious. Far from granting such dances religious freedom, they argued that the government should restrict them just as it should any behavior it found immoral in white society. In this way, the crusade against Indian dances was also an attempt to shore up the faltering Christian establishment in Indian affairs and, indeed, to defend the very idea of a "Christian America."

The Assimilationist Case against Indian Tradition

In the years just before the dance controversy, the missionary establishment would find many reasons to renew its concerns about Indian dancing. For one thing, advocates of assimilation worried that the extravagant praise bestowed on Indian ceremonies by artists, writers, and anthropologists would undermine their own "civilizing" efforts. According to Board of Indian Commissioners chair George Vaux, the art colony in Santa Fe had a "deleterious and undesirable effect upon the Pueblo Indian in that it encourages him to retain his immemorial manner of dress and spoils him by offering him easy money to pose for paintings when he might be better employed at the handles of a plow." In his view, the "painters" were "merely clogging the wheels of progress by making the Indian lazy and shiftless."[4] Anthropologists met with similar criticisms. As the Franciscan Fridolin Schuster put it, the "archaeological and ethnological outfit of Santa Fe" was doing "nothing towards the advancement or progress of the Indians," but only encouraged them "to retain their old pagan and superstitious customs, [and] would make of the Indians a show, a circus, a sort of living museum." Some assimilationists would conclude that such influences had actually reversed Indian "progress," negating the impact of government and missionary educational efforts and so making direct intervention against Indian ceremonies and traditions necessary once more.[5]

At the same time, assimilationists had to respond to critics who pointed to the number of educated Indians returning to traditional practices as evidence that Indians were permanently inferior, racially incapable of becoming "civilized." Assimilationists had long blamed the evident corruptions and inadequacies of the BIA for the slow "progress" of the Indians, but this explanation began to ring hollow after decades of reforms had made no discernible difference. In this context, they began to believe that Indians needed more than just a good education and a level playing field in order to achieve true progress. Rather, they would increasingly argue that certain indigenous traditions had a "degrading" effect that could prevent Indians from absorbing the lessons of civilization. The problem appeared far more serious among tribes like the Pueblos, where strong tribal governments and powerful cultural norms could pressure returned students to participate in the ceremonies, and where so many "artists and scientists" actively encouraged the perpetuation of indigenous traditions. If a tribe was permitted or even encouraged to force its young people to participate in "degrading and horribly immoral" ceremonies—and Johnson claimed that the Pueblos did exactly this—then they could never fulfill their promise and "uplift" their tribes to civilization. In this view, the decline of the most degrading Indian ceremonies would not just naturally result from education. Instead, their direct suppression increasingly seemed a necessary part of government assimilation policies.

Johnson's own career suggests that early twentieth-century crusades against alcohol and peyote also encouraged a new crackdown on indigenous traditions. Johnson gained notoriety as a temperance activist in Nebraska during the 1890s, when he posed as a brewer in order to uncover and incriminate pro-alcohol businessmen. BIA commissioner Francis Leupp enlisted him to enforce liquor laws among Indians in Oklahoma in 1906 and then named him chief special officer in charge of ending the illegal alcohol
[...] all Indian reservations.[6] Like his allies in the Indian Rights Associa-
[...] ally focused blame on liquor traffickers and cor-
[...] 1911 he joined with Clara True and the Women's
[...] ion to defend Juan Cruz against murder charges
[...] ndent C. J. Crandall. Cruz, a Santa Clara Indian
[...] an, had accidentally killed another Indian after the

in Indian Affairs

latter resisted arrest for liquor sales. To discredit Crandall, Johnson and True accused him of selling liquor to Indians, and succeeded in having him transferred to another agency. In his account of the conflict, Johnson praised Santa Clara's temperance activists as devout Christians far superior in moral character to the BIA's "crew of wriggling, squirming, sword-swallowers." Far from condemning the dance ceremony that the Indians staged to celebrate Cruz's eventual acquittal, Johnson praised the dancers' "fantastic attire" and affirmed its performance as a celebration of the pueblo's accomplishments in temperance work.[7]

From the beginning, however, Johnson's efforts to combat substance abuse had led him to condemn at least one kind of Indian tradition. Native Americans in southern Texas and northern Mexico had used the peyote cactus in religious ceremonies for centuries, finding spiritual benefits in its mildly hallucinogenic effects. From the late nineteenth century, more and more Indian tribes across the west adopted peyote as a religious manifestation of a growing pan-Indian consciousness. Many credited "Grandfather Peyote" with healing powers against alcoholism, disease, and despair, and anthropologist James Mooney thought so highly of the peyote tradition that he would help Indians in Oklahoma formally incorporate the Native American Church in 1918 to help legitimate it as an authentic religion.[8] However, assimilationists and missionaries (both Protestant and Catholic) condemned peyote as a dangerous drug and a "race menace," and lobbied for laws to prohibit its transport and use.[9] As chief special officer, Johnson brought his forceful tactics to bear against peyote as well as alcohol. In 1909, for example, he bought out and burned the entire stock of the seven businesses in Laredo, Texas, that handled peyote.[10] He was so vigilant in his antipeyote efforts that Native American Church members still recount stories of his "unholy reign of terror."[11] Johnson and like-minded moral reformers characterized the movement's religious claims as merely a cloak for drug trafficking. As they saw it, peyote was a dangerous drug and so by definition could not be part of legitimate religion.

Johnson's later allegations against the Pueblo ceremonies repeated these themes. His 1924 article condemned peyote use as "highly destructive, more so than alcohol," claiming that it combined the effects of cocaine and opium and associating it with the "immorality" of the traditions perpetuated by Taos Pueblo's "pagan leaders."[12] Ironically, peyote was not prevalent among the Pueblo Indians, who generally saw it as inconsistent with their traditions. Taos did have a small group of peyote devotees, but the tribal council opposed the practice and worked with the BIA and the local Catholic priest to combat peyote use among its people.[13] By linking peyote with the Pueblo ceremonies, though, Johnson turned his prohibitionist crusade for public morality into a condemnation of all Indian ceremonialism. The triumph of prohibitionism in the Eighteenth Amendment (1920) no doubt encouraged him and other assimilationists to reconsider outright suppression along with education as a viable tool for eliminating traditions they found problematic.

Meanwhile, missionaries and government agents were expressing renewed concerns about the moral influence of Indian dances. Missionary critiques of the Hopi ceremonies came to the BIA's attention in 1920. Hopi traditionalists had asked a sympathetic superintendent to ban a Protestant missionary from the reservation because he was disturbing the peace with fire-and-brimstone sermons condemning their ceremonies. Commissioner Cato Sells sent Inspector Evander Sweet, a former Methodist minister, to investigate. Sweet did not even bother to speak with the traditionalists. Instead, he gathered testimony from local whites and Hopi Christians who claimed that "their ceremonial or 'religious' dances" included "unprintable and unspeakable immoralities." Sweet's informants told of ceremonial clowns who "took off their Gee string to show the women themselves," of skits depicting "adultery and prostitution," and of a dance in which female performers exposed their "sex organs" as an erotic invitation to the male observers. His cover letter called the Hopis "promiscuous adulterers" who opposed Christianity just so they could continue their "unspeakable practices," and he sought government action to support the Christians on the reservation. Setting the tone for the dance controversy, he concluded that this "scrap" was "simply a case of Paganism vs. Christianity." Surely "no one in the Indian Office," he wrote, would "lend his influence to perpetuating such unspeakable practices under the guise of 'Hopi religion.'" Whatever else the Hopi ceremonies might be, it was clear that in Sweet's view they were not real religion.[14]

The accounts in Sweet's file were not completely fabricated. Some Hopi ceremonies did include sexual symbolism designed to increase the fertility of the earth, the crops, and the people. Hopi Christians testified that at the start of the women's *marawu* ceremony in September men and women gave each other models of sexual organs carved out of watermelon rinds or clay. Critics called these models "immoral" and assumed they signified a sexual invitation, but within the context of Hopi tradition they were symbols of fertility.[15] The sexual antics sometimes performed by Hopi clowns, a focus of particular condemnation in the Sweet report, were also understood as invocations of fertility. Don Talayesva, a Hopi leader who grew up in the 1920s, defended tribal ceremonies against allegations of immorality in his autobiography by explaining how clowns pantomiming intercourse were assuring that the crops would grow. "Well, white man, you want to see what goes on, don't you?" he wrote. "You have spoiled our prayers and it may not rain. You think this business is vulgar, but it means something sacred to us. This old *katcina* is impersonating the Corn Maiden; therefore we must have intercourse with her so that our corn will increase and our people will live in plenty. If this were evil we would not be doing it." Interpreting Talayesva's account, anthropologist Barbara Babcock explains that "seemingly vulgar antics can be sacred . . . associated with fertility and rain, with societal and cosmic regeneration and renewal." Talayesva understood the antics of the Hopi clowns as crucial to the continued vitality and prosperity of his people.[16]

Clowning served other purposes as well. Anthropologists from the early twentieth century on have pointed out that sexually explicit skits could serve as a mode of community discipline, providing moral sanction by making fun of socially unacceptable actions. Elsie Clews Parsons argued in *Pueblo Indian Religion* that the "ritual obscenity and gluttony" she observed among Zuni clowns should be understood as a form of "inverse speech, as departure from normal behavior," and that these clowns effectively served as "sheriffs or disciplinary enforcers of propriety."[17] Zuni leader Virgil Wyaco further explains in his recent autobiography that the clowns remind the people how badly they behaved "before the gods instructed them in correct behavior."[18] Ironically, in some cases Pueblo clowns were almost certainly making fun of mainstream American culture and even of the tourists who observed them. A shocked white woman from Bernalillo, New Mexico, reported in 1924 that she had seen a Santo Domingo man and woman go "through the performance of a hula-hula dance" followed by "the movements of sexual intercourse in pantomime." She interpreted the clowns' performance as evidence that the Pueblo dances were immoral, but for Indians themselves such clowning could serve as a way to ridicule and critique the sexually charged popular dance styles of the 1920s.[19]

The testimony of Hopi Christians against indigenous ceremonies reveals the intensity of their conflict with traditionalists on the reservation. The absence of an indigenous Catholicism left educated young Hopis more inclined than their counterparts in the New Mexico pueblos to accept the message of Protestant missionaries, who demanded that converts completely reject native traditions. Many Hopi Christians had spent years at government or missionary boarding schools, had not participated in tribal ceremonials for many years, and had never been initiated into any of the Hopi religious societies. Their affidavits described events they had witnessed as children, interpreting what they remembered in terms of their current Christian commitments. At the same time, some Hopi Christians drew far more from indigenous traditions than their missionary mentors recognized. The Hopi Christian Hongeva Hooker believed that the missionaries fulfilled a prophecy, which he had heard from his grandmother, that "some day someone would come to the Hopis and bring them the knowledge of the right way." A few years later, Tulawetstiwa—another Christian who had contributed an affidavit to Sweet's report—would publicly burn his clan's "altar and idols." He and his fellow converts believed that this act fulfilled a prophecy that the ceremonies would eventually be corrupted and must then be destroyed. Even as they adopted the Protestant condemnation of Hopi ceremonies, these Hopi Christians continued to understand their lives from within the frameworks of Hopi culture.[20]

Meanwhile, condemnations of Hopi and Pueblo "immorality" by missionaries, reformers, and government agents reflected cultural disputes that had little to do with the Indians. In the 1910s and 1920s, Christian moral reformers were fighting a losing battle against a popular culture that seemed intent on destroying the sexual ethics of Victorian America. They railed against the explicit nature of jazz and swing dance styles, against dance halls and other gathering places that provided the opportunity for sexual contact between young men and women, against bohemian intellectuals like Parsons who advocated trial marriage, and against the growing prevalence of divorce in the teens and twenties. When they alleged that Indian ceremonies included or encouraged "adultery," "free love," and "orgies," Sweet and other Christian assimilationists revealed their anxieties about the new mores of the larger society. This larger context added to the urgency of the assimilationist campaign against Indian dancing.[21]

Bureau of Indian Affairs officials in Washington responded to Sweet's report with a new crackdown on Indian dancing. Assistant Commissioner Edgar B. Meritt, a lawyer originally from Arkansas, was so appalled that he took it upon himself to draft a new circular letter instructing BIA superintendents all around the country not to tolerate such ceremonies. Newly appointed commissioner Charles Burke, a former South Dakota congressman, was a committed assimilationist who had chaired the House Committee on Indian Affairs. Although he knew little about the Indians of the Southwest, he was eager to curry favor with the missionary establishment, and in February 1921 he was glad to sign and release the circular as his own. "Circular No. 1665: Indian Dancing" attempted to show balance and restraint by deeming some Indian dances "not inconsistent with civilization," but its primary aim was to instruct superintendents that they should enforce "existing regulations" against any Indian dances that retained "elements of savagery or demoralizing practices." Recall that the Religious Crimes Code of 1883, which had never been rescinded, authorized imprisonment or other punishments for Indians who participated in any tribal ceremonies that BIA agents found offensive. The new circular deemed "educational processes" and "patient advisory methods" preferable if possible but approved the use of "punitive measures" whenever necessary.[22]

The missionary establishment, well beyond local missionaries like those on the Hopi reservation, was also becoming more vocal in its critiques of Indian dancing. These concerns were evident in a major survey of religious conditions on all Indian reservations, funded by John D. Rockefeller and conducted by the Home Missions Council of the Federal Council of Churches between 1920 and 1922. G. E. E. Lindquist, a prominent missionary leader widely recognized as an authority on Indian affairs, directed the survey and published its results in 1923 as *The Red Man in the United States*. Lindquist advocated a gradual and moderate approach to assimilation, rejecting boarding schools like Carlisle that had tried to "civilize" by eradicating everything Indian in favor of local schools that would preserve the "natural affections" and allow Indians to maintain those indigenous traditions that he judged worthwhile. Still, in his view certain traditions clearly needed to be eliminated. Like "Pussyfoot" Johnson, he especially condemned "the new and insidious cult of peyote (the Indian's cocaine) that has sprung up of recent years and spread at an alarming rate through the reservations," which he believed "threatens to rival the malign influence of the medicine man and to exceed that of the 'firewater' whose place it is in some instances taking." He judged some Indian dances almost as harshly. Although most of these had once been "connected with religious observances," he believed that "under modern conditions" they had "developed into some of the strongest influences for race demoralization and degeneracy." Relying on the Sweet report, he singled out the "secret dances" of the Pueblo Indians as "characterized by unbridled license."[23]

After the survey, the Home Missions Council organized a series of regional conferences designed to coordinate local Protestant mission efforts. At the conference in Albuquerque, delegates decried "the recrudescence of heathenism in the recent increase in the number of tribal dances and the return of former dominating forces of paganism," and they divided responsibility for missions to the various pueblos among the Episcopal, Presbyterian, and Brethren churches. Local Catholic leaders understandably saw this agreement as an aggressive anti-Catholic move. The Protestants had "decided that we Catholics have not done our duty in the past with respect to the Indians," Father Fridolin Schuster reported angrily, and were now more determined than ever to "invade all the Pueblos to make Christians of the Pueblo Indians." Despite the BIA's efforts to ensure parity between them, Catholic and Protestant missionaries continued to see each other as rivals for Indian souls and for authority in Indian affairs. Schuster feared that under Burke's administration the Protestants had reclaimed their old advantage, leaving Catholics with little hope for fair treatment.[24]

At the Home Missions conference in South Dakota, missionaries complained that the Indians were holding more dances and other ceremonies than they had in former years. This may well have been true. A postwar economic crisis was devastating many small farmers in that region, and Indian communities—already impoverished as a result of allotment policies—were hit especially hard. In response to economic hardship, Plains tribes including the Lakota traditionally performed dances as a form of prayer for better times. Giveaway ceremonies, which served to redistribute material resources to those most in need, often accompanied the dances. Instead of understanding such ceremonies as a way of coping with crisis, though, missionaries believed they were "injurious to the industry of Indian people" and therefore a primary cause of the problem. Hoping to determine new strategies to stop the dances, they called for a joint conference of missionaries and BIA personnel in the region. Commissioner Burke, who was seeking a way to regain missionary support after the negative publicity over scandals including the Bursum Bill, was no doubt sincerely concerned about the Indians of his home state and personally convened this meeting.[25]

Burke's "Supplement to Circular No. 1665," sent out in February 1923, repeated verbatim the recommendations developed at the South Dakota conference. The new guidelines called for completely banning dances considered especially "objectionable," restricting the Indians to one approved event per month (only during daytime hours and not at all during months busy with planting and harvest), and forbidding Indians younger than fifty from attending any dances at all. The commissioner did not insist on uniform or strict implementation, asking that agents adapt these guidelines to the varying circumstances on each reservation and attempt "gentle persuasion" before taking any coercive measures. To ensure that the Indians took the policy seriously, Burke penned a "Message to All Indians," asking tribal leaders on every reservation to lead their people toward the voluntary abandonment of all "useless and harmful performances." If they would not do this, he warned rather ominously, "some other course will have to be taken." Apparently discouraged that both agents and Indians had not taken his first dance circular seriously, Burke hoped that this new directive would be specific enough to bring meaningful change. To create accountability, he directed his agents to send a report within a year on the results of their efforts. Shaped by the agenda of the missionary establishment, both of Burke's dance circulars represented a renewed effort to bring Indian dancing, judged as "degrading" and "immoral," to an end either by persuasion or by force.[26]

The Controversy Begins

When they received the Commissioner's "Message to All Indians," Pueblo leaders uniformly refused to curtail their ceremonies in any way. In their initial responses, some tribal councils simply informed their superintendents that the new policy was not relevant to them. Because Burke had warned against "the neglect of stock, crops, gardens, and home interests,"

Cochiti Pueblo's governor and tribal council pointed out that they held most of their dances in the winter rather than in the busy agricultural seasons. The fact that they lived on far less land per person than whites considered necessary for survival in arid New Mexico, and had done so long before any Europeans had arrived, should be proof enough that they did not "waste time" in their ceremonies. As Zia's governor poignantly wrote, "We are not doing anything bad or wrong, in our old custom way." These initial Pueblo responses did not directly challenge the logic of the circular and did not explicitly define the ceremonies as a "religion" that merited constitutional protection. Instead, they simply insisted that their own "customs" were not immoral and had never interfered with their livelihood in any way.[27]

Some months later, San Ildefonso's tribal council expanded on this argument by defending the dances as a positive cultural heritage, which they explicitly differentiated from their Christian religion: "we have accepted the white man's religion, are Christians, and we live as such. Every Indian child is baptised in the Christian Church by the consent and request of its parents, and our children are trained in the Christian religion. But we also teach our children reverence and love for the memorials of their ancestors, and we believe we have a right to do this." This statement, drafted with the help of a sympathetic day school teacher, defended the Pueblo dances not as a separate "religion," not even as a part of Catholic observance, but as ancestral "memorials" with no bearing on their Christianity. In Pueblo historical experience, defining ceremonial traditions as "custom" rather than "religion" had prevented their repression as a direct competitor to Catholicism. In Protestant-dominated America, naming their religion as "Christian" suggested that their "customs" had no reason to clash with Protestant religion any more than it did with Catholicism.[28]

The Isleta progressive Pablo Abeita opposed the new policy as an impediment to the progress he wanted for his people. "I wonder if [Burke] realizes how the Indians will feel about it" and "how much it will hurt us Pueblo Indians," he wrote. As we have seen, Abeita was a lifelong participant in Isleta's ceremonial life and considered the dances a positive part of tribal identity rather than an impediment to the Pueblos' progress. But he diplomatically avoided any direct defense of the ceremonies in his correspondence with the Bureau of Catholic Missions, arguing instead that this "latest instruction" would take his pueblo "back at least fifteen years" by creating "dissatisfaction among the every-day Indian." Here Abeita pointed out that offending and alienating Native Americans was no way to help them achieve the progress he desired: "There are certain rules or regulations of the Department that if enforced would do an immense lot of good and there are other rules that if enforced will harm the Pueblos that would make the Indians lose faith with the Department or Uncle Sam."[29]

The new dance circular also had political implications in the ongoing controversy over Pueblo lands. Father Schuster advised the Laguna Indians not to participate in any formal protests against the circular because he feared that "any foolish or hasty action" on their part might inspire retribution from the BIA in the form of a less favorable land bill. Although Commissioner Burke's assimilationist motivations were no doubt sincere, he may also have hoped for political advantages in the Pueblo land disputes. According to Colonel Twitchell in Santa Fe, Burke intended his dance policy to punish the Pueblos and their modernist allies for the Bursum Bill's defeat. Other observers concluded that the commissioner was pursuing a "divide and conquer" strategy. Burke intended to "irritate the artists" and "line up many Protestant people with him," argued Roberts Walker of the Eastern Association, thereby sowing dissension in the anti–Bursum Bill coalition and leaving the way open for the BIA to take the lead once again in shaping the Pueblo lands legislation.[30]

More immediately, the opponents of Pueblo land rights used the circular to discredit the Indians' claims. Responding to demands that the government increase levels of aid to the Pueblos, Burke himself blamed the Indians' poverty on their overindulgence in dancing rather than their loss of land.[31] Settlers' attorney A. B. Renehan seized on the circular as an opportunity to advance the claims of his clients. "Burke did not command, as a master should," he wrote, but only "pleaded patiently and paternally" for the "cessation from evil dances." The land rightfully belonged, he argued, to the racially superior "pioneers" of European derivation who had tamed the desert landscape and the "savage foe." The Espanola Chamber of Commerce mailed copies of Renehan's diatribe to every member of Congress, hoping this would influence votes on the pending lands bill. Once again, the rhetoric of paganism functioned as a political tool operating against Indian interests.[32]

The All-Pueblo Council met in May 1923 to forge a unified Pueblo response to the new threat. Delegates from twelve pueblos—not including Laguna, Zuni, Taos, Picuris, Tesuque, and San Ildefonso—sent a resolution informing the commissioner that they did not "hold or have any dances, races, or other tribal customs merely for the fun there is in it. It all has a solemn meaning to us." Despite reassurances from their superintendents that the order would not be applied to them, these Pueblo leaders feared that, unless the commissioner actually rescinded the policy, he could at any time find them "guilty of defiance" and implement forceful measures. They reminded Burke that former secretary of the interior A. B. Fall had guaranteed that the government would not interfere with the Pueblo "customs, elections, etc." and demanded that the BIA honor that promise. The council's statement also appealed to the constitutional guarantee of religious freedom, arguing that Pueblo ceremonies were an Indian form of devotion to a common God: "One way of worshipping our God is by dancing, singing, praying and fasting. You know better than we do that the Constitution of these United States gives the rights and liberty to all people to worship according to their own consciences." The Pueblo subcommittee that framed this resolution—council chairman Sotero Ortiz of San Juan, Antonio Abeita of Isleta, and Alcario Montoya of Cochiti—may have been influenced by previous modernist appeals for religious freedom. But no reformers were present at this meeting, and the Indians certainly did not employ modernist conceptions of "primitive religion." By naming their ceremonies as worship, the council used language that would be comfortable and familiar to the American Christian mainstream. Without defining their ceremonies as a religion distinct from Christianity, these Pueblo leaders demanded their own right to religious freedom. This resolution would be the council's only involvement in the dance issue for almost a year.[33]

If Commissioner Burke had hoped for political benefits from his dance policies, he was sorely disappointed. Instead, the new circular ignited a firestorm of opposition not only from Native Americans but from a more politically influential constituency: the modernists who had so recently mobilized on behalf of Pueblo land rights. At their instigation, condemnations of the dance policy soon appeared in the *New York World*, the *New York Times*, and other papers around the country.[34]

The art and business communities of Santa Fe reacted directly against the new circular as a threat to the cultural riches of the Pueblos. The *Santa Fe New Mexican*, edited by New Mexico Association member Dana Roberts, commented that "the utter injustice of misrepresenting their ceremonials as evil and foolish, harmful and depraved, should arouse the widest indignation." Editorials ridiculed the government's assimilationist agenda as a misguided attempt to replace the Indians' "natural" grandeur with the trivialities of "civilization." "The prayer for rain is immoral and the Eagle dance is wicked; the harvest celebration is indecent and the marvelous Shalako is risque," the editors mocked. "Let us put a vest on the turquoise sky, censor the breeze in the tops of the pine trees, tie a gingham apron on the high priest, and set the governor, stately in his native dignity, to work washing dishes in a restaurant." These were ceremonies with untold archaeological value, they argued, which "bring hidden prehistoric times down to the present." Suppressing them would contradict the best of both artistic and scientific opinion. Finally, the editors portrayed the commissioner as a bullying fool with no concept of the meaning and the value of the Pueblo ceremonials. "Pin-headed vandalism is the issue," they concluded.[35]

The *New Mexican* expressed particular concerns about the new policy's potential impact on the state's tourist industry. The Pueblo Indians were "the greatest drawing card for visitors from all over the country and the world in New Mexico," one editorial noted, making any suppression of their ceremonies potentially "a serious blow to the prosperity . . . of central New Mexico." Civic leaders had been working hard to draw attention to the Pueblo ceremonies as the centerpiece of the state's attractions, and they were bound to be angry at a policy that threatened to eliminate them. "The world is aflame to hear of it," as one editorial put it; "therefore let us destroy the living evidence and put it where we will have to excavate it." All of the state's civic organizations, the paper argued, should mobilize against this threat to "one of the greatest business assets of all time." As these editorials reveal once again, the primitivist discourse of modernist artists and anthropologists was closely tied to the commercial interests of Santa Fe's tourist economy. Despite the critiques of commercialism from art colony members like Luhan, some of the most vocal critics of the dance circular were Santa Fe's business and community development leaders who feared negative repercussions on the area's economy.[36]

These financial concerns blended, sometimes uncomfortably, with protests based on religious freedom grounds. Any enforcement of Burke's order would be "subversive of [the Indians'] religious liberty and suppressive of their racial life," the *New Mexican* argued, and would therefore directly violate the U.S. Constitution. At least one reader criticized the paper for focusing too much on the circular's financial implications. "I think we are choosing the wrong weapon on the bigoted head of 'we who are enlightened with wisdom from on High' when we attempt to preserve something sacred as a commercial asset," wrote Mrs. O. S. Emblem. Instead, she argued that Americans must learn to appreciate the religious value of the Indian dances, which she articulated in primitivist terms as a more authentic and more "natural" religion. "We are Christians, to be sure—but we are Americans also; and being American Christians we at least try to be big enough to hold in sacredness things which we must admit are a little bigger and nearer to God than anything we have so far attained in our own religion. We can learn much, if we are big enough to realize it, from these true children of Nature. So there is sufficient religiously, to be gained from them without even considering the commercial value of their dances." Emblem signed her letter, "A subscriber who stands for 'Freedom to worship God in our own way.'" Emblem argued that the virtues of the Pueblos' religion were sufficient reason to preserve them, and that something so sacred should not be sullied through commercialization.[37]

Quickly the argument for religious freedom emerged as the favorite modernist strategy for defending the Pueblo ceremonies. "These so-called dances are largely religious ceremonies," as the Eastern Association on Indian Affairs put it to Interior Secretary Hubert Work, "and under the terms of existing agreements with the U.S. the Indians are free to practice their own religion or the religion of their choice." The letter further criticized the BIA for framing "orders for the Indians in accordance with advice of" missionaries from a particular religion: "In Arizona and New Mexico, where most of these Indian dances occur, the majority of the tribes are baptised Christians of the Roman Catholic faith and have been so since the Spanish Conquest." Because the Indians' "own church makes no objection to these dances," and the order was made "at the instance of the representatives of other churches," they argued that the order amounted to "an affront to the dignity and prestige of the Roman Catholic Church and an offense against the religious liberty that is guaranteed to the rest of us but would thus be withheld from our wards." Like the Pueblos themselves, in this formulation the Eastern Association argued for religious freedom on behalf of the Pueblos' Catholicism rather than any clearly articulated indigenous religion. From the beginning, though, this modernist campaign against the dance circular was also an attack on the lingering strength of the Protestant establishment in Indian affairs.[38]

Stung by so much negative publicity, the BIA immediately began to back-pedal. Southern Pueblos superintendent H. P. Marble, who throughout his tenure was relatively sympathetic to Indian traditions, had immediately supported the Pueblo leaders' own argument that, because their dances did not "interfere with the work upon their farms," the circular did not apply to them. The recently appointed BIA inspector Adelina Otero-Warren, who was a friend of Clara True's and part of a prominent Hispano family in New Mexico, quickly endorsed this view. According to the *Albuquerque Herald*, Otero-Warren and Burke had both indicated that the circular applied not to the Pueblos but only to the Sioux whom the missionary recommendations had originally targeted. When the Santa Fe Chamber of Commerce asked whether Indian dances could still be performed in its city's annual fiesta, Burke replied that the new dance policy was not intended to restrict such events or to negatively affect New Mexico's tourist economy in any way.[39]

When the Indian Rights Association held its annual board meeting in April 1923, controversy was swirling around the dance circular. Concerned that the growing wave of criticism would force Commissioner Burke to retract the policy, the IRA leapt to his defense. In a widely distributed statement, the board established its basic talking points on this issue for the year to come. They expressed regret that Burke's "efforts . . . to check certain vicious, immoral and degrading dances" had inspired "protests from some intelligent groups"—whom they charitably suggested must be acting in "ignorance of the real facts"—against "governmental interference with the 'ancient and sacred rites of the Indians.' " From the IRA's perspective, these dances were anything but sacred. The "secret dances" in particular, they charged, were "of a bestial and revolting character, too filthy to be described in public print, which would not be tolerated for an instant in any civilized community by local police authority." In their view, such dances could be understood only as criminal immorality and were certainly not religion in any meaningful sense of the term. The Home Missions Council and other Protestant missionary organizations immediately agreed.[40]

Catholic opinion was far more ambivalent, although the Eastern Association was wrong to suggest that the church actually approved of the Pueblo dances. Father Schuster, who had worked so closely with modernist reformers against the Bursum Bill, had mixed opinions about Burke's circular. While his essays for the *Indian Sentinel* continued to portray the dances held on Pueblo saints' days in positive terms, he shared the BIA's goal of eliminating those ceremonies he considered un-Catholic and advised the Indians not to actively protest a policy that he believed to be ultimately in their best interests.[41] "In conscience I cannot countenance the dances, as they are pagan," he wrote to William Hughes at the Bureau of Catholic Indian Missions. But he stopped short of endorsing the new policy, arguing that direct government pressure on the Pueblos would be counterproductive: "If the orders in that circular are enforced it will only make the Pueblo Indians more determinate [sic] to continue their dances. It is a delicate situation. Even if the Commissioner wanted to abolish the Pueblo dances, I fail to see how he can succeed. It would require a regiment of soldiers in each pueblo and even then the Indians would sneak out into the hills and hold their dance." This "untimely circular" would only make the Indians "sullen and more determined than ever to retain what customs they have and to revive others." Schuster's dislike for the Protestant missionaries who had motivated the circular, and his suspicions that Burke favored them, no doubt entered into his judgments in this matter. For the time being, he—along with the other priests stationed in the Pueblos—would remain out of the fray.[42]

Despite Schuster's hesitations and the ongoing Protestant-Catholic conflicts, the Bureau of Catholic Indian Missions quickly joined in the missionary establishment's affirmation of Burke's circular. According to an editorial in the *Indian Sentinel*, this was a measure that would meet the approval of "both Catholic and Protestant" missionaries as well as "progressive Indians." Like its Protestant counterparts, the BCIM argued that the current "attacks on the Indian Office" did not serve the Indians' real interests but reflected "the desire of false friends of the Indians to exploit them for profit or amusement." The IRA was of course delighted with this development. To refute the Eastern Association's argument that the circular discriminated against Catholics, one IRA mailing pointed to the *Indian Sentinel* piece as evidence that on this matter Burke enjoyed broad-based, nonsectarian support. "This is an instance where Catholic and Protestant missionaries are in hearty accord," the IRA wrote in triumph. Rather than emerging from local missionary sentiment, the BCIM's enthusiasm for the dance circular served to demonstrate Catholic allegiance to the government's assimilationist program and helped build a tentative Protestant-Catholic alliance against the secularizing threat of the new modernist reformers.[43]

The Sweet report on the Hopi dances, which became known as the "secret dance file," provided the primary basis for assimilationist condemnations of Indian dancing during the controversy. As soon as modernists began criticizing the circular, and even as Burke publicly backed away from applying it to the Pueblos, Assistant Commissioner Meritt gave this file to the IRA in hopes that it could use it in Burke's defense.[44] For that purpose, the IRA adopted a strategy of innuendo rather than full disclosure. In letters and bulk mailings, IRA secretary Matthew Sniffen informed the association's members and correspondents that the affidavits in the file were "too filthy to be described in public print" and "of so vile a character that they are not permitted circulation in the mails." The reference here was to the Comstock laws, a legacy of nineteenth-century moral reform that made it illegal to mail anything considered lewd, lascivious, or obscene. To prove that they were not exaggerating matters, Welsh and Sniffen repeatedly invited "anyone interested in the welfare of the Indians" to visit Washington or Philadelphia to view the file and judge the allegations for themselves. Sniffen and S. M. Brosius, the IRA's Washington lobbyist, personally carried copies to New York and the Southwest to build support for Commissioner Burke's policies. Such tactics increased the impact of the immorality allegations, inviting readers to fill in the blanks and imagine the worst.[45]

The IRA attempted to invalidate objections based on religious freedom by insisting that such "immoral" dances could not be truly religious and could therefore be legally suppressed. The board's very first statement argued that the Supreme Court's decision excluding polygamy from religious freedom claims (Reynolds, 1876) should also apply to the Pueblo ceremonies. According to Sniffen, the commissioner was merely "seeking to eliminate vicious practices that are marked by unbridled license," which, like the Mormon practice of polygamy, could in no way "be sanctioned under the guise of a 'sacred religious rite.'" Sniffen applied parallel logic to peyotism. In the IRA pamphlet Timely Indian Facts, alongside his comments on the dance issue he condemned peyote as a harmful drug being falsely sold to Indians as religion. Those who call peyotism "religion," he argued, "give full license to the 'dope' habit and enable a clique of mixed-bloods and others to create a demand for the peyote buttons by assuring its devotees that it is the Indian's religion and cannot be interfered with." Although Sniffen acknowledged that the peyote ceremony may once have been a "real religious rite," he was convinced that "conditions have radically changed, and now peyote is being pushed as 'dry whiskey' and a substitute for cocaine, etc." In his view the

The Struggle for Authority in Indian Affairs   153

Matthew Sniffen.
Courtesy Historical
Society of Pennsylvania,
Philadelphia.

Pueblo dances and the peyote ceremony alike were immoral, should be illegal, and could certainly not be considered as part of any legitimate religion.[46]

By arguing that the police should suppress immoralities in Indian and white dances alike, the IRA tried to convince skeptics that it was advocating equality rather than discrimination. Most dances among both whites and Indians were "harmless and should not be interfered with unless they . . . deprive their votaries of the strength to attend the ordinary duties the next day," Welsh wrote, "but there are others which are immoral and naturally fall under the inspection of the police." The "secret dances" of the Pueblos, Sniffen claimed, "would not be tolerated for an instant in any civilized community by local police authority." Stopping such ceremonies would simply be holding Indians to "the ordinary laws of decency" that must apply to all citizens in a civilized society. These statements reflected a certain amount of wishful thinking. Protestant moral reformers were certainly concerned about the recent "dance craze" that was making sexually charged dances increasingly popular in the white middle class, but they rarely succeeded in restricting them. When Burke privately informed him of a Minnesota law that did "regulat[e] public dance houses and actually prohibit[ed] certain objectionable dances," Sniffen eagerly publicized this as a precedent for suppressing dances judged immoral. "Local police authority [in white communities] is not supposed to permit dances (public or private) that are obscene or immoral," he wrote to archaeologist Warren Moorehead, "and on various occasions 'spicy parties' have been unceremoniously stopped by the police." Rather than religion, the IRA defined the Pueblo dances in terms of secular immoralities that had to be controlled.[47]

As they struggled to defend Burke's circular, IRA representatives returned again and again to their foundational conviction that Indians must embrace the twin blessings of Christianity and civilization. "It must be apparent to any thoughtful person who has examined the facts," Welsh wrote, "that there is no midway resting place between the policy of civilization on the one hand, which involves, sooner or later, the practical abandonment of old heathen customs, and that of retrogression, which would leave the Indian undeveloped, uncivilized, insuring his disintegration and final extermination by his own inherent vices." Again, the choice was stark. "The Indians must either be led . . . to a position in which they can maintain themselves in competition with white civilization, or else they must sink into a sort of gypsy life where it will be impossible to help them to anything better." If this could not be done, he warned, then "the work of Indian civilization for which Catholic missionaries and Protestant missionaries, wise thinkers and earnest citizens have long and patiently labored will be deprived of a harvest." The future of the Indian, he told one correspondent, relied on "the time-honored ideals of Uncle Sam," including "a definite, elevating knowledge of that Divine Creator . . . whose purposes for mankind have best been declared by the greatest teacher which the Hebrew race produced." Welsh remained committed to the Protestant establishment's synthesis of Christianity and civilization, which he believed essential for Indian progress and indeed for the future of the nation as a whole.[48]

Welsh and Sniffen presented themselves as the moderate, enlightened, and nonsectarian advocates for Indian rights. As Sniffen told one correspondent, "My own Church affiliations are with the Episcopalians, and my Creed is mainly the Golden Rule. Denominational lines make very little difference to me, and I like to judge people by what they do rather than what they profess." Despite their direct support for Protestant missions, Welsh and Sniffen presented this as a cause that reasonable people of any faith, or even no faith, must embrace. As Sniffen wrote in the *Southern Workman*, "all thoughtful people, especially those who believe that the Indian should be regarded as a human being and not merely as an ethnological specimen," would support the commissioner's efforts to "advance [the Indians'] moral, material, and spiritual progress." The choice seemed clear, immediate, and inevitable. As Sniffen put it, "We have to reckon with a juggernaut called 'civilization' that cannot be checked, and the point that concerns us most from the practical standpoint, is to adapt the Indian to meet the inevitable change that he must face." If they were to survive in the modern world, these reformers believed, the Indians must abandon their "heathen vices" and embrace a civilization founded on Christian values.[49]

With those values increasingly threatened in the larger culture, this task seemed more urgent and more difficult than ever before. Aware that some people questioned the link between civilization and Christianity, Sniffen pointed to all of the "activities of a humanitarian nature," including the work of the IRA, "that would not exist but for Christianity." He admitted rather mournfully "that to a considerable extent the church has lost its grip on present day affairs," but he insisted that this problem was not the fault of Christianity as a religion but rather of "the failure of many who are looked up to as its leaders."[50] In a letter to Interior Secretary Hubert Work, Welsh assigned blame, both for the current attacks on Burke's circular and implicitly for the broader challenge to Christian civilization, on the misguided cultural elites who were rejecting Christianity in favor of the "primitive" mentality of the Indians. "I am convinced that at the root of the Indian dance attack," he wrote, "is the strange wide-spread belief that affects many modern minds, in literature, art, music, religion, philosophy to the effect that primitive man had more that is excellent in all the range of human mentality than the race has gained from the greatest of Christian teachers. 'Back to Nature' is their cry. It is to some a captivating theme, but there are dangerous flaws in it, as a careful perusal of the reports in your office on the secret dances will show, or a visit to the ultra impressionist picture show now going on at the Pennsylvania Academy of the Fine Arts will convince those who visit it." Welsh perceptively linked the opposition to the dance circular, and to its Christian and assimilationist premises, with the primitivism of modernist artists and intellectuals.[51]

Making the Case for Pueblo Religion

Most critics of Burke's dance circular absolutely rejected the idea that the Pueblo Indian dances were "immoral." Some of these were moderate reformers who did not dispute the circular's assimilationist premises but opposed such a coercive approach. The archaeologist Warren Moorehead, a member of the Board of Indian Commissioners, had long supported the "humanitarian" work of missions and education as the best way to accomplish the gradual assimilation that he believed the Indians must eventually accept. His book *The American Indian in the United States* (1914) had asked his fellow scientists to renounce their view of the Indian "not as a man but as a . . . specimen [to be] duly catalogued, described, and placed in an exhibition case." But Moorehead made it quite clear that he considered the "secret dance file" an unreliable source, informing Sniffen that he had never seen any "immoral dances" and that none of the archaeologists or ethnologists he knew would approve of any dance that was "actually immoral." In the end, he viewed this as a trivial issue that only diverted attention from more important problems in Indian affairs. He told Sniffen that if the IRA could only refocus its concerns, "Your powerful institution and your large membership and the amount of money you raise place you in a position to do a great work."[52]

Other critics rejected the allegations of immorality in far stronger terms. In the battle against the Bursum Bill, John Collier had already denounced the "general opinion" that "the Pueblo Indians kept things secret because they were wicked, disgraceful in some way," as an unwarranted justification for "invading their sanctuaries." These were "slanderous statements," he told the House Committee on Indian Affairs, with no substantiation from any of "those, like Frank Cushing and [Charles] Lummis and others, who have lived among them." As he put it in a *Sunset Magazine* piece on the land issue, "The Pueblo Indian is the most modest being I have ever known, also monogamous and conventionally moral." When Burke released his circular, Collier was preoccupied with fundraising and the effort to pass a strong Pueblo lands bill, and he devoted little immediate attention to the new attack on Pueblo ceremonies. Fearing that too much attention might add visibility to the charges, he argued that the "'secret documents'" should "be dealt with [only] incidentally." But he continued presenting Pueblo traditions in glowing terms in his writings on the land controversy and hoped that other writers would also "[deal] in a positive way with the Pueblo religions."[53]

When Collier finally turned his full attention to the dance issue early in 1924, he would blast the "propaganda" against the Pueblos as "a sheer and unmitigated slander," completely unsubstantiated and "contradicted by the united testimony of all anthropologists." Lummis himself, then near the end of his career, joined the fray to defend the "modesty of mind and body" that he had found among the Pueblos. "I am frank to say," he wrote to the *New York Times*, "that there is no New England village of which it could be quite as unintelligent to ascribe these orgies as it is to ascribe them to a New Mexico Pueblo." Over the course of the controversy, Collier, Lummis, and other reformers would become increasingly vocal in defending the Pueblos' moral virtue, a virtue that they presented in conventional Victorian Protestant terms. By insisting that the Pueblos exemplified the very moral standards their opponents were defending, they tried to invalidate the central argument for suppressing the ceremonies.[54]

Many of the Pueblos' cultured supporters turned the comparison with white dances to the Indians' advantage. "You have [immoral dances] in the city of Philadelphia and I would suggest that [you] take an interest in stopping some of the Pagan dances occurring there," Moorehead told Sniffen. Others agreed. "In twenty-five years of observing Pueblo ceremonies," wrote School of American Research and Museum of New Mexico director Edgar Hewett, "I have seen a few vulgar exhibitions as side episodes—nothing like so flagrant as may be seen any evening in Chicago, London, Paris, Naples or Cairo." Lummis informed the *New York Times* that there had never "been a Pueblo dance so provocative, so suggestive, so un-modest, as the average 'American' Dance in our average Society." By taking public stands in defense of the Pueblo dances, these established scientists and writers lent considerable cultural authority to the cause. If the Pueblo dances were to be compared with popular dances in America and around the world, many observers agreed that by any moral standard the Indians came out ahead.[55]

In a very different line of defense, a few of the IRA's critics questioned the idea that moral standards could be truly universal. Ralph Miller, a disaffected IRA member from Washington, D.C., who had never been to New Mexico, pointed to "history and sociology" for evidence that "morals [are] a matter of community feeling." "The Mohammedan" could have "a half-dozen wives" while the "Western European has one wife," he pointed out, and both were seen by their societies as "equally moral." Because U.S. policies had long recognized Indians as "a separate community," Miller argued that they had both the moral and legal right to follow their own "religious and moral traditions" whether or not they appeared moral to the majority of white people. Those who did not like this could simply "stay away." The Chicago attorney Robert Catherwood went so far as to argue that even sodomy—though "morally wrong and illegal in Christian countries"—might "in savage or other non-Christian lands . . . be so interwoven with religion or custom as to be both legal and moral." Miller and Catherwood were far less interested in the reality of Pueblo practice than in advancing the argument that one society had no basis for condemning the standards of another. With these appeals to cultural relativism, which as we have seen was increasingly influential among America's cultural and intellectual elites, these critics challenged the universalizing claims of Victorian Protestant moral standards. But this was always a minority position among the Pueblos' defenders, advanced primarily by those like Miller and Catherwood who had little direct knowledge of the Indians. It proved less compelling to both reformers and Indian leaders with a stronger investment in the practical concern of defending the Pueblo dances.[56]

Anthropologists and reformers with personal knowledge of the Pueblos tended to advance a more subtle and culturally grounded relativism, interpreting the Indian ceremonies as fertility symbolism that did not imply any "immorality" even in mainstream American terms. A *Ladies' Home Journal* article on the controversy quoted Hewett to the effect that among these Indians "all creation of new life in both vegetable and animal worlds" was "a sacred thing." "I have learned much of such symbolism, but I have yet to find the first bit of evidence of the obscene." The artist Mary Colton, who accompanied her archaeologist husband on extensive research trips in the Southwest, informed Welsh that she found Burke's policy "narrow and shortsighted." "It is true that some of the dances symbolize the growing of corn and the bearing of children and this I have heard people say is obscene," but like Hewett she found that "the creation of all new life is sacred to the Indian, and he sees no wrong in offering up a public prayer for the greatest blessing of mankind." Colton advocated "building upon [Indian] culture as we find it" rather than arbitrarily destroying it. Grounded in firsthand knowledge of the Pueblo ceremonies and in the new anthropological theories of culture, such perspectives rejected assimilationist ideology to advocate an implicitly relativist sensitivity to Indian norms.[57]

Refuting the allegations of immorality cleared the air for what had already become the most important line of attack—the denunciation of Burke's circular as a violation of Indian religious freedom. The Pueblos were "an ancient mature race," wrote Hewett, and "coercive authority over them as to their religion is unwarranted under our government, a violation of our institutions, and repugnant to fair-minded men." Of course, this argument was only persuasive to the extent that the Pueblo dances could be located as an integral part of a bona fide religion, and toward this end reformers expanded on the arguments they had already developed in the land crisis.[58]

Some appealed to theories that sought the essence of human religion in its "primitive" beginnings. In the late eighteenth and early nineteenth centuries, Protestant scholars engaged in polemics against Catholicism had claimed that "the Popish and Pagan religions" shared common origins in the worship of the "generative powers." Subsequent historians of religion found sexual symbolism in the religions of India, ancient Greece, Japan, Judaism, and early Christianity, and by the twentieth century writers seeking alternatives to conventional Christianity were celebrating the sexual impulse as the basic foundation of all religion. Thus it was that Mary Austin could write with a certain primitivist nostalgia that among the Hopi Indians "procreation is still associated with worship."[59] Freudian and Jungian ideas could also be harnessed in support of this theory. In classic psychoanalytic terms, Austin explained the outcry against the Pueblo ceremonies as a product of "the inhibitions and repressions forced upon our pagan ancestry, particularly the inhibition of our innate wish to preserve for the sex impulse its pagan sanctity, its mystical connotations, of which Christianity has so utterly bereft it." And as Roberts Walker put it, "some of the pious moth-balls may resent the fact that occasionally the generative or fructifying processes are celebrated, just as they were in Greece and Egypt. To such persons, I should recommend a shocked perusal of what Doctor Jung has to say about the Christian religion in that connection." For Austin and Walker, Christianity's repression and denial of the "pagan sanctity" of sexuality explained some of the virulence of the campaign against the Pueblo dances.[60]

Mabel Dodge Luhan suggested that the healthy sexuality she saw in the Pueblo ceremonies made it far more "virile" than Christianity. Infuriated by the negative publicity against the ceremonies, she urged Elizabeth Shepley Sergeant to "write a fine article about religious freedom and the incompatibility between those emasculated religions and the virile religion of the Indian that has retained its vigor and its life just because it has symbolically a sexual basis."[61] Here Luhan represented the "primitive" vitality of Indian religion in masculine terms, presenting Christianity as "emasculated" precisely because it had lost the sexual basis of ancient religion. This gender coding suggested the work of early twentieth-century theorists like G. Stanley Hall, who tried to tap the secrets of "primitive" masculinity in hopes of curing the "neurasthenic" ailments they found in "overcivilized" men.[62] By casting aspersions on the masculinity of Christianity, Luhan also echoed the discomfort with "feminized" religion then so prevalent among both liberal and conservative Christians.[63] But rather than supporting any of their proposals for revitalizing what she saw as a thoroughly corrupted Christianity, Luhan defended Indian religion as the virile, natural, and authentic alternative.

Modernists also appealed to theories that placed dance itself at the origins of religion, a tactic that helped refocus debate away from the controversial topic of sexuality. Austin wrote, after suggesting that "early man" found power in the dance, "Who can doubt that the Allness is moved by our singing, since it immediately begins to throb in us as the dance progresses?" In his autobiography, Collier would quote the British psychologist Havelock Ellis, whose book *The Dance of Life* (1923) identified the spellbinding power of dance as the original impulse behind all the arts along with religion. For Ellis, dance was the most "essential . . . part of all vital and unregenerate religion." Collier may not yet have read Ellis in 1923, but he was already finding the heart of religion in ceremonial dancing. "Symbolic pantomimes, mystic signs, and a kind of emotional ecstasy are the very soul of religion in its great original moments, in its strange and profound beginnings in the childhood of all races." And he too attributed the persecution of Indian religions to Christianity's distance from what he believed had also been present in its origins. The Indian "religion . . . includes so much that ascetic Christianity has cast out from religion and committed to the world and the devil that it has been natural for our white missionaries and Indian Agents to believe they were dealing merely with barbaric social amusements." From this perspective, dance was not only a valid religious practice; it was at the very heart of the human religious impulse, far more authentic as religion than Christianity itself.[64]

At other times, modernists suggested that the term "dance" inherently misrepresented the religious character and solemnity of the Pueblo ceremonies. Emma Estabrook, secretary of the newly formed Massachusetts branch of the Eastern Association on Indian Affairs, adopted this approach after Herbert Welsh wrote to the *Boston Herald* to condemn those who defended what he called "grossly immoral and degrading" Pueblo dances. Estabrook, who would write several books celebrating Pueblo and other Native American cultures, had been unable after many inquiries to find any hint of immorality in the Pueblo ceremonies. "Much could be written in favor of their 'dances' or more correctly religious ceremonies. My husband and I have witnessed many Pueblo dances and have always come away with a sense of having found a seriousness and dignity of deportment in refreshing contrast to the modern dancing of our 'civilized' neighbors." The noted anthropologist C. Hart Merriam argued more forcefully against the use of "dance" as a word that "has prejudiced the American people against something which they should favor." "To us the term implies amusement," whereas "to the Indian the term implies religion, a religious ceremony." Knowing that most Americans would associate dancing with entertainment and often with sexually compromising behavior, some modernists tried to eliminate these associations by adopting a more unambiguously religious vocabulary.[65]

Another way to move away from the category of secular dancing was to argue that the Pueblo ceremonies were superior in both aesthetic and religious terms to some of the most popular religious movements in white America. "I have never known [the Pueblo and Hopi dances] to be carried out with anything but deep sincerity and real beauty of rhythm, gesture and plan," Roberts Walker wrote to Burke. Betraying his own bias in the complex terrain of American Christianity, Walker suggested that Pentecostalism represented a far more serious infringement of religious propriety than the Indian ceremonies. "You and I do not go to witness Marathon dancing contests or the Holy Rollers' 'religious' observances," he continued, "but if we did, we should be more anxious to abolish them than you possibly can be to abolish the snake dance." Moorehead framed a similar defense of peyote religion, which he compared favorably to the "menace" he saw in Pentecostalism. "We have the Holy Rollers religion increasing in Oklahoma, Arkansas, Texas, South Dakota and elsewhere," he wrote. "If you have never attended one of their meetings I advise you to do so. Nobody is protesting against it and what they do is far worse than the peyote ceremony." Whether the problem was religious deviance or morally questionable dancing, Walker and Moorehead asked white Americans to reform their own society before they criticized Indian ceremonies too harshly.[66]

Modernists continued to argue for the religious legitimacy of the Pueblo dances by comparing them to culturally normative examples of authentic and praiseworthy religion. Mason Green of the Eastern Association's Massachusetts branch wrote to the *Boston Herald* that "these ancient dances for luck in hunting, for rain, and for good crops are religious observances—prayers to the Great Spirit," and must be respected as such. "Why should they not worship with their feet as well as with their lips?" he asked. "Perhaps the commissioner has repeated the Psalm, 'Let them praise his name in the dance.'" Over the next few years, like-minded reformers including Charles Lummis and John Collier would continue to point to the "ancient Israelites" to demonstrate the religious validity of dancing. The Indian dances were "strictly and exclusively religious ceremonials as devout and as inspired as when King David 'danced before the Lord,'" Lummis wrote to President Coolidge in 1924, and equivalent in meaning to the Israelites' "dances around the Ark of the Covenant." By comparing the Pueblos to the heroes of the biblical narrative, modernists cultivated the sympathies of a predominantly Christian public.[67]

Christian devotional practices provided another useful comparative reference. In the hearings on the Bursum Bill, Collier had defended the Pueblos' right to manage their own internal affairs on the grounds that their ceremonial secrets were "just as holy as are the secrets given to Catholic priests in the confession." Citing Ellis, he later claimed that early and medieval Christians had also accepted or even practiced religious dancing: "In the great age of Christianity, dancing . . . was usual in the Cathedrals. The Catholic mass itself is a beautiful and awesome dance-drama. [And] in Dante's paradise, Christ danced forever with those who on earth had been warriors of God."[68] When Alice Corbin Henderson interpreted the corn dance as "a beautifully archaic, conventionalized symbol of fertility," she also named it as a kind of prayer and compared its function to the Catholic Eucharist. This was "an organic paean in praise of life—a rain-prayer, true enough, but something more powerful than prayer because it brings to pass through expression that which it desires to accomplish. It is a ceremony like that of the eucharist; the seed of the corn becomes flesh."[69] Such comparisons made the argument for religious freedom more persuasive. Edgar Hewett wrote that the "so-called dances" of the Pueblos were "prayers . . . of intense sustained fervor" and should therefore be protected by the constitutional principles that "guarantee every one the right of religious worship." Interference in the Indians' ceremonies "is just as vicious as interference with Catholic mass or Protestant sacrament." By interpreting the Pueblo ceremonies through a Christian vocabulary, these modernists identified the Pueblo dances as religion in terms that the dominant culture was likely to accept.[70]

In sum, modernists insisted that the Pueblo ceremonies deserved the same degree of acceptance and protection as the practices of any other religion. "As far as I can understand," Estabrook wrote, "all broad-minded men and women who really know the Pueblo Indians agree that they should have the same religious freedom for which Mr. Storey's ancestors and mine may have come to this country." By redefining the Pueblo ceremonies as "religion" in public debate, modernists claimed the high ground as the true defenders of American values.[71]

Fighting for Moral Authority

Faced with such opposition, assimilationists struggled to reclaim their standing as the presumed mainstream voice in Indian affairs. Their campaign against Pueblo dances gained momentum from a July 1923 letter in the Arizona *Coconino Sun* by Otto Lomavitu, one of the Hopi Christians who had contributed an affidavit to Sweet's report three years earlier. Now Lomavitu used the dance controversy as a new opportunity to attack the Hopi ceremonies and the traditionalists who practiced them. Praising the "government teacher and missionaries" for having "crushed" the "endless religious ceremonies" and replaced them with "better learning and religious instruction," he argued that the remaining dances had so little legitimate religious meaning and exerted such a "degrading" influence that 45 percent of the Hopi people no longer wished to continue them. The dances were "preserved . . . only for the benefit of the tourist," he wrote, who "stretches out his covetous hands to a poor, dust-covered Hopi . . . only to sneer when meeting him on his own town streets." Even the financial profits of the tourist industry went not to any of the Hopis but to white business owners in nearby towns, "whose pocket books swell to triple size during those days as the tourists find lodging and boarding" in their establishments. For these reasons, Lomavitu praised Burke's circular, asking critics to stop interfering so that the Indians could simply "follow out his orders the best we can." He concluded by linking Christianity to American identity as firmly as any member of the Protestant establishment: "We owe all our education and civilization to the man in Washington besides our greatest benefactor, the Almighty God. We must pay our debt by becoming better citizens."[72]

Commissioner Burke and his defenders publicized Lomavitu's letter as evidence that "progressive" and Christian Indians welcomed the dance policy. "Perhaps the very best of all answers given to the cultured and misguided friends . . . may be found in a letter from a Hopi Indian living at Oraibi, Arizona," Welsh wrote in his next mailing to IRA members. "Otto Lomavitu . . . thinks that his people ought not to be encouraged by foolish tourists and lovers of luchre hotel and cafe proprietors, to maintain the filthy and degrading practice of the snake dance under the specious plea that it is a religious ceremony." In New Mexico, the *El Paso Herald* affirmed Lomavitu's account as evidence that the BIA and the IRA, "in full accord for once," were acting wisely on this issue. The *Herald* writer related his own experience traveling to the snake dance several years earlier, when he "remembered meeting a group of well dressed and intelligent Hopi who had stopped by the roadside for refreshment. 'Suppose you are all on the way to the snake dance,' I volunteered. One tall young man drew himself erect and resentfully shot back the answer: 'Not by a long sight! I'd have you understand we're Christians!'" Simultaneously condemned as commercial spectacle, immoral paganism, and impediment to civilization—all of which were rhetorically opposed to true religion—the snake dance had become a centerpiece in the struggle to define and regulate Indian dancing. This enthusiasm for Lomavitu's letter also signaled a new direction for the IRA, which over the next year would increasingly reorient its antidance efforts to focus on "progressive" Indians who did not want to participate in the tribal ceremonies.[73]

While many modernists shared Lomavitu's dismay at the tourist industry, they refused to accept his conclusions about the Hopi Snake Dance. Roberts Walker advised Commissioner Burke that the tourists ought to be regulated rather than the Indians. Walker nostalgically invoked his own experience of this ceremony "when it was a penance to get across the desert, as I did in 1897, with a pack-train in August to witness this dance." He expressed regret for the trains and automobiles that provided such easy access to the

Hopi mesas, making "the whole business . . . distressingly popularized and touted," and he blamed any lapse in religious meaning on the commercialization that had accompanied so many touristic spectators. "If the Government could find some method of allowing the Indians to hold their ceremonies in peace and seclusion, this dance could not possibly hurt anybody," he told Burke. If the BIA really wanted to address this problem, the commissioner should "prohibit, or rigidly restrict, attendance" on the part of tourists, not place any restrictions on the snake dance itself.[74]

Walker contended that Lomavitu did not represent any significant number of Hopis and attributed his letter to the unfortunate influence of conservative Protestant missionaries on the reservation. "It was a disgusting letter," he told one correspondent, "written by, or perhaps merely signed by, a craven sycophant of the psalm-singing revival-convert order." As a self-described liberal Protestant disturbed by the strength of fundamentalism in the contemporary religious scene, Walker linked the dance controversy to the narrow conceptions of religion and morality held by his more conservative counterparts: Whereas the Catholic Church allowed "freedom of action to the individual and, perhaps as a corollary, [enjoyed] century-old association with the arts in all their branches, Protestant missionaries get much exercised if the standards of conduct of savage tribes do not conform in all respects to the (theoretical) standards of conduct of the Third Methodist Episcopal Church of Akron, Ohio." The Hopi snake dance as he had witnessed it was "a dignified and sincere service that need not upset anybody, except prudish mothballs who like to prevent other people from doing almost anything." Walker painted anyone who opposed such ceremonies as a narrow-minded religious fanatic who should not be permitted to destroy the core American values of democracy and individual freedom: "To stop the dance by an order would be un-Christian and un-Constitutional. The only people who should be allowed to stop it are the Indians themselves." By placing the circular's defenders outside the boundaries of authentic Christianity as well as American values, Walker attacked the credibility and authority of the missionary establishment in Indian affairs.[75]

Modernists deliberately positioned themselves—and not the circular's defenders—as moderate voices representing the consensus in Indian affairs. Walker accused Sniffen of trying "to isolate and stigmatize 'artists and archaeologists,'" pointing out that both groups had expert opinions that demanded respect and that, in any case, there were many "hard-headed businessmen" in Santa Fe as well as lawyers like himself who objected to the circular. In an impressive full-color bulletin, "Concerning Indian Dances," the Eastern Association insisted that "the testimony of many distinguished men and women who have lived with the Indians and made a life-long study of their customs and habits" must be given priority over the unreliable "gossip" and "folklore" of "ignorant, uncultivated whites" who had produced the allegations against the Pueblo dances. Statements by the distinguished anthropologists Elsie Clews Parsons, Pliny Goddard, F. W. Hodge, and Herbert Spinden established the scientific basis for religious freedom. Spinden attributed the allegations to "ignorance, scandal, and intolerance," condemning "Christian churchmen of many creeds" for "the grossest exaggeration" in their depiction of Indian ceremonies, and for "advocating inhuman modes of conversion in this blindness of their zeal." Instead, he advocated a scientifically disinterested stance that would ensure the Indians the religious liberty they deserved. By working to secure the place of anthropology as the foremost authority in Indian affairs, modernists presented a formidable threat to the missionary establishment.[76]

With the dance circular framed as an assault on Indian religion, the IRA found itself losing the battle for public opinion. At least a few longtime members found its uncompromising focus on Christian civilization to be an increasingly uncomfortable fit with their own convictions. The Hopis "had carried on their dances and their traditions for an astonishingly long period of time before any 'foolish tourists and lovers of luchre hotel and cafe proprietors' came along to encourage them," wrote the Chicago attorney Arthur Aldis, and no government had any right to forbid them from continuing to do so. Even if there were "some features of which we do not approve from our standards," he believed that "the peaceful and excellent record of these Indians over several centuries" should be enough to prove that the ceremonies were beneficial overall. Stansbury Hagar, another IRA member and lawyer in Chicago, informed Welsh that, contrary to the dance policy, he was convinced that "for the sake of the Indian, both as an individual and as a citizen . . . every possible encouragement should be given to native religion." Hagar applied the liberal idea that all religions in essence were the same, interpreting the differences among religions as racially distinctive pathways toward the same truths: "No one path is much, if at all, superior to any others. Forms of religion are unimportant. Each people develops those best suited to it; but each people can see truth most clearly in its own religion."

Aldis, Hagar, and others like them informed Welsh that they could not remain members of an association that interfered with Indian religious freedom in the name of Indian rights.[77]

Some assimilationists agreed with the Pueblos' defenders that Indian dances were morally superior to popular white dances. R. Newberne, a BIA inspector sent to Zuni in 1924 to investigate complaints about the health situation there, considered the "primitive" Zuni dances a "waste of time" but denied that they were "vulgar and obscene." "If they must dance," he concluded, "it is better that they should adhere to their native ceremonial dances in which only the men indulge than that they should learn the modern dances of white society, many members of which fox-trot, and turkey trot and bear-hug themselves to the divorce courts, or a worse predicament." Although Newberne considered all dances undesirable, he saw the Pueblo dances as preferable to the dances that he thought caused divorce and other disruptions in "white society." Similarly, the Franciscan Barnabas Meyer concluded his description of a saint's day feast at Tesuque Pueblo with the comment that Indian dances had "none of the levity, the refined sensuality, the languid grace, the voluptuous movements that characterize some of the [modern] dances . . . and lead many an unsuspecting young man and young woman to moral degradation and, often, to physical ruin." Such statements demonstrated a deep discomfort with popular "modern" dances and more broadly with the changing sexual mores in American culture. They also help explain why even those who shared the IRA's assimilationist goals were not necessarily persuaded by their allegations against the Pueblo ceremonies.[78]

The few efforts at consensus building during this period ended up reinforcing the growing gulf between a missionary establishment that insisted on assimilation and the modernists who celebrated Indian traditions. Soon after his appointment as secretary of the interior, Hubert Work decided to appoint an advisory council, charged with forging agreement on future directions for federal Indian policy, to convene in December 1923. Work selected for his "Committee of One Hundred" a diverse group, including scientists, missionaries, reformers, and other recognized experts in Indian affairs. John Collier and Stella Atwood sat alongside Herbert Welsh, G. E. E. Lindquist, William Hughes of the Bureau of Catholic Indian Missions, and the populist politician and fundamentalist Christian William Jennings Bryan, soon to defend biblical creationism against evolutionary theory in the famous Scopes trial. Knowing how difficult it would be for this group to agree on anything, Work asked Warren Moorehead to plan ahead "to reconcile the differences." "If we can all agree on major propositions, as the Secretary requests," Moorehead told Sniffen, "we shall have achieved the great purpose."[79]

In New Mexico, Pablo Abeita was characteristically skeptical about the council's prospects. "I understand that sometime this coming fall the Secretary of the Interior is going to have a conference with one hundred men from all over the country," he wrote to Hughes. "These men are supposed to be interested [in] Indians . . . everybody is interested in Indians except the Indian himself, he is never consulted, they just simply give him what looks good to the giver and not to the receiver."[80] In fact Secretary Work did include a few well-educated and well-connected "representative" Indians, most prominently Robert Yellowtail of the Crow Nation in Montana, who had earned a law degree from the University of Chicago and would later serve as the first Native American superintendent of a BIA agency; and the Winnebago Henry Roe Cloud, an ordained Presbyterian minister who was the first Native American to graduate from Yale University and later headed Haskell Institute in Lawrence, Kansas. Both made important contributions to this meeting and to the direction of reform more generally.[81] But, as Abeita suggested, Work never considered that current tribal leaders—most of whom lacked Yellowtail and Cloud's credentials—would also have vital perspectives on the issues affecting their future.

In the summer and fall of 1923, the Eastern Association on Indian Affairs invited like-minded reform organizations to a series of conferences to prepare for the advisory council meeting. The New Mexico Association, the American Indian Defense Association, and the Indian Affairs committees of the American Anthropological Association and American Association for the Advancement of Science all joined in a tentative agreement on questions of education, industry, health and sanitation, land tenure, irrigation, religion, tribal autonomy, and the "organization of administration and inspection that will best accomplish these ends." Matthew Sniffen felt quite optimistic after he attended one such meeting, concluding that even though the anthropologists and "radicals" tended to "dwell upon the cultural and ethnological side of the question," they now seemed "ready to admit that the Indians should be under the same laws that apply to the whites."[82] But where he understood the call for "religious and social freedom in all matters not directly contrary to public morals" as an overdue acknowledgment that some Indian dances must be restricted, modernists assumed the primacy of religious freedom and demanded a high standard of "expert evidence" before any Indian ceremony could be judged "immoral or unsanitary."[83]

The council's preliminary agreement accurately represented the views of moderate anthropologists and reformers like Moorehead who insisted that although Indians would ultimately need to adopt Christianity and civilization, the government had no right in the meantime to prohibit any ceremonies not actually proved immoral. These moderates rejected Burke's circular because they found the allegations against the Pueblo ceremonies implausible and insisted that those who wanted Indians to adopt either Christianity or civilization should seek to build on the indigenous traditions rather than suppress them. "The best education of our Indian wards," wrote Herbert Spinden, "would be achieved by developing, instead of destroying, their pride of race." F. W. Hodge told his fellow delegates at the full advisory council meeting in December that the Pueblo ceremonies had "a hopeful, soulful, spiritual faith, without which no religion can subsist," arguing that if instead of suppressing the indigenous traditions they could be "used as a foundation," then "Christianity will get somewhere, and perhaps much more rapidly than starting anew and building up over generations." Here Hodge suggested that the Indians possessed something that—although perhaps not religion in itself—was an authentic "spiritual faith" that could provide the foundation for the development of Christianity. In the end, although they defended the Indians' right to practice indigenous traditions, Hodge and other moderates saw these as a precursor to the true religion of Christianity.[84]

These moderate voices notwithstanding, the illusion of agreement between the increasingly polarized extremes had shattered well before the advisory council even met. Sniffen and his fellow assimilationists overruled modernist objections to pass a resolution at the meeting "endorsing the action of Commissioner Burke in endeavoring to have the Indians eliminate immoral and degrading practices from their dances." The IRA's annual report concluded in satisfied tones that "an impartial view of the Commissioner's letter, so caustically criticized, reveals no intention of destroying the arts and crafts, the religious rites and ceremonies of the red men." But modernists were not about to accept this conclusion. An enraged Elizabeth Shepley Sergeant wrote in the *New Republic* that the committee's presentation to President Coolidge had been hijacked so that "the missionary and 'extreme right' view of the Indian question" appeared to be the "reasoned conclusions of [its] deliberations." Rather than building consensus on the issue of Indian dancing, the Committee of One Hundred had only deepened the struggle for authority in Indian affairs.[85]

Despite its triumph at the Committee of One Hundred, the Indian Rights Association found itself struggling to convince constituents of the justice of Burke's circular. Welsh seemed bewildered at the strength of the opposition. "A very large body of intelligent and influential people, archaeologists, writers, artists, their relatives and sympathizers, have held the opinion that these old customs—which we well know in one form or another militate against the civilization of the Indian, holding him back in the communal state which is inconsistent with modern life—ought to be preserved," he wrote to IRA members in the fall of 1923. "I have been kept busy in answering either individually or generally their appeals and attacks which have come in almost by every mail and which have teemed in the newspapers."[86]

One of the IRA's strategies for reclaiming its mainstream image was to insist that the new campaign was fully consistent with constitutional principles of freedom, principles that the IRA believed it had always supported. "There seems to be a great deal of confusion in the minds of many people regarding whether or not the Commissioner's appeal (it was not an ORDER) to the Indians was warranted," Sniffen wrote to one skeptical correspondent. Agreeing that "any proper tribal, ceremonial or religious dance could not be legally stopped by the Government," he insisted that because the circular affected only "immoral and improper dances," it did not interfere with legitimate Indian liberties. "We have always concluded that the Indians 'should be allowed the same liberty of action that other inhabitants of the U.S. enjoy,' and in at least one instance, we established the correctness of that position by action in the U.S. Courts." Because they did not see the dances in question as legitimately religious, Welsh and Sniffen simply could not comprehend why modernists denounced the dance circular as a violation of Indian religious freedom.[87]

In January 1924 the IRA launched the *Indian Truth*, a new monthly bulletin intended to "tell our friends at regular and short intervals just what is needed." In the first two issues, editor Matthew Sniffen spared no effort to reestablish the IRA's reputation as a voice of moderation. He praised John

Collier's work in bringing a second Pueblo delegation to Washington that January to raise support for the struggle over the land bill and even affirmed the educational and entertainment value of the Indians' "songs and ceremonial dances." Commenting on a debate in *Forum* magazine over the direction of Indian policy, Sniffen chided Flora Seymour of the Board of Indian Commissioners, who "evidently considers herself a part of the Indian administration," for painting an overly "bright picture" that ignored the "many instances of exploiting the Indians within our own generation." On the other hand he found Seymour's opponent Mary Austin "extreme in her sweeping condemnation of the Indian educational work," arguing that while "the 'inestimable treasure of culture' is not as general" as Austin suggested, "the native arts and crafts have been encouraged to a greater degree than she realizes, and rightly so." Despite their many disagreements, he went so far as to claim that all "the friends of the Indian" had long advocated "the general policy outlined by Mrs. Austin."[88]

However, for the rest of the year the *Indian Truth* devoted much of its attention to challenging the credibility and authority of the "artists, scientists, and writers" who defended Pueblo dances. Sniffen used "the amusing incident of 'We-Wha,'" who pulled off "the best joke the American Indian ever played," to mock "the gullability and unreliability of some scientists." After ethnologist Matilda Coxe Stevenson had taken We-Wha to Washington and presented this "wonderfully intelligent Zuni woman" to President Grover Cleveland, he explained, "We-Wha proved to be a man, and the father of four children!" He contended that anthropologists and others who attended and admired some Pueblo dances "often fail[ed] to learn the whole truth" and that scientists could "say, with all honesty, that they have not witnessed immoralities connected with the dances" because the Pueblo Indians excluded all outsiders from their "secret dances." On this basis, assimilationists attacked anthropologists as "sentimentalists" who knew very little about real conditions among Indians. According to former Presbyterian missionary teacher Mary Dissette, now serving as librarian at the Santa Fe Indian School, "To hear the sentimental outcry for the preservation of the Indian puts a person who has spent a life time in Indian villages in a state of dumb despair. . . . If any of these people had ever tried to carry out the educational policy of the government in a place where that government apparently had no control they might sing a different song." From the perspective of the IRA and its allies, missionaries and BIA agents who had devoted years of their lives to the cause of Indian "progress" knew far more than any anthropologist or artist about the real impact of Indian ceremonies.[89]

The circular's supporters were convinced that the dances in question contradicted foundational "moral laws" that were essential to a civilized society. Secretary Hubert Work answered San Ildefonso Pueblo's protest by claiming that, if the Indians wished "to perpetuate the integrity of their race," they must honor "the laws of nature, or moral laws" that were "ordained by that Supreme Being who created all of us and who has been worshiped by nearly all tribes and races in their own way since the beginning." Work defined these laws in terms of sexual mores and behaviors. "It is contrary to these moral laws to exaggerate the sex instinct of man, or become subservient to it." Determined not to appear bigoted or ignorant of Indian diversity, he acknowledged that not all Indian dances fit this description and commended the Tewas' "desire to cherish the customs and traditions of their forefathers." But he asked them to judge their own ceremonies by asking, "Does the motive of a particular dance corrupt good morals or invite the neglect or loss of property, and are the rites and symbols illustrating it unbecoming to normal, healthy manhood and womanhood?" Work was so pleased with this letter that he released it to the press in order to clarify the Interior Department's position on the issue.[90]

In keeping with classic social evolutionary theory, Secretary Work asserted the superiority of the white race even as he insisted that other races had the same potential. "The White Man did not make these laws" but had "adopted some of them into his beliefs and customs"—and implicitly was the most advanced in fulfilling them. Work presented these "moral laws" as among the most important factors in the Indians' effort to achieve full racial equality: "The Indian, no more than the White Man, can not afford to contribute to his own spiritual and physical downfall by indulging in practices which appeal to lower animal emotions only." Other assimilationists shared these views. Dissette argued that nothing could be worse for any race than "ignorance of [the moral] laws and transgression of them in sex precocity and sex promiscuity." If the "artists, scientists and writers" were taken seriously, "we must . . . cease teaching those things on which we grew up and on which this great American nation has prided itself . . . and have a different moral standard for each class." Work, Dissette, and other assimilationists insisted that theirs was an all-American call for moral equality, for Indians to improve their race and join the American mainstream by adopting the same standards that whites had (however unevenly) already adopted.[91]

For assimilationists these moral laws, with Christianity as their acknowledged source, formed the necessary foundation of American civil society. According to Herbert Welsh, in order to be consistent with its civilizing mission the government must actively encourage Indians to "seek a Saviour whose essential moral concepts are now woven into federal and state statutes." Although he conceded that the "old pagan party" could not be prevented from worshiping "their idols and their rain gods," Welsh saw this "old religion" as fundamentally incompatible with the moral standards of civilization. "The old religion, which is closely akin to all the old nature-worships, and which will not tolerate religion and civil freedom as we understand these twin great blessings, utterly ignores the sanctity of home and of monogamous marriage." Work argued in the *Saturday Evening Post* that both Indians and "white Americans . . . must stand for a religion fundamentally such as Christ taught, through whatever forms symbolize it to his own understanding." Despite this gesture to the liberal ideal of religious pluralism, Work went on to say that the "ordinances" of "Indian religion" must be modified "into harmony with the forms of the Christian religion which civilization has approved, from which our rules of life are drafted and upon which our Government is founded." Any tradition that wished to claim the title "religion" must conform itself to Christianity—which as the one true religion was the only real source for morality and civilization.[92]

Welsh argued that even non-Christians must recognize the relevance of the "moral laws." Alongside Protestants and Catholics, he wrote, Burke's policy must be supported by "persons who profess no religious faith but who want to see these Indians taken out of the hunter and stone age type of civilization and brought into a state where they can mingle on equal terms with other people." Indeed, "secret dances such as exist among the Pueblos, which are grossly immoral . . . cannot be tolerated or supported by any decent people at this state of the world's history." He pointed to the "secular" concerns of education and economic growth to explain why all clear-thinking Americans must support the dance policy. "The time for their cessation has certainly come unless these Indians are to be considered as archeological, or artistic, or literary pets who are to have no concern with American taxation, with American education, with American farm or commercial life." By emphasizing public morality and widely shared American values, assimilationists could distance themselves from a constitutionally impermissible insistence on Indian conversion to Christianity. In response to the outcry against the dance circular, the IRA had been forced to concede the Indians' right to religious freedom—at least in principle—and to defend its own position in secular as well as Christian terms. But this was a secularism very much defined according to Protestant Christian norms.[93]

The Battleground of Women's Rights

In their efforts to cast the dance circular as progressive policy, assimilationists turned to a group of female reformers who approached Indian affairs through the lens of women's rights. One of these was Edith Dabb, secretary of the YWCA Committee on Indian Affairs and a member of Secretary Work's Committee of One Hundred, who precipitated a flurry of debate in December 1923 by praising Burke's policies in the *New York Times* and the *New York Tribune*. Dabb focused on the education and advancement of young women, the founding priorities of the YWCA. Indian girls who were just learning "to enjoy a carefree girlhood" in the boarding schools, she charged, were too often "called back to the reservation . . . and made to take part in the ceremonial dances, which mean for them child marriage and usually motherhood . . . at the very age when they should be getting the most out of their education."[94] Dabb had no direct knowledge of the Pueblo Indians, but several BIA superintendents had charged that tribal leaders deliberately encouraged sexual promiscuity during the dances so that the girls would become pregnant and stay at home.[95] And although these allegations were originally motivated by the effort to enforce compulsory education, Dabb refocused them to condemn Indian dancing as a primary contributor to the downfall of young girls. Burke's policy should receive widespread support "on behalf of these mute sacrifices to the cruelties of tradition," she argued, because it was "the duty of the government" to "protect the young girls of the race" from "vicious elements" such as these.[96]

Female missionaries and moral reformers within New Mexico also supported Burke's circulars out of concern for the rights of Indian women. Dissette argued that the sexual immorality she had seen in the Zuni dances led directly to female subordination. She alleged that Zuni men resented any educational efforts for the girls because their "round of debasing customs [depended] entirely on keeping their women in ignorance." Zuni ceremonies encouraged "sex precocity and sex promiscuity," she charged, causing too many promising young schoolgirls to become pregnant and drop out of school. Furthermore, the ceremonies provided the foundation for "male supremacy" by instilling the idea that girls were good only "to bear children and to grind corn." Certain that women's rights depended on Victorian standards of sexual morality, Dissette detailed the steps she had taken over the years to educate Zuni girls and protect them from sexual exploitation. Like so many other female Protestant missionaries, Dabb and Dissette were convinced that Indian women were the helpless victims of "heathenism" and could be saved only by "Christian civilization." They concluded that in order for Indian women to progress, some indigenous ceremonies would need to be forcibly suppressed.[97]

Once again, not all assimilationists found these allegations convincing. Northern Pueblos Superintendent C. J. Crandall fully embraced the government's "attempt to educate these Pueblos in our Christian civilization." In his own jurisdiction, he enforced compulsory school attendance for all Pueblo children, banned the use of indigenous languages in the schools, required American-style haircuts, and insisted that students paint only "civilized" rather than indigenous subjects in their art classes.[98] But Crandall completely rejected the idea that Pueblo tribal leaders were deliberately "encouraging school girls to go wrong." As he wrote to one colleague, "You and I know that the standard of morals in the pueblos are different from ours . . . that marriage awaits all Pueblo girls; that there are no old maids; that there are no divorces; that motherhood is honored . . . [and] that there are few if any illegitimate children." On this occasion at least, Crandall found the mores of Pueblo culture more wholesome than those of white America.[99] Similarly, although Episcopal bishop Frederick Howden of Santa Fe denounced the "artists, archaeologists, etc" for exploiting the Indians, he determined after a personal investigation that the Pueblo dances did not lead to a "large number of illegitimate births" and that teachers at the Santa Fe and Albuquerque Indian schools had very few complaints about sexual immorality among the students. Howden warned that direct attempts at controlling the Pueblos' "public exhibitions" would only increase the number of "surreptitious and secret dances, which I strongly suspect are beyond the control of the Government," and proposed instead that BIA superintendents work on gradual reform from within the Pueblos.[100]

Despite skepticism from people like Crandall and Howden, the IRA eagerly embraced the women's rights argument as further justification for Burke's dance policy. Welsh had long decried the alleged violation of Pueblo women. "Civilization," he told the relativist Ralph Miller, "is not consistent with a religious dance in which a young Pueblo Indian girl, educated in a Government or missionary school . . . is required to submit her physical body to the loathsome embraces of a heathen Indian man of her tribe, and who is not her husband, under penalty of punishment by beating, by order of the Cacique [tribal chief] of the Pueblo in question, if she refuses to obey." Did Miller really believe that "our civilization, civil rights, and citizenship should be kept out of the Indian Pueblos," Welsh asked, subjecting young women to such "unspeakable outrage?" Pussyfoot Johnson's infamous article on Indian dances detailed the charges by Dissette, whom he called "a veritable saint among the Pueblo Indians," that "little girls were debauched in these dances under the guise of 'religious liberty.'" "I myself," he claimed, "have rescued and educated more than one Indian girl who had become a victim of such hideous affairs." The defenders of Burke's circular hoped that concern for Indian girls among female reformers and the public at large would add new credibility and urgency to their cause.[101]

In particular, they hoped that such appeals would attract support from the nation's key women's organizations. This was not a foregone conclusion. Dabb claimed that the YWCA's belief "in the full development of the women of every nation" led to a unanimous protest "against the tribal dances and its support of Commissioner Burke in his attempt to abolish them," but her publicity was always aimed in part at the skeptical within the organization, and she had enough critics that she was forced to solicit letters of support to defend herself before the YWCA president.[102] The IRA also hoped to reverse the policies of the nationally influential General Federation of Women's Clubs, where Stella Atwood and John Collier had built support for modernist views on religious freedom. With the leadership of female moral reformers like Clara True, local chapters in Arizona, New Mexico, Utah, and Oklahoma—all states with high Indian populations—openly objected to the actions of Atwood's Indian Welfare Committee in order to support what they believed to be the best interests of Indian women.[103] Many Catholic women came to share this view. According to True, the Catholic missionary sisters of the Drexel Indian School of Santa Fe contributed logistical support to the campaign against Indian dances because they "realized that we were working with a view to the protection of their pupils in the practice of Christianity and civilized living at home." All of these women found the allegations against Pueblo ceremonies convincing enough to support the IRA's crusade.[104]

Modernist feminists countered these charges by praising Pueblo society as a model for women's liberation, using the controversy as an opportunity to advance their own ideas about women's roles. "No feminist could ask for a better position for women than the position of the Hopi and Zuni women who own their houses, control their offspring, choose their mates, and contribute to the economic, political and religious life," wrote Elsie Clews Parsons. Even the women of the Rio Grande Pueblos, whom she admitted had somewhat lower status than their Hopi and Zuni counterparts, she found on the whole to be "more independent and respected than the bulk of the white women of the State."[105] Parsons particularly ridiculed Dabb's claim that Pueblo "medicine men" violated young women, arguing that the requirement for priests and performers to remain sexually abstinent during ceremonies, in combination with the relatively high status of Pueblo women, made such allegations "more misleading than any similar arraignment she might undertake of our own physicians and bishops." At other times Parsons seemed to celebrate a degree of sexual experimentation in Pueblo society, which she had long argued would give women (along with men) greater freedom. For a woman so critical of the gender inequalities of U.S. society, Pueblo traditions seemed feminist indeed. In her words, "for American white women to be perturbed about the social position of American Pueblo women is farce for the gods of them all."[106]

Expressing a far more romantic primitivism, Mabel Dodge Luhan celebrated the "natural" modesty of Pueblo women and the sexual symbolism of their ceremonies. Despite her image as a "new woman," Luhan longed to emulate the specifically feminine power she saw in "the Indian women sheltered in their shawls . . . held close and protected from encroachments," and praised these women as models of modesty and domesticity.[107] Countering the allegations of immorality, she argued that the dose of sexuality in Pueblo dancing actually helped create more natural and therefore healthier and saner people. "Of course they worship creation, and we know that almost all their symbols are sexual as in all the ancient religions. But just because their religion is alive, and because in their daily life they are not inhibited, they do not revert to orgiastic over-compensations, and in their ceremonies *never*, I believe, approach each other libidinously . . . Furthermore they have not got sex *on the brain* like the missionaries and others whose religion has been given the purification of civilization." Explaining that the Taos Indians were *"horrified* at bringing it into speech, letter, and discussion . . . *ashamed* to think 'their pueblo' could ever come under any such consideration," she expressed rage that "the purest people I know . . . should be accused of monstrous orgies, forced humiliations of an obscene nature, and all the rest of the things these missionaries say." Luhan believed that the "natural" sexuality apparent in Pueblo ceremonies and in all of Pueblo life prevented them from developing the sexual obsession apparent in the missionaries.[108]

Not all of the modernists who countered Dabb's charges were interested in the question of women's rights. In a letter to the *New York Times*, John Collier ignored the Indian girls who were Dabb's primary concern and absolutely denied her charges that the Pueblo ceremonies were in any way immoral. He reframed Dabb's allegations as a reflection of the problems faced by Indian young people who returned from boarding schools alienated from the indigenous traditions. "They are subjected to vigorous Christianization," the products of a "governmental policy of turning all Indians into imitation white men ashamed of their tribal naiveties and splendors and alienated from and embittered towards their elders." He recommended the colonial policies of "England, Russia, Germany, and France" as a far preferable solution. Each, he claimed, had helped "the aboriginal races toward a transition which would blend the white man's culture with their culture and enable them to incorporate modern technologies in their native activity." As he had done so many times before, Collier approached this problem not by challenging the basic colonial politics of Indian affairs but by suggesting administrative strategies that would at least respect indigenous traditions.[109]

Perhaps the most substantive response to Dabb was the Eastern Association's bulletin "Concerning Indian Dances." The impressive lineup of anthropologists who contributed to this publication conceded that "immoralities" existed in contemporary Pueblo life, but like Collier they laid the blame on government and missionary assimilation programs. "Ironically enough," wrote Parsons, "the fact that children are born in some cases to girls of an earlier age is largely due . . . to particular conditions of familiarity between the sexes unusual in Indian life, and to the general influence of the boarding school in breaking down Indian life and authority." Archaeologist F. W. Hodge wrote that over the course of thirty years of research he had witnessed countless ceremonies at Zuni—which of all the pueblos adhered "most closely to its primitive customs and beliefs"—and had seen no evidence of immorality. "Not only are the Zuni ceremonies especially of a highly sacred and circumspect character, but the native priests who direct them are the most thoroughly religious men, white or red, I have ever known." And after Herbert Spinden condemned the "blindness" of those who would "alienate [Indian children] forever from their parents," he asked, "Is it not time that we gave the remnant of our Red men a share of that religious freedom which our ancestors found in America?" Once again, the case for religious freedom relied on defending the fundamental morality and religious character of the Pueblo ceremonies.[110]

The General Federation of Women's Clubs would emerge as a central battleground between the controversy's competing visions of feminism. Although far from a radical, Stella Atwood clearly favored the modernist take on these questions. The Pueblos were "not an inferior race," she told a writer for the *Ladies Home Journal*, and she pointed to the status of Indian women to prove it. "The Indian woman has peace of mind as a matter of course, what American women are frantically groping for. The Indian woman sings at her work, contemplates the stars and finds inspiration in the hills and deserts. She does this not because an apostle of the latest psychic fad has told her to do it at a lecture costing two dollars for admission; she does it because it is her nature to do so." Like Luhan, she found a "natural" sense of domestic peacefulness and freedom among Indian women.[111] And despite the opposition of the women's clubs in so many of the southwestern states, Atwood won a vote of confidence at the General Federation board meeting in 1923. "I made up my mind before I went to Atlanta that I would have a complete show-down," she wrote afterward, "that there would be no mincing of policies or words." Atwood told the president that if she did not have the confidence of the board she would "join a more courageous and aggressive organization," perhaps the League of Women Voters. In the end, the board adopted a resolution giving her its full "moral support," endorsing the continued employment of John Collier as her research associate, and authorizing her "to employ a lawyer for counsel should this become necessary."[112]

At least for the time being, assimilationists had found themselves unable to sway the largest women's organization in America. As it cast about for another way to defend the dance circular, the IRA increasingly embraced the cause of Pueblo progressives who had rejected the tribal ceremonies. By casting these progressives as the victims of religious persecution, the IRA could refocus the debate away from the BIA's persecution of Indian dances and present itself as a supporter of "real" religious freedom for individual Indians.

❖

FIVE

The Implications of Religious Freedom

"Resolved," wrote the newly created Council of Progressive Pueblo Indians in May 1924, "That we love our homes, our towns and villages and our people, and our Christian God more, and we are sorry that some of the Pueblo officials are cruel toward many of us and try to make slaves of us under pretense of alleged ancient customs . . . [using] these means to punish and persecute us for secret reasons because of our refusal to take part in secret and unchristian dances. . . . That liberty to practice one's religion should be equal and not limited alone to those whose beliefs and ceremonies may be ancient, but those who disagree with one group in religious matters should have the right to stand fast in that disagreement in favor of their own beliefs without being subjected to religious persecution," and "That the Bureau of Indian Affairs should not encourage the tribal governments in tyranny and persecution, by holding up the hands of these tribal governments in matters which ordinary common sense shows are tyrannical and have religious persecution at bottom."[1]

When Pueblo progressives appealed for religious liberty against what they called "persecution" from tribal leaders, they revealed one implication of identifying Indian ceremonies as "religion." If these traditions were religion rather than "custom" or "community work," then the tribe could not require participation from all its members without violating the constitutional principle of religious freedom. By encouraging and publicizing the progressives' complaints, the Indian Rights Association was able to refocus the dance controversy away from its allegations of immorality in the ceremonies, and it worked to present itself once again as the champion of Indian rights and progressive values. Although the assimilationist opposition to "pagan" dancing remained grounded in the conviction that Christianity and Euro-American civilization were superior, the progressives' cause—once it was identified as a matter of religious freedom—was one that few Americans would deny.

The Indian Citizenship Act, which Congress passed in June 1924 to grant U.S. citizenship to all Native Americans, formed an important part of the background to these religious freedom disputes. Although the measure was intended to guarantee equal rights for Indians as citizens, most Indians had opposed it because they feared it would further erode tribal sovereignty, culture, and land rights. Ultimately the act made little difference in either direction, because the Supreme Court had already ruled that Indians could be both citizens and government wards, and for better or for worse the Bureau of Indian Affairs oversight continued much as before. Becoming citizens did not even give the Pueblos voting rights, because New Mexico along with several other states continued to use the Indians' status as non-taxpayers to bar them from voting until the mid-twentieth century. But it made tremendous symbolic difference in the dance controversy, where both sides used it to argue for their vision of equal rights for Indians. Assimilationists focused on the rights of individual progressive Indians who no longer wanted to participate in "pagan rites," arguing that their commitment to Christianity and civilization was necessary for productive citizenship and must therefore be embraced by all Indians. On the other hand, modernists and Pueblo traditionalists insisted that as citizens Indians had the right to practice tribal religions without interference from the government.[2]

As the controversy began to fade from public view, the BIA imposed a compromise solution that guaranteed the Indians' right to continue their tribal ceremonies as long as tribal leaders promised to give the same religious freedom to individual tribal members who may not want to participate. Identifying the Pueblo ceremonies as religion provided effective protection against direct government suppression, but it also forced Pueblo leaders to accept newly individualistic norms of ceremonial participation—norms based on Euro-American concepts of religion as a private affair. By solidifying the identification of Indian traditions as legitimate religions that could not constitutionally be restricted, the dance controversy undermined assimilationist premises and so contributed to the decline of the Christian establishment in Indian affairs. The Christian condemnation of "heathenism" was no longer credible as a basis for government policy, and gradually Christian missionaries would lose their special status as government-endorsed civilizing agents on the reservations. The Interior Department began to re-create its Indian policy on the basis of scientific and secular authority, implementing the secularization long sought by modernist reformers. Yet even the "secular" vision of the modernists, as implemented by John Collier when he became commissioner of Indian Affairs, required Indians to transform indigenous traditions in the name of progress. As the Pueblo experience demonstrates once again, the "secular" is a culturally specific concept, carrying assumptions that are often an uneasy fit with religious minorities.

Defending Pueblo Religion: Confrontations at Zuni and Taos

Pueblo Indians entered into the dance controversy in earnest in mid-1924, when tribal leaders and modernist reformers saw evidence that the BIA had embarked on an all-out war on Pueblo religion. Events at Zuni and Taos convinced John Collier to refocus his reform energies from land to religion, and his involvement encouraged the All-Pueblo Council to do the same.

At Zuni, the trouble began with a conflict over ceremonial secrecy at the Shalako festival in 1923. Zuni governor Latario Luna and kiva priest Komosana gave permission for Owen Cattell, a filmmaker working with the Heye Foundation who had already taken footage of several summer ceremonies, to film certain portions of the Shalako as long as he maintained a respectful distance. But many Zunis found the very presence of the camera offensive, and by popular demand the chief priest of war demanded that Cattell stop filming midway through the ceremony. Zuni's minority faction—called "Catholics" because they had supported the reestablishment of the Catholic mission at Zuni two years earlier—complained that the governor had acted improperly, violated the trust of the people, and therefore had to be removed from office. Final decisions regarding the appointment and dismissal of tribal officers were in the hands of the pueblo's six high priests, under the leadership of Sun Priest Tsatsana. On this occasion Tsatsana's nephew and designated successor Seowtewa, who belonged to the Catholic faction, ordered Governor Luna and his officers to resign. When Luna refused, Seowtewa enlisted the help of BIA superintendent Robert Bauman—who had gained permission for the Catholic mission despite the opposition of tribal leaders—to confiscate the governor's canes of office. The next day Seowtewa named replacements from the Catholic group, initiating a bitter dispute over the legitimacy of tribal officials not appointed in the traditional way by consensus of all six high priests.[3]

Suddenly out of power, the majority faction protested the superintendent's support for Seowtewa as a coup d'etat designed to force Catholicism on the tribe. The members of this faction were friendly with modernist reformers and anthropologists—hence their trust of Cattell—and were often called "Protestants" not because of any affiliation with the local Christian Reformed missionaries but for their opposition to the Catholic mission. After Bauman had brought in the mission, complained "Protestant" leader Lorenzo Chaves, he had gone on to force Zuni children to attend the new Catholic school, directed Mexican employees to attend ceremonies despite traditional Zuni objections to their doing so, and had now taken the drastic step of replacing the legitimate tribal officers with candidates who also supported the growth of Catholicism at Zuni.[4] Collier learned about these events when he came to Zuni in mid-January to discuss land issues, and he immediately demanded that Bauman return the governor's canes to Tsatsana in order to restore what he considered legitimate tribal authority. Bauman refused, insisting that he had simply provided support for new tribal officers who he believed had been properly installed.[5] C. V. Safford, the BIA inspector who investigated the crisis the following month, agreed with Bauman that the new Zuni officers were legitimate and blamed the disturbance on the "interference" of Hodge and other outsiders in Zuni affairs.[6] For Collier and for the ousted Zuni leaders, this report simply provided new evidence of the BIA's duplicity. "Zuni believes that the Government, acting for the Catholic missionaries, has committed itself to a destruction of the historical fabric of the tribe," wrote Collier, "and particularly the religion which stands as a barrier against Christianization." From that time on, religious freedom would be a primary focus of Collier's activities.[7]

It is important to note here that both the "Protestant" and "Catholic" factions at Zuni were trying to protect their ceremonial traditions. Komosana explained to Safford that he had given Cattell permission to film the ceremonies because—less than a year after Burke's dance circular—anthropologist F. W. Hodge had assured him that this would help persuade the government not to suppress Indian dances. "They told me that they were going to take the pictures from the very beginning and the making of the Shalakos," he told Safford, "so they will be sent back East and the people will see them and believe about our dances and they should keep our religious secrets like we have before, peacefully, friendly and happily." However, his "Catholic" opponents argued that filming the Shalako violated Zuni standards of ceremonial secrecy and that the film might in some way "be used . . . to cause forcible suppression of the religious ceremonies." Seowtewa suspected that the filmmakers only wanted to make a profit for themselves, and in his closing statements to Safford expressed a general mistrust for all reformers. "In the future we do not want any outsiders to come in and interfere with our religious ceremonies, since we have everything settled through you [the BIA] . . . because we all want to keep our own religion."[8]

The Zunis' distrust of "outsiders" grew from the violations they had experienced not only from missionaries and government agents but from the accepted norms of anthropological research. At Safford's recommendation, all six of Zuni's high priests asked the BIA to warn Hodge against any further "interference" in their affairs. Hodge had been conducting archaeological excavations in the Zuni environs for many years and was well known to the Zunis—hence Komosana's trust—but now the Zunis' underlying suspicions of his work surfaced. "The excavation [he] has done is where our fathers lived," they said. "Suppose we Indians make excavations like the white men, digging out your fathers, mothers, and all of your relatives, how would you feel if we put them in the show cases and let everybody see them, would you like it?" Even though some of them had been on friendly terms with Hodge, the "Protestant" as well as "Catholic" high priests maintained a strong distaste for archaeological research and its violation of ancestral remains. These Zuni factions disagreed over the advantages of working with anthropologists and reformers on one hand, or missionaries and government agents on the other. But as we have seen, all of them demonstrated deep commitment to the ceremonies that they already defined as their own religion.[9]

In May 1924 a growing crisis at Taos Pueblo emerged as the new focal point for the religious freedom controversy. That January, Taos governor Antonio Romero and his tribal council had asked Commissioner Burke for permission "for some school children to be absent from school for our Indian religious." They informed the commissioner that they intended to take three boys out of school for eighteen months, and six other boys for six months. "All our young and us has passed this," they wrote, "and [we] cannot go without it."[10] Taos's religious societies selected several seven- to ten-year-old boys each year, the various societies taking turns from one year to the next, for extensive rites of initiation. During this time "the priests and medicine men and ancients of the Pueblo convey to them the story of Pueblo life in all its phases," attorney A. B. Renehan reported to Burke, including instruction in "their rites and rituals, their traditions, the uses of herbs and their medical qualities, application and effect." The boys were permitted "no association with other children or people except the ancients," slept in the kiva "under watch and ward of one of the old men," and ate only indigenous foods such as "corn and corn products, squashes and other traditional vegetables . . . [and] the flesh of wild animals and fish and wild birds." Not all Taos boys received this training, but those who did became "the depository of Pueblo learning of all kinds," eligible for positions of religious and political leadership within the tribe and responsible to pass their knowledge on "to later generations." Even though Renehan believed the Indians must ultimately abandon such traditions, the Taos leaders convinced him that the boys' absence from school would not be "a serious detriment" because they were "acquiring knowledge of a useful character," and he advised Burke that to "forcibly and despotically" forbid such traditions would devastate the pueblo.[11]

These initiation practices became an issue in 1924 because the BIA had only just expanded the day school at Taos so that it was large enough to enroll all the pueblo's children.[12] Now that the school had the capacity, BIA officials wanted all the children to attend. Superintendent Crandall proposed a compromise allowing the boys to stay away for "ten days or two weeks," but despite his desire to maintain good relations with the pueblo, he could not countenance more. The Indians' request squarely contradicted his conviction that Christianity and civilization necessarily went hand in hand. "To grant this request for the period stated in the letter," he wrote to Burke, "would almost mean a surrender of our attempt to educate these Pueblos in our Christian civilization." The "religious instructions" the Indians wanted to impart were not "in the Christian religion, but in the ancient customs, legends, and rites of the Pueblo." The goal of the initiation was to pass on to the next generation "their ancient religion, if religion it may be called." Crandall clearly did not see the indigenous traditions as legitimate "religion" at all.[13] Burke followed Crandall's advice, informing the Indians that he could not compromise "the principle of common school education" and so they would be permitted to withdraw children "not more than two weeks each year" for the tribal initiations. While he wanted to preserve the Indians' "freedom of religious faith," he was confident that their children could complete any additional requirements after school hours or in the summer months.[14]

There the matter rested for more than two months, until Burke visited Taos that April on a tour of the region with Interior Secretary Hubert Work and learned that the boys had still not been returned to school. "At the close of the meeting," Crandall told the BIA's chief supervisor of education, "I ordered the governor to return the boys the following Monday to school." The commissioner and the superintendent reacted to the Indians' resistance as a full-scale challenge to their authority—a struggle that they articulated in the language of colonial control. "If the Moros become hostile in the distant Philippines, we generally find a way to settle them," Crandall wrote. "The question in my mind is, if we must submit to the pagan demands of these Indians here right at home." Crandall hoped that the commissioner would authorize him to "arrest the governor and a few of the leading men and incarcerate them in jail." Yet he insisted that enforcing this policy would not unfairly discriminate against what he considered a dubious Indian religion. "Every white man in no matter what state he lives must send his child to school, and he is not allowed to keep him out to study Catholicism or Protestantism or any other ism. The question is, shall we concede this to poor Loh?"[15] BIA officials pointed to a recent case in Iowa as a precedent establishing their authority to enforce school attendance, but in private they remained uncertain of their legal standing. "If we find we have the power," Burke told Crandall, "[we] may give the Taos Indians a lesson, that sooner or later the Pueblos have got to learn."[16]

Taos refused to budge, and as the standoff continued, the pueblo's leaders increasingly spoke of their own tradition as a religion in its own right. After a series of consultations and meetings, they informed Burke that they could never "comply with this order, no matter what the penalty may be, because this order would violate our religion and also destroy it." Comparisons to Christianity, intended to make their traditions acceptable and comprehensible to non-Indian officials, also reinforced the idea of a separate indigenous religion. "We have a Bible which is not printed," they wrote, "but is passed on by memory from the old to the young, and it contains our knowledge of God, our forms of prayer and our rules of life." To make it clear that they valued the education provided at the government school, Taos's tribal leaders proposed that the boys who had been "transferred for a year . . . for their religious training" in the pueblo should afterward "remain in the Government school for an additional year." They could not simply move the tribal initiations to the summer vacation, as Burke had suggested, because, as Governor Romero later explained, their calendar was fixed "just like Easter, and Christmas that comes on the 25th of December." In both cases "they have the same day and don't change it." The tribal initiations were a "fundamental requirement" of Taos religion, the council wrote. If they were not continued "our religion would soon die out from the souls of our people . . . and we, and our ancestors who live through us, would pass away from this earth." They reminded Burke that the Treaty of Guadalupe Hidalgo as well as the state and federal constitutions guaranteed them religious freedom, and they threatened to take their case to court if necessary. "We think that white people in our position would consider that they were . . . defending the Constitution and the fundamental liberty of America when they refused to obey such an order from an administrative official."[17]

This crisis marked a turning point for Pueblo Indian leaders beyond Taos, who began increasingly to adopt the language of "religion" and "religious freedom" as the most promising way to defend their ceremonies. The All-Pueblo Council, called together this time by Taos, linked Burke's dance circular to the recent events at Zuni and Taos as evidence of a concerted attack on all Pueblo religion. The council's resolution asked "all Pueblo Indians, all Indians, and all the people of the U.S." to support them in a struggle for "our most fundamental right of religious liberty." For the first time, it publicly denounced the allegations of immorality in the Pueblo ceremonies as "shamefully untrue and without any basis of fact or appearance, and contrary to the abundant testimony of white scholars who have recorded our religious customs." It condemned the commissioner's circular on Indian dances as "an instrument of religious persecution," and called his order to return the Taos boys to school an effort to "destroy the ancient good Indian religion of Taos." Finally, they challenged the continued privileges given to Christianity in the government schools: "When our children go to school, as they all must do and we want them to do, they are compelled to receive the teachings of the Christian religion no matter what the parents or the clan may desire," sometimes without even a choice of denomination. Such religious instruction inevitably caused "division . . . between the parents and the children," and if the Indians were now "forbidden to instruct our own children in the religion of their fathers," then "the Indian religions will quickly die and we shall be robbed of that which is most sacred and dear in our life."[18]

Pueblo Indians from all over New Mexico were especially enraged at reports that Secretary Work (though some believed it had been Commissioner Burke) had called them "half-animals." As Governor Romero remembered, Work had actually said that "the artists—some of these artists, some near artists—don't like to see you dressed like a citizen and go around like a citizen. They rather see you wild, like an animal, so that they could get better material for their model."[19] Work's intention was to convince the Indians that the artists did them more harm than good, and Burke vociferously denied that either he or the secretary had called them "half-animals."[20] But Work had clearly compared Indians who wore indigenous clothing and practiced their own traditions to animals, a sentiment consistent with centuries of racialized discourse on "primitives," and this had touched a very sore nerve. "When issuing [his] order to the Taos Pueblo," the All-Pueblo Council wrote, "the Commissioner denounced the old customs and religions and he used harsh words about us who are faithful to the religious life of our race. He called us 'half-animal.'" As this episode suggests, the Pueblos' mounting crusade for religious freedom was also a struggle to be recognized as fully human.[21]

John Collier played an active role in the deliberations of the All-Pueblo Council and encouraged its new emphasis on religious freedom. No delegates were present from Zuni at the May meeting, largely because its new governor mistrusted the council's agenda, and Collier reported to the council that the BIA had already interfered with tribal initiations in that pueblo. When Zuni's high priests complained to Inspector Safford that Bauman did not allow them to take their children out of school "for religious instructions and for initiation in the winter and spring months," the inspector had refused to intervene, despite the explanation from Zuni leaders that "we cannot change our dates any more than the white people can change the date of Christmas, or change the date of New Year." The Zunis had been fighting this particular battle for quite some time, as Bauman's predecessors had also refused to allow children to leave school for tribal initiations. But by highlighting this exchange in the transcript of Safford's investigation, Collier identified this Zuni dilemma for the first time as part of a larger Pueblo struggle for religious freedom. He also noted that "at Zuni the children are required to have religious training in Christianity," even though the vast majority of Zunis "are not Christians at all, but have only their Indian religion." These reports from Zuni reinforced the idea of an indigenous religion separate from Catholicism and helped convince the delegates that religious freedom was a concern not only for Taos but for all the Pueblos.[22]

Collier's speech to the All-Pueblo Council argued that the Pueblo traditions must be understood as a religion with as much legitimacy as any other. He offered the analogy of "wonderful buildings which it took thousands of years to build," explaining that Indian religions were just as important to humanity as Catholicism, Judaism, or any other religion. When the Ku Klux Klan had managed to pass a law in Oregon "forbidding the Catholics to take their boys out of school for religious education," he told the delegates, the Catholics went to court on religious freedom grounds and the law was declared unconstitutional. As Indians and now citizens they had the same constitutional right "to practice their own religion, their own prayers and ceremonies and dances, to have their own holy days, to educate their own children in the Indian religion." The "effort to destroy the Indian religion" had been "going on for a whole life time," he reminded them, and now the time had come to "stop it by going into court and proving that your religion is a religion, and getting the court to say that you shall be free like other people to practice your religion." In the event that they ended up in court, Collier promised full support, financial and otherwise, from the General Federation of Women's Clubs and the American Indian Defense Association.[23]

Just as he had done during the land disputes, Collier appealed to the sympathies of a predominantly Christian public by comparing the Indians' situation to the religious persecution suffered by the early Christians. "In just such manner," he wrote, "the provincial Roman governors developed their indictment against the Christian religion, as an incestuous, sodomitic cult of torture and of anarchism, while in their day long gone they persecuted Christianity." Collier argued that the current case was actually more egregious because the Pueblos were a tiny group who "have no wish to make converts" and "seek no power," while the early Christians were a real threat to the Roman Empire. In a later article aimed at Protestant readers, he extended this comparison to the persecutions many Protestant denominations had faced early in their histories: "There is no ancient denomination which does not remember that it was once as the Indians are." Such comparisons strengthened the identification of Pueblo traditions as religion, adding weight to their demands for religious freedom.[24]

By arguing that Indians had a religion of their own that must be granted the same rights held by Protestants and Catholics, modernists and Pueblo Indians challenged the privileged status that Christianity still held on Indian reservations. The *Santa Fe New Mexican* observed in characteristically mocking tones that the Interior Department had blown the situation far out of proportion. "The federal government is prepared to take all possible measures for the defense of American institutions threatened by this menacing Pagan dictator and supreme ruler of Taos who wants to keep two small boys out of school to teach the insidious doctrines of the Great Spirit, this Great Spirit lacking any Methodist, Baptist, Catholic, Presbyterian, Dutch Reformed or Campbellite affiliations."[25] Modernists insisted that any religion, whether Christian or not, must be granted its constitutional right to religious freedom. Cash Asher, the AIDA's associate executive and a former journalist, wrote a piece in the *New York Times* condemning the BIA's actions at Taos as "another manifestation of our official policy of stamping out Indian tribal life." Asher clearly considered the missionary influence a big part of the problem in Indian affairs: "We continue to persecute and proselyte these first Americans, among other crimes forcing them to send their children to denominational schools—denominational schools supported in part by tribal money conscripted by the Government for that purpose." In a direct challenge to the lingering Christian establishment, Asher sent telegrams to this effect to all Democratic members of Congress along with press releases to newspapers around the country.[26]

Not all of the dance circular's opponents shared Collier's and Asher's optimism about the Pueblos' chances in court. Even the AIDA's lawyer, A. A. Berle, warned that "actions running counter to the accepted ideas of public welfare have been held not to be protected under [religious freedom] laws" and that the Taos case might be decided against the Indians on those grounds. Just as ominously, he suggested that "the idea of withdrawing children from public schools for the purpose of training in a sect or tribe," when that training was not otherwise similar to the public school education, would likely not be found "permissible under American law and customs."[27] Members of the Eastern Association and the New Mexico Association, who already disliked Collier because of their conflicts over the land legislation, saw the new campaign as further evidence of his dangerously overzealous nature. The "hullabaloo" raised by Collier, wrote Francis Wilson from Santa Fe, had made it impossible for more level-headed parties to settle the matter "quietly with the Commissioner." "The Indians are now placed in a terrible position to my mind," Wilson wrote, "that of open opposition to the Government and of having challenged the Government to force their hands." Should the case go to court, Wilson, like Berle, feared that the Indians would lose. In New York, Roberts Walker spelled out additional reasons for that fear. Despite what Collier or he himself might believe the Indians merited in the way of religious freedom, he thought there was too great a risk "that the maintenance of Christianity will be favored by the courts and that the Indian ceremonials will be denounced as 'pagan,' 'barbaric,' and otherwise read out." Walker blamed Collier for "threatening [the Indians] with extinction" by causing a public showdown that was sure to end badly. In his opinion, a legal confrontation was bound to turn against the Indians because American courts were still governed by a virtual Christian establishment.[28]

When the IRA caught wind of the Taos controversy, it demanded that the BIA enforce its compulsory education requirements and refuse to capitulate to the "pagan" demands. Herbert Welsh urged Secretary Work to move forward with Burke's original proposal: "Thus will an incipient but dangerous rebellion against the authority of the U.S. and its constitution be nipped in the bud."[29] The IRA inevitably saw these events in the context of its ongoing campaign against Indian dances. Matthew Sniffen had just arrived in New Mexico to gather information on the Pueblo controversies when he learned about the crisis at Taos, and under the circumstances he took special note of the rumors he was able to gather concerning that pueblo. "It is said" that at the invitation of the Taos Indians "Navajo men . . . have sexual intercourse with the Taos women to prevent too much inbreeding, and thus keep up the strength of the Taos Indians." Another story—even more scandalous and equally unfounded—held that Taos sacrificed two boys every four years "as a sacrifice to the Water God."[30] Assimilationists used such rumors to discredit the Pueblo claims to religious freedom. BIA inspector Adelina Otero-Warren, a consistent ally of the IRA, told Burke that the "evidence" Sniffen gathered made a mockery of Collier's comparison of "the cacique training to that given to boys intending to become rabbis or priests."[31] When time dragged on and neither Burke nor Crandall took decisive action, Sniffen wrote in frustration that their delay had created the "opportunity (which was readily seized) to outside influences to arouse an attitude of defiance." The situation at Taos had only confirmed the IRA's convictions about the duplicity of the modernist reformers and the "degrading" quality of Pueblo ceremonies, here set directly against the "civilizing" benefits of education.[32]

Under pressure from both modernists and assimilationists, the Department of the Interior struggled to find an effective policy for handling the standoff. Convinced that Collier was fomenting rebellion among the Pueblos, government officials seriously considered seeking a court injunction to keep him out of all Indian land. The commissioner's legal counsel also advised that "from a legal standpoint" the BIA could almost certainly "put these children back in school and successfully resist any attempt of the Pueblo authorities to take them from our institutions for training in religious pagan practices." But the AIDA's publicity tactics proved too powerful for this course of action. Characteristically, Burke tried to deflect criticism by insisting against all evidence that he had not issued any "orders" at Taos but had simply "requested" that the Indians return the boys to school. Despite his fears that consenting to Taos's request would mean "surrender to the Indian government," by May 1924 Superintendent Crandall was recommending "leaving the Indians in suspense" over the summer because "in view of the fuss it will stir up . . . drastic steps would be unwise."[33] Burke finally announced at the end of the school year that he was handing the whole matter to Secretary Work for a final decision, to be announced by the end of the summer, which he guaranteed would do no "violence to any religious rights of the Indians." Even though lawyers on both sides of the controversy had concluded that the BIA would probably win in court, the commissioner did not want to risk further adverse publicity. By September, he hoped, reformers' attention would have shifted away from Taos.[34]

The Pueblo Progressive Movement

In the meantime, Pueblo progressives were beginning to adopt the language of religious freedom as a way to strengthen and publicize their case against the conservative tribal leaders. The first to articulate the progressive cause in these terms were not Indians but local assimilationists reacting against the modernist campaign. One of these was Nathan Bibo, a member of a pioneering Jewish family in New Mexico who had lived near Laguna Pueblo in the 1870s and was now an insurance agent in Bernalillo. Bibo entered the fray of the controversy in the fall of 1923 with opinion pieces in the *Santa Fe New Mexican* and the *Albuquerque Journal*. "All those very interesting articles on the Pueblo Indian question" were "doing great harm to the young generation of the Pueblo Indians," he claimed. In his view, the "meddling artists or writers" were only encouraging a "self-constituted, old-time fanatic clique" of Pueblo leaders who forced their "educated young folks" to participate in "the old customs and rites." Denying that the government had ever "tried to interfere with the old customs of the older set of the Indians," Bibo turned the question of religious freedom on its head. "While the old set have their right to believe what they please," he asked, "why should they be permitted to interfere with the religion or way of more modern living of the children educated in government schools or other institutions?" In short, Bibo depicted the Pueblo tribal leaders as the perpetrators rather than the victims of religious freedom violations.[35]

Mary Bryan, who lived near Santa Clara Pueblo as Clara True's longtime companion, introduced the Pueblo progressives to the Indian Rights Association as an ideal solution to the religious freedom impasse. Bryan was originally from Philadelphia, the daughter of an IRA member, and she described two cases that seemed tailor-made to bolster the faltering case against the Pueblo dances: "Edward Hunt and his family, Indians of the Pueblo of Santa Ana, are in need of liberty to worship God according to the dictates of their own consciences instead of bowing in reverence to the old tribal gods on pain of expulsion from the tribe and confiscation of their lands." A similar conflict had developed at Cochiti Pueblo, where self-identified progressive Joseph Melchor had protested the governor's requirement that he help maintain community ditches that he did not even use. Bryan was convinced that, as with Hunt, the Melchor family was being penalized because it had "thrown off the yoke of the tribal religion." Even though Inspector Adelina Otero-Warren had filed a report recommending "a policy of protection to the young," she complained, Commissioner Burke refused to take any action without the approval of the superintendents in the field. And according to Bryan, both Northern Pueblos superintendent Crandall and Southern Pueblos superintendent Marble favored "the old pagan element" and so were actually contributing to the problem.[36]

For the most part, Bryan's allegations matched the stories told by Hunt and Melchor themselves. Edward Hunt, a member of a progressive family from Acoma Pueblo, was a devout Protestant educated at the Presbyterian Menaul Indian School in Albuquerque and at St. Catherine's in Santa Fe. His sister was married to Nathan Bibo's brother Solomon, who had been named Acoma's governor six times in the 1890s and in that capacity pressured the tribe to moderate or abandon its ceremonies. Hunt had regularly conflicted with more conservative tribal officials ever since, partly because his family was less and less willing to take part in the ceremonies.[37] He finally left Acoma with his wife and children in 1918, mostly because he felt the tribe had not allotted them enough land. The Hunts were officially "adopted into Santa Ana" soon afterward and established a farm near one of that pueblo's satellite villages. Every year after that, Santa Ana's governor had asked the family to take part in the pueblo's ceremonies, and each time it refused. After four years of these exchanges, the tribal council denied the family access to the community's pastureland and to the irrigation ditches. It also warned, Hunt recalled, that "if we did not conform to their pagan rules we would be expelled from our land and our home." Leo Crane, then super-intendent for the Southern Pueblos, sympathized with the Hunts and in-sisted that the tribe allow them to keep their land and water rights even without their ceremonial participation. The following year a new set of tribal officers —who according to Hunt only "wanted to get rid of me"— charged that he had failed to contribute his share of labor to the irrigation ditch. By this time, Marble had replaced Crane as superintendent, and he informed the family it must either obey the tribal officers or move else-where. At the advice of the BIA attorney, Hunt agreed to "a fair price for all my possessions and improvements" and in the fall of 1923 seemed resigned to leaving Santa Ana. He told Ralph Twitchell, then working as a BIA lawyer in Santa Fe, that he and his family simply hoped to "work in freedom" and live as "real American citizens." Hunt, who insisted that he could not "ob-serve two religions as they [the Santa Ana people] do," had clearly come to think of the indigenous ceremonies as a "pagan" religion incompatible with his Christian faith. But he did not yet conceive of his dilemma in terms of religious freedom.[38]

Joseph Melchor's case seems to have had more to do with labor patterns and ditch work than it did with ceremonial obligations. Several years earlier his father Juan Pedro Melchor, one of the older men in Cochiti Pueblo's progressive party, had been working far away from the pueblo and failed to "go home to dance four days at Christmas as was the requirement." When he and his wife refused to be punished for this absence, as the elder Melchor told Twitchell and Otero-Warren in their initial investigation, the tribal council had "put us out of the customs" entirely—meaning that they were banned from future ceremonies. Asked to clarify this point, Melchor assured Otero-Warren that even before that banishment he had not wanted to "worship those idols" because he was "sworn to believe in one God and not in the strange gods of that people." But his testimony suggests that he had originally stayed away from the Christmas ceremony not primarily out of religious conviction but because his work made it too difficult to return home in time, and that it was the council's ban that prevented him from participating thereafter. At least some of Cochiti's leaders apparently understood this banishment as applicable to all the privileges of pueblo life. According to Juan Pedro Melchor, the next year's governor had "[torn] down our fences," thereby reclaiming his land for the tribe, and had been making trouble for the family ever since.[39] The current tribal officials were now accusing his son Joseph Melchor of failing to do his assigned share of work on the irrigation ditches and had confiscated his land as well. Tribal leaders claimed that this case had nothing to do with the ceremonies and everything to do with the Melchors' refusal to do their fair share of the ditch work.[40] And the Melchors themselves devoted more attention to protesting the governor's work assignments than to the question of ceremonial participation.[41]

However, some Pueblo progressives immediately understood these events through the lens of religious freedom. John Dixon, who as Cochiti's former Indian judge was the acknowledged leader of the pueblo's progressive faction, claimed in a statement to attorney A. B. Renehan that the Cochiti authorities had often allowed many tribal members who did not use water from a ditch to avoid working on it. They were treating the Melchor family differently, he said, only because they did not "take part in either the public or the secret dances of the Indians." Dixon—at least as filtered through Renehan's report—understood the Melchors' plight as a contest between Christianity and an indigenous religion. "In his opinion," Renehan wrote, "the Christian Indians of the Pueblo are confronted with a contest brought against them by the Indians who recognize their ancient rites, beliefs and customs, to compel them to sacrifice their conscientious belief in their Christian religion in favor of the ancient religion or religious beliefs of the Pueblo generally." If the government refused "to protect them" now, the report concluded, all "the Christian Indians of the Pueblos" would "be treated as outlaws and made to suffer persecution because of their religious belief in one true God." Perhaps through Renehan's encouragement, Dixon was beginning to demand the BIA's protection for Pueblo progressives in the name of religious liberty.[42]

Whether Pueblo leaders had in fact forced unwilling tribal members to participate in the dances is perhaps a matter of interpretation. As we have already seen, Pueblo Indians traditionally understood their ceremonies not as "religion" but as part of the shared work of the community. When BIA officials in Santa Fe investigated Hunt's complaints in April 1924, Santa Ana's Governor Daniel Otero claimed at first that Hunt had been penalized solely for his refusal to do his share of the ditch work. Inspector Otero-Warren was not satisfied with this response and asked whether Hunt had been required "to take part in the pagan ceremonies as part of his community work." The governor answered that "besides ditch work" Hunt would of course need "to do . . . the customs, to take part in these ceremonies, as he agreed to when he came into the Pueblo." Inspector C. V. Safford's interview with the Cochiti officials a few months later yielded much the same result. Asked whether the pueblo's forthcoming Christmas dance was "for the benefit of the whole Pueblo, and the whole world . . . hard work, which you believe necessary to bring the rain and good crops and good for all the people?" Governor Luis Ortiz responded, "Yes." The man who dances in the pueblo, council member Alcario Montoya testified, "is benefitting his people." Such ceremonies benefited the whole community by bringing rain and a good growing season, and by maintaining the balance and harmony of the whole earth. For this reason, all tribal members were expected to contribute in one way or another to the pueblo's ceremonial life.[43]

Hunt's refusal to do so had apparently perplexed the Santa Ana officials. "I never knew of anybody else in that pueblo who would not conform to the customs," Daniel Otero told the BIA investigators. Porfirio Montoya, Santa Ana's "lieutenant ditch boss," hastened to explain that although "everybody takes part" in dancing during the "general Fiesta days," nobody would be expected to participate or even attend all pueblo ceremonies. Most were populated solely by those "that are willing," he said—and "there are others that they are not allowed unless they are a member. They may look on, but they cannot take part." In other words, participation in some ceremonies was restricted to members of the sponsoring religious society. Montoya insisted that Hunt had never been forced to participate even in the saint's day fiesta. "Of course we cannot force him," he told his interrogators. "We cannot make him dance."Hunt had not conformed to pueblo expectations for either land rights or ceremonial participation, and the tribal council saw no alternative but to expel him.[44]

Enforcing such participation was certainly within the traditional bounds of a Pueblo governor's authority. Asked whether he would be upset if his son were "forced" to participate in "religious ceremonies," Taos governor Antonio Romero answered that "if he is a member" of one of the pueblo's societies, then he would of course be required to take part in its activities. The question was moot because all the boys wanted "to be a member" anyway, he explained. But if one of his sons had not wanted to join, Romero would insist that he do so because the training these societies provided was "a fine study"—one that he himself valued as much as the education he had received in the government schools. Speaking at the height of Taos's struggle to defend its tribal initiations, Romero astutely framed his response in terms of education. If the U.S. government could enforce compulsory school attendance, he implied, then Taos could also require its own brand of education— one that its people found equally valuable. Romero certainly considered ceremonial participation one of the obligations incumbent on society members, and it is not difficult to imagine him enforcing this as part of his responsibilities as governor. His answer suggested an alternative to the growing move toward defining the Pueblo ceremonies as religion. Defending the ceremonies in terms of tribal education would have circumvented the question of individual religious liberty, but no doubt this would also have been difficult to justify to assimilationist officials who did not see indigenous traditions as worthy subjects for education.[45]

In the meantime, the BIA's investigations into the Hunt and Melchor allegations contributed to the reconceptualization of Pueblo ceremonies as a religion distinct from Catholicism. H. J. Hagerman, former territorial governor of New Mexico and now the BIA's special commissioner for the Navajo, asked Daniel Otero near the beginning of the Hunt investigation whether any returned students were "in any way discouraged from following their religious belief by the Pueblo authorities." Otero replied simply, "Why, no!" He was surprised by the question because the answer seemed so apparent. He himself was a Catholic, he testified, and "all of my Pueblo Indians belong to the Catholic church." Why then would he or other Santa Ana officials have discouraged their young people from practicing Catholicism? Hagerman seemed to find the conversation equally disorienting. "At the same time," he asked, "in order to obtain the privileges of the Pueblo . . . they must also conform to non-Christian customs and ceremonies?" And then, "Does the Catholic Church approve of that?" Inspector Otero-Warren stepped in at this point to defend her church, which was in her words doing everything it could "to enlighten the Indians so that when they are strong enough to withstand the influence of the Pueblo authorities that they will of their own accord give up their pagan customs." A few minutes later BIA attorney Burton Livingston asked Otero, "Now these customs that he was supposed to perform, are they against the Catholic religion?" Tentatively the governor answered, "I think so, yes." After the preceding discussion, it would have been hard for him to answer in any other way. His interrogators had presented the ceremonies as "pagan" and "non-Christian"—opposed to and incompatible with Christianity. From the perspective of Pueblo tradition, this redefinition had its perils. If dancing was a part of community service, then by all rights a governor could require tribal members to participate. But if dancing was redefined in terms of "paganism"—or more positively as a distinctively Indian religion—then the same exercise of authority appeared as a violation of the progressive Indian's religious freedom, an all-American value that nobody wanted to assault.[46]

Progressive Indians from Santa Clara, Cochiti, San Juan, and Santa Ana Pueblos met for the first time in May 1924, when they formed the Council of Progressive Pueblo Indians expressly to counter the voice of the All-Pueblo Council. Although Clara True originally proposed the meeting to coincide with Matthew Sniffen's visit, the progressive Indians quickly made the council their own. The twenty-five progressives in attendance were eager to adopt a common platform, but they expressed a wide range of grievances. Some were most concerned that the pueblo governors allocated community work unfairly, that conservative tribal leaders blocked "progress" of one kind or another, or that the conservative factions in their pueblos had a monopoly of power. Not all of the group were interested in protesting the "customs" or "ceremonies" as such. Marejildo Roman of Santa Ana commented that he saw no problem "with the dance in my village" because, as Daniel Otero and Porfirio Montoya had also said, "everybody comes willing to dance." Instead he complained that the current cacique, Manuel Pena, had usurped the position of "this man right here, Felipe Montoya, [who] is supposed to hold that position." In other words, Roman was not really interested in challenging the "customs," either the dances or the traditional systems of pueblo leadership, but in ensuring that the powerful position of cacique went to the man he supported.[47]

Those who emerged as the council's leading voices, however, defined religious liberty as perhaps the most important issue they faced. John Dixon, elected chair as the council's first order of business, welcomed his fellow delegates as men who "have been trying to get ahead and not to go back as to the ways of years past"—which he believed meant that "we do not want to take part in any Indian ceremonials." He had plenty of support among the delegates. Joseph Montoya of San Juan, another graduate of Carlisle Indian School, responded to Roman's comments by insisting that the central issue was the imposition of the "pagan customs" on educated younger people like himself who did not want to participate in them. Sniffen, Schuster, Otero-Warren, and True all spoke at length to the progressive delegates, each of them presenting religious liberty as a matter of individual conscience. By the end of the meeting the council was ready to approve a set of resolutions—drafted by A. B. Renehan—which demanded justice for the Hunts and Melchors, proposed tribal elections as well as various reforms in the system of community work, and most importantly called for "religious liberty and a voice in the management of our pueblo affairs which we do not now have on account of our refusal to conform to outgrown customs." The council as a body, if not all its members, had come to see its cause largely in terms of religious liberty.[48]

Convinced that Indians must embrace the ideals of "progress" and "civilization," these progressives unequivocally rejected the primitivist admiration of the modernists. Joseph Montoya explained in a letter to the *Santa Fe New Mexican* that he and other progressives wished to "meet new conditions with the will to be men among other men, not curios taking dimes from tourists." He challenged John Collier in one particularly scathing letter to adopt the "Stone Age . . . habits of living" that "the Caucasian race" had practiced long ago when they too were "pagans." Unless Collier would be "satisfied to continue in that life" himself, Montoya wrote, then he should "be honest enough to cease . . . imposing upon the simplicity of the Indians when you tell them you are trying to save an ancient religion with its customs." In Montoya's eyes it was impossible to move beyond "primitive ignorance" without abandoning "paganism," because Christianity was inextricably linked to progress in civilization: "The medicine man must give way to the welfare worker," and "local tribal governments accountable to nobody but the stone images who cannot audit accounts must give way to administrations based on some degree of representative government. . . . Our real friends are those who preach the gospel of preparation for competitive life to us, not those who would try to preserve us as a 'priceless heritage' working out his destiny in a clay pot which for a season adorns some white man's curio shelf and then is cast into outer darkness with other undusted relics of forgotten fads." Rather than serving Pueblo interests, Montoya believed, the modernist romanticization of Pueblo traditional ceremonies grew out of the antiquarian curiosity, aesthetic ideals, and economic self-interest of artists, writers, scientists, and tourists. Over such friends, he and other Pueblo progressives preferred those who preached a practical gospel of progress.[49]

Of course, this did not mean that the progressives shared the full agenda of their assimilationist allies. After the progressive council meeting, Sniffen visited a number of pueblos, hoping that one-on-one interviews with progressive Indians would provide new evidence both about their plight and of the alleged immorality in the tribal ceremonies. Despite his leading questions to that effect, though, very few of the progressives he interviewed gave any credence to the idea that the ceremonies were sexually immoral. Even John Dixon insisted in response to Sniffen's queries that the "secret dances" did not include "anything bad." He conceded that some "bad things" were "done by the clowns—koshares" in the public dances, who performed what he called "dirty tricks." But when Sniffen asked if the tribal leaders took "young girls and put them in the estufas with men," Dixon replied that, even if such things had occurred in the past, they had been "forbidden by the Government" and so were no longer practiced. The critique he volunteered was one based on religious conviction—that the performers in the "secret dances . . . are men [yet] they represent themselves as the Gods."[50] Manuel Mondragon of Taos, another progressive who had quarreled with his pueblo's authorities because he and his children refused to dance, even more firmly refuted Sniffen's suggestions of sexual immorality in the dances. When asked, "Do you feel that there are some wrong doings connected with some of these ceremonies?" Mondragon responded simply, "The only thing is that they interfere with the progress of the children. I don't know of any

Manuel Mondragon, 1903. Courtesy National Anthropological Archives, Smithsonian Institution, Suitland, Maryland, INV 06327200.

immorality connected with them." Dixon, Mondragon, and other progressives who avoided the ceremonies did so not because they thought them immoral but because they were convinced these practices were incompatible either with their Christian faith or with tribal advancement toward "civilization." Although Bibo, Schuster, and other non-Indians continued to make allegations about sexual immorality in the Pueblos, the progressives had little interest in discrediting their people in this way.[51]

Despite the much-publicized cases of Hunt and Melchor, many of the self-identified progressives among the Pueblo Indians, like Pablo Abeita, actually continued to participate in the traditional ceremonies. Laguna, widely considered the most progressive pueblo, had leaders who were suspicious of John Collier and refused to join in the All-Pueblo Council's petitions for religious freedom. But Laguna also declined to send delegates to the progressive council and insisted that the BIA not "interfere with our customs or dances as long as we do not violate the law."[52] The delegates from Santa Clara Pueblo, the largest contingent at the progressive council, were silent on the question of dances. This group, it turns out, had a complex identity that did not neatly fit the IRA's image of "progressive" Indians. Many of the same names had appeared on a petition to the Bureau of Catholic Indian Missions just four years earlier asking for support in a dispute with the governor. At that time, they advocated returning to the equitable distribution of labor on the irrigation ditches that had "been a custom among our people for many years"—an appeal based on tradition rather than progress.[53] The factional conflict at Santa Clara originated in the pueblo's basic division between Winter and Summer moieties, a structure common to all the Tewa pueblos. Each moiety traditionally had its own cacique, directed the pueblo's ceremonial affairs for its designated half of the year, and named the governor in alternate years.[54] But at Santa Clara the Summer People had gained a significant demographic majority, and for several decades had apparently claimed the right to name all of the pueblo's governors.[55] The minority Winter People began to embrace progressive sentiments partly because they hoped that an alliance with assimilationists and BIA officials would provide a new advantage. Although a few of the pueblo's more radical progressives apparently stopped participating, throughout the period the "progressive" Winter People of Santa Clara as well as the "conservative" Summer People continued to hold the ceremonial dances appropriate to their moieties.[56] In other words, the factional conflicts in many pueblos had internal histories that had little to do with any outside reformer's agenda.

Especially because it came at a time of serious threats to Pueblo land, culture, and sovereignty, this increasingly vocal opposition movement infuriated the All-Pueblo Council. Along with its modernist allies, the council tried to marginalize and discredit the progressives as a small group of troublemakers being exploited by their white supporters. "It is a proven fact that you are only a few persons, a Bunch of [dis]gruntled fellows who refuse to do your share of work in your own pueblos," retorted a group of All-Pueblo Council leaders that June. "The same people who had been against the Pueblo Indians when the original Bursum Bill [was] first introduced are misleading you," the council warned, "or at least with their aid you are carrying out your work, to destroy your people."[57] They pointed out that settlers' attorney A. B. Renehan had drafted the progressive council's resolutions, and none other than Clara True had initiated its first meeting. These advisers, they believed, were deliberately stirring up dissention within the pueblos at the time they most needed to remain unified. With the newly appointed Pueblo Lands Board about to begin its deliberations, thousands of acres of disputed land were at stake. If the Pueblos were preoccupied with internal battles, they would not be able to effectively present their cases before the board.[58]

Although these charges were not entirely fair, the very existence of the progressive council did tend to weaken the Pueblo cause. The progressives certainly believed that they were working for the best interests of their people, and some like Abeita and Dixon had labored long and hard for Pueblo land rights. But their complaints against the Pueblo governors—especially when the IRA gave them added publicity—probably added credibility to Renehan's suggestion that these Indians did not deserve the land they still possessed.[59] Furthermore, as the All-Pueblo Council feared, factional conflicts made it more difficult for the Pueblos to shape a common defense before the Lands Board. Acoma and Laguna refused to participate in the council's actions during this period, largely because their leaders did not trust Collier and wanted to maintain a positive relationship with the BIA.[60] Many other pueblos experienced internal dissent on how best to deal with the land issues. In their desire to work with the BIA, Joseph Montoya of San Juan and Benjamin Naranjo of Santa Clara advised the All-Pueblo Council that they should not retain lawyers to represent them before the board. "We are wards of the government," Naranjo told the delegates that July, and "it is up to us to look up to the government instead of fighting the government." The council disagreed, voting to accept the AIDA's offer to hire independent counsel on its behalf. But the self-presentation of the progressives as the educated vanguard of their people almost certainly damaged the All-Pueblo Council's credibility in the eyes of BIA and Lands Board officials.[61]

The All-Pueblo Council's evolving statements on religion not only were directed at the BIA and the larger U.S. public but served as a direct repudiation of the progressive movement. Although called to address the crisis at Taos, the council's May 5 meeting took place just a few days after the first progressive council meeting, and its "Declaration to all Indians and to the People of the United States" concluded with a clear appeal to the newly visible dissidents: "Most of all, we say to all the Pueblos whom we represent. . . . This is the time of the great question. Shall we peacefully but strongly and deathlessly hold to the religion of our fathers, to our own religion, which binds us together and makes us the brothers and children of God? There is no future for the Race of the Indians if its religion is killed."[62] Where at least a few progressives advocated abandoning this "pagan" religion in the name of Christianity and progress, traditionalists insisted that its preservation was the most important condition for the future of their tribes.

Pueblo leaders also began to employ the language of religion as a way to argue against the presence of Protestant missions. According to Superintendent Chester Faris, the governor of Jemez Pueblo advised his people to stay away from the Presbyterian mission because "he had always hoped that his people would not be divided in religion." "We have our Indian religion," the governor explained, "and most of us are Catholics and that would seem enough." Where many Pueblo Indians had previously rejected Protestantism on the grounds that they were already Catholics, now this Jemez leader openly distinguished between Catholic and Indian religions. But because BIA officials considered religious affiliation an individual rather than tribal choice, the governor's claim that these two religions justified the exclusion of Protestant missionaries would not hold.[63]

Neither the All-Pueblo Council nor individual tribal leaders consistently employed the new terminology. That July, the All-Pueblo Council's first direct reply to the progressives' resolutions would apply the more traditional Pueblo usage of "religion" for Catholicism and "custom" for indigenous tradition. "The caciques don't harm you," wrote a committee of council leaders. "How many times have you been punished or prosecuted because you didn't want to take part in any dance?" Challenging their opponents' rejection of Indian "paganism," these leaders accused the "progressives" of straying from their common Christian faith: "If you are Christians as you claim, and progressive as you claim you wouldn't say those falsehood[s] of your own people. Our Catholic religion forbids us to tell falsehood against our neighbor. . . . You are not forced to believe in the customs if you don't want."[64] In a later and more polished statement, the Pueblos' predominantly Catholic identity became the primary basis for rejecting the allegations of religious persecution. "As you know, we are all Christians," the council wrote to Superintendent Crandall, "those few men who proclaim themselves Christian Progressives are no more Christian nor different Christian than we. . . . We protest against a great fraud which is being put over on the public, when these men sign a statement prepared by White men that they are Christian Indians being persecuted by us heathen or pagan Indians." Here, as they had done for many years, the council defended Pueblo interests by emphasizing their Catholic identity rather than a distinct indigenous religion.[65]

Starting in the spring and summer of 1924, the Indian Rights Association offered enthusiastic support to the progressive movement in the Pueblos. This was not an entirely new direction for the IRA. Its *Thirty-ninth Annual Report* (1921) had claimed that the Pueblo Indians were "dominated by the old-time pagan element that usually aimed to suppress all progress along modern lines"—information that Sniffen privately credited to Leo Crane, then superintendent for the Southern Pueblos.[66] But the association had not taken any particular action on the issue at the time, and the following year Welsh largely ignored a charge from Clara True that the Pueblo young people were being forced into "compulsory service to the old gods of the tribe and participation in ceremonials which are not printable."[67] Now things were different. With modernist reformers and the All-Pueblo Council apparently winning the battle for public sympathy, the Hunt and Melchor stories appeared as an ideal way to reframe the controversy. "The artist-writer-scientist combination are howling about 'religious liberty' for the Pueblos," wrote Sniffen, "and the incidents reported by Miss Bryan would seem to be their idea of 'liberty!' "[68] Sniffen and Welsh were soon circulating Bibo's condemnations of the "old-time fanatic clique" in the Pueblos and devoted regular attention to the issue each month in the *Indian Truth*. Through the Pueblo progressives, they hoped once and for all to establish the basic fairness and all-American values of the assimilationist cause.[69]

These new religious freedom allegations presented quite a puzzle for BIA officials, most of whom wanted to "civilize" the Indians without stirring up too much controversy. A few, like Inspector Otero-Warren and attorney Ralph Twitchell, actively supported the progressive cause as the only effective way to fulfill the government's "civilizing" goals.[70] Others found this approach overly controversial and, in their work with Indians, actually counterproductive. Faced with the practical problems of administering day-to-day Pueblo affairs, Superintendent Crandall recognized the tribal officers' need for meaningful authority. He instructed Joseph Melchor "to do any community work that may be ordered by the officials" whether or not he directly benefited or "whether your land is one side of the river or the other," and insisted that the tribal governor had "a perfect right to take your land or your father's land" if he refused "to comply with the general orders invoked and practiced in the pueblo."[71] Although Crandall shared the IRA's worry that "the returned student who tries to make progress is handicapped and held down by the old ancient customs," and promised to support any Indian under such circumstances, he was certain that this sort of coercion had not happened under his charge. Instead of blaming modernists for the conflicts at Santa Ana and Cochiti, Crandall accused True and Otero-Warren of undermining his authority and that of the Pueblo leaders by encouraging the progressives to continue their protests.[72] Commissioner Burke was inclined to agree. Throwing reluctant support to the tribal governors in the name of democratic principle, Burke had advised the progressives of Santa Clara Pueblo "to bide their time, and in the near future they would probably have a majority of the votes, and then could turn the tables upon the ignorant members of the Pueblo who are now in control." Both Burke and Crandall insisted that as long as the "old faction" had the majority and was not breaking any laws, the progressives needed to respect its governing authority.[73]

Frustrated by the government's apparent unwillingness to enforce the dance circular or to support the Pueblo progressives, the IRA turned from praising Burke to condemning what it saw as his capitulation to the nation's "archaeological, artistic, and literary interests."[74] Welsh appealed to influential contacts such as Senator Wharton Pepper of Pennsylvania, a fellow Episcopalian from Philadelphia, and Senate Majority Leader Henry Cabot Lodge of Massachusetts. He hoped they would intervene with the Interior Department, or even with President Calvin Coolidge, to "strengthen Commissioner Burke and Secretary Work in their original idea that progress and morality should be maintained in these Indian pueblos, and not the reverse."[75] When Sniffen learned of Burke and Work's plans to visit New Mexico that April—the occasion of their confrontation with the Taos tribal council—he sent the secretary copies of Bryan's letters demanding "vigorous action on the part of the authorities to uphold the constitutional rights of individual Indians to religious liberty."[76] Brosius mined past BIA annual reports for evidence that the "progressive element" among the Pueblos was being suppressed and argued by appealing to precedent that the government had the power "to dominate the affairs of the Pueblos" and should exercise it "without further hesitation or delay in protecting the Pueblos who aspire to better living." If the Department of the Interior refuses to do this, he wrote, then "Congress should be appealed to for authority to so act."[77]

The turning point in these arguments was the IRA's insistence that religious freedom must apply first of all to the individual Indian rather than to the tribe as a whole. The "white pagans" who called for religious liberty for the Indians were erroneously applying religious liberty "to the group" rather than to "the individual," Sniffen wrote, and so "intolerantly and arrogantly interfering with the right of the individual to worship God according to the dictates of his own conscience."[78] As we have already seen, such arguments implied a basic conception of "religion" itself as a matter of internal subjectivity and individual conscience, an understanding of religion that originated in Enlightenment philosophy and has long been dominant in American culture.[79] These Enlightenment ideals motivated the provision in the First Amendment to the U.S. Constitution that "Congress shall make no law respecting an establishment of religion, or prohibiting the free exercise thereof," and so set the tone for the nation's legislative and interpretive traditions. It was therefore quite easy for Sniffen to find precedent to oppose what he called the "group" theory of religious liberty. He pointed to the New Mexico state constitution's guarantee of "perfect toleration of religious sentiment" to every "inhabitant" of the state as proof that religious freedom was legally intended to apply to individuals and not to "an entire community." The latter interpretation, he wrote, "would mean liberty for a ruling minority to tyrannize a majority, in which the right of the individual is ignored."[80] Sniffen also cited an 1890 Supreme Court decision, *Crowley v. Christensen*, on the restrictions of liberty as "freedom of restraint under conditions essential to the equal enjoyment of the same rights by others."[81] Cultural norms, legal precedent, and constitutional mandate all supported the idea that religious freedom applied to individual persons rather than to a community as a whole.[82]

This argument for individual religious freedom would prove compelling even to modernists. All reformers, no matter how skeptical they were of the IRA's agenda, conceded the basic argument that individual Indians must not be forced into ceremonial participation. "I did not hear of the case that you mentioned in your letter," Eastern Association Secretary Amelia White replied to one of Welsh's missives—continuing that of course "religious intolerance is always to be deplored, whether Christian or pagan."[83] Collier would not concede the point quite so easily. When Sniffen asked after the May All-Pueblo Council meeting whether he "thought Indians should be compelled to participate in the old-time ceremonies against their will," Collier replied only that this "would be a hard question to answer."[84] A complete answer, he explained in a later exchange with Welsh, would require stepping back from the immediate situation to denounce a situation in which "missionary work" and "the aggression of the Indian Bureau" had caused some Indian children to become "rebellious against the instructions and disciplines." Collier argued that because virtually all the Pueblo Indians were Christians, the idea that this was a case of "pagans" persecuting "Christians" was ludicrous. Following the All-Pueblo Council's lead, he insisted that the Hunt and Melchor cases were disputes about the allocation of ditch work and had nothing to do with religious freedom. The "broadly social view" that all tribal members should share in work that benefited the community as a whole had clashed with the "narrowly individualistic and unphilosophical and anti-social view," adopted by the "so-called Christian Progressives," in which those who did not personally "water their fields" from a particular ditch no longer needed to contribute to its maintenance. But in the end he too agreed that the individual as well as the tribe "should be free to choose their own way of worshipping" and that "the use even of parental authority in religious matters" was unacceptable and in any case counterproductive for "the religious life of the child." With the ceremonies defined in terms of religion, even Collier could not deny that an individual Indian should have the right to refuse participation in them.[85]

Excited by this new focus for the IRA's crusade, Sniffen naturally turned for financial and political support to the Protestant missionary establishment that remained the association's most important constituency: "This Hunt matter ought to stir up the Home Missions Council and all Protestant Church organizations"—essentially all "Church people" who believe in "real religious liberty." Sniffen hoped that these groups still carried enough political weight to influence BIA policy. "It may be that the Indian Office fears to take any action . . . because of the artist-writer combination, but if the Home Missions Council should begin to make a fuss concerning 'religious liberty,' it will put the Bureau between the devil and the deep sea."[86] When he decided that April to visit New Mexico to personally investigate the situation, he appealed to the mission boards and their supporters to fund the trip. As he told his good friend Edith Dabb, the situation involved "religious liberty for the young people as well as the pagan and revolting dances." The progressives' demand for religious liberty, in other words, served as a new vehicle for the assimilationist condemnation of "pagan" tradition. Despite the IRA's insistence that it supported religious freedom for both "pagans" and "Christians," this campaign was in large part an effort to defend the status of Christian missions in Indian affairs.[87]

Sniffen began his trip to New Mexico in May 1924 by meeting with allies in Santa Fe who reinforced his optimism about the progressives' future. Although he expected Crandall to "[favor] the old pagan reactionaries," in person he found that the superintendent was willing "to protect the young and progressive members of the Pueblos." He secured a copy of John Dixon's testimony from A. B. Renehan, and Ralph Twitchell showed him the transcript of the BIA's investigations into the Hunt and Melchor cases.[88] Twitchell had immediately defined the issue as one of "paganism" against Christianity and progress. "If these Indians are successful in driving this man [Hunt] out of the Pueblo," he wrote to Burke, "simply because he refuses to accept the pagan teachings of the caciques and play the hypocrite, as [the Indians] do in worshipping the Christian God in the church and the pagan monstrosities in the kiva, then every effort directed by the government to the education of these benighted pagans is wasted and thrown away." Convinced that Hunt's case would "appeal with great force to all fair-minded American citizens," he advised as much publicity as possible. Twitchell blamed the problem on the "propaganda" being spread by certain "altruistic individuals" who were "almost without exception . . . Bolshevik in their thoughts and code of morals," and exerted "insidious influences . . . making for the ultimate destruction of the Indian rather than for his future benefit. The lives of some of these people (Mrs. Mabel Dodge-Sterne-Lujan, for example) are a living force in the destruction of all that we care to see embodied in the make-up of an upright American citizen." In his view those calling for the preservation of the Pueblo ceremonies were themselves immoral, un-American, and un-Christian (which amounted to much the same thing), and so it was easy for him to believe that they were encouraging the "immorality" and "paganism" he saw in the Indian dances.[89]

Despite his initial skepticism about the dance circular, Father Fridolin Schuster at Laguna Pueblo emerged around this time as an important ally in the IRA's efforts. This was by no means inevitable. Alongside his suspicions of the Protestant-oriented IRA and his initial skepticism about Burke's dance circular, he and other Catholic clergy had long considered Clara True an anti-Catholic troublemaker. Schuster had initially mistrusted Otero-Warren as well, but by early 1924 he had come to respect her as an honest and "conscientious inspector" who had "won the universal confidence of the Indians."[90] With her encouragement, Schuster attended the progressive council meeting that May and then toured the Pueblos with Otero-Warren, True, and Sniffen. He saw the cause primarily in terms of strengthening Catholicism in the Pueblos. This movement was one "for which we missionaries have long hoped and prayed," he wrote. "It is [the Indians'] endeavor to worship the Christian God in the Christian way (which in this case means the Catholic Faith)."[91] Father John Woods of the Bureau of Catholic Indian Missions, in New Mexico for several months recuperating from an illness, echoed Schuster's sentiments. "The progressive group is entirely Catholic," he wrote to his superiors in Washington, "and they allege that after having received a Christian education, they hardly think it proper that their children should return home from Convent schools and government schools and be compelled to participate in . . . these wild orgies of Indian dances." Despite their long-standing enmity, the cause of the Pueblo progressives had brought Protestants and Catholics together—in New Mexico as well as in Washington—in a common attack on Indian "paganism."[92]

The IRA's most important resource in New Mexico was undoubtedly Clara True, who did more than anyone else to shape the association's advocacy on behalf of the Pueblo progressives. Sniffen had full confidence in True as the ideal advocate for the cause, and when he learned that the Rockefeller Foundation had awarded the IRA $5,000 in "seed money" to hire a new financial secretary he unhesitatingly recommended her to the board. Although the understanding was that she would eventually make her "permanent headquarters" in Philadelphia for fundraising purposes, Sniffen told her that "for the time being" she could set her own agenda and "may be able to do a good deal from Santa Fe."[93] Her first priority was to present the progressives' case—in terms of women's rights as well as religious freedom—at the biennial convention of the General Federation of Women's Clubs in Los Angeles that June. For that purpose, she called a second meeting of the Progressive Pueblo Council, held on May 27 specifically to authorize delegates to go to California. She told the delegates that this convention was critical because the federation represented "practically a majority of the voters of the U.S." and so wielded enormous political power especially in an election year. Unless the progressives took action immediately, she warned, the convention would follow Stella Atwood's recommendation to "endorse the resolutions of the Santo Domingo meeting." Ultimately, True feared that the Interior Department would bow to political pressure and implement the

All-Pueblo Council's resolutions, which she believed would "stop all progress" and "put the Pueblo Indian affairs three hundred years back." To
represent them in Los Angeles the council selected Joseph Montoya from
San Juan; Juan Pedro Melchor, John Dixon, and Francisco Chavez from
Cochiti; and three representatives from Santa Clara.[94]

The General Federation's convention in June 1924 became a showdown
event between competing reformers in the dance controversy. There, five
thousand clubwomen from around the country had the opportunity to judge
the competing appeals for religious freedom. Atwood worked to ensure their
continued support by circulating the All-Pueblo Council resolutions, secured sympathetic coverage from the *Los Angeles Times*, and highlighted the
Pueblos' cause during her address to the convention. Collier, still serving as
Atwood's research agent, arranged for a delegation from the All-Pueblo
Council to appear at the convention and gave a presentation arguing that the
government's misguided effort to "civilize" the Indians had become an outright attack on Indian religion. "The Pueblos have been ordered arbitrarily
to discontinue their ancient customs and forms of worship," he told the
clubwomen, "and the demoralizing effect has been such as in time will cause
the complete disintegration of the tribe unless the rulings of the Indian
Bureau are withdrawn."[95] Collier also enlisted Charles Lummis, who was
quite popular among the California women's clubs as a speaker on Indian
topics, to help with publicity for the event. In a widely circulated pamphlet,
Lummis interpreted the Pueblo ceremonies as the central acts of a religion
that actually exceeded Christianity in beauty, antiquity, and ethical value. All
Pueblo dances were "reverent, decent and devout," and represented "a noble
and beautiful Faith," he wrote, "a Faith which was old when the Man of
Nazareth walked the earth, a Faith of such high and reverent ideals that no
Galahad of ours could falter at following." Warning the clubwomen that the
commissioner had called for "a careful propaganda . . . to educate public
opinion against the Indian dance," Lummis called the delegation of Pueblo
progressives "renegade Indian hirelings of the Bureau . . . the entering
wedge of a campaign to destroy the whole Pueblo system and drag from
under the feet of the Indians the last acre of their lands." The women of the
nation must "throw your mighty influence to save the Indians from this
agony and outrage from a blind political bureaucracy." Although the federation failed to endorse the All-Pueblo Council resolutions, at the time Collier
remained optimistic that it would do so.[96]

To counter the publicity from Atwood and Collier, True and Otero-Warren planned a presentation that clearly articulated the issue as one of Christianity against paganism. Because Atwood controlled the time allotted to Indian affairs, it was no easy matter for them to be granted a hearing on the convention floor. But together they managed to enlist an impressive coalition of women's club leaders, and with the help of the Bureau of Catholic Indian Missions they gained support from Catholic leaders in Los Angeles as well. When the request came from the head of the Catholic women's clubs in California, General Federation president Mrs. Thomas G. (Alice Ames) Winter—who apparently wanted to avoid the appearance of anti-Catholicism—finally agreed to allow the progressives ten minutes immediately after Atwood's presentation.[97] Mrs. Walter McNabb (Helen Guthrie) Miller, Atwood's immediate superior in the federation, sympathized with the progressive cause and agreed to introduce Otero-Warren to the convention. After a brief address "pleading for the upholding of the Christian religion," Otero-Warren gave the floor to the Los Angeles attorney Ida May Adams, a member of the Indian Welfare League of California who had coauthored the Indian Citizenship Act. In the name of Indian rights, she appealed to the "Christian women of America" for the progressive Indians who were being persecuted "because they worshipped the Christian God." The progressive delegation did not speak but stood at Adams's introduction and "received vigorous applause." Convinced that they had carried the day, True and Otero-Warren framed a resolution "that all Christian Indians should be protected." The statement finally adopted by the Resolutions Committee was a compromise that called for "a reorganization of the Indian Bureau so that ALL Indians may receive justice." Certain that such an investigation would validate her point of view, True claimed this as a clear victory for the progressive cause.[98]

The IRA was convinced that the Pueblos' future depended on eliminating Collier's influence in the federation, and this task remained incomplete. "The Pueblo question has been made a storm center by John Collier," wrote Sniffen, "and because he claims to have the backing of the Federation of Women's Clubs, the Indian Bureau is afraid of him, and is unwilling to take a firm, common sense stand in defense of its own recognized policy."[99] Toward this end, the association joined forces with the New Mexico Federation of Women's Clubs, whose president Grace Baer was a close friend of Otero-Warren's; and with the New Mexico Association on Indian Affairs, which agreed with many of Collier's views but thought his tactics counterproductive.[100] This coalition tried to convince the federation's executive committee, scheduled to meet that September, to remove Atwood from her position as chair of the Indian Welfare Committee. True drafted a letter warning against "a propaganda as ruinous to the Pueblo Indians as it is unjust to the government of the United States," which Baer forwarded to the executive committee along with a copy of Pussyfoot Johnson's article on the Pueblo dances.[101] Meanwhile, members of the New Mexico Association spread rumors that Collier was "a violent red" and a "propagandist" who received a huge salary and expense account. For the time being, Collier and others successfully refuted these allegations, and Atwood retained her position.[102] Their opponents, however, soon gained enough influence to place limits on Atwood's activities, and the new president of the federation informed her that the position of "research agent" was no longer necessary—effectively ending Collier's affiliation with the organization. A few years later, Atwood herself was forced to resign. By the late 1920s, the federation had moved away from the political radicalism it briefly embraced early in the decade, and in Indian affairs it would focus on the less controversial movement to support Indian arts and crafts.[103]

The cause of the Pueblo progressives had temporarily renewed the assimilationist crusade, and for most of the next year the IRA maintained a steady beat of publicity portraying indigenous traditions as part of a degrading and immoral "paganism" that must ultimately be replaced with Christianity. This discourse undergirded self-consciously colonialist policies of suppression. Leo Crane, whose popular essays and books on his experiences as a superintendent attracted the IRA's praise, concluded an account of Hopi resistance to compulsory education and land allotment by commenting that "Priestcraft and sorcery, superstition and cruelty, differ very little among primitive peoples."[104] In another passage Crane characterized the Pueblos in general as "benighted and evil . . . savages very like those who beat the awesome drums in [Joseph] Conrad's *Heart of Darkness*."[105] Conrad's novel, a classic in the modernist canon, has generally been read as a critique of European assumptions of superiority and the violence intrinsic to imperialism. Yet, as the Nigerian writer Chinua Achebe has pointed out, Conrad depicted Africans as the repressed irrational Other, and Africa as the "heart of darkness" where Europeans risk losing civilization's tenuous hold and regressing to the violent savage within. Crane's reference suggests that Achebe has accurately gauged the popular impact of Conrad's primitivism. In the context of the dance controversy, the *Heart of Darkness* intensified the image of the Pueblo traditions and all "paganism" as savage and cruel.[106]

Against Collier's claim that British colonial authorities were tolerant of indigenous traditions, assimilationists insisted that the relevant comparison was to practices the British had actually outlawed. India was a favorite point of reference. Edith Dabb likened the fate of young girls in Pueblo ceremonial life to suttee and child marriage in India, noting that British administrators did "not feel compelled" to permit such practices "because of their antiquity and picturesqueness."[107] Because Pueblo progressives complained of a traditionalist monopoly of power in the Pueblos, assimilationists also condemned the Pueblos' "theocratic" system of tribal governance—a reference to the appointment of tribal governors by caciques who supposedly enforced participation in "paganism" and forbade any "progress." The cultural critic and essayist Harvey Watts, a good friend of Herbert Welsh's, wrote in this vein that the British had outlawed "immoral" practices, including "vice, crime, infanticide . . . and especially self-immolation which have figured as allowable under the vile and hideous theogony of India."[108] As postcolonial theorists have amply demonstrated, such depictions of (East) Indian traditions themselves need to be understood as distorted products of British colonial discourse.[109] But for the IRA and like-minded assimilationists, these comparisons reinforced the construct of a worldwide "paganism," believed to be intrinsically degrading and oppressive. In both cases, these were self-serving fantasies, allowing reformers to believe themselves benevolent while they justified the destruction of indigenous practices in the name of progress.

Assimilationists drew on scholarship in comparative religions to strengthen their attacks on the Pueblo ceremonies. One example was the sensationalized claim that the Pueblo ceremonies involved "phallic religion." Pussyfoot Johnson's infamous article, written that summer in response to the crisis at Taos, claimed that the "secret" Pueblo dances were "the survival of an ancient Phallic worship, much more degrading than the Phallic worship of the Ancient Greeks and Hindus."[110] Such critiques were aimed as much at the modernist reformers as at the Indians themselves. Leo Crane, ridiculing the "sensationalists" who were defending "religious liberty among the dangerous barbarians," opined that "the views of priests and ministers, the affidavits of eye-witnesses, the testimony of Indians who had emerged from the twilight zone and had accepted both education and Christianity, all availed nothing against those who would demonstrate that a Pueblo cacique, having a phallic doctrine to uphold, was being denied his 'religious right' to enslave and debase the helpless of his community." In a single sentence, Crane managed to portray modernists as misguided fools and the Pueblos as dangerous theocratic pagans, whereas those who condemned the dances appeared as honest and upstanding Christians who possessed the only legitimate moral and cultural authority.[111]

The trope of phallic religion was far more ambivalent than such slanders could admit. It had originated among eighteenth- and nineteenth-century antiquarians and scholars who theorized that sexuality, especially in the form of phallic symbolism, was central to many of the world's religions. One of the first of these was Richard Payne Knight, whose 1780 Discourse on the Worship of Priapus set out to demonstrate "the similitude of the Popish and Pagan religion," and their common obscenity in contrast to an enlightened Protestantism. But by the turn of the century, occultists, theosophists, and others seeking alternatives to Christianity celebrated phallic worship as one of the primal sources of religion.[112] Writing in defense of the Pueblo ceremonies, a romantic primitivist like Mary Austin could characterize the Indians' "phallic rites" as "life-increasing ceremonies" for "a society where procreation is still associated with worship."[113] The more scientifically minded Elsie Clews Parsons, who held that some Zuni ceremonies were undoubtedly of a "phallic character," had long since rejected the idea that this made them immoral on the grounds that the Zuni version of "phallicism" required "ceremonial continence."[114] For assimilationists, though, the very concept of "phallic worship" placed the Pueblo traditions within a worldwide category of "paganism" that deserved only eradication.

Assimilationists used biblical references to ancient "pagans" to solidify their condemnation of Pueblo traditions. The allegation that the Pueblos practiced sodomy gained traction because it seemed to link the Pueblos with the biblical condemnation of Sodom and Gomorrah. Pussyfoot Johnson publicized this charge when he described the religious initiation of Taos as "a two years course in sodomy under pagan instructors." He offered no evidence to support this claim, and the only reference to "sodomy" in the "secret dance file" applied not to Taos but to Jemez and came from an obviously prejudiced source.[115] Nevertheless, Welsh quickly picked up on this idea and extrapolated a connection to the "pagans" and "idolaters" of the Bible. Because "the religion of the New Mexican Pueblos . . . goes back to unlimited spaces of time in human history, it is quite natural that it should resemble this ancient religion practiced by the people of Sodom and Gomorrah."[116] Welsh thought this charge so important that when the *New York Times* omitted it from his published letter to the editor, he complained that his "principal point" had been omitted.[117] Assuming that the Bible accurately described the rites of "pagans" in all times and places, he proceeded to draw on biblical scholarship to elucidate the Indians' offenses. William Smith's *Dictionary of the Bible*, a popular reference guide for Protestant ministers and Sunday School teachers, claimed that the Sodomites had practiced "abominable and unnatural" rites identical to the "nature worship of Ashtoreth, or the Greek Astarte." Welsh applied these charges to the Pueblos, adding that these "vices" involved "carnal communication between members of the human species and animals."[118] He also cited lectures by biblical scholar Rev. Dr. Stuart L. Tyson to claim that the "nature worship of the Goddess Astarte and Ashtoreth" involved rites in which "young women . . . submitted themselves to the basest treatment from the vast number of nature worshippers, merchants and business-men from all over the Roman Empire."[119] In Welsh's mind, the conveniently amorphous sins of Sodom offered further insight into the Pueblos' transgressions.[120]

Convinced that the Pueblos were caught in a self-defeating cycle of paganism that punished dissenters, assimilationists argued that the government must intervene at least enough to enable the progressive Indians to practice the education they had been given in the government schools. And if the Pueblo leaders were the "pagan" idolaters of the ancient world, then it only made sense to identify the progressives with the heroes of the biblical narrative. Clara True, characterizing the Pueblos generally as "the Sodom and Gomorrah of the modern world," pointed to the promise in Genesis 18 that God would spare even Sodom if ten righteous men could be found. "I have found ten righteous men," she wrote. "Whether I can keep them alive or not remains to be seen."[121] Sniffen appealed to a different biblical source—one even more popular in missionary condemnations of "idolatry"—when he claimed that the "progressive Christian Indians" were being persecuted because "they will not bow the knee to Baal."[122] And Welsh saw courage in the progressive Pueblos comparable to that so famously exhibited by the biblical hero Daniel, thrown to the lions because he refused to worship the Babylonian king. On the basis of vague allegations that Bibo promised to substantiate (but never did), he wrote that several Indians "had been put to death by secret strangling in a dark room because they would not bow the knee to the images which Nebuchadnezzar, the Babylonian king, had set up."[123] Using such comparisons, assimilationists hoped to mobilize enough public pressure so that the BIA would be forced to actively support the Pueblo progressives and suppress the alleged abominations of Indian "paganism."

Because they believed that Christianity was the most advanced religion in both evolutionary and ethical terms, assimilationists simply assumed that Indians given the benefit of an education would abandon "paganism" if they had the option to do so. The "tribal pagan priests," Sniffen and True wrote in a resolution they drafted for the Dutch Reformed Church, "resent the practices of any ethical religion, or one superior to their own debased nature worship."[124] In contrast, Sniffen believed, Indians who had "absorbed the fundamentals of the Christian religion" would "naturally find the old pagan ceremonies and dances—some of them of a most indecent and revolting nature—very repugnant."[125] In the end, these reformers did not consider indigenous traditions to be legitimately religious—a categorical exclusion that they assumed rather than argued. This is evident in a Presbyterian mission board's resolution in support of the commissioner's dance circular, which thanked BIA personnel for "the encouragement that they give to the efforts of all religious denominations and sects to bring religion into the thought and life of the Indians."[126] Sniffen made the same assumption when he denied that the BIA forced Christianity on the Indians. He pointed to the BIA policy of allowing Indian parents to select "religious instruction" for their children "from the local Catholic or Protestant ministers or none at all. . . . At one school," he concluded, "the Superintendent has a group classed as 'pagans' who receive no religious instruction."[127] By excluding "paganism" from what counted as religion, assimilationists made their advocacy for the Pueblo progressives appear to be the only logical position. They believed Christianity inextricably linked with progress, morality, and civilization—and, as true religion, it certainly merited protective efforts that "paganism" did not.

Assimilationists caricatured the Pueblo leaders as enemies of progress, but in reality the Indians were often quite ready to make use of new technologies. To support their claim that "paganism" prevented Indians from adopting modern agricultural methods, Sniffen and Brosius accused tribal officers at Jemez and Santo Domingo of punishing progressives for using a cultivator rather than planting their corn by hand. In fact, the Indians had very practical reasons for their prohibition against cultivators. Repudiating the IRA's logic, Southern Pueblos superintendent Chester E. Faris noted that the Jemez man who had tried to use a cultivator had no schooling outside the pueblo, while ironically the tribal officers who forbade him from doing so had attended government and missionary schools and were widely known as "progressives." Faris went on to explain that these Indians did not use the cultivator because it was incompatible with well-established methods of irrigation and impractical for the size and configuration of their fields: "The fact that by the use of the hoe they grow better corn than do their neighbors and . . . took first prize on corn at the Albuquerque fair has been their justification to all inquiry." He also pointed out that these Indians had eagerly adopted other modern technologies including "the steel breaking plow, the thresher, the mower, the dropper, the wagon, buggy, and many other implements that offer practical return." Like any other people, the Pueblos were sometimes resistant to change, but Faris—himself no fan of what he called "paganism"—reported that they quickly embraced innovations that improved their farming methods.[128]

When the Pueblos did oppose new methods, their reasons often had to do with the agenda of those who introduced them rather than any intrinsic incompatibility with indigenous tradition. In 1925 Superintendent Crandall complained to Burke that Santo Domingo refused to accept a nurse and a home economist from the Red Cross, a refusal that Crandall and others attributed to power-hungry "caciques and medicine men." But Santo Domingo's leaders made it quite clear that they objected not to health care in itself but to the broader cultural changes these workers were trying to implement. A petition from the pueblo complained that these workers "force[d] themselves into the houses of our people" and asked questions about "many things which do not concern health." The tribe had learned through bitter experience not to trust outsiders of any kind. "We don't wish to have any outsiders in the pueblo," the council wrote, "as history has taught us that that will mean the end of our pueblo life." They preferred their "own ways" to the "white man's medicine" and insisted in any case that they had "hardly any sickness in our Pueblo." At the same time they promised to take any children with trachoma or other serious illnesses "to Albuquerque to the clinic for treatment until well." Santo Domingo leaders were clearly suspicious of the "white man's medicine," but their most important objection was not to the medical treatment as such but to the presumptions of the Red Cross workers in interfering with other aspects of Pueblo life.[129]

By claiming that tribal religions prevented the Indians from accepting modern health care, assimilationists helped the government avoid responsibility for a broken system. Reformers of all varieties were concerned about the rates of diseases such as tuberculosis and trachoma among the Pueblos and lobbied the BIA to send more doctors and nurses and otherwise improve its health care services. The AIDA attributed these problems to government mismanagement, corruption, and cultural insensitivity. Collier explained that when the AIDA established an effective clinic at Taos to treat an epidemic of syphilis in 1923, it was "able to secure the active cooperation of the whole so-called archaic, governing life of the pueblo." But then the BIA took over the clinic, and after three months "closed it absolutely with no single case cured"—even as a doctor "found treating syphilis with hydrogen peroxide" remained in BIA employment.[130] Collier went on the attack, arguing that under current policies Indians were "dying at a sensational rate from neglect of medical aid; being rapidly pauperised through acts of an Indian Bureau responsible neither to the Indians nor the courts; [and] denied the elementary Constitutional rights."[131] In contrast, the IRA claimed that these health care problems were a product of the "autocratic rule" of "pagan leaders," given strength by misguided artists and scientists. "The Collier organization is committed to a continuation of the old order of things among the Pueblos," wrote Sniffen, "and so long as those Indians are flattered as to the 'superiority' of their old customs, they will resist the introduction of modern medical science, and any effort to improve their health conditions will fail." Sniffen suggested that Collier's energies would be better spent persuading the Indians "to welcome modern medical treatment instead of opposing it."[132] By blaming indigenous traditions for poverty and health problems among the Indians, assimilationist reformers obscured and excused systemic issues of poverty, colonial history, and government culpability.

The Concluding Compromise: Religious Liberty for All?

By the time the dance controversy faded, both traditionalists and progressives in the Pueblos had won guarantees of religious freedom. As Burke had promised, the Bureau of Indian Affairs announced a compromise solution to the standoff at Taos before the new school year began that August. Superintendent Crandall informed Taos's governor and tribal council that the BIA would grant their request to keep two boys out of school each year for the full period of their religious initiations, as long as they were returned to school immediately thereafter to complete their education. To compensate for the time lost they would be required to stay in school an additional year, as the Indians had initially proposed. Even though he had previously written off this idea as a "surrender to the Indian government," Crandall now concluded that it gave him new leverage on behalf of the progressive Indians. The progressive council had not focused attention on Taos, but a few weeks earlier Crandall had received a report that the Taos progressive Manuel Mondragon and his daughter had been punished because she did not participate in a recent dance. "I explained to [the Taos council] that we wanted full personal and religious liberty granted," he informed Burke, "and that we expected the same in return; that I should insist in the future that returned students spending their vacation in the pueblo should not be forced and compelled to take part in the dance or dances against their desire and wishes." Accused of violating the religious freedom of both "pagan" and Christian Indians, he and Burke saw this as a winning compromise that should satisfy the demands from both sides of the controversy. Crandall believed that the Taos decision placed him "in a better position to protect the returned student and the progressive Indian." Now that the BIA had clearly demonstrated its commitment to religious freedom, he could be more forceful in his demands that the tribal leaders do the same.[133]

Predictably, this announcement did not satisfy any of the reformers active in the controversy. Although modernists welcomed the decision at Taos, the AIDA would continue to publicize the BIA's other ongoing violations of Indian religious freedom. Collier pointed out that Commissioner Burke had quite recently distributed Pussyfoot Johnson's essay to justify his actions in the dance controversy. As long as the commissioner continued to hand out this sort of propaganda, Collier could see only hypocrisy in the promise of religious freedom at Taos.[134] Meanwhile, the IRA characterized the compromise as disastrous policy that would only encourage defiance by the "pagan" leaders at Taos and other pueblos. "This is a complete surrender on the part of the Indian Bureau," wrote Sniffen, "and Collier will not be slow to tell the Indians that they have won a great victory—or rather that he has won it for them. Naturally, it is apt to encourage them to be more defiant—even though they were told by Crandall that they must respect the rights of the Indians who did not wish to participate in the dances and ceremonials." As long as Crandall refused to act on behalf of Hunt and Melchor, Sniffen could not believe that the superintendent sincerely supported the progressive cause.[135]

For the Taos Indians themselves, Crandall's call for religious freedom forced a public redefinition of ceremonial participation as a matter of individual conscience. BIA school superintendent H. B. Peairs, who was with Crandall at the August meeting, reported that after a great deal of hesitation the Taos war chief had stepped forward to say that the tribe "would consider the right of the Indian young people to make their own decision with reference to religious and other ceremonies, and that the old Indian people would not compel the returned students to participate in any of their ceremonies if it were against the wishes of the people."[136] By defining and defending their tribal initiation in terms of religion, Taos's tribal council had found a way around a compulsory education policy that would otherwise have effectively ended these traditions. With this success came the necessity to recognize the right of individuals to refuse participation in the ceremonies. What I am suggesting is not that this right of refusal never previously existed, but that Pueblo leaders would have been unlikely to discuss the ceremonial dances in quite this way before they began using the language of religion and religious freedom. The religious freedom defense was effective as a discursive strategy for protecting Pueblo traditions from outright government suppression. Accompanying it was a degree of implicit individualism, derived from dominant American conceptions of religion, which forced traditionalist Pueblos to conceive of ritual responsibilities in newly individualistic terms.

Pueblo leaders soon began to apply the religious freedom defense not only to ceremonial dances and rites of initiation but also to other aspects of tribal life, especially in questions of sovereignty and governance. In 1925 one All-Pueblo Council petition "to the President of the U.S., the Congress, and our Friends the American People" once again protested against the BIA's efforts to restrict ceremonial dances, now linking the dance circular to new disputes over tribal governance as further proof of the government's "interference in religious liberty." The petition complained that Superintendent Crandall had arrested Taos Pueblo's entire tribal council because he disagreed with its decision to whip two young men, Joe Sandoval and Juan Gomes, who attended a religious ceremony "dressed in non-ceremonial costumes."[137] From Crandall's perspective, the Taos council had to be punished because it had violated the previous year's agreement to grant religious freedom to any individuals unwilling to participate in the ceremonies. At his request, an assistant U.S. attorney filed charges against the tribal council. With AIDA lawyers defending the Indians, a federal district judge ruled that his court had no jurisdiction in this case. Crandall believed that this decision meant the end of the BIA's attempts to balance competing claims to religious freedom. If returning students were "to be sent back to the village to be publicly whipped, humiliated, and brought down to a level with the most primitive Indians in these villages," he complained, then all the BIA's efforts at educating the Indians were pointless. Although Crandall claimed that the BIA granted religious freedom to all parties, he clearly continued to see Christianity as a far more beneficial influence than the tribal ceremonies.[138]

Taos leaders argued that Crandall was the only one who had violated the religious freedom agreement. They insisted that the tribal council had not interfered with the young men's religious freedom because nobody had been forced to attend, but if they did come, they were required to dress in proper ceremonial attire. If governors were not permitted to exercise their legal authority within the pueblo, if they were to be undercut by the superintendent at every turn, then there would be no way for them to maintain an effective tribal government, a government that was part of the religious system of the tribe. Supported by the All-Pueblo Council, Taos leaders interpreted Crandall's actions as a direct attack on Pueblo religion. They protested that the superintendent had deliberately arrested the governor and tribal council "immediately before the most sacred and mandatory of the yearly religious ceremonies of the Taos tribe" and had done so with deliberate intent "to destroy the religious constitution of the Pueblo, to humiliate and render powerless the tribal officers, and to nullify our ancient tribal self government. . . . We appeal for fair play in the treatment of our religions."[139] Because the Pueblos' systems of governance were intertwined with their religious traditions, Pueblo leaders insisted that tribal sovereignty must be protected under religious freedom guarantees. In the end, the judge ruled that jurisdiction in this case belonged to the tribe, marking a small but significant success for the Pueblos' defense of tribal sovereignty. Whether or not their religious freedom argument played a part in this victory, it illustrates the ways in which Pueblo leaders defined their religion quite expansively in order to defend tribal sovereignty.

The factional disputes at Santa Clara were quite different from the situation at Taos, but they too centered around tribal governance and ended with a religious freedom compromise. Questions of tribal governance gained center stage when, encouraged by the BIA, Santa Clara's progressives proposed at the end of 1924 that the next governor be chosen by democratic election rather than in the traditional way by the cacique. The progressives, a group essentially equivalent to the pueblo's Winter People, had previously sought simply to restore their traditional balance of power with the Summer People. Even though their appeal to Inspector Otero-Warren that spring had indicated that they no longer wanted "to follow the old customs of our ancestors," they had demanded only that at least one of the leading officers "be selected from our party."[140] But in May the progressive council had condemned the "cacique government" as "essentially despotic and arbitrary," and the progressives learned that Laguna Pueblo had already implemented a system of elections—a fact that won it considerable praise from the BIA. That December, hoping for a chance at leadership in the coming year, the Santa Clara progressives proposed that the new governor be chosen by lot. Anticipating that their traditionalist opponents would reject this idea on religious grounds, they insisted that this proposal would require "no change in any purely religious custom."[141] Crandall used their proposal as an opportunity to encourage a change in the pueblo's system of government. He wrote to the Santa Clara tribal council that its "ancient form of government" was undemocratic and therefore "contrary to the spirit and practice of the American people," and he asked each faction to field a candidate for "a general election." If the factions could not agree to this or another plan of their choosing, he warned that the BIA might simply overrule them both and appoint its own choice for the next year's governor.[142]

The tribal council members refused, justifying their position through the all-American values of democracy and religious freedom. First, it claimed that its system should be unobjectionable to advocates of democracy because it was the will of the pueblo's majority. "As the majority of our people want to select our governor according to our ancient custom, we think we are living in the American spirit." Next, as the progressives had anticipated, they

Santa Clara Pueblo Council members (left to right) Santiago Naranjo, Manuel Tafoya, Leandro Tafoya, Victoriano Cisneros. Photograph by Barbara Freire-Marreco Aitken, Courtesy Arizona State Museum, University of Arizona, Tucson.

appealed to the principle of religious freedom. "The conduct of the government of our Pueblo is a part of our religion, and we know that if we are citizens of the U.S. then we are guaranteed freedom in our religious customs and observations."[143] Eventually, they would offer to renew the older tradition of giving the caciques of the Winter and Summer People the right to name the governor in alternate years. They pointed out that this plan would actually be fairer to the progressives because they would be able to name the pueblo's governor every other year, while elections would always favor the majority party of conservatives.[144]

Thus began the most divided period in Santa Clara's history. Clara True, and through her the IRA, saw the conflict as an opportunity to unseat the pueblo's religious hierarchy by installing young progressive leaders. With her encouragement the progressives called a general election. As expected, because most tribal members refused to participate, the progressive candidate won the election.[145] Meanwhile, AIDA lawyers supported the tribal council's religious freedom defense with the opinion that the government had "no right to interfere with the religious liberty of the people of Santa Clara nor to disturb their form of government," and they offered legal help if necessary.[146] According to long-standing custom, on New Year's Day the cacique of the Summer People selected Victoriano Sisneros as the pueblo's governor. Each faction refused to recognize the other faction's governor, and so for the next three years Santa Clara Pueblo had two competing sets of tribal officials.[147]

The traditionalist leaders' demands for religious freedom directly shaped the BIA's response to this crisis. Santa Clara's division caused serious problems for the BIA as well as for the pueblo, because each of the governors was claiming the right to allocate tribal funds, irrigation rights, and shared labor responsibilities. Burke and Crandall hoped to push the Indians toward democratic elections, but they hesitated to interfere any further in part because they feared stirring up further controversy. The Pueblos would "oppose very vigorously any drastic steps taken" to change their system of government, Crandall wrote, because it was "a part of their pagan or religious organization." For that reason, he determined that, despite the IRA's advocacy for the progressives, it was best to let Santa Clara settle these conflicts on its own.[148] From Washington, Burke had already reached the same conclusion. Fearing yet another storm of protests on religious freedom grounds, the BIA simply avoided action for as long as possible.[149]

The final resolution of this crisis included a religious freedom compromise very similar to that implemented at Taos. The BIA finally decided to step in for economic reasons, because it needed a legitimate governor to negotiate terms for harvesting timber on the pueblo's land. Assistant Commissioner E. B. Meritt visited Santa Clara in December 1927 to work out a solution, and both conservative governor Juan Gutierrez and progressive governor Desiderio Naranjo promised to abide by his decisions. The new plan focused on the allocation of water and community work, historically the most serious points of conflict between the factions. Both parties agreed that Gutierrez would serve out the current year as governor for the entire pueblo, but Meritt decreed that in future years each moiety would select a candidate for a general election. Finally, in a reprise of the Taos compromise, Meritt instructed the Indians that he would guarantee their religious freedom—the BIA would not interfere with Santa Clara's ceremonial dances—as long as the tribal government did not require any unwilling person to participate in the dances. Soon after Meritt's departure the conservative party complained that Gutierrez had been forced to sign the agreement and protested once more against the idea of elections, which the pueblo would not actually implement for another decade.[150] Santa Clara's factions continued their disputes, but after Meritt's visit they did recognize a single governor once more. Despite a variety of complaints, the BIA saw the so-called Meritt Plan as an ideal compromise that they would try to impose in other pueblos as well.[151]

Santa Clara's leaders adopted a newly individualistic understanding of ceremonial participation as they struggled to defend their system of governance. In a subtle departure from traditional norms, the tribal council insisted in a letter to Meritt that their traditions already provided individual religious freedom. "Under our ancient form of government and the form of government that we are now seeking to re-establish, no male or female is required to participate directly or indirectly in the dances or religious observances; that is a matter which they must and have a right to decide by themselves."[152] As in the earlier crisis at Taos, traditionalists were framing participation in the ceremonial dances as a matter of individual conscience. Here—perhaps more than at Taos—this shift seems to have been internalized. Chester Faris, the new Northern Pueblos superintendent, wrote a few years later that Santa Clara along with most of the other pueblos was "getting more and more tolerant" in regard to ceremonial life, and that dancing was no longer "forced upon those unwilling to recognize it as community obligation."[153] Embracing the category of "religion" and employing the religious freedom defense had brought a subtle shift from the ceremonies as a community obligation to seeing them as a religious practice that individuals had the right to refuse.

These changes in Pueblo governance and ceremonial life must be understood as one step in a much longer process of cultural adaptation to outside rule. The office of governor had not always been a part of Pueblo "tradition" but was originally a Spanish imposition intended to separate religious and civil authority in the Pueblos. The Spanish wanted to strip the existing tribal leaders—whom they called by the originally Caribbean term "cacique"—of their political authority. Instead, the Pueblos had made the caciques responsible for selecting the governors, who handled all tribal business with the outside world and effectively shielded the caciques from having to engage with colonial authorities directly. As the BIA and the reformers of the 1920s recognized, the caciques had remained the ultimate authorities over all of Pueblo life. The new religious freedom controversies heightened factionalism in pueblos like Santa Clara and brought increased BIA attention to Pueblo governance. The pressure to elect Pueblo governors democratically would continue with Collier's Indian Reorganization Act of 1934, when several pueblos including Santa Clara did adopt written constitutions providing for elective governments. This system continued the process—begun when the Spanish imposed the office of governor—of separating religious leadership from a secularized government. But within most pueblos, where the caciques have maintained the power to name and endorse candidates, that separation has never been complete.[154]

By defining themselves as the defenders of Pueblo religion, using the tools of the American legal system if necessary, Pueblo leaders of the 1920s had shaped a new traditionalism based partly on American categories of religion and religious freedom. In concert with modernist reformers, Pueblo traditionalists recognized that naming their practices "religion" could provide a valuable tool for self-defense. They understood that constitutional guarantees of freedom of religion were a foundational element of American civil discourse. Successfully defining any aspect of Pueblo life as part of an authentic religion, then, could help defend it from government suppression. The Pueblos and their modernist defenders had managed to successfully label the dance ceremonies as "religion" within the public discourse, and thereby to defeat attempts by Christian assimilationists and the BIA to directly forbid them. When BIA policies threatened to further erode tribal sovereignty, Pueblo leaders responded by insisting that their traditions of governance were also religion and therefore equally defensible in terms of religious freedom. Pueblo leaders insisted on liberal democratic religious freedoms and protections as a way to protect their claims to tribal identity. Despite the individualism built into the liberal system, their survival today demonstrates that they were largely successful. Their appeal to religion should not be understood as an imposition of Western ideology but as an indigenous strategy of resistance, contributing to the ongoing adaptation of Pueblo traditions.

In historical perspective, the dance controversy represented a tenuous victory for the Indians and reformers who fought against the assimilationist policies of the Christian establishment. Although Burke's dance circular would not be repealed until some years later, the demand for Indian religious freedom had largely prevented their enforcement. The IRA and its missionary allies—both Protestant and Catholic—failed to convince the BIA, the Congress, or the general public that the Pueblo dances were "immoral" enough to merit suppression. Furthermore, the extremes of the IRA's allegations in the dance controversy damaged its reputation and influence among other reform agencies, in Congress, and with the BIA. The missionary establishment would never fully recover.

Disappointed with the dance controversy's results, the IRA gradually shifted focus to other issues in Indian affairs. Welsh and Sniffen had regained some momentum by reframing the controversy in terms of religious freedom for individual Christian Indians, but even in this arena they found the BIA unwilling to fully support the progressives in the very cases that they had championed. The association's shift in focus began in the spring of 1925, when the board determined that Clara True had not fulfilled the primary responsibilities of her position—she had insisted on returning to New Mexico rather than staying in Philadelphia to raise funds—and informed her that her services were no longer required.[155] True expressed considerable disillusionment with an organization that seemed to care more for its bottom line than for the ideals it espoused. "As long as the Progressives were a 'cause' they were interesting to the IRA," she wrote, "but the organization has to live on contributions to 'causes' and . . . no society can financially afford to hang on to the cause through the trials and tribulations of a long-drawn out struggle requiring endless persistence and patience not worth a tinker's dam to raise money upon."[156] Indeed, after several more months of advocacy failed to bring results, Pueblo concerns almost entirely dropped out of IRA publicity materials. By the end of the 1920s Welsh actually found it necessary to ask BIA personnel whether the "practices of the old heathen party" still presented a problem among the Pueblo Indians.[157]

Of course, the fight for Indian religious freedom was far from over. For a decade after the controversy, John Collier and the AIDA continued to generate publicity condemning the government's ongoing and taken-for-granted campaign against Indian religion. "Among the powers asserted by the Indian Bureau," Collier wrote, "are the censoring of the religious observance of the Indians and the arbitrary determination of the descent of Indian property. Religious observances which encourage 'wasteful generosity' are forbidden to Indians," and boarding schools designed to "[annihilate] the child's pride as an Indian" required students to submit to "compulsory Christian teaching." Through all of this, he pointed out, the Indians had no right of appeal except to the same Interior Department that operated the BIA.[158] Government agents on the ground in New Mexico and elsewhere continued to work closely with missionaries and to assume that Indians must abandon "paganism" and become Christians. In 1926 Southern Pueblos superintendent Chester Faris used this logic to bemoan Jemez Pueblo's opposition to its Presbyterian mission: "While a majority of the Jemez people are nominally Catholics, perhaps all too many are yet under the shadow of paganism to a degree that the light of Christianity has made but slight penetration." Many in the BIA continued to see Christianity as a prerequisite for civilization, and did not consider Indian traditions worthy of consideration as legitimate religions. Native American religious traditions were and still are quite different from mainstream American ideas about what counts as religion, making Indian religious freedom an elusive goal indeed.[159]

Nevertheless, after the controversy a wide array of decision makers and opinion shapers, at least in principle, accepted the legitimacy of Indian religion, and so Christian assimilationists could no longer assume public approval for policies directly attacking "paganism." In 1928 the Institute for Government Research released a report on Indian affairs that offered a devastating critique of assimilationist policy and recommended wide-ranging changes in government policy along with increased appropriations for Indian health and education.[160] Over the next few years, Collier gained increasing influence in the U.S. Congress, and both reformers and lawmakers increasingly questioned the idea of Christian missions as an integral part of government Indian policy. When Burke's successor, Commissioner of Indian Affairs Charles Rhoades, released a circular letter in 1931 asking agents to work closely with missionaries, AIDA activist Charles de Y. Elkus articulated what was becoming an increasingly prevalent critique. "I have no objection to missionary efforts, although my own reactions, intellectually and philosophically, are against them, but I do very definite protest, and believe that there are sufficient of like opinion to make themselves felt, against the Government lending its authority to missionary effort and spending tribal funds, without proper tribal authority, for such purposes. . . . Freedom of religion is not limited to the whites nor to those who are not technically wards of the Government, nor are the Indians excluded from this freedom. The churches have a right to do missionary work, but they have no right to do it as a part of a Government program."[161] Lewis Meriam, the lead author of the 1928 report, had given tentative support to Rhoades's circular but backpedaled after he read Elkus's comments: "We have, I believe, made considerable progress in the past two years in having the government undertake activities which were previously largely neglected or left largely to missionaries." More and more reformers and policy makers saw direct missionary involvement in Indian affairs as a violation of the separation of church and state and took for granted the principle that Indians had the right to practice their own religions, "pagan" or not.[162]

The limits of this new Indian religious freedom were imposed by the dominant cultural concept of "religion" as an individual and private affair. This was apparent both in the struggles of individual pueblos like Taos and Santa Clara and in the All-Pueblo Council and AIDA's fight against a series of bills intended to limit the scope of tribal authority. The Leavitt Bill, drafted by Burke and introduced early in 1926, would have applied federal civil and criminal statutes to all Indians, abolished "Indian custom" marriage and divorce, and given the BIA's "Indian Courts" authority over any crimes not covered by federal law. Pueblo leaders objected to this bill largely on religious freedom grounds, insisting on the integrated and communal quality of Pueblo religion. "Our whole tribal structure, all the ties that bind us together, will dissolve if our tribal authority is taken and we are denied to worship according to our customs," wrote Acoma Pueblo to the House Committee on Indian Affairs.[163] Vidal Sanchez of San Felipe proposed a thought experiment applying the policy to white Americans. "The ceremony which the Indians have, has been carried on before any white man ever dreamed of sailing to what is now the Great American Continent. So why should now we be obliged to abolish our ceremonies. Suppose we as Indians ask the white people to quit their religion and follow ours. What will be the result?"[164] Acknowledging that the jurisdictional questions needed to be resolved, the All-Pueblo Council recommended that the bill be drastically amended so that "where Indian tribal authority exists and Indian custom continue operative, such tribal authority and custom shall prevail in all civil and criminal matters other than felonies." For the Pueblo Indians, interference with tribal sovereignty and governance was also interference in tribal religion.[165]

The Leavitt Bill's supporters saw things very differently. The Eastern and New Mexico Associations on Indian Affairs supported this legislation because—like the IRA but without the latter's overtly Christian bias—they had come to believe that the Pueblo governments were too intertwined with tribal religious authority and needed modernization. The *Santa Fe New Mexican* argued that the ideal solution for the Pueblos would be to find "a middle ground between a vanished culture . . . and [the] alleged suppression of 'progress' among the younger element."[166] After the AIDA and the All-Pueblo Council convinced Congress not to pass the Leavitt Bill, the New Mexico Association worked with BIA lawyers on new legislation specifically designed to limit tribal authority over returned students. Echoing the IRA's earlier arguments, BIA attorney Walter Cochrane explained that members of "the younger generation" who returned from school and tried "to put into effect some of the things they have learned" were invariably "forced either to give up their new ideas or else suffer a series of petty persecutions which either eventually force them out of the Pueblo entirely or else force them to return to the ways and customs of their forefathers." Margaret McKittrick of the New Mexico Association endorsed the view of the "younger generation" that Indians should have the right "to dance or not to dance as the individual sees fit" and that tribal governors should be restrained from imposing excessive punishments for any offense.[167] In short, these reformers were convinced that tribal systems of governance had to be modernized for the sake of the educated members of the tribes. Like most Americans they defined religion as a matter of individual conscience and therefore supported educated Indians who chafed at the limitations and restrictions of traditional life.[168]

The moderate reformers of the Eastern and New Mexico Associations saw a future for Indian "religion" only in the rather confined sphere of an aestheticized and privatized ceremonial practice. While they had vehemently defended the Indians' right to practice their ceremonies, they were convinced that the Indians would need to abandon other aspects of their indigenous traditions—religious or not—in order to receive the benefits of modernity. Like assimilationists, they believed that Indian religion interfered with advances in Indian health care and would therefore need to be restricted. Instead of advocating Christian missions, they called for professional health care and social workers to "modernize" the Indians through secular methods. "To get any good out of modern medical care," wrote Roberts Walker, "you must discard the cacique and the medicine man and a whole theology of beliefs and learn strange new things about diet and ventilation and prophylaxis and bodily hygiene."[169] Walker's view of Pueblo tradition was patronizing and overly negative. Recent research affirms the therapeutic value of a wide variety of indigenous traditions whether or not they make sense according to the Western medical model, and as Collier had already suggested, many Indians have found it entirely possible to incorporate indigenous and Western healing methods. But from Walker's perspective, the Pueblos would be better off if they abandoned tribal methods of governance, agriculture, and health care—leaving only the ceremonies as that part of the tradition that fit the dominant conception of "religion."

Moderate reformers saw no inconsistency between their celebration of the Pueblo ceremonies as "religion" and their critique of Pueblo medicine and governance. Their goal of separating the Pueblo's government and health care from their religion reflected the dominant culture's ideas about the proper sphere of religion in human society. In post-Enlightenment Euro-American culture, "religion" was not only a matter of individual conscience but also was clearly distinct from the state. Alice Corbin Henderson, who had so eloquently extolled the aesthetic and spiritual beauties of the Pueblo dances, wrote that she hoped the Pueblos' "transition . . . between church and state" could be "made gradually . . . so that all the old customs will not be lost by a forced or destructive change from outside."[170] Pueblo Indians had not previously recognized any separation between spheres of "government" and "religion" and so had quite naturally moved to apply religious liberty to defend their systems of government. Cultural modernists like Collier, who had come to value the integrated and communal quality of Pueblo tradition, did the same. The new bill, the AIDA proclaimed, "would destroy the self-government of the Pueblo tribes, create lawlessness within the Pueblos and injure the cultural and religious life of the Indians."[171] But, as Henderson reveals, redefining the ceremonies as "religion" was a modernizing step, bringing along with it the dominant assumptions about the meaning and role of "religion" that created new pressures to separate the ceremonies as "religion" from other aspects of Pueblo life.

◆

SIX

Religious Freedom and the Category of Religion into the Twenty-First Century

Throughout the twentieth century and into the twenty-first, Native American efforts to achieve religious freedom have been essential to a broader fight for cultural survival. Their struggles have involved pivotal concerns such as the right to use peyote in religious ceremonies, the repatriation of human remains and sacred objects held in museums, the use and ownership of sacred lands, and the (mis)use of Indian religious practices by non-Native spiritual seekers. But these campaigns have borne only limited success, and religious freedom for Native Americans remains an elusive goal.

As in the dance controversy, dominant conceptions of religion are among the factors that impede its achievement. The category of religion, as it continues to be understood in mainstream American culture, is a product of Euro-American (and primarily Protestant) historical development and leaves little space for the integrated, communal, and land-based qualities of indigenous traditions. To make the case for religious freedom, Indians have had to represent their traditions according to prevailing concepts of what counts as religion. This appears to be a necessary and sometimes successful move within the American legal system, and it has often helped engender public sympathy for Indian claims. Yet it continues to have its drawbacks. State and federal courts and government agencies alike tend to uncritically deploy dominant concepts of religion that—despite Indian efforts to challenge and expand them—have led to judgments against Native Americans in many cases. Meanwhile, as in the dance controversy, reframing indigenous traditions as "religion" has added in subtle ways to the pressures that continue to transform indigenous cultures.

The point here is not that Indians should not use the term religion or that they are falsely applying it. The dominant Euro-American culture has defined and continues to define religion and religious freedom in ways that do not fit Indian cultures and traditions. At the same time the concept of religion—along with related terms like the "sacred"—have become part of contemporary indigenous cultures, and Indians make use of these concepts in ways that do not necessarily fit the dominant mold. All parties will benefit from understanding these definitional problems. If the term "religion" is taken to imply separation from a "secular" sphere and is understood as exclusively a matter of individual conscience, then applying it to Indian traditions can seriously misrepresent them and ultimately contribute to the pressures that continue to transform them. As I argued in the introduction, all human traditions experience complex and often ambivalent historical evolutions, and there is no point in mourning the loss of an imagined past purity of tradition. The changes that result from employing terms like "religion" and the "sacred" may be necessary to enable Indian cultures to survive at all. Understanding these dynamics offers Native Americans a greater measure of control over their own cultural development. In the final analysis, for contemporary Native Americans this language helps provide not only inner strength and motivation in efforts to revitalize indigenous traditions to meet contemporary needs but also a way to communicate something of the power and beauty of these traditions across cultural boundaries.

The contemporary fight to legitimize the religious use of peyote illustrates both the necessity for and the ambivalent consequences of religious freedom claims for Native Americans. As it spread among Plains tribes in the late nineteenth century, peyote religion demonstrated Native American adaptations to American Protestant norms. The Comanche leader Quanah Parker, healed from battle wounds through peyote administered by a Lipan Apache medicine woman, reported that Jesus Christ had told him in a vision to take this medicine to all Indians. The peyote tradition he founded stressed a distinctively Indian way of being religious but accepted Christ as a primary focus of worship. "The White Man goes into his church and talks about Jesus," he said. "The Indian goes into his tipi and talks with Jesus." Other peyote traditions were even more committed to a Christian identity, with meetings that included many features of a Protestant service such as Bible readings, hymn singing, and baptism for new members. Parker and other leaders combined elements of Christianity with the rites of those tribes that had been using peyote for centuries. In the midst of the poverty and cultural dislocation that so embittered reservation life, the new peyote religion blended Protestant themes of individual salvation and morality with a more indigenous emphasis on healing and communal well-being. In addition to its obvious Christian elements, this new pan-Indian peyote religion introduced Protestant-style evangelical fervor to indigenous contexts and spread quickly among the Plains Indians and beyond.[1]

Despite these Christian associations, peyote religion met with fierce opposition from America's Christian establishment. We have already seen that early twentieth-century missionaries and reformers like Pussyfoot Johnson considered peyote a dangerous drug and dismissed Native American claims that this was the central rite of a legitimate religion. The Native American Church incorporated as a church in 1918 largely to strengthen peyote's religious legitimacy in the eyes of the law. By furthering the movement of peyotism into a recognizable religion in Euro-American terms, this move created a stronger foundation for religious freedom claims. Anthropologists and other non-Indian supporters pointed to the Christian character of peyote religion as evidence that it was a beneficial influence on Native Americans, a legitimate religion that would help assimilate them to mainstream American life.[2] But the cultural prejudices against this move were powerful, and state and federal legislatures continued to propose and pass laws specifically targeting peyote use. In *State v. Big Sheep* (1926), the Montana Supreme Court affirmed one such law and refused to take the Indian defendant's religious freedom argument seriously. The justices rejected the Native American Church's claim to Christian identity—and the religious legitimacy of peyote in general—by reasoning that peyote was mentioned nowhere in the Bible. Evidently, the Montana court had not yet been touched by the secularizing trends in legal institutions that on a national level had already made openly Christian claims less acceptable as the basis of legislative reasoning.[3]

The complexities of the peyote controversies are apparent when we consider the historical opposition to peyote from many Native American tribal governments. Tribal opposition originated in some cases from a traditional resistance to infringement on communal tradition and in others from modernized tribal governments that adopted federal and state antidrug measures. Taos Pueblo's tribal council bitterly opposed a small peyote group in the 1920s and 1930s primarily because the council considered it inconsistent with the indigenous communal tradition. In addition, it condemned peyote as a dangerous drug that menaced social welfare, and on those grounds sought aid from the BIA and the Catholic Church in fighting the peyote group. When John Collier became commissioner of Indian Affairs in the 1930s, he reversed his predecessors' policies on the Native American Church. Collier defined peyote worship as a legitimate religion and insisted that the Taos tribal council allow religious freedom for peyote users. After the religious freedom compromise of the dance controversy, the tribe could no longer demand conformity to communal ceremonial norms and—with the peyote ceremonies defined by the commissioner as religion rather than drug abuse—eventually had to concede religious freedom to the peyote group. Despite his continued celebration of Indian communalism, Collier's policies pushed Native Americans further toward the individualized and voluntaristic conception of religion implicit in the American tradition of religious freedom.[4]

Peyote religion was perhaps the most significant of many pan-Indian religious movements that emerged as a result of colonial impositions. The Ghost Dance, given even more attention at its height in 1890, was suppressed by the government before it could become a clearly defined religion in its own right. Because such pan-Indian movements by definition traveled across tribal lines, they helped develop the notion of a generalized "Indian religion"—a significant departure from older indigenous patterns in which religious, cultural, and tribal identities were coextensive. Thus, the Native American Church readily embraced the idea of religious freedom as an individual right not only out of resistance to restrictive tribal governments like that at Taos but also because of its pan-Indian and evangelical character. Having taken on various Protestant characteristics, peyote religion found American legal guidelines on religion to be a relatively comfortable fit.

These and other pan-Indian religious movements helped shape the concept of a unified "Indian religion," representing a significant transformation in Native American traditions. In the 1970s, the American Indian Movement reached for grounding in the traditions of a variety of spiritual leaders, including the Lakota medicine man Crow Dog. By introducing ceremonies that originated in specific tribal contexts to movement events all over the country, the movement furthered the emergence of pan-Indian religious consciousness. Starting with the work of Vine Deloria Jr., contemporary Native American scholars have worked more systematically to identify and celebrate shared philosophies and values across Native American traditions.

As these scholars are certainly aware, defining qualities of Indian religion in general—thereby distinguishing it to some extent from particular cultural contexts—runs the risk of upsetting the seamless integration and holistic lifeways that they otherwise cherish as integral to tribal cultures. In other words, when Native American traditions are defined as "religion," they may necessarily develop certain similarities to dominant conceptions of religion in America.[5]

Despite its general conformity to Euro-American ideas about religion, the Native American Church's long struggle for religious freedom is far from over. The first major court decision to affirm its religious legitimacy was *People v. Woody* (1964), when the California Supreme Court identified peyote as a Native American sacrament and affirmed the right of Native Americans to use it on religious freedom grounds. Using the "compelling interest" test that the Supreme Court had established for free exercise cases, the court ruled that the Navajo defendants' First Amendment rights outweighed the state's interest in regulating the use of peyote. The cultural climate of the 1960s, a time of increased public interest in Native American traditions and of countercultural experiments with mind-altering drugs and "alternative" spiritualities, no doubt helped determine the outcome of the *Woody* case. But the decision governed only California, and in many other areas the "war against drugs" of the 1980s would bring increased penalties for peyote use along with other controlled substances. Some federal and state agencies created religious exemptions for Native American Church members, but these rights varied by agency and locale.[6]

The issue finally came before the U.S. Supreme Court in *Employment Division, Department of Human Resources of Oregon v. Smith* (1990), seen by many legal scholars as the most important religious freedom case in twentieth-century America. Codefendants Alfred Smith and Galen Black, Klamath Indians working at a drug counseling center, were fired and then denied unemployment benefits because they had used peyote in a Native American Church service. The Supreme Court formally accepted the religious legitimacy of peyote but ruled that the state was not obliged to create special exceptions to facilitate this or any other religious practice. As long as a law was universally applicable and not directed specifically against religious practice, it could not be held to violate the constitutional guarantee of free exercise. The decision reversed a half century of free exercise jurisprudence that, as in the *Woody* case, required the state to demonstrate a compelling interest for any law that even indirectly interfered with a practice judged central to a religious tradition. It also confirmed what many Indians had feared—that the American Indian Religious Freedom Act (AIRFA), passed by the U.S. Congress in 1978 in an effort to give Indians the full measure of religious liberty, was not robust enough to provide full legal protection. It is telling that the court announced this philosophical reversal in a case that dealt with a Native American tradition whose religious legitimacy had been suspect, despite its many "Protestant" traits, for so much of its history.[7]

Many religious organizations saw the *Smith* decision as a threat to religious liberty for all Americans and joined with Native American activists to seek legislative redress. The Religious Freedom Restoration Act (RFRA) of 1994 attempted to reinstate the compelling interest test by requiring state and federal agencies to honor religious freedom unless they had no other way to accomplish a vital state interest. Three years later the Supreme Court ruled portions of RFRA unconstitutional, insisting that Congress did not have the authority to impose this policy on the states. Since then, religious freedom advocates have succeeded in passing mini-RFRAS at the state level in a growing number of states, and the U.S. Congress passed a more limited law protecting the religious rights of prison inmates and also ensuring that religious groups would not be restricted in their use of land. This battle between Congress and the Court over the limits of religious freedom has extended beyond Native American issues, and in the meantime the Native American Church has actually gained some ground. In 1996, the American Indian Religious Freedom Act Amendments included a mandate that the government grant religious exemptions for Native American Church members to use peyote, and most federal and state agencies today do recognize this exemption. Peyote has been at least partially assimilated into dominant understanding of religion. Journalists and judges have affirmed the analogy, first made by Native American Church members and their supporters, of peyote ceremonies to the Christian use of wine as a sacrament. Despite the Smith decision and many other barriers along the way, its use by Native American Church members is now generally accepted—although not guaranteed by the courts—on religious freedom grounds.[8]

In the early years of the twenty-first century, neither peyote ceremonies nor Indian dances are directly threatened by the kind of alliance between missionaries and government that existed at the time of the Pueblo dance controversy. While most evangelical Protestants still consider Indian ceremonies to be incompatible with Christianity, the secularization of Indian affairs ensured that they could no longer shape federal Indian policy. Some Indian Protestants today shun tribal ceremonies, but others have found creative ways to blend indigenous and Christian traditions. In some Native communities, conversion to Christianity (whether Protestant or Catholic) provided a means for preserving aspects of indigenous tradition and culture in very difficult circumstances.[9] For the past half century, the Catholic Church has largely welcomed indigenous dancing as a legitimate part of Native American Catholicism. Robert Sanchez, archbishop of Santa Fe from 1974 to 1993, worked to strengthen Pueblo Catholicism by insisting— in keeping with the eighteenth-century Franciscan accommodation with Pueblo practice—that local priests accept indigenous dances as a legitimate part of Catholic worship. For most Pueblo Catholics, as Martin Vigil explained in the 1920s, the traditional dances are simply an indigenous form of prayer. In 1989 Sanchez inaugurated an annual Native American Liturgy at Santa Fe's Saint Francis Cathedral, an event that includes Pueblo ceremonial dancing. His successor, Michael Sheehan, has followed Sanchez's lead in affirming Indian traditions. Their approach is consistent with the Second Vatican Council's expression of openness to the interpretation and practice of Catholicism in culturally relevant ways around the world.[10]

In the meantime, many Native American communities are struggling to revitalize indigenous languages, cultures, and religious traditions. Indian communities are plagued with poverty, alcoholism, violence, and other problems that were caused or exacerbated by the U.S. government's long campaign to destroy Indian ways of life and are perpetuated by continued economic and cultural discrimination. Tribal leaders do not always agree about how to solve these problems, but many have concluded that the best way to save their communities is to reinforce cultural pride. Many tribes have initiated educational programs and even special summer camps to teach indigenous languages and traditions to the children. By the end of the twentieth century, Native Americans had gained control of the remaining historic "Indian schools," including one in Santa Fe with a predominantly Pueblo student body, where children had once been forcibly confined and taught that indigenous ways of life were inferior. Children at these schools are now encouraged to respect and practice Indian traditions including

ceremonial dancing.[11] The rise of the intertribal pow-wow movement, although far removed from the religious context of tribal ceremonies, has also
helped many Indian tribes increase the pride in and practice of traditional
dances among their young people.[12] The Red Power movement and the
broader increase in Native American political activism, with grounding
and inspiration from indigenous religious traditions, has had much the
same effect.[13]

Although the Pueblo Indians never experienced the geographic dislocation or the level of cultural persecution and devastation suffered by many
tribes, such pan-Indian movements have also supported the continued flour-
ishing of Pueblo religious ceremonies. For more than a century, New Mexico's tourist industry has marketed Indian dances as one of the state's most
distinctive charms, and any recent list of tourist attractions includes the
dates of the Pueblos' most popular public dance ceremonies. The Pueblos
have not always welcomed this publicity and the resulting crowds at some of
their religious events, but they have for the most part successfully managed
the tourists who flock to their ceremonies and have sometimes found ways
to share in the profits. In addition, the Pueblos have often benefited from
the "Indian ceremonials," intertribal events that display a variety of Native
American dances for the tourist market. Today most such ceremonials are
managed by Indians. Although their intertribal and commercial character
distinguish them from village ceremonies, the dances maintain a degree of
religious significance for the majority of Indian people who perform and
witness them.[14]

Ironically, perhaps the most direct threats to Native ceremonies today
result from overly enthusiastic admirers of all things Indian. Native American activists have presented a strong critique of New Agers and other similar
groups, such as the Smoki in Prescott, Arizona, in the 1930s, who appropriate indigenous religious practices for their own purposes. According to these
critics, it seriously violates the ceremonies to practice them out of their
tribal context, without the direction of recognized and experienced tribal
religious leaders, and to combine them with other rituals of completely
different origin. Such performances can undermine indigenous traditions by
introducing distorted views of a ceremony even within its tribe of origin,
and certainly among young urban Indians who may be seeking a return to
tradition. Indian traditions generally hold that certain kinds of ceremonial

and sacred knowledge are powerful—so powerful that invoking them without proper qualifications or outside their intended context can be dangerous —and that such knowledge can be weakened by being too widely shared. Some Native American critics condemn such casual appropriation of Indian ceremonies as nothing less than a new variety of cultural genocide, threatening the cultural integrity and the very survival of Native religious traditions. They charge that white Americans have already stripped Native Americans of their land, resources, and political independence, and that "whiteshamans" and "plastic medicine men" are now taking the only thing left: their religion. When non-Indians insist on their right to conduct Indian ceremonies and teach Indian religion, they are at best disrespectful and at worst perpetuating cultural genocide.[15]

There are of course more positive ways to look at these New Age activities. The New Age movement can inspire interest in and increase the general public's knowledge about Native American cultures, and in this way it has the potential to create new support for Indian causes. Some Native Americans who are concerned about environmental as well as cultural destruction share with New Agers the hope that the dominant culture can learn from indigenous ethics and philosophies to honor the natural balances and cycles of the earth. Vine Deloria himself defended New Age enthusiasts for their attempts, clumsy and partial though they may be, at taking seriously the insights and practices of Native American religious traditions.[16]

Whatever their consequences, it is worth pointing out that New Age appropriations of Indian ceremonies are based in dominant concepts of religion as a matter of individual conscience, as a separate sphere of life that is largely disconnected from community or land, and as a commodity that can be easily chosen and changed. These concepts of religion, especially the last, are in many ways a product of American cultural history. The notion of religion as commodity is encapsulated in Robert Bellah's well-known discussion of the mix-and-match spiritual eclecticism he called "sheilaism." Indians are not the only ones who find this attitude problematic. Most Christians would likewise be offended by eclectic religionists who saw fit to practice communion or other sacraments without any ordained leadership or even any professed Christian faith, or in combination with rites originating in other religious traditions. For Indians, the primary issue is not belief but that these ceremonies are an integral part of each community's life and of its ties to the land, not part of some separable "religion" that can be exported, and are meant to be practiced in the context of the tribal community.[17]

In this case, constitutional guarantees of religious freedom work against Native American demands. New Age practitioners insist on their right to hold sweat lodges and vision quests as a matter of their own religious freedom. Religion cannot be owned, they say, and anyone has the right to participate in religious practices no matter what their origin. Pueblo Indians found in the 1920s that demanding religious freedom required them to grant that same liberty to individual tribal members who did not wish to participate in the ceremonies. The identification of Indian ceremonies as religion has also helped opened the door for New Age practitioners to insist on religious freedom grounds that they have the right to include those ceremonies in their own practice of religion. Now that Indian ceremonies are recognized by the dominant culture as "religion," there is no legal basis for denying non-Indians the free exercise to practice them.[18]

The discourse of religion has proved useful for Native American tribes seeking the return of cultural artifacts and human remains from museums, universities, and private collections—a significant part of contemporary Indian cultural revitalization efforts. Whether for profit or in the name of scientific research, private collectors, bounty hunters, and scientists long considered it their right to collect artifacts from tribal lands. For many years, anthropologists routinely participated in the theft and illicit purchase of ceremonial objects such as masks and altars from religious sites and considered both recent and ancient Indian graves simply as archaeological sites to be excavated for skeletal remains and burial objects. Convinced that Indian cultures were doomed to disappear, most anthropologists until the late twentieth century were blind to the threat posed by their own collecting activities. Many tribes vehemently protested the theft of objects whose loss negatively affected their religious practice, and they decried the desecration of their ancestors' graves. As they pointed out, scientists had no difficulty respecting the sanctity of non-Indian graves. For most of the century, their only legal recourse was the Indian Antiquities Act of 1908, which outlawed private collecting on Indian lands. From an Indian perspective the law was fatally flawed, because it was designed to facilitate rather than limit scientific excavations, and even against bounty hunters it imposed only limited penalties.[19]

As Indian political activism became more assertive during the 1970s, several tribes initiated more forceful demands for the return of artifacts and/or human remains. Arguing that many stolen items were central to tribal religion, Indian leaders quickly began to appeal to the legal principle of religious freedom as one basis for the repatriation of artifacts. Among the most noted cases was that of the Zuni Ayahu:da, the "war gods" Masewi and Oyoyewi. In Zuni traditional practice, wooden Ayahu:da figurines are carved by ceremonial specialists, used in the kiva, then placed in shrines on specific mountain peaks where they serve as spiritual guardians. Zuni leaders initiated a persistent campaign for the repatriation of the numerous Ayahu:da on the grounds that their loss had created "an imbalance in the spiritual world," causing many problems on the Zuni reservation and around the world. This imbalance could be corrected only by returning them to their mountain shrines. Because they are intended to gradually decompose in their mountain shrines, a symbol of the cyclical nature of life and the power of the spirit world, museum curators violated the purpose of the Ayahu:da not only by keeping them from the mountain shrines but by artificially preserving them in climate-controlled conditions. In 1979 this cause drew attention in the *American Indian Law Review*, where attorney Bowen Blair argued that the First Amendment and the newly passed American Indian Religious Freedom Act offered the best legal recourse for the recovery of these and other tribal artifacts. But, as in so many other areas, AIRFA proved ineffective, and this strategy never gained much support.[20]

Greater success came with the Native American Graves Protection and Repatriation Act (NAGPRA) of 1990, legislation inspired in part by the Zuni campaign and specifically intended to facilitate the return of Indian artifacts and human remains. NAGPRA provided a concrete process and resources for implementation, obliging all public institutions and any private museums that have received federal funds to review their collections and contact the relevant tribal leaders to initiate a process of returning "human remains, funerary objects, sacred objects, and objects of cultural patrimony" to the tribes of origin. As these specifications suggest, the law's proponents did not limit their appeal to religious freedom, insisting that Native American claims to cultural property and ancestral remains—rights generally granted without question to other American citizens—must also be recognized as basic civil and human rights. But the testimony for the act and at subsequent hearings on its implementation relied heavily on religious freedom appeals, emphasizing the inseparability of Native religion, law, and culture that bestows a sacred quality to all the remains and artifacts covered by the act. Alongside testimony to Congress about the historic violation of Indian religious and civil rights, this emphasis on the sacred added considerable gravity to the cause and no doubt helped sway Congress to almost unanimously pass the act.[21]

NAGPRA's implementation has resulted in the return of many artifacts and human remains to the relevant tribes. The Zuni are a famous success story. After two decades of persistent but respectful appeals to humanitarian ethics—and after 1990 to NAGPRA—the tribe had successfully recovered eighty Ayahu:da from a variety of museums and private collections and returned them to their rightful places in the mountains. Many museum curators and anthropologists have praised NAGPRA and have found that its procedures have helped them build positive and cooperative relationships with Native Americans. Indian religious leaders have helped some curators better understand and interpret their collections; such collaborations have already reshaped museum standards for displaying and curating Native American artifacts. Meanwhile, Native American tribal museums are growing as Indians reclaim their artifacts and take charge of the public representation of their own histories and cultures. But the act is not perfect. Some Indian scholars and activists have complained that too many institutions have tried to exempt themselves from its provisions and that artifacts have allegedly disappeared from several museum collections before Indians could reclaim them.[22]

This process too reveals the complex consequences of defining indigenous practices in terms of religion. The Zuni appeal for the Ayahu:da emphasized the significance of Zuni religion for all aspects of Zuni life. According to a statement by Zuni religious leaders in 1978, religious items such as these "are the essence of our Zuni culture." Yet the very language of "religion" implies a separate sphere in Zuni culture—the nonreligious—to which such statements would not apply. The same is true of the Zuni Tribal Council's 1978 resolution on the Ayahu:da and other "items of sacred religious significance." The council deferred to the Zuni religious leaders "because this effort ultimately involves protection and return of objects which are intimately bound up with the traditional religious practices and doctrines of the Zuni Tribe." By deferring to the religious leaders on a matter defined as religious, the tribal council implied its own sovereignty in other "non-religious" affairs. The statement thus reveals a greater degree of separation between tribal government and religion than was present in 1923, when the high priests were very clearly the highest authority in all matters of Zuni life. With certain spheres of Zuni life marked off as "religion," other parts had come to be defined as "secular" and therefore the proper jurisdiction of the tribal council. Defining both ceremonies and artifacts as "religion" had proved strategically useful because it enabled the argument for religious freedom. At the same time, the language of "religion" helped further a separation of spheres in Zuni life.[23]

The "sacred" is a concept closely tied to "religion"—indeed, the two are often defined in relation to one another—and its definitional quandaries are no less severe. Given the centrality of the sacred in the NAGPRA process, it should be no surprise that its definition has been a central point of dispute. The act's cosponsor, Senator Daniel Inouye of Hawai'i, remembers that during preliminary hearings scientists and museum curators expressed the fear that "if native people were allowed to determine what is 'sacred,' they might deem everything as 'sacred,'" and so have a legal foundation for reclaiming every Native American artifact in the nation's museums. Inouye claims that this fear has proved groundless and that the act has been largely successful for all parties concerned,[24] but many Native Americans are less positive about NAGPRA's results. They have protested that the National Park Service, which provides oversight to the repatriations process, has favored the scientific and museum community and defined the "sacred" so narrowly that many legitimate claims are refused. Rosita Worl of the Sealaska Heritage Foundation, which represents a coalition of Alaskan tribes, recommended in 1999 that Congress amend the act to provide a broad definition of the sacred that does not require proof that an object was sacred to ancestors but recognizes that "all cultural processes, including religion, evolve" and takes into account "the phenomenon of religious renewal."[25]

Despite NAGPRA, in several prominent cases the courts have favored scientific research over Native American religious and cultural claims. The most important of these is the case of Kennewick Man, a human skeleton found in 1996 near Kennewick, Washington, on land owned by the Army Corps of Engineers. Initial research determined that the remains, known to affected Indian tribes as the Ancient One, were approximately nine thousand years old. Convinced that NAGPRA's provisions applied and that there was sufficient evidence of cultural affiliation, the corps announced its intention to turn Kennewick Man over to the tribes. The Confederated Tribes of the Umatilla Indian Reservation, Nez Perce Tribe, Confederated Tribes and Bands of the Yakama Nation, Confederated Tribes of the Colville Reservation, and the Wanapum Band agreed that the remains should be reburied according to traditional tribal practice. When one scientist argued that the skeleton had "Caucasian" features and therefore represented a separate human migration to the Americas not culturally or biologically related to contemporary Native Americans, the tribes appealed to oral and religious tradition to substantiate their claims. "From our oral histories, we know that our people have been part of this land since the beginning of time," wrote Umatilla religious leader and board of trustees member Armand Minthorn, "and, our elders have told us that Indian people did not always look the way we look today." Minthorn explained that the religion of the tribes required the immediate reburial of the Ancient One. "Our religious beliefs, culture, and our adopted policies and procedures tell us that this individual must be re-buried as soon as possible," he wrote. "Our elders have taught us that once a body goes into the ground, it is meant to stay there until the end of time." Minthorn appealed to NAGPRA as the strongest legal basis for the tribes' claim: "We are trying to ensure that the federal government lives up to its own laws, as well as honoring our policies, procedures, and religious beliefs."[26] Extensive studies sponsored by the Department of the Interior supported the Indians' claim, and validated the corps' initial decision to give them the remains for reburial.[27]

A small group of scientists filed suit to prevent the transfer, insisting that the Indian tribes could not prove cultural affiliation to Kennewick Man and therefore had no rights to the remains under NAGPRA. These scientists discounted the Indians' religious freedom claims, arguing that absent clear evidence of cultural affiliation, the Indians' religious convictions could not be permitted to dictate government policy and inhibit scientific research. As the case went to court, tribal leaders continued to base their appeal in part on religion. Seeking public sympathy and support, the tribes identified themselves as guardians of mainstream American values of religious freedom and human rights—and insisted that the case did not involve any fundamental conflict between science and Indian religion. "We have tried to explain to the public and scientists that our religious and cultural beliefs mandate that we rebury the remains of this individual as soon as possible," wrote former Umatilla tribal chairman Don Sampson. "This case is about fundamental human rights, not about science versus religion," wrote the Umatilla tribes during the district court hearings. The Indians insisted that they had no objection to scientific research as long as it was appropriately conducted. "We use science every day to help in protecting our people and the land," wrote Sampson, "but we do reject the notion that science is the answer to everything and therefore it should take precedence over the religious rights and beliefs of American citizens." Sampson called the anthropological research on Kennewick Man methodologically flawed because it employed nineteenth-century notions of racial identity and argued that the scientists involved were not respected by the scientific mainstream.[28]

In the end, neither religious freedom nor NAGPRA proved strong enough to support the Indians' claim. The federal district court ruled on behalf of the scientists, and then—on the grounds that the Indians' case was based purely on "religious and spiritual" rather than legal grounds—rejected the tribes' appeal for a stay to prevent further research until the case was decided in appeal. In a press statement denouncing this decision, the tribes minimized the role of religion in their claim by explaining that the judge was wrong to call their claims "strictly religious." "The Native American Graves Protection and Repatriation Act was made law to ensure that tribes have the same rights non-Indians have to protect their ancestors," they pointed out. "We object to scientific study because the ancient one is our ancestor, and that the claimant tribes, by law, have a right to determine who, if anyone, should study his remains."[29] A month later, the Ninth Circuit Court of Appeals did grant the stay on research but then, in February 2004, issued a final ruling that the tribes did not have valid legal claim to the remains because the court did not find any proof of cultural affiliation. The tribes did not appeal the case before the Supreme Court partly because they lacked funding to do so and partly because they feared "that an unfavorable Court decision could become law" and further damage other Indian claims. Instead, they began working to amend NAGPRA to provide better protection.[30] Meanwhile, groups such as Friends of America's Past, who want to ensure that ancient remains are available for scientific research, have proposed revisions designed to limit Indian claims under NAGPRA. To date, neither side has been successful, and NAGPRA's future remains unresolved.[31] In this case, repatriation efforts—

grounded in a broader appeal to human rights and religious freedom—clashed with the claims of scientific research and lost.

Perhaps the most important religious freedom issues for Native Americans today center around efforts to protect and regain control of the places that are central to their cultural integrity and traditions. Native Americans have traditionally considered the natural world and its creatures not as objects to be owned but as living beings that must be treated with respect, and with whom the people must interact for various purposes. Through centuries of experience, as Vine Deloria has explained, Indians have found that certain features of the natural landscape have intrinsic power and must be treated "in the light of reverence."[32] These sites are generally associated with the origins of the people, with events of the mythological past, and with the powers of the earth. They are places where tribal members go to pray or hold vision quests; where medicine men and women go to gather healing herbs, materials for ceremonies, and to renew their power; or where specific ceremonies are periodically held to renew the balance of the earth. "The most important aspect of sacred places," Deloria writes, "is that they mark the location and circumstances of an event in which the holy became an objective fact of existence." These places are vital to the preservation and revitalization of Indian tradition, and Indians have employed the term "sacred" in an effort to communicate their power and significance to non-Indian ears.[33]

When the U.S. government confined Native Americans to reservations in the nineteenth century, some tribes were forcibly taken from their homelands and far away from their sacred places. Others were assigned reservations encompassing only a small fraction of their ancestral lands, and over the decades the federal government demanded that they relinquish more and more of that land. Many of the sacred places are mountains, lakes, rock formations, or other sites of extraordinary natural beauty, and many of them were incorporated into the National Forest or National Park systems. Others were claimed by white settlers and became private lands. Whatever the situation, tribal members and religious leaders continued to make pilgrimages to their sacred places to pray and to benefit from the powers found there. They often made these visits in secret, hoping to protect these places and to avoid trouble with landowners or federal land managers—especially during the long decades when Indian ceremonies were banned outright. By the late twentieth century, the federal government was making efforts to accommodate Native American religious practice, yet more and more of the places sacred to Indians were being destroyed or threatened by developments such as mining, logging, road building, dams, or recreation and tourism. Through all this history, Indians sought the means to regain their sacred places or at least to protect them from destruction. Especially in the late twentieth century, Indians have appealed to constitutional guarantees of religious freedom as a primary legal argument to prevent the development of sacred lands.

One of the few successful efforts to regain tribal ownership of sacred land was Taos Pueblo's long struggle for Blue Lake and its environs. Blue Lake, located high in the Sangre de Cristo Mountains, was taken from Taos in 1906 when President Theodore Roosevelt included it in an addition to the National Forest Reserve. The tribe never agreed to that move, and over the years the Indians protested that the timber harvesting, livestock grazing, and recreational uses that the Forest Service permitted were desecrating the lake, damaging their shrines in the area, and polluting their water supply. Gradually the pueblo's leaders developed a legal strategy focused on the positive religious significance of the site. As tribal cacique Juan de Jesus Romero put it in the 1960s, "Our Blue Lake wilderness keeps our water holy, and by the water we are baptized. If our land is not returned to us, if it is turned over to the government for its use, then that is the end of Indian life. . . . It is our religion that holds us together." They would finally succeed in 1970, when by act of Congress the region was finally returned to the pueblo. The case has been hailed as an important precedent because for the first time the government returned land to Indians on the basis of its religious significance.[34]

Efforts to defend sacred lands in the courts have been far less successful. In a series of cases in the 1980s, Indian tribes argued that specific actions planned by federal government agencies would violate sacred places and so interfere with their free exercise of religion. The tribes in these cases were not in any immediate sense asking for the transfer of the land to tribal ownership but hoped to prevent various kinds of development that threatened to destroy its sacred character. In every case, courts used narrow interpretations of what counted as "religion" in order to rule that the government's plans did not interfere with any constitutional right. In *Sequoyah v. Tennessee Valley Authority* (1980), Cherokee plaintiffs argued that the completion of a dam on the Little Tennessee River would flood areas crucial to

Cherokee tradition and would destroy "sacred sites, medicine gathering sites, holy places and cemeteries, and will disturb the sacred balance of the land." The Sixth Circuit Court of Appeals ruled that although the Cherokees clearly "have a religion within the meaning of the Constitution," the government's action did not infringe on the Indians' constitutional rights because "the overwhelming concern of the affiants appears to be related to the historical beginnings of the Cherokees and their cultural development . . . it is damage to the tribal and family folklore and traditions, more than particular religious observances, which appears to be at stake." In other words, the justices did not consider the Cherokees' historical beginnings, cultural development, and tribal folklore to meet the court's standard of being a "central" or "indispensible" part of the religion. They implicitly defined religion as something separate from each of these things, a division between cultural spheres that does not exist in Cherokee or other indigenous traditions. The language of religion, essential in order to put forward the religious freedom claim, once again seemed to inhibit a holistic understanding of Indian tradition. In contrast, non-Indian free exercise claims have rarely been held to the standard that the practice be central or indispensable to the religion concerned.[35]

The sacred land cases reflect the incompatibility between Native American and Euro-American conceptions of land as well as religion. The basic principles of the American legal system make it difficult for judges to view religion as anything but a particular sphere of human beliefs and activities, or land as other than an object controlled by property rights. In *Badoni v. Higginson* (1980), Navajo plaintiffs protested that the recent expansion of Lake Powell had flooded their sacred sites in the vicinity of Rainbow Bridge National Monument and called for restrictions on the tourists who were drinking beer, defacing the bridge, and disrupting religious ceremonies in the monument area. Although the district court acknowledged that the tourists were disruptive and the flooding had "drowned" the Navajo gods, it determined that the First Amendment could not justify disrupting the government's right to manage the land as it saw fit. Viewing land only in terms of property, the justices could not understand that for the Navajo the land itself was a religious presence and ignored the historical injustices that had originally robbed the Indians of ownership and access to the site. Imagining a person who claimed that the Lincoln Memorial in Washington, D.C., was a "sacred religious shrine to him," they concluded that the courts could not "enjoin all other visitors from entering the Lincoln Memorial in order to protect his constitutional right to religious freedom." The Tenth Circuit Court of Appeals affirmed the lower court's ruling, reasoning that the government's need to maintain high water levels in Lake Powell outweighed the Indians' interest in the flooded sites, and that restricting tourist traffic would amount to a violation of the establishment clause by giving undue privilege to Navajo religion. Because the flooding and tourist activity effectively destroyed important Navajo religious practices, however, this decision suggested that Indians had no meaningful First Amendment rights on public lands.[36]

Throughout the 1980s, the courts remained unable to comprehend Indians' relationships with their sacred places. In *Wilson v. Block* (1983), the Court of Appeals for the District of Columbia Circuit ruled that a ski resort on the San Francisco Peaks in Arizona—the home of the Hopi Kachinas and the physical embodiment of one of the Navajo Holy Ones, essential to religious practice for these and at least four other tribes—did not violate the Indians' free exercise of religion because, although the development project may cause "spiritual disquiet," it did not prevent them from believing in the holiness of the peaks.[37] In *Crow v. Gullet* (1983), the court applied the reasoning from *Sequoyah* and *Badoni* to argue that the National Park Service's proposed expansion of tourist facilities at Bear Butte in the Black Hills—ironically intended to display to tourists the very religious practices that they would damage—did not violate any First Amendment rights of the Lakota and Tsistsistas (Cheyenne) Indian plaintiffs. The Indians argued that disturbing the natural qualities of the Butte would irreparably damage their holy place and so inhibit their religious liberty. The justices not only rejected that reasoning but went so far as to claim that the new parking lot, restroom, trails, and so forth would help to facilitate Indian religious activities and that the park service had already done enough (perhaps too much, they hinted) "to afford special treatment and privileges to American Indian religious practices at the Butte." Once again the court raised the specter of religious establishment and failed to consider the Indians' understanding of the land itself as a religious entity that would be violated by the development.[38]

The final and most significant case in this series was *Lyng v. Northwest Indian Cemetery Protective Association* (1988), in which the U.S. Supreme Court determined that a logging road proposed by the U.S. Forest Service through the sacred "high country" of the Yurok, Karok, and Tolowa Indians did not violate their constitutional rights. In 1977 the Forest Service announced plans to build a logging road directly through this part of the Siskiyou Mountains so that private companies could harvest timber. The service's own commissioned report on the project determined that the undisturbed high country was essential to the Indians as the center of the world—a holy reality where one could communicate with the powers of the universe—and that by disturbing the network of sacred trails and prayer sites that covered the region the road construction and logging would do irreparable harm to "the very core of Northwest religious beliefs and practices." The anthropologists who wrote the report cautioned that the words "religion" and "sacred" should not be taken to mean only a set of ritual activities performed at specific places and that the plan to fence off specific prayer sites for Indian use was a serious distortion of the Indians' way of understanding these sites that would do little to preserve free religious expression. "Any division into 'religious' or 'sacred' is in reality an exercise which forces Indian concepts into non-Indian 'categories,' and distorts the original conceptualization in the process," they wrote. That analysis recognizes the problems inherent in the use of terms like "religion" and the "sacred" to describe Indian traditions. In Euro-American culture, these imply distinct and opposed spheres of religious and secular and of the sacred and the profane, which are not operative in Indian traditions. Forest Service administrators refused to follow these recommendations, justifying the existing plan as the best way to improve the administration of the area, to enable logging activities that would stimulate employment in the regional timber industry, and to provide recreational access to the region.[39] When the tribes and allied environmental groups brought suit, the district court and the Ninth Circuit Court of Appeals both ruled in their favor. They found that the "use of the [undisturbed] high country is 'central and indispensable' to the Indian plaintiffs' religion" and that the government's interests in the road were not "of the highest order" and so could not justify a violation of the Indians' free exercise.[40]

The Supreme Court disagreed, reversing its own precedents to find that, because the road's primary purpose had nothing to do with the Indians' religion, it did not violate their constitutional rights. In this case, as it would in the *Smith* decision two years later, the Supreme Court rejected its own compelling interest test to rule that the free exercise clause was violated only if the government directly prohibited or penalized the free exercise of religion. Further, even though Justice Sandra Day O'Connor's majority opinion formally acknowledged the Indians' view of land as a sacred entity, the decision treated land simply as property to be used and managed at the government's pleasure. "Whatever rights the Indians may have to the use of the area," O'Connor wrote, "those rights do not divest the Government of its right to use what is, after all, *its* land." The court found that the Forest Service had complied with its obligations under AIRFA by commissioning the original report on the cultural impact of the logging road and that nothing in AIRFA required the government to follow the recommendations in the report. In his dissenting opinion, Justice William Brennan rebuked the decision in the strongest possible words. "Today, the Court holds that a federal land-use decision that promises to destroy an entire religion does not burden the practice of that faith in a manner recognized by the Free Exercise Clause," he wrote. "Given today's ruling, that freedom amounts to nothing more than the right to believe that their religion will be destroyed." The case, he wrote, "represents yet another stress point in the longstanding conflict between two disparate cultures—the dominant western culture, which views land in terms of ownership and use, and that of Native Americans, in which concepts of private property are not only alien, but contrary to a belief system that holds land sacred."[41]

Given the spectacular failure of the courts to recognize sacred land claims on First Amendment grounds, Native Americans have turned to other legal strategies that do not rely completely on religious freedom. Perhaps the most important is the National Historic Places Act, first enacted in 1966 to create a National Register of Historic Places and amended in 1992 to explicitly include Indian sacred sites. The amendments recognized the rights of tribes not to disclose sensitive information, allowed for the creation of independent tribal preservation offices and legally granted Indian tribes the right to administer sacred sites on their own reservation lands. Under this act any development project requires a thorough review of the property to determine whether such sites are present, and after adequate documentation and tribal consultation the site may be given a measure of protection through placement on the National Register of Historic Places.

The Park Service's procedures for nominating Native American sites for the National Register highlight the complications of religion in federal policy, justifying the inclusion of religious sites not in terms of religious freedom but for their cultural and historical significance. *National Register Bulletin* no. 38 developed guidelines for identifying sites of "traditional cultural significance," with special attention to Native American sacred places. Noting the American Indian Religious Freedom Act mandate to review federal policies to ensure Indian religious freedom, the bulletin recognized that NHPA criteria had often been interpreted "in a manner that excludes historic properties of religious significance to Native Americans from eligibility." Specifically, absent other justification for National Register listing, these criteria called for excluding religious properties "because of the necessity to avoid any appearance of judgement by government about the merit of any religion or belief." The fact that in "most American Indian societies, the clear distinction made by Euroamerican society between religion and the rest of culture does not exist," wrote anthropologists Patricia Parker and Thomas King, made this criterion generally inappropriate for Native American sites. "The fact that a property is used for religious purposes by a traditional group . . . or is described by the group in terms that are classified by the outside observer as 'religious' should not by itself be taken to make the property ineligible, since these activities may be expressions of traditional cultural beliefs and may be intrinsic to the continuation of traditional cultural practices." Excluding such sites would "result in discriminating against the group by effectively denying the legitimacy of its history and culture" and would be "ethnocentric in the extreme." In other words, Parker and King had to justify the inclusion of religious sites in the register, and—despite their acknowledgment of the conceptual differences between cultures—nominations for National Register listing must necessarily demonstrate that the site has broad "cultural and historical" rather than only "religious" signficance.[42]

Recent Indian sacred land claims have appealed to the full arsenal of NHPA, AIRFA, and the First Amendment, often in conjunction with the Environmental Protection Act when the development threatened ecosystems and endangered species. Results have been mixed. In *Apache Survival Coalition v. United States* (1994), the Ninth Circuit Court of Appeals ruled that the construction of an observatory complex on the top of Mt. Graham in southern Arizona should be permitted to continue despite the mountain's importance to the San Carlos Apache. This case faltered in part because of divisions within the tribe and the tribe's failure to respond initially to inquiries from the National Forest Service and the University of Arizona—

the lead institution in the observatory project—for consultation on the mountain's cultural significance. At the same time, both the Forest Service and the judges who heard the case employed concepts of land and religion that invalidated the Indians' claim. In its initial review of the proposal under NHPA guidelines, the Forest Service had located what it termed three "shrines" on Mt. Graham's summits and called for consultation with the tribe only to "mitigate" the project's effects on these shrines. This idea that the "shrines" were the important sites to be protected reflected little understanding of the indigenous concept of the mountain itself as a sacred and powerful presence, and protecting them in isolation could not have satisfied the Apache's concerns. The NHPA, applied only to specifically designated shrines on the mountain, did not provide any meaningful supplement or alternative to arguments based on religious freedom.[43]

In several other cases, federal courts have upheld government policies restricting the public use of sacred sites in order to accommodate Indian practices. In *Bear Lodge Multiple Use Association v. Babbitt* (1999), an association of recreational rock climbers challenged the Forest Service's voluntary ban on climbing during the month of June—the most important month for Lakota and other tribal ceremonies at Bear Lodge. The Tenth Circuit Court of Appeals found that the park service's accommodation to Indian religious practices and its efforts to educate the public about "the religious and cultural significance of the Monument to some American Indians" did not amount to a violation of the establishment clause.[44] Similarly, in *National Arch and Bridge Society v. Alston* (2004), the same court upheld a Park Service plan that asked visitors to the Rainbow Bridge National Monument to voluntarily refrain from walking under the bridge in deference to Native American religious beliefs. In both cases, the court determined that the non-Indian plaintiffs had not suffered the legal standard of an "injury in fact" and therefore did not have standing to present a constitutional challenge in the case; and that the government policies in question represented a "reasonable accommodation" to rather than an unconstitutional establishment of Indian religion.[45]

Most recently, in *The Access Fund v. United States Department of Agriculture* (2007), the Ninth Circuit Court of Appeals upheld the U.S. Forest Service's decision to ban recreational climbing at Cave Rock, a formation on the eastern shores of Lake Tahoe that is sacred to the Washoe Indians. The Washoe know the 360-foot high, 800-foot wide dome as the site of an epic confrontation at the time when their people came into being, and as the gathering place of the "water babies" who possess medicinal knowledge and power that only trained medicine men know how to safely access. The rock suffered structural violation in 1937 and again in 1951 when the state blasted tunnels through the rock to accommodate a highway that had formerly circled the lake side of the formation. Cave Rock has been a popular site for rock climbing since the 1980s, and in recent years "sport climbers" have drilled permanent bolts into the rock, installed seating and a permanent masonry floor inside the cave, cemented over certain cave openings, and marked up cave walls with graffiti. While the Washoe were not pleased when the tunnels were blasted through the rock, tribal religious leaders indicated that climbing caused more harm than the highway because the cars pass through quickly and so absorb little power. The climbers, on the other hand, have sustained and intimate contact with the rock with potentially dangerous results for them as well as for the Washoe people.[46]

The outcome of this case shows both the strengths and the limitations of NHPA guidelines for protecting Indian sacred places. In 1998 the Forest Service nominated the dome for the National Registry in recognition of its role as "traditional cultural property," its archaeological value, and its historic importance as a transportation corridor. Its new management plan aimed to preserve the site's "historic and cultural" characteristics by restricting its use to "non-invasive activities" that were current during the lifetime of the famed Washoe medicine man Henry Rupert (d. 1965). The plan banned rock climbing activities as a violation of the site's "heritage resource" and called for the removal of the masonry flooring in the cave along with the bolts installed along climbing routes. Noting the guidelines in *National Register Bulletin* no. 38, the Forest Service emphasized that "the fact that traditional history and culture at Cave Rock are sometimes discussed in religious terms does not diminish the site's historical or cultural significance to the Washoe people," and that the site's significance was "not based on 'Washoe religious doctrine' but rather on the secularly-derived historical and ethnographic record." When the Access Fund, a climbing advocacy group, challenged the ban on the grounds that it violated the establishment clause, the district court and then the Ninth Circuit Court of Appeals determined that court precedents permitted reasonable accommodation to religion and that under NHPA guidelines the government had demonstrated the "cultural and historical" importance of the site outside of its religious significance to the

Washoe people. "The fact that Cave Rock is a sacred site to the Washoe does not diminish its importance as a national cultural resource," the court concluded. The court found that, according to the well-established test formulated in *Lemon v. Krutzman (1971)*, the policy did not violate the establishment clause because it had a clear "secular" purpose, did not have the primary effect of advancing or endorsing religion, and did not create "excessive government entanglement" with religion. The policy "provides for general public use and access well beyond members of the Washoe Tribe," the court noted, permits other recreational "activities that are incompatible with Washoe beliefs," and did not require the Forest Service to "monitor" or "develop expertise on Washoe religious worship or evaluate the merits of different religious practices or beliefs." In order to receive National Register protection, in other words, the site must be defined primarily in terms other than "religion."[47]

In essence, the court found that the Forest Service's policy was not an unconstitutional establishment of religion because it did not completely accommodate Washoe religious tradition, which would have required banning all recreational uses of Cave Rock. The ban on climbing was permissible because the court was convinced it had a "secular" rather than "religious" purpose; on the other hand, excluding all non-Washoe would serve only to facilitate Washoe religion. For this reason Washoe tribal leaders pointed out that, while they were grateful for the decision, the situation was still not ideal because the policy was "not based on tribal rights to practice their tradition but rather on National Register historic status. . . . The ban on rock climbing is a significant victory, but at the same time it demonstrates that the United States still lacks legislation that understands sacred places to be the sites of ongoing worship and protection, practices that are sometimes disturbed simply by the presence of humans and activities that appear to be non-invasive." The government has found no way to fully accommodate ongoing Indian tradition regarding sites defined as "religious" without running up against the establishment clause.[48]

In fact, the First Amendment has sometimes directly impeded the protection of Native American sacred sites. At Bear Butte in South Dakota, where the Lakota and Tsistsistas Indians lost their appeal to stop the construction of tourist facilities, the tribes and their supporters have continued to protest against interference by New Agers and other tourists in indigenous religious ceremonies. More than two hundred mostly Lakota people attended a rally held during the summer solstice in 1994 to protest the state's inaction against what some of them called "spiritual genocide." They complained that "New Age charlatans" were "charging fees to people who want to experience sweats, quests, and bogus Pipe ceremonies at Bear Butte" and demanded that the park limit access to sacred areas to "authorized Indians" and close the park entirely during Indian ceremonies. One protestor, Bill Miller of the Cheyenne River Sioux, told a reporter that "the New Agers holding ceremonies and placing crystals on Bear Butte" were like "someone barging into a Christian denomination church sanctuary to hold mock ceremonies and leave behind false idols." State park administrators had attempted to ameliorate the situation and to educate the public about the site's significance to Indians with a display at the visitor's center and with signs asking visitors to leave prayer ties, feathers, and flags unmolested. But a park manager explained that it was "unrealistic to suggest that the state should discriminate" among various religious groups that want to use the site and that, while the park system wanted to accommodate "consecrated use" by Indians, "at the same time we've got an obligation to the general public." In this case the constitutional principle of religious freedom appears to work against the Indians' efforts to protect Bear Butte as a sacred place. Park administrators must grant free exercise rights to New Agers as well as to Indians, and any effort to limit religious expression at the site to Indians would surely be challenged as a violation of the establishment clause.[49]

Advocates for Native American religious freedom met their most recent defeat in *Navajo Nation v. U.S. Forest Service* (2008), where the Ninth Circuit Court of Appeals ruled that the Arizona Snowbowl ski resort on the San Francisco Peaks could use reclaimed sewage water to make artificial snow, despite arguments by the Navajo, Havasupai, White Mountain Apache, Yavapai-Apache, Hopi, and Hualapai tribes that this activity would seriously infringe on their free exercise of religion. These tribes each have different traditions around the Peaks, but all of them consider the mountain a vital sacred site. Havasupai subchief Dianna Uqualla explained that, although all land is sacred, this mountain is "more sacred" than any other place, "like our tabernacle, our altar to the west." Even this comparison, shaped by Western conceptions of sacred places, does not quite communicate the significance of a mountain that for these tribes is itself a sacred and powerful living entity. For them, the use of reclaimed water—whether or not it meets scientific standards of purity—will irreparably damage the purity of this mountain.

Navajo practitioner Larry Foster testified that from a Navajo religious perspective there could be no way to purify water "reclaimed through sewage, wastewater . . . mortuaries, [or] hospitals," and that the use of such water would be a far more serious infringement on the Peaks than the existing ski resort (the Indians' efforts to prevent the initial development of the Snowbowl were defeated in *Wilson v. Block* [1983]). Foster explained that if the San Francisco Peaks "were to be poisoned or given [these] foreign materials that were not pure, it would create an imbalance. . . . We would not be able to go there to obtain herbs or medicines or do our ceremonies, because that mountain would then become impure." Despite such testimony the court found that "the sole effect of the artificial snow is on the Plaintiffs' subjective spiritual experience" rather than on their religious practice as such, that such an effect did not impose a "substantial burden" on free exercise, and that ruling in the Indians' favor would give "one religious sect a veto over the use of public park land," thereby depriving "others of the right to use what is, by definition, land that belongs to everyone." In an extensive dissenting opinion, Judge W. Fletcher argued that this decision reflected a faulty understanding of RFRA, the "substantial burden" standard, Native American religion, and (citing William James) the nature of all religion as "subjective spiritual experience." He also pointed out the "tragic irony" that the United States, which had originally taken "this land from the Indians by force," was now using "that forcible deprivation as a justification" for refusing to recognize the Indians' rights to religious freedom.[50]

Throughout this history, Native American religious freedom has faltered on the inability of the courts and the larger society to understand Indian conceptions of the sacred. Dominant cultural concepts of religion and land are not easily reconciled with the foundational importance of land in indigenous religious traditions. Courts have been hesitant to violate the establishment clause by allowing what they believe would be special accommodations for Indian religion. Even on the rare occasions when legal decisions have protected Indian sacred sites, the specter of the establishment clause has clearly limited those protections. The Interior Department is mandated by AIRFA, NHPA, and by President Clinton's Executive Order to accommodate Native American religious sites and practices, and they are taking steps to do so. But government agencies also have a broader mandate to accommodate multiple uses, some of which will be incompatible with Native American conceptions of the land. The government or the courts may sometimes determine that these uses are overly invasive, as they did at Cave Rock and the San Francisco Peaks. But the courts have made it clear that if the government were to fully accommodate Indian conceptions of these sacred sites—by restricting all non-Washoe access at Cave Rock, for example—this would amount to an unconstitutional establishment of Indian religion.

Native American activists and their allies have been working hard over the past several years to improve this situation. The National Congress of American Indians, the Sacred Land Film Project, and other groups are advocating passage of a "Native American Sacred Lands Act," first introduced in Congress in 2003. This legislation defines "sacred land" as "any geophysical or geographical area or feature which is sacred by virtue of its traditional cultural or religious significance or ceremonial use, or by virtue of a ceremonial or cultural requirement, including a religious requirement that a natural substance or product for use in Indian tribal or Native Hawaiian organization ceremonies be gathered from that particular location." It would prohibit development in areas designated as Indian sacred land, require government agencies to "accommodate meaningful access to and ceremonial use of sacred lands . . . avoid significant damage to sacred lands," and "consult with Indian tribes and Native Hawaiian organizations prior to taking significant actions or developing policies affecting Native American sacred lands." Finally, the act would authorize the transfer of sacred lands "into trust for the benefit of the Indian tribe or Indian tribes for which the land is considered sacred, on the condition that the Indian tribe[s] . . . manage the land in perpetuity to protect that sacredness." Wherever possible, the best solution would be this return of sacred lands to Native Americans so that Indians themselves can preserve and protect the quality and integrity of their most treasured places. Such a step would at long last take seriously the unique quality of indigenous relationship with the land and would acknowledge and offer a degree of restitution for the historic injustices that stripped Indians of all their lands.[51]

This chapter has outlined the ongoing challenges of religious freedom for Native Americans, with particular attention to the definitional problems of the terms "religion" and the "sacred." Pursuing religious freedom claims necessarily requires defining certain aspects of a tradition through these concepts. But terms like "religion" and the "sacred" originated outside Native American traditions and continue to carry the kinds of cultural baggage that are very difficult to unravel. As we have seen, the U.S. legal system is shaped by dominant conceptions of religion as a matter of belief, ritual, and individual conscience; and of the land as objectified property with no intrinsic relationship to those spheres of life defined as religious. Under the First Amendment, religious freedom must be granted to all—New Agers as well as Native Americans—a formulation that serves the New Age movement's individualized and transportable forms of religion far better than it does the community- and land-based indigenous traditions. When the courts apply the establishment clause to forbid all but very limited accommodations to Native American religious traditions on public lands, the U.S. Constitution appears to provide no way to recognize Native Americans' prior claims to this land or to rectify the historic injustices that stripped them of it.

The depth of this challenge is evident in the United States' decision to vote against a historic Declaration on the Rights of Indigenous Peoples, passed in the United Nations by a margin of 144 to 4 in September 2007. The declaration's measures include guarantees that indigenous peoples "have the right to manifest, practice, develop and teach their spiritual and religious traditions, customs and ceremonies . . . the right to maintain, protect and have access in privacy to their religious and cultural sites," and "the right to own, use, develop and control the lands, territories and resources that they possess by reason of traditional ownership or other traditional occupation or use." Joining the U.S. in opposition were Australia, Canada, and New Zealand—all fearing that their politically active native populations would gain too much leverage in their struggles to reclaim indigenous land.[52]

When Native Americans and others define indigenous traditions in terms of religion, this is a conceptual shift that may also have implications within the tradition. To some degree, setting apart certain ceremonies or certain land as "religious" or "sacred" creates a new distinction between these spheres of life and others that come to be marked in opposition as "secular" or "profane." As in the dance controversy, the introduction of such terms may change the ways in which Native Americans view their own traditions. However, at least in North America, the language of religion and the sacred has become too deeply embedded in contemporary Native American cultures to consider its abandonment. These concepts have become indigenous ones, and Indians have actively reinterpreted them to fulfill indigenous needs. In his study of the Kiowa gourd dance, anthropologist Luke Lassiter points out that Indians often speak of the sacred in ways that do not fit with the sacred-secular dichotomies of academic theory. "Terms like *sacred* or *religious* have very different meanings to [Indian community members] than they do for academics," he writes. "When *we* say it's 'sacred,' it means we respect it," commented one of his informants. "We have to take care of it, to pass it on to our children. It's our way of life, and it goes with us all the time, every day." Scholars who "use *sacred* to distinguish ritual from that which is secular . . . may ignore the fact that the meaning of terms such as *sacred* and *religious* are contested, situational, and multifaceted within their community contexts." Events like the Gourd Dance may be highly valued and meaningful in indigenous terms, but rather than being set apart as "sacred" or "religious," they are "intrinsic to peoples' everyday lives." In the end, Native Americans may redefine the language of religion more than it changes them.[53]

Whatever their implications within indigenous cultures, the concepts of religion and the sacred have become essential to the struggle for cultural revitalization. In an evaluation of "lessons learned" in Native American struggles for sacred land, the Sacred Land Film Project concludes that "grounding actions in spirituality" provides "strength and courage for the struggle."[54] The concepts of religion and the sacred provide a deeply meaningful way to communicate the significance and power of indigenous traditions to contemporary Indians and non-Indians alike. It is no accident that Indians have tried to explain the importance of sacred sites by comparing them to churches and cathedrals, or that they have explained dance and peyote ceremonies as Indian forms of prayer. These identifications, like the terms "religion" and the "sacred" themselves, may not be capable of communicating the full meaning of particular places and traditions to non-Indian people. Yet they convey something of the depth of their importance within Indian tradition, and given the high value ascribed to religion in American culture, they provide an important starting point for the more extensive work of cultural translation that must follow.

NOTES

Abbreviations of Archival Sources

AAIA Papers   Association on American Indian Affairs Papers. Department of
                     Rare Books and Special Collections, Princeton University
                     Library. Princeton, New Jersey.

BCIM Records   Bureau of Catholic Indian Missions Records. Series I,
                     Correspondence. Marquette University Archives. Milwaukee,
                     Wisconsin.

Boas Papers   Franz Boas Papers. American Philosophical Society. Philadelphia,
                     Pennsylvania.

Cassidy Collection   Ina Sizer Cassidy Collection. Archives of the Laboratory of
                     Anthropology/Museum of Indian Arts & Culture. Santa Fe, New
                     Mexico.

Collier Papers   John Collier Papers. Manuscripts Division, Sterling Library, Yale
                     University. New Haven, Connecticut.

Duke Collection   Doris Duke American Indian Oral History Collection. Center for
                     Southwest Research, General Library, University of New Mexico.
                     Albuquerque, New Mexico.

Hewett-ALA   Edgar Hewett Collection. Archives of the Laboratory of
                     Anthropology/Museum of Indian Arts & Culture. Santa Fe, New
                     Mexico.

Hewett-CHL   Edgar L. Hewett Collection. Fray Angélico Chávez History
                     Library. Santa Fe, New Mexico.

IRA Papers   Indian Rights Association Papers. Pennsylvania Historical
                     Society. Philadelphia, Pennsylvania.

Luhan Papers   Mabel Dodge Luhan Papers. Beinecke Library, Yale University.
                     New Haven, Connecticut.

NAA   Smithsonian Institution National Anthropological Archives.
                     Suitland, Maryland.

NARA-NPCa   Northern Pueblos Agency, General Correspondence file, 1904–
                     1937. Records of the Bureau of Indian Affairs, RG 75. National
                     Archives and Records Administration. Denver, Colorado.

NARA-NPCb   Northern Pueblos Agency, General Correspondence file, 1912–
                   1938. Records of the Bureau of Indian Affairs, RG 75. National
                   Archives and Records Administration. Denver, Colorado.

NARA-NPLB   Northern Pueblos Agency, Correspondence, Reports, and Other
                   Records Relating to the Pueblo Lands Board, 1918–1932. Records
                   of the Bureau of Indian Affairs, RG 75. National Archives and
                   Records Administration. Denver, Colorado.

NARA-NP Records   Central Classified files, 1907–1939, Northern Pueblo Records.
                   Records of the Bureau of Indian Affairs, RG 75. National Archives
                   and Records Administration. Washington, D.C.

NARA-SA   Records of the Special Attorney for the Pueblos, Miscellaneous
                   Correspondence 1908–1935. Records of the Bureau of Indian
                   Affairs, RG 75. National Archives and Records Administration.
                   Denver, Colorado. Consulted on microfilm.

NARA-SFIS   Santa Fe Indian School, Correspondence, Accounts and Other
                   Records, 1911–1935. Records of the Bureau of Indian Affairs, RG
                   75. National Archives and Records Administration. Denver,
                   Colorado.

NARA-SPC   Southern Pueblos Agency, General Correspondence file, 1911–
                   1935. Records of the Bureau of Indian Affairs, RG 75. National
                   Archives and Records Administration. Denver, Colorado.

NARA-SP Records   Central Classified files, 1907–1939, Southern Pueblo Records.
                   Records of the Bureau of Indian Affairs, RG 75. National Archives
                   and Records Administration. Washington, D.C.

NARA-VPJ   Various Pueblo Jurisdictions, Consolidated Correspondence and
                   Other Records, 1911–1934. Records of the Bureau of Indian
                   Affairs, RG 75. National Archives and Records Administration.
                   Denver, Colorado.

NARA-Zuni Records Central Classified files, 1907–1939, Zuni Records. Records of the
                   Bureau of Indian Affairs, RG 75. National Archives and Records
                   Administration. Washington, D.C.

Parsons Papers   Elsie Clews Parsons Papers. American Philosophical Society.
                   Philadelphia, Pennsylvania.

PCUSA   Board of National Missions (PCUSA) Division of Church
                   Strategy and Development Records, 1871–1972. RG 301.7.
                   Presbyterian Historical Society. Philadelphia, Pennsylvania.

Pueblo Collection Pueblo Indians Collection. New Mexico State Records Center
                   and Archives. Santa Fe, New Mexico.

Renehan Papers   Renehan-Gilbert Papers. New Mexico State Records Center and
                   Archives. Santa Fe, New Mexico.

Speck Collection   Frank G. Speck Collection. American Philosophical Society. Philadelphia, Pennsylvania.

SWAIA Records   Southwestern Association on Indian Affairs Records. New Mexico State Records Center and Archives. Santa Fe, New Mexico.

White Papers   Amelia E. and Martha White Papers. School of American Research. Santa Fe, New Mexico.

Introduction

1. Grant, *Taos Today*, 10–11.

2. Ibid., 11–13, 17–22.

3. A. R. Manby to Rev. William Ketcham, November 6, 1910, reel 51, BCIM Records; Curtis in Wood, *Taos Pueblo*, 72.

4. Grant, *Taos Today*, 103–4.

5. Bodine, "The Taos Blue Lake Ceremony," 91–105, includes Matilda Coxe Stevenson's account of the ceremony—the most detailed ever published—based on her interviews with informants in 1906.

6. Quote is from Jung, "The Pueblo Indians," 42. On Blue Lake and Taos culture, see Brandt, "On Secrecy," 123–46; Bodine, "Taos Pueblo," 263; and Parsons, *Taos Pueblo*, 98–100. On the pueblo's struggle to regain Blue Lake, see Keegan, *The Taos Pueblo and Its Sacred Blue Lake*, 52.

7. C. Smith, *The Secular Revolution*.

8. On Collier and the transformation of federal Indian policy, see Daily, *Battle for the BIA*; Kelly, *Assault on Assimilation*; and Philp, *John Collier's Crusade*.

9. W. Smith, *The Meaning and End of Religion*, 15–79; J. Smith, "Religion, Religions, Religious," 179–96; Hultkrantz, *The Religions of the American Indians*, 9.

10. I am indebted to my colleague Tod Swanson at Arizona State University for this insight.

11. Wenger, " 'We Are Guaranteed Freedom,' " 89–113.

12. Charles Burke, "Circular No. 1665: Indian Dancing," April 26, 1921, reel 40, IRA Papers; Charles Burke, "Supplement to Circular No. 1665: Indian Dancing," February 14, 1923, reel 38, IRA Papers; Herbert Welsh to Hon. George Wharton Pepper, March 27, 1924, reel 87, IRA Papers.

13. Because these cultural elites challenged "modernity," many historians follow Lears, *No Place of Grace*, to call them "anti-modernists." However, literary critics and art historians have long identified the modernist movements in art and literature with primitivist critiques of "modern civilization," and for this reason—following S. Smith, *Reimagining Indians*—I find the term "modernists" more accurate. For a defense of the term "modernist anthropology," see Manganaro, *Modernist Anthropology: From Fieldwork to Text*.

14. My understanding of primitivism is shaped by Dilworth, *Imagining Indians*, 4–7; and Torgovnick, *Gone Primitive*.

15. Wenger, "Modernists, Pueblo Indians, and the Politics of Primitivism," 101–14.

16. Johnson, "Ancestors before Us," 327–46; Nabokov, *A Forest of Time*, 63, 147; Linnekin, "Cultural Invention and the Dilemma of Authenticity," 446–49; White, "Using the Past," 217–305.

17. Nabokov, *A Forest of Time*, especially 42–48.

18. Wenger, " 'We Are Guaranteed Freedom,' " 89–113.

19. King, *Orientalism and Religion*, 35–41; Balagangadhara, *"The Heathen in His Blindness—,"* 46.

20. King, *Orientalism and Religion*, 97–114. For broader reflections on the category of "world religions," see Masuzawa, *The Invention of World Religions*.

21. Chidester, *Savage Systems*, 11.

22. The definition of religion is Clifford Geertz's, and the critique is from Asad, *Genealogies of Religion*, 43. For a counterargument in defense of Geertz, see Schilbrack, "Religion, Models of, and Reality," 429–52.

23. Fitzgerald, *The Ideology of Religious Studies*, 6; Balagangadhara, *"The Heathen in His Blindness—"*; Lash, *The Beginning and the End of "Religion."*

24. J. Z. Smith, *Relating Religion*; Peterson and Walhof, *The Invention of Religion*; McCloud, *Making the American Religious Fringe*; Burris, *Exhibiting Religion*; Schmidt, *Hearing Things.*

25. Strenski, "On 'Religion' and Its Despisers," 113–32.

26. Chidester, *Savage Systems*; Tweed, *Crossing and Dwelling*; J. Z. Smith, "Religion, Religions, Religious."

27. Peterson and Walhof, *The Invention of Religion.*

28. These movements have inspired some scholars to defend the Western construct of an at least somewhat privatized religion as necessary to a modern and religiously diverse democratic society. See Lincoln, *Holy Terrors.*

29. C. Smith, *The Secular Revolution.*

30. Asad, *Formations of the Secular*; Fessenden, *Culture and Redemption.*

31. Gulliford, *Sacred Objects and Sacred Places*; Mazur, *The Americanization of Religious Minorities.*

Chapter 1

1. Wyaco, Jones, and Riley, *A Zuni Life*, 1–2, 97–104; Tedlock, "Zuni Sacred Theatre," 93–110; Parsons, "Notes on Zuni," 183–215.

2. Wyaco, Jones, and Riley, *A Zuni Life*, 97–99.

3. Elizabeth Shepley Sergeant, "Principales Speak," *New Republic* 33 (February 7, 1923): 273–75.

4. Sando, *Pueblo Nations*, 6–9; Gutierrez, *When Jesus Came*, xx–xxix.

5. Gutierrez, *When Jesus Came*, 46, 55–58, 81–82.

6. Spicer, *Cycles of Conquest*, 155–61; Vecsey, *On the Padres' Trail*, 129–33, 34–40; Sando, *Pueblo Nations*, 61–79.

7. Whiteley, "Reconnoitering 'Pueblo' Ethnicity," 484–86.

8. Sando, *Pueblo Nations*, 9, 263.

9. Spicer, *Cycles of Conquest*, 165–69; Vecsey, *On the Padres' Trail*, 141–42.

10. Vecsey, *On the Padres' Trail*, 143–44.

11. Brandt, "On Secrecy," 124–26; Parsons, *Pueblo Indian Religion*, 1:433–44.

12. Parsons, "Taos Field Notebook," July 1922, Parsons Papers.

13. Gutierrez, *When Jesus Came*, 165. See also Ramón Gutierrez, introduction to Parsons, *Pueblo Indian Religion*, 2:v–vi.

14. Quote is from Vecsey, *The Padres' Trail*, 143.

15. Wright, "How Many Are 'a Few'?" 219–37.

16. Pulido, *The Sacred World of the Penitentes*.

17. Lamadrid, *Hermanitos Comanchitos*; see also J. Brooks, *Captives and Cousins*, for a sophisticated treatment of cultural exchanges (including those conducted through human captivity) among Mexicans, Pueblo Indians, Comanches, Apaches, and other Plains and Southwestern tribes through the colonial period and into the nineteenth century.

18. Kessell, *The Missions of New Mexico*, 11–21; Vecsey, *On the Padres' Trail*, 151–53. Lamy's campaign to Americanize the Mexican-American Catholics in his diocese was championed in Cather, *Death Comes for the Archbishop*.

19. U.S. Office of Indian Affairs, *Sixty-first Annual Report of the Commissioner of Indian Affairs to the Secretary of the Interior*, 540–49.

20. Daniel Dorchester, "The City as a Peril," *National Perils and Opportunities: The Discussions of the General Conference, Held in Washington, D.C., 1887, under the Auspices and Direction of the Evangelical Alliance* (New York, 1887), 32, cited in Handy, *A Christian America*, 89.

21. Holm, *The Great Confusion in Indian Affairs*, 1–3; Prucha, *The Great Father*, vol. 1.

22. Hinsley, "Zunis and Brahmins," 170–75; Spicer, *Cycles of Conquest*, 169–71. The Pueblos' only armed resistance to U.S. rule was in the Taos Revolt of 1847, which killed the new U.S. governor. This revolt was an expression of Mexican nationalism, showing the Pueblos' close ties with their Hispano neighbors.

23. Keller, *American Protestantism*; Walker's quote is from U.S. Office of Indian Affairs, *Annual Report of the Commissioner of Indian Affairs for 1872*, 141.

24. Keller, *American Protestantism*, 1–4; Hamburger, *Separation of Church and State*, 193–251.

25. Baird, *Religion in America*, 259.

26. U.S. Office of Indian Affairs, *Annual Report of the Commissioner of Indian Affairs for 1882*, vii.

27. The original 1870 assignments, made before these guidelines were formally developed, gave the Catholic Church responsibility for none of the reservations. Keller, *American Protestantism*, 34, appendix 1; Prucha, *The Churches and the Indian Schools*, 2.

28. U.S. Office of Indian Affairs, *Annual Report of the Commissioner of Indian Affairs for 1871*, 389–91.

29. Prucha, *The Churches and the Indian Schools*, 2.

30. Baird, *Religion in America*, 579.

31. Dorchester, *Christianity in the United States*, 380–97.

32. Handy, *A Christian America*, 82–100.

33. McGreevy, *Catholicism and American Freedom*.

34. U.S. Office of Indian Affairs, *Annual Report of the Commissioner of Indian Affairs for 1873*, 269.

35. Sheldon Jackson, "Missionary Tour through New Mexico," *Rocky Mountain Presbyterian* 4, no. 12 (December 1875).

36. Franchot, *Roads to Rome*, analyzes nineteenth-century Protestant fascination and repulsion with Catholicism, including the tendency to equate Catholicism with Native American religions.

37. Jackson, "A Missionary Tour through New Mexico," *Rocky Mountain Presbyterian* 4, no. 11 (November 1875). While Montezuma was certainly present to some extent in Pueblo lore as a culture hero, these missionaries exaggerated his importance in Pueblo religious life and refigured his significance in messianic terms.

38. Mrs. J. W. Partridge, "A Plea for New Mexico," *Rocky Mountain Presbyterian* 8, no. 8 (August 1879).

39. U.S. Office of Indian Affairs, *Annual Report of the Commissioner of Indian Affairs for 1882*, 130.

40. U.S. Office of Indian Affairs, *Annual Report of the Commissioner of Indian Affairs for 1881*, 140–41; *Report of the Commissioner of Indian Affairs for 1898*, 207–9; and other annual reports.

41. Keller, *American Protestantism*, 219–22; Prucha, *The Great Father*, 519; Holm, *The Great Confusion in Indian Affairs*, 4–6.

42. On evolutionary theory and nineteenth-century U.S. Indian policy, see especially Dippie, *The Vanishing American*, 102–11; Hinsley, *The Smithsonian and the American Indian*, especially 81–189; and Hoxie, *A Final Promise*, 114–45.

43. Welsh, *Report of a Visit to the Great Sioux Reserve*, 1–49. Biographical information on Welsh is from Hagan, *The Indian Rights Association*, 1–5.

44. Board of Indian Commissioners, *Annual Report of the Board of Indian Commissioners*, 1016.

45. Welsh, *Report of a Visit to the Navajo, Pueblo, and Hualapais Indians*, 6, 47–48.

46. Father Anselm Weber to Father Besset, May 5, 1911, reel 56, BCIM Records.

47. Prucha, *American Indian Policy in Crisis*, 143–51.

48. Welsh, *Report of a Visit to the Navajo, Pueblo, and Hualapais Indians*, 48.

49. Dippie, *The Vanishing American*, 165–95; Hoxie, *A Final Promise*, 70–81, 147–87; Prucha, *The Great Father*, 618–40, 761–62.

50. Olson and Wilson, *Native Americans in the Twentieth Century*, 56; Daily, *Battle for the BIA*, 38.

51. J. Martin, *The Land Looks after Us*, 84–97; Moses, *The Indian Man: A Biography of James Mooney*, 52–73. For more detailed information on Wovoka and the Ghost Dance, see Hittman and Lynch, *Wovoka and the Ghost Dance*; and Mooney, *The Ghost-Dance Religion*.

52. J. Brown and Edwards, *Encyclopedia of Religious Knowledge*, 604, 899; Herzog, Schaff, and Jackson, *A Religious Encyclopaedia*, 5:178–80, 443–44; 8:298; W. Smith and Cheetham, *Dictionary of Christian Antiquities*, 1:761–63, 810–12; 2:1536–46.

53. John Menaul, "Characteristics of Pueblo Indians," *Home Missions Monthly* 6, no. 4 (February 1892): 80.

54. U.S. Office of Indian Affairs, *Sixty-first Annual Report of the Commissioner of Indian Affairs to the Secretary of the Interior*, 540–49.

55. Masuzawa, *In Search of Dreamtime*.

56. Cushing and Green, *Cushing at Zuni*, 24, 137, 55, 304, 241, 327.

57. Bourke, *The Snake-Dance of the Moquis*, 255–59, 169–70; Porter, *Paper Medicine Man: John Gregory Bourke and His American West*, 126–27.

58. U.S. Office of Indian Affairs, *Sixty-first Annual Report of the Commissioner of Indian Affairs to the Secretary of the Interior*, 549.

59. Pietz, "The Problem of the Fetish," 105–23; Murray, "Object Lessons," 199–217.

60. Parezo, "Matilda Coxe Stevenson," 38–62, quote on 41; Fowler, *A Laboratory for Anthropology*, 111–14; McFeely, *Zuni and the American Imagination*, 43–74.

61. Stevenson, "Zuni Religion," 137.

62. Stevenson, *The Zuni Indians*, 382.

63. Ibid., 406.

64. Crane, *Indians of the Enchanted Desert*, 16–18, 175–79, 276.

65. Ibid., 148–75. Crane's actions echoed those of former Hopi superintendent Charles Burton, described in chapter 2 and in Whiteley, *Deliberate Acts*, 91–97.

66. Jacobs, *Engendered Encounters*, 24–55. On the women's missionary movement, see Hill, *The World Their Household*; Hunter, *The Gospel of Gentility*; Robert, *American Women in Mission*. On women missionaries in the Southwest, see Yohn, *A Contest of Faiths*.

67. Mary Dissette to Capt. C. E. Nordstrom, August 19, 1897, box 8, folder 31, PCUSA.

68. On the expanding concerns of women's organizations in the period, see Scott, *Natural Allies*; and Epstein, *The Politics of Domesticity*.

69. Mary Dissette to Capt. C. E. Nordstrom, August 19, 1897, box 8, folder 31, PCUSA.

70. Daily, *Battle for the BIA*, 38–40; Hoxie, *A Final Promise*, 147–238.

71. Indian Rights Association, "Twenty-ninth Annual Report," 1912, reel 104, IRA Papers; Indian Rights Association, "Thirty-eighth Annual Report," 1920, reel 104, IRA Papers.

72. Board of Indian Commissioners, *Annual Report of the Board of Indian Commissioners*, 1009.

73. U.S. Office of Indian Affairs, *Annual Report of the Commissioner of Indian Affairs for 1872*, 301.

74. Ibid.

75. Prucha, *The Churches and the Indian Schools*, 3–4, 8.

76. U.S. Office of Indian Affairs, *Annual Report of the Commissioner of Indian Affairs for 1887*, 179–80, 248.

77. Prucha, *The Churches and the Indian Schools*, 4–9. Quotes are on 6 and 9.

78. Hamburger, *Separation of Church and State*, 219–32; Prucha, *American Indian Policy in Crisis*, 292–397; see also Thomas, Peck, and De Haan, "Reforming Education," 355–94.

79. *Proceedings of the Lake Mohonk Conference* (1889), 16–34, cited in Kvasnicka and Viola, *The Commissioners of Indian Affairs*, 196.

80. Prucha, *The Churches and the Indian Schools*, 10–20.

81. U.S. Office of Indian Affairs, *Sixty-first Annual Report of the Commissioner of Indian Affairs to the Secretary of the Interior*, 159–61; Prucha, *The Churches and the Indian Schools*, 22–25.

82. U.S. Office of Indian Affairs, *Sixty-first Annual Report of the Commissioner of Indian Affairs to the Secretary of the Interior*, 162–63.

83. U.S. Office of Indian Affairs, *Annual Report of the Commissioner of Indian Affairs for 1885*, 157.

84. Father Barnabas Meyer, O.F.M., to Rev. William Ketcham, April 21, 1911, reel 56, BCIM Records.

85. Hanks, "Lamy's Legacy," 399.

86. Rev. Fridolin Schuster to Rev. William Ketcham, May 22, 1917, reel 85, BCIM Records.

87. Examples include Sister Mary Philip, "The Peace-Loving Pueblo," *Indian Sentinel* 3, no. 3 (July 1923): 106–7; Fridolin Schuster, "How Pueblo Honor the Holy Child," *Indian Sentinel* 3, no. 4 (October 1923): 171; and William Hughes, "Who's Who among Catholic Indians: The Pueblo Sacristan," *Indian Sentinel* 3, no. 3 (July 1923): 132.

88. Rev. A. Docher to Rev. William Ketcham, February 12, 1917, reel 85, BCIM Records.

89. Rev. Fridolin Schuster to Rev. William Ketcham, December 9, 1910, reel 51, BCIM Records.

90. Wilken, *Anselm Weber, O.F.M.*, 168.

91. Jerome Hesse to Rev. William Ketcham, December 1, 1915, reel 75, BCIM Records.

92. Rev. William Ketcham to Commissioner Cato Sells, April 20, 1915, reel 75, BCIM Records.

93. Dolan, *The American Catholic Experience*, 294–320; Gilberto M. Hinojosa, "Mexican-American Faith Communities in Texas and the Southwest," and Jeffrey M. Burns, "The Mexican Catholic Community in California," in Dolan and Hinojosa, *Mexican Americans and the Catholic Church, 1900–1965*, 11–83, 148–50.

94. Rev. William Ketcham to Commissioner Cato Sells, April 20, 1915, reel 75, BCIM Records; Rev. Fridolin Schuster to Msgr. William Ketcham, January 13, 1920, reel 97, BCIM Records; Vecsey, *On the Padres' Trail*, 161.

95. Hughes, "Who's Who among Catholic Indians: The Pueblo Sacristan," 132; Vecsey, *On the Padres' Trail*, 159–70, 182–93.

96. Wilken, *Anselm Weber, O.F.M.*, 160; Matilda Coxe Stevenson to Mr. Holmes, February 25, 1907, box 2, Correspondence with Matilda Coxe Stevenson 1890–1918, Records of the Bureau of American Ethnology, NAA; Pandey, "Factionalism in a Southwestern Pueblo," 103–6, 151–66. Weber blamed Stevenson for influencing the Zunis against the mission, but Chavez and Stevenson both insisted this was the tribe's own decision.

97. Rev. Anthony Kroger to Rev. William Hughes, February 27, 1922, reel 107, BCIM Records; Vecsey, *On the Padres' Trail*, 141–58; Wilken, *Anselm Weber, O.F.M.*, 160–72.

98. U.S. Office of Indian Affairs, *Report of the Commissioner of Indian Affairs* (1903), 219.

99. Rules Regarding the Religious Instruction of Catholic Indian Pupils in the Government School at Albuquerque, New Mexico, March 1, 1907, reel 71, BCIM Records.

100. Prucha, *The Great Father*, 777–79.

101. Father Jerome Hesse to Rev. William Ketcham, July 20, 1911, reel 56, BCIM Records.

102. Rev. Fridolin Schuster to Mr. Charles Lusk, March 27, 1918, reel 85, BCIM Records.

103. Rev. William Ketcham to Rev. A. Docher, August 4, 1916, reel 80, BCIM Records.

104. Charles Lusk to Rev. Barnabas Meyer, January 10, 1913, reel 67, BCIM Records; Prucha, *The Churches and the Indian Schools*, 189–203.

105. U.S. Office of Indian Affairs, *Report of the Commissioner of Indian Affairs* (1921), 37.

106. Valentine, "General Regulations for Religious Worship and Instruction of Pupils in Government Indian Schools," March 12, 1910, file 806.3, NARA-SPC.

Chapter 2

1. Luhan, *Edge of Taos Desert*, 31–33, 68. On Luhan, see Rudnick, *Mabel Dodge Luhan*; Burke, "Finding What They Came For"; S. Smith, *Reimagining Indians*, 188–206.

2. Carr, *Inventing the American Primitive*; Lears, *No Place of Grace*; Dilworth, *Imagining Indians*.

3. Rodriguez, "Art, Tourism, and Race Relations in Taos," 144–60; Dilworth, *Imagining Indians*.

4. Scholars who share this more sympathetic view of the modernists include Rudnick, *Mabel Dodge Luhan*; S. Smith, *Reimagining Indians*; and Jenkins, *Dream Catchers*.

5. Tylor, *Primitive Culture*; Kuper, *The Invention of Primitive Society*, 80.

6. Morgan, *Ancient Society*, 6–7, 553–54; Styers, *Making Magic*, 103–04; Worster, *A River Running West*, 60–66, 437–66.

7. Stevenson, *The Zuni Indians*, 414, 20.

8. Culin is cited in McFeely, "Palimpsest of American Identity," 157. For more on Culin, see McFeely, *Zuni and the American Imagination*; Pandey, "Factionalism in a Southwestern Pueblo," 111–48.

9. Fiske and Lummis, *Charles F. Lummis*, 5–18; S. Smith, *Reimagining Indians*, 119–44.

10. Quotes are from Thompson, *American Character*, 35; Lummis, *A Tramp across the Continent*, 249; and Lummis, *Letters from the Southwest*, 18–20, 132.

11. Thompson, *American Character*, 116–55, "people of Mars" quote on 55. Ambrosio Abeita is said to have loaned the U.S. government tens of thousands of dollars to pay its troops in New Mexico during the Civil War. See Lummis, *Mesa, Cañon and Pueblo*, 445; and Sando, *Pueblo Nations*, 181.

12. Thompson, *American Character*, 155–71.

13. Fiske and Lummis, *Charles F. Lummis*, 112–17; S. Smith, *Reimagining Indians*, 136–39.

14. Lummis, *Some Strange Corners*, 167–74. Lint Sagarena, "Re-Forming the Church," 118–34, has argued that such mythologizing of the Spanish past served as a way to justify the United States taking over the Southwest from Mexico, which Americans stereotyped as a racially mixed, corrupt, and otherwise inferior nation.

15. Lummis, *Some Strange Corners*, 69–73; the points about Lummis's Hispano persona and his infantilization of Indians are from S. Smith, *Reimagining Indians*, 119–44.

16. Lummis, *Tramp across the Continent*, 142; Lummis, *Some Strange Corners*, 1–5; Lummis, *Mesa, Cañon, Pueblo*, 213–29; Fiske and Lummis, *Charles F. Lummis*, 71–74. Bandelier, *The Delight Makers*, is the archaeologist's own effort to use fiction to publicize his research on the Pueblos.

17. Lummis, *Some Strange Corners*, 5, 45, 56; Lummis, *Land of Poco Tiempo*, 253.

18. Lummis, Easton, and Brown, *Bullying the Moqui*, 14–19, 31–34, 43.

19. Daniel Dorchester, "Report of Superintendent of Indian Schools," in U.S. Office of Indian Affairs, *Sixty-first Annual Report of the Commissioner of Indian Affairs to the Secretary of the Interior*, 547.

20. Lummis, Easton, and Brown, *Bullying the Moqui*, 22–23.

21. Gibson, *The Santa Fe and Taos Colonies*, 3–49; Carr, *Inventing the American Primitive*, 212–17. Quote is from Paul A. F. Walter, "The Santa Fe-Taos Art Movement," *Art and Archaeology* 4 (December 1916): 335, cited in Gibson, 13.

22. This and the following paragraph are based on the paintings that appear in Woloshuk, *E. Irving Couse*.

23. The same is true of his treatment of pottery, weaving, and other Indian crafts.

24. Dilworth, *Imagining Indians*, 101–3; Rodriguez, "Art, Tourism, and Race Relations in Taos," 148.

25. Forrest, *The Preservation of the Village*, 34–54; Phoebe S. Kropp, " 'There is a little sermon in that': Constructing the Native Southwest at the San Diego Panama-California Exposition of 1915," in Weigle and Babcock, *The Great Southwest of the Fred Harvey Company and the Santa Fe Railway*, 36–46; Dilworth, *Imagining Indians*, 16–20, 77–124; Chauvenet, *Hewett and Friends*, 97–108, 135–61.

26. Kuper, *The Invention of Primitive Society*, 127–31.

27. Quote on Eskimo is in Stocking, *Race, Culture, and Evolution*, 148; Boas, *The Mind of Primitive Man*, 251–78; Boas, *The Ethnography of Franz Boas*, 280–81, 290–92. My reading of Boas is especially shaped by Silverman, *Totems and Teachers*, 1–19; and R. Martin, *The Languages of Difference*, 165–88. On Boas and the concept of culture, see Stocking, *Race, Culture, and Evolution*, 195–233.

28. T. Kroeber, *Alfred Kroeber*, 26–27; Hollinger, *Science, Jews, and Secular Culture*.

29. Boas, *The Mind of Primitive Man*, 203–6; Martin, *The Languages of Difference*, 165–88.

30. A. Kroeber, *Anthropology*, 298–302, 363–70; T. Kroeber, *Alfred Kroeber*; A. Kroeber, *Zuni Potsherds*; A. Kroeber, *Zuñi Kin and Clan*.

31. A. Kroeber, *Anthropology*, 370, 480–84, 455. On the European invention of "world religions" as a category, see Masuzawa, *The Invention of World Religions*.

32. Deacon, *Elsie Clews Parsons*, 1–77, Stein quote on 1; and Zumwalt, *Wealth and Rebellion*, 16–97.

33. Deacon, *Elsie Clews Parsons*, 97–103; quote is in Desley Deacon, introduction to Parsons, *Fear and Conventionality*, xiv.

34. Parsons, *The Old-Fashioned Woman*, 227–37.

35. Cited in Deacon, *Elsie Clews Parsons*, 65.

36. Parsons, *Fear and Conventionality*, 205–18.

37. Stocking, "The Ethnographic Sensibility of the 1920s," 216–17; Parsons, *Pueblo Indian Religion*, 1:xxxvi.

38. Deacon, *Elsie Clews Parsons*, 85–87, 145–201, 222–24; Zumwalt, *Wealth and Rebellion*, 123–44. Jacobs, *Engendered Encounters*, 56–105, examines the relationships between Parsons's feminism, cultural relativism, and primitivism.

39. Benedict, *Patterns of Culture*; Handler, "Ruth Benedict," 164–78.

40. Parsons, *Pueblo Indian Religion*, 1:xxxiii–xxxiv.

41. Elsie Clews Parsons, "Ceremonial Dances at Zuni," *El Palacio* 8, no. 10 (November 15, 1922): 119–22; Parsons, *Pueblo Indian Religion*, 1:xxxiii–xxxiv; 2:1068–73; Deacon, *Elsie Clews Parsons*, 228–30.

42. Rudnick, *Mabel Dodge Luhan*, 1–100; quote is from Lois Palken Rudnick, introduction to Luhan, *Intimate Memories*, vii.

43. Stansell, *American Moderns*, 100–111, 311–38; Rudnick, *Mabel Dodge Luhan*, 100–106, 121–41.

44. Luhan, *Movers and Shakers*, 468, 511–12, 533; Rudnick, *Mabel Dodge Luhan*, 129–37. On New Thought, see Satter, *Each Mind a Kingdom*.

45. Luhan, *Movers and Shakers*, 534–35.

46. Luhan, *Edge of Taos Desert*, 62–66, 280–81, 333.

47. Ibid., 174–95, 232; Rudnick, *Mabel Dodge Luhan*, 154–56, 181–83.

48. Luhan, *Edge of Taos Desert*, 65.

49. Ibid., 84–85, 126. Luhan helped initiate a vogue for collecting *santos*, which are still prized by collectors and tourists as an authentic New Mexican "folk art."

50. Ibid., 34, 80–82.

51. Ibid., 221–22, 283; Mabel Dodge Sterne to John Collier, November 21, 1922, reel 3, Collier Papers.

52. Luhan, *Edge of Taos Desert*, 65–66; DeWitt, *Taos*, 68.

53. Luhan, *Edge of Taos Desert*, 9.

54. Ibid., 197.

55. Morrill, *Taos Mosaic*, 110, cited in Jacobs, *Engendered Encounters*, 104.

56. P. Deloria, *Playing Indian*; Huhndorf, *Going Native*. Deloria and Huhndorf both provide a more nuanced analysis than my summary suggests, showing how white Americans have used Native traditions as an antidote to the anomie of industrial society.

57. Luhan, *Edge of Taos Desert*, 197, 225.

58. Ibid., 223; Rudnick, *Mabel Dodge Luhan*, 165.

59. Luhan, *Edge of Taos Desert*, 222; Luhan, *Winter in Taos*, 215.

60. Henri, *The Art Spirit*, 112–13.

61. V. Brooks, *John Sloan*, 92–93.

62. Sloan to Hewett, New York, June 2, 1922, Hewett Collection, Museum of New Mexico, Santa Fe, cited in Gibson, *The Santa Fe and Taos Colonies*, 151. Sloan's essay on modernism is from *Forum* magazine in 1925, cited in Loughery, *John Sloan*, 274; Couse is quoted in Alice Corbin Henderson, "A Painter of Pueblo Indians," *El Palacio* 10, no. 10 (April 15, 1921): 2–76; and Blumenschein and Phillips in V. Brooks, *John Sloan*, 19.

63. Burlin, *The Indians' Book*, xxi.

64. Austin, *The American Rhythm*; Castro, *Interpreting the Indian*, 7–19.

65. Harriet Monroe, "In the Chapel of Nicholas V," *Atlantic Monthly* 92 (1903): 409, cited in Schultze, "Harriet Monroe's Pioneer Modernism," 53; Monroe, "In Texas and New Mexico," *Poetry*, September 1920, 326–28, cited in Weigle and Fiore, *Santa Fe and Taos*, 18; and Monroe, "The Grand Cañon of the Colorado," *Atlantic Monthly* 84 (1899): 818–19, cited in Schultze, "Harriet Monroe's Pioneer Modernism," 54.

66. Marsden Hartley, "Tribal Esthetics Dance Drama," *El Palacio* 6, no. 4 (November 15, 1919): 53–54; Henri, *The Art Spirit*, 144–45.

67. Alice Corbin Henderson, "The Dance-Rituals of the Pueblo Indians," *Theatre Arts Magazine* 7 (April 1923): 109–14.

68. Luhan, *Intimate Memories*, 150; John Sloan, introduction to Collier, *Patterns and Ceremonials*, 5; Shelton, *Ruth St. Denis: A Biography of the Divine Dancer*, 157–58, 76–77; Daly, *Done into Dance*, especially 114–15; De Mille, *Martha*, 175–77.

69. Austin, *Earth Horizon*, 360–61; Gibson, *The Santa Fe and Taos Colonies*, 155–59.

70. Loughery, *John Sloan*, 306–9; Pfister, *Individuality Incorporated*, 160–64.

71. Henderson, "A Painter of Pueblo Indians," 2–76; Babcock, "Mudwomen and Whitemen," 180–95. For a related critique of Indian art and the politics of authenticity, see Clifford, *The Predicament of Culture*, 193–206.

Chapter 3

1. Council of All the New Mexico Pueblos, "An Appeal to the People of the United States from the Pueblo Indians of New Mexico," November 5, 1922, box 317, folder 2, AAIA Papers.

2. Mabel Sterne to Austin, December 1922, in Austin and Pearce, *Literary America, 1903–1934*, 173.

3. Kelly, *Assault on Assimilation*, 190–206; Sando, *Pueblo Nations*, 107–16, 204; *U.S. v. Ruperto Archuleta, et al.*, New Mexico District Court, 1921, Renehan Papers.

4. L. A. Dorrington, "Report of Meeting with Northern Pueblo Officials at San Juan Pueblo," November 30, 1921, file 154, NARA-NP Records; Pablo Abeita to Rev. William Ketcham, December 1915, reel 75, BCIM Records; Pablo Abeita to Charles Lusk, March 20, 1924, reel 119, BCIM Records.

5. Isleta Governor and Officials to Pueblo Governors, December 19, 1910, Santiago Naranjo Papers, Fray Angélico Chávez History Library, Santa Fe; Council of All the New Mexico Pueblos, "Petition to Washington," January 20, 1911, file 046, Hewett-ALA. For more detailed discussion of these jurisdictional disputes and their links with the battles over land, see Kelly, *Assault on Assimilation*, 193–98.

6. Parsons, *The Pueblo of Jemez*, 9.

7. Coleman, *American Indian Children at School*; Adams, *Education for Extinction*; Hyer, *One House, One Voice, One Heart*; and McKinney, "History of the Albuquerque Indian School," 109–38.

8. John Dixon to John Collier, November 14, 1922, reel 4, Collier Papers; H. P. Marble to Commissioner of Indian Affairs, October 20, 1922, file 066, NARA-SP Records.

9. Antonio Montoya to Samuel Beahm, February 9, 1923, file 63, NARA-VPJ.

10. Council of All the New Mexico Pueblos, "Petition to Washington," January 20,

1911, file 046, Hewett-ALA; Leo Crane to C. R. Kopplin, January 3, 1921, file 070, NARA-SPC.

11. Superintendent Marble to Antonio Montoya, March 5, 1923, reel 41, IRA Papers; H. P. Marble to Alcario Montoya and John Dixon, February 12, 1923, file 63, NARA-VPJ.

12. Kelly, *Assault on Assimilation*, 209–16; Philp, *John Collier's Crusade*, 28–32. Shortly after this episode, Fall was forced to resign after a series of scandals, their effect perhaps exacerbated by the public outrage over the Bursum Bill.

13. Pablo Abeita to Rev. William Ketcham, December 5, 1913, reel 67, BCIM Records; Sando, *Pueblo Nations*, 181–82; Pablo Abeita to Rev. William Ketcham, October 7, 1921, reel 102, BCIM Records.

14. Sando, *Pueblo Profiles*, 48.

15. Abeita gave this speech at the meeting of the U.S. Indian Pueblo Council in Santa Fe on November 7 and 8, 1928. Minutes were entered into the record of the U.S. Senate, *Hearings on S. Res. 79 and 308 (70th Cong.), and S. Res. 263 and 416 (71st Cong.)*.

16. Pablo Abeita to Rev. William Ketcham, January 3, 1910, reel 56, BCIM Records; Pablo Abeita to Rev. William Ketcham, February 8, 1911, reel 56, BCIM Records; Pablo Abeita to Rev. William Ketcham, December 1915, reel 75, BCIM Records; Sando, *Pueblo Nations*, 181–82.

17. Pablo Abeita to Rev. William Hughes, October 23, 1922, reel 107, BCIM Records.

18. Rev. Fridolin Schuster to Rev. William Hughes, July 22, 1922, reel 107, BCIM Records; Rev. William Hughes to Rev. Robert Lucey, December 20, 1922, reel 107, BCIM Records; Letter to Mrs. Markoe, October 14, 1922, reel 37, IRA Papers.

19. Elizabeth Shepley Sergeant, "Notes on Pueblo Indians," n.d., 1922, reel 5, Collier Papers; Council of All the New Mexico Pueblos, "An Appeal to the People of the United States from the Pueblo Indians of New Mexico," November 5, 1922, box 317, folder 2, AAIA Papers.

20. Pablo Abeita to Rev. William Hughes, October 23, 1922, reel 107, BCIM Records.

21. Collier, *From Every Zenith*, 24–25, 29–30; Philp, *John Collier's Crusade*, 4–7.

22. Collier, *From Every Zenith*, 19–20, 22–24.

23. Ibid., 38–48, 61–63; Philp, *John Collier's Crusade*, 7–9.

24. Collier, *From Every Zenith*, 69–71; Philp, *John Collier's Crusade*, 9–22.

25. Collier, *From Every Zenith*, 115–19; Philp, *John Collier's Crusade*, 22–24; Kelly, *Assault on Assimilation*, 109.

26. John Collier, "The Red Atlantis," *Survey* 49 (October 1, 1922): 16–19, 63–66; Collier, *From Every Zenith*, 126.

27. Collier, *From Every Zenith*, 126, 161; Collier, "The Red Atlantis," 16–19, 63–66; John Collier, "The Pueblos' Last Stand," *Sunset Magazine* 50 (February 1923): 19–22, 65–66.

28. Stella Atwood, "The Case for the Indians," *Survey* 49 (October 1, 1922): 7–11; Philp, *John Collier's Crusade*, 26–27, 32–33.

29. Elizabeth Shepley Sergeant to Norman Hapgood, November 14, 1922, reel 5, Collier Papers; Mary Austin to Mabel Dodge Sterne, December 5, 1922, Luhan Papers; Fergusson, "Justice for the Pueblo Indians," 665; Witter Bynner, "From Him That Hath Not," *Outlook* 133 (January 17, 1923): 125–27; Elizabeth Shepley Sergeant, "Principales Speak," *New Republic* 33 (February 7, 1923): 273–75; Alice Corbin Henderson, "The Dance-Rituals of the Pueblo Indians," *Theatre Arts Magazine* 7 (April 1923): 109–14; John Collier, "The American Congo," *Survey Graphic* (August 1923): 467–76.

30. Announcement of the Formation of the Eastern Association on Indian Affairs, 1923, reel 113, BCIM Records; New Mexico Association on Indian Affairs, "Bulletin No. 1: The Pueblo Land Problem," 1923, reel 5, Collier Papers; Pablo Abeita to Rev. William Ketcham, October 7, 1921, reel 102, BCIM Records; American Indian Defense Association, "Announcement of Purposes of the American Indian Defense Association, Incorporated," n.d., 1923, box 2A, White Papers. See also Zumwalt, *Wealth and Rebellion*, 257–62; Kelly, *Assault on Assimilation*, 215–54.

31. Ortiz, *The Tewa World*, 13–28; Parsons, *Pueblo Indian Religion*, 1:270–310; Collier, "The American Congo," 467–76.

32. U.S. House, *Hearings on H.R. 13452 and H.R. 13674*, 348; Pueblo of San Ildefonso Report, March 24, 1922, file 154, NARA-NP Records.

33. Interview with Martin Vigil, Tesuque Pueblo, 1970, No. 764, Duke Collection.

34. U.S. Senate, Subcommittee on Public Lands and Surveys, *Hearings on S. 3865 and S. 4223*, 189–93.

35. Ibid., 207.

36. Ibid., 116.

37. Ina Sizer Cassidy to Dr. Samuel Elliot, December 6, 1922, file 006, Cassidy Collection; Ina Sizer Cassidy, "Preserve the Pueblos," n.d., [1922], file 006, Cassidy Collection.

38. Collier, "The American Congo," 467–76; Collier, "The Pueblos' Last Stand," 19–22, 65–66.

39. John Collier, "Politicians Pillage the Pueblos," *Searchlight* 7, no. 8 (January 31, 1923): 15; John Collier, "Plundering the Pueblo Indians," *Sunset Magazine* 50 (January 1923): 21.

40. Collier, "Politicians Pillage the Pueblos," 15; Sniffen, "Minutes of the Advisory Council on Indian Affairs," December 12, 1923, reel 39, IRA Papers; Lears, *No Place of Grace*, 141–81.

41. Collier, "Politicians Pillage the Pueblos," 15; Leontis, *Topographies of Hellenism*; Ferris, *Silent Urns*. Admiring studies of ancient Greece published in this period included Van Hook, *Greek Life and Thought*; and Greene, *The Achievement of Greece*.

42. Collier, "The Pueblos' Last Stand," 19–22, 65–66.

43. U.S. House, *Hearings on H.R. 13452 and H.R. 13674*, 219–22, 236.

44. Collier, "Plundering the Pueblo Indians," 21–25, 56; John Collier to Rev. William

Hughes, October 8, 1922, reel 107, BCIM Records; Collier, "The American Congo," 467–76.

45. Collier, "The Pueblos' Last Stand," 19–22, 65–66.

46. Mabel Dodge to John Collier, November 21, 1922, Collier Papers, cited in Kelly, *Assault on Assimilation*, 227; John Collier to Ina Sizer Cassidy, November 26, 1923, file 005, Cassidy Collection.

47. Pablo Abeita to Charles Lusk, March 20, 1924, reel 119, BCIM Records.

48. "Are the Pueblo Indians to Be Robbed of Their Heritage?" *Current Opinion* 74 (February 1923): 213–14; Lawrence, *Selected Letters*, 211; Lawrence, "New Mexico," 33–36.

49. "Pueblo Indians Have Danced for Centuries; Red Men Asked to Quit It All in a Year's Time," *Santa Fe New Mexican*, April 25, 1923, 6; Stanton, "Processing the Native American," 59–84; Torgovnick, *Gone Primitive*, 168–74.

50. "The Last First Americans," *Nation* 116 (November 29, 1922): 570; U.S. Senate, Subcommittee on Public Lands and Surveys, *Hearings on S. 3865 and S. 4223*, 113.

51. U.S. House, *Hearings on H.R. 13452 and H.R. 13674*, 20–21.

52. Alice Corbin Henderson to Roberts Walker, November 20, 1922, box 317, folder 2, AAIA Papers.

53. John Collier to Mabel Dodge Luhan, February 2, no year, Luhan Papers; Kelly, *Assault on Assimilation*, 130–31.

54. Spence, *Dispossessing the Wilderness*. Thanks to Sherry Smith for pointing out this irony and guiding me to Spence's work.

55. John Collier, "The Indian and Religious Freedom" (San Francisco: The Indian Defense Association of Central and Northern California, 1924), reel 9, Collier Papers.

56. Frank G. Speck, "Pueblo Statement," 1922?, Speck Collection; Frank G. Speck, "Educating the White Man up to the Indian," n.d., Speck Collection.

57. U.S. Senate, Subcommittee on Public Lands and Surveys, *Hearings on S. 3865 and S. 4223*, 137.

58. Elizabeth Shepley Sergeant, "Principales Speak," *New Republic* 33 (February 7, 1923): 273–75.

59. J. D. DeHuff, "How Shall We Educate the Indian?" *El Palacio* 8, no. 5 (September 1, 1922): 59–64.

60. "Draft New Policy on Indian Welfare," *New York Times*, June 10, 1923, 2:3.

61. DeHuff, "How Shall We Educate the Indian?" 59–64; "Indian Play Most Delightful; Costumes, Dances All Clever," *Santa Fe New Mexican*, June 5, 1924; J. D. DeHuff to the Commissioner of Indian Affairs, November 16, 1923, file 310, NARA-SFIS; J. D. DeHuff to Commissioner Charles Burke, June 10, 1924, file 063, NARA-SFIS; McDowell, "Report to Hon. George Vaux on the Santa Fe Indian School," May 4, 1925, file 296, NARA-SFIS.

62. Collier, "The Red Atlantis," 63; Collier, *From Every Zenith*, 203.

63. John Collier, "Our Indian Policy," *Sunset Magazine* 50 (March 1923): 13–15, 89–93; Collier, "The Red Atlantis," 19–20; Collier, "Politicians Pillage the Pueblos," 15–19.

64. Kelly, *Assault on Assimilation*, 239–54.

65. John Collier to Francis C. Wilson, April 13, 1923, box 317, folder 4, AAIA Papers.

66. Francis Wilson, "Wilson Reply to John Collier Makes Clear What Friends of Pueblo Indian Have Gained," *Santa Fe New Mexican*, October 18, 1923. See also Kelly, *Assault on Assimilation*, 252–57.

67. Kelly, *Assault on Assimilation*, 229–30, 252, 276; Mary Austin to Robert Brown, March 31, 1923, box 2A, White Papers; Roberts Walker to Jack Vollmar, February 9, 1923, box 317, folder 4, AAIA Papers; Roberts Walker to Margaret McKittrick, November 8, 1923, box 317, folder 6, AAIA Papers; "Shocking," *Santa Fe New Mexican*, December 4, 1923; Rev. Fridolin Schuster to Rev. William Hughes, November 19, 1923, reel 113, BCIM Records. See also Forrest, *The Preservation of the Village*, 56–57.

68. Roberts Walker to Alice Corbin Henderson, January 30, 1924, box 318, folder 1, AAIA Papers; Roberts Walker, letter to the editor, *Forum*, February 19, 1924, box 318, folder 2, AAIA Papers.

69. Roberts Walker, "On John Collier," July 23, 1923, box 2A, White Papers.

70. Indian Rights Association, "Thirty-ninth Annual Report," 1921, reel 104, IRA Papers; S. M. Brosius to Matthew Sniffen, November 4, 1922, reel 37, IRA Papers; S. M. Brosius to Matthew Sniffen, December 1, 1922, reel 37, IRA Papers.

71. Stella Atwood to S. M. Brosius, November 10, 1922, reel 37, IRA Papers.

72. S. M. Brosius to Herbert Welsh, August 8, 1923, reel 39, IRA Papers; S. M. Brosius to Matthew Sniffen, March 15, 1924, reel 40, IRA Papers.

73. Jacobs, *Engendered Encounters*, 30; Clara True, "The Experiences of a Woman Indian Agent," *Outlook* 92 (June 3, 1909): 331–36; and Ronnie Peacock, "Biographical Timeline of Clara True," compiled in preparation for her M.A. thesis at the University of Northern Colorado, and kindly shared with me July 2, 2001.

74. Superintendent Horace J. Johnson to Rev. William Ketcham, January 13, 1921, reel 102, BCIM Records; Horace J. Johnson to Matthew Sniffen, March 13, 1922, reel 37, IRA Papers.

75. Pueblo of Santa Clara Report, March 24, 1922, file 154, NARA-NP Records; Pueblo of San Ildefonso Report, March 24, 1922, file 154, NARA-NP Records.

76. Clara True to A. B. Renehan, n.d., 1921, Renehan Papers; *U.S. v. Ruperto Archuleta, et al.*, New Mexico District Court, 1921, Renehan Papers.

77. Clara True to S. M. Brosius, October 29, 1922, reel 37, IRA Papers; S. M. Brosius to Matthew Sniffen, November 4, 1922, reel 37, IRA Papers; Alice Corbin Henderson, "Death of the Pueblos," *New Republic* 33 (November 29, 1922): 11–13.

78. S. M. Brosius to Matthew Sniffen, December 1, 1922, reel 37, IRA Papers.

79. Council of All the New Mexico Pueblos, "Statement," August 25, 1923, reel 39, IRA Papers.

80. Kelly, *Assault on Assimilation*, 295–99; Philp, *John Collier's Crusade*, 104–5, 18.

Chapter 4

1. William E. Johnson, "Those Sacred Indian Ceremonials," *Native American* 24, no. 13 (September 20, 1924): 173–77.

2. Council of All the New Mexico Pueblos, "To the President of the United States, the Congress, and Our Friends the American People," August 31, 1925, reel 9, Collier Papers.

3. Jacobs, *Engendered Encounters*. On Victorian and post-Victorian gender roles, see Smith-Rosenberg, *Disorderly Conduct*; D'Emilio and Freedman, *Intimate Matters*; Filene, *Him/Her/Self*.

4. *Santa Fe New Mexican*, December 28, 1919, cited in Gibson, *The Santa Fe and Taos Colonies*, 150.

5. Rev. Fridolin Schuster to Rev. William Ketcham, March 7, 1919, reel 93, BCIM Records.

6. It was in these years that Johnson's predilection for nighttime sleuthing earned him a reputation as a "pussyfoot," a nickname that would stick for the rest of his career. See McKenzie, *"Pussyfoot" Johnson: Crusader-Reformer-a Man among Men*, 65–101; and "William E. Johnson," Anti-Saloon League Website, <http://www.wpl.lib.oh.us/AntiSaloon/Leaders/william_johnson.html>, consulted December 21, 2005.

7. Clara True to Rev. William Ketcham, March 18, 1911, reel 56, BCIM Records; William E. Johnson to Rev. Haelterman, March 13, 1911, reel 56, BCIM Records; Johnson, "The Story of Juan Cruz" (Laurel, Maryland, 1912), IRA Papers.

8. Stewart, *Peyote Religion*, 219–26; Moses, *The Indian Man: A Biography of James Mooney*, 179–205.

9. Joint committee on Indian Missions of the Home Missions Council, "Program: Conference of Christian Workers among Indians," September 24–26, 1919, reel 130, IRA Papers; C. M. Weisenhorn, "The Peyote Evil," *Indian Sentinel* 1, no. 4 (October 1920): 172–73; Roundy, "Joint Committee on Indian Missions Meeting Minutes," June 21, 1922, reel 37, IRA Papers.

10. U.S. Office of Indian Affairs, *Report of the Commissioner of Indian Affairs* (1909), 14.

11. K. Trout and Mark Hoffman, "Faith, Belief, and the Peyote Crisis," *Entheos: The Journal of Psychedelic Spirituality* 1, no. 2 (Winter 2002), <http://www.entheomedia.org/peyote_crisis.htm>, consulted December 21, 2005. For more details on Johnson's anti-peyote campaign, see Stewart, *Peyote Religion*, 134–47.

12. Johnson, "Those Sacred Indian Ceremonials," 173–77.

13. Charles Lusk to Charles Burke, July 29, 1921, reel 102, BCIM Records; Wood, *Taos Pueblo*, 33–34.

14. Daily, *Battle for the BIA*, 41; Evander Sweet, "Memorandum on Burris Charges," February 6, 1921, Manuscript 7070, NAA.

15. Evander Sweet, "Exhibit A: Affidavits of Hopi Indians Residing at Oraibi, Arizona, Regarding the Moral Character of the Ceremonial Dances among the Hopi Indians," February 6, 1921, Manuscript 7070, NAA; Dockstader, *The Kachina and the White Man*.

16. Talayesva and Simmons, *Sun Chief*, 109, cited and discussed in Babcock, "Arrange Me into Disorder," 112.

17. Parsons, *Pueblo Indian Religion*, 1:438–39, 2:805.

18. Wyaco, Jones, and Riley, *A Zuni Life*, 53. See also Ortiz, "Ritual Drama," 135–62; and Hieb, "Meaning and Mismeaning: Toward an Understanding of the Ritual Clown," 163–96.

19. Statement of Mrs. Julius (Blanche) Seligman, May 4, 1924, file 150, NARA-NP Records; Jacobs, *Engendered Encounters*, 137–38.

20. Evander Sweet, "Exhibit B: Affidavits of Hopi Indians Residing at Polacca (First Mesa), Arizona, Regarding the Moral Character of the Hopi Ceremonial Dances," February 6, 1921, Manuscript 7070, NAA; Whiteley, "Burning Culture," 46–85.

21. This paragraph is based on Jacobs, *Engendered Encounters*, 121. She cites May, *Great Expectations*, 167; and D'Emilio and Freedman, *Intimate Matters*, 112–16, 223–26.

22. Charles Burke, "Circular No. 1665: Indian Dancing," April 26, 1921, reel 40, IRA Papers; Daily, *Battle for the BIA*, 41.

23. Daily, *Battle for the BIA*, 43; Lindquist, *The Red Man in the United States*, 40–41, 68–69, 269.

24. Elmer Higley and Bertha Eckert, "Utilizing the American Indian Survey," March 1922, reel 37, IRA Papers; Rev. Fridolin Schuster to Rev. William Hughes, May 13, 1922, reel 107, BCIM Records.

25. Daily, *Battle for the BIA*, 42–43.

26. Charles Burke, "Supplement to Circular No. 1665: Indian Dancing," February 14, 1923, reel 38, IRA Papers; Charles Burke, "A Message to All Indians," February 24, 1923, reel 38, IRA Papers.

27. Alcario Montoya and Cochiti Pueblo to Mr. Marble, March 15, 1923, Indian Correspondence, folder 109, SWAIA Records; Governor Isidro Shije to Margaret McKittrick, March 28, 1923, Indian Correspondence, folder 109, SWAIA Records.

28. San Ildefonso Pueblo to the Secretary of the Interior, January 16, 1924, reel 9, Collier Papers.

29. Pablo Abeita to Charles Lusk, March 10, 1923, reel 113, BCIM Records.

30. Rev. Fridolin Schuster to Rev. William Hughes, March 30, 1923, reel 113, BCIM Records; R. E. Twitchell to Gerald Cassidy, March 8, 1923, box 1, Pueblo Indian Land

Matters Scrapbooks, Fray Angélico Chávez History Library, Santa Fe, New Mexico; Roberts Walker to Miss A. E. White, March 23, 1923, box 317, folder 4, AAIA Papers; Roberts Walker to Denis Riordan, March 30, 1923, box 317, folder 4, AAIA Papers.

31. Charles Burke to Edgar Hewett, March 7, 1923, file 046, Hewett-ALA.

32. Espanola Chamber of Commerce Settlers Committee and A. B. Renehan, "The Pueblo Indians and Their Land Grants," 1923, reel 128, IRA Papers; Margaret McKittrick to Roberts Walker, December 8, 1923, box 318, folder 1, AAIA Papers.

33. "Don't Dance for Fun of It, Indians Tell Commissioner," *Santa Fe New Mexican*, April 11, 1923, 6.

34. "Commissioner Burke's Silly Order," *New York World*, March 9, 1923; "Preserving Indian Dances," *New York Times*, May 8, 1923.

35. "Moral Vandalism," *Santa Fe New Mexican*, March 8, 1923.

36. Ibid.; "Action Needed," *Santa Fe New Mexican*, March 9, 1923.

37. Mrs. O. S. Emblem, "Duty under Constitution to Guarantee Religious Freedom," *Santa Fe New Mexican*, March 10, 1923.

38. Eastern Association on Indian Affairs to Hubert Work, March 23, 1923, file 017, Cassidy Collection.

39. "Don't Dance for Fun of It, Indians Tell Commissioner; "No Order Has Been Issued Forbidding Pueblo Dances Indian Bureau Announces," *Albuquerque Herald*, March 11, 1923; Charles Burke to Walter Danburg, May 10, 1923, file 073, NARA-NPCb.

40. Matthew Sniffen, "Extract from the Minutes of a Regular Meeting of the Board of Directors of the Indian Rights Association," April 4, 1923, reel 39, IRA Papers; Rodney W. Roundy to Matthew Sniffen, April 9, 1923, reel 39, IRA Papers; Home Missions Council, "Indian Missions: Achievements, Adjustments and Advances in Christian Cooperation," 1923, reel 130, IRA Papers.

41. Fridolin Schuster, "How Pueblo Honor the Holy Child," *Indian Sentinel* 3, no. 4 (October 1923): 171.

42. Rev. Fridolin Schuster to Rev. William Hughes, March 30, 1923, reel 113, BCIM Records.

43. "Indian Dances," *Indian Sentinel* 3, no. 2 (April 1923): 58–59; Matthew Sniffen, "Timely Indian Facts," May 15, 1923, reel 104, IRA Papers; and Matthew Sniffen, "Ban on Indian Dances," *Southern Workman* (May 1923): 209–10.

44. Matthew Sniffen to S. M. Brosius, April 7, 1923, reel 87, IRA Papers; S. M. Brosius to Matthew Sniffen, April 9, 1923, reel 39, IRA Papers.

45. Indian Rights Association, "Forty-first Annual Report," 1923, reel 104, IRA Papers; Matthew Sniffen to Amelia E. White, May 1, 1923, reel 87, IRA Papers; S. M. Brosius to Matthew Sniffen, April 9, 1923, reel 39, IRA Papers; Matthew Sniffen to S. M. Brosius, April 7, 1923, reel 87, IRA Papers.

46. Matthew Sniffen, "Extract from the Minutes of a Regular Meeting of the Board of Directors of the Indian Rights Association," April 4, 1923; Matthew Sniffen to Warren

Moorehead, June 5, 1923, reel 39, IRA Papers; Matthew Sniffen, "Timely Indian Facts," May 15, 1923, reel 104, IRA Papers.

47. Sniffen, "Ban on Indian Dances," 209–10; Herbert Welsh, letter to the editor, *Record*, May 3, 1923, reel 87, IRA Papers; D'Emilio and Freedman, *Intimate Matters*, 223–26, and plates 47–51; Charles Burke to Matthew Sniffen, May 19, 1923, reel 39, IRA Papers; Matthew Sniffen to Warren Moorehead, June 5, 1923, reel 39, IRA Papers.

48. Herbert Welsh, letter to the editor, *Record*, May 3, 1923, reel 87, IRA Papers; Herbert Welsh to Ralph Miller, June 13, 1923, reel 39, IRA Papers; Herbert Welsh to Matthew Sniffen, June 14, 1923, reel 39, IRA Papers.

49. Matthew Sniffen to Jennie B. Dunham, April 11, 1923, reel 87, IRA Papers; Sniffen, "Ban on Indian Dances," 209–10.

50. Matthew Sniffen to Jennie B. Dunham, April 11, 1923, reel 87, IRA Papers.

51. Herbert Welsh to Hubert Work, May 9, 1923, reel 39, IRA Papers.

52. Moorehead, *American Indian in the United States*, 17–18; Warren Moorehead to Matthew Sniffen, June 20, 1923, reel 39, IRA Papers.

53. U.S. House, *Hearings on H.R. 13452 and H.R. 13674*, 220, 235; John Collier, "The Pueblos' Last Stand," *Sunset Magazine* 50 (February 1923): 19–22, 65–66; John Collier to Elizabeth Shepley Sergeant, October 4, 1923, reel 4, Collier Papers.

54. John Collier, "The Indian and Religious Freedom" (San Francisco: The Indian Defense Association of Central and Northern California, 1924), reel 9, Collier Papers; Charles Lummis, letter to the editor, *New York Times*, September 18, 1924, reel 5, Collier Papers.

55. Warren Moorehead to Matthew Sniffen, June 20, 1923, reel 39, IRA Papers; Edgar Hewett, "My Neighbors, the Pueblo Indians," *El Palacio* 15, no. 8 (October 15, 1923): 123–34; Charles Lummis, letter to the editor, *New York Times*, September 18, 1924, reel 5, Collier Papers.

56. Ralph Miller to Herbert Welsh, June 5, 1923, reel 39, IRA Papers; Robert Catherwood to Herbert Welsh, May 13, 1925, reel 42, IRA Papers.

57. Charles Selden, "Women Saved the Pueblos," *Ladies' Home Journal*, July 1923, 18–19, 128; Mary Colton to Herbert Welsh, July 17, 1923, reel 39, IRA Papers.

58. Hewett, "My Neighbors, the Pueblo Indians," 123–34.

59. Verter, "Dark Star Rising: The Emergence of Modern Occultism, 1800–1950," 71–87; Mary Austin, "Cults of the Pueblos: An Interpretation of Some Native Ceremonials," *Century Magazine*, November 1924, 32.

60. Austin, *Taos Pueblo*, 12; Roberts Walker to Doctor Julien E. Benjamin, September 18, 1923, box 317, folder 5, AAIA Papers.

61. Mabel Dodge Luhan to Elizabeth Shepley Sergeant, June 10, 1925, reel 5, Collier Papers. Even though she reported the Pueblos' horror at the allegations of sexual immorality, it is worth noting here that, like the moralists she condemned, Luhan depicted the "primitive" in highly sexualized terms.

62. Bederman, *Manliness and Civilization*, 84–88; Taves, "Feminization Revisited," 304–24.

63. See, for example, DeBerg, *Ungodly Women*; Curtis, *A Consuming Faith*; and Bederman, "'The Women Have Had Charge of the Church Work Long Enough,'" 432–65.

64. Ellis, *The Dance of Life*, 34–62; Collier, *From Every Zenith*, 136–7; John Collier, "Indian Dances Defended," *New York Times*, December 16, 1923, 6; John Collier, "Persecuting the Pueblos: The Indian Bureau Denies Its Wards Religious Liberty," *Sunset Magazine* 53, no. 7 (July 1924): 50, 92–93; Austin, *The American Rhythm*, 24–26.

65. Herbert Welsh, "Why Indian Dances Are Bad," *Boston Herald*, August 26, 1923; Mrs. H. K. Estabrook to Mason Green, August 26, 1923, reel 5, Collier Papers; Emma Franklin (Mrs. H. K.) Estabrook to Herbert Welsh, August 27, 1923, reel 39, IRA Papers; Emma Franklin Estabrook, "Those Indian Dances," *Boston Herald*, August 26, 1923; C. Hart Merriam in Matthew Sniffen, "Minutes of the Advisory Council on Indian Affairs," December 12, 1923, reel 39, IRA Papers. See also Lummis to Coolidge, August 2, 1924, reel 5, Collier Papers.

66. Roberts Walker to Charles Burke, June 11, 1923, box 317, folder 5, AAIA Papers; Warren Moorehead to Matthew Sniffen, May 24, 1923, reel 39, IRA Papers.

67. Mason Green, "Those Indian Dances," *Boston Herald*, August 22, 1923; Charles Lummis to President Calvin Coolidge, August 2, 1924, reel 5, Collier Papers. See also Charles Lummis, letter to the editor, *New York Times*, September 18, 1924, reel 5, Collier Papers; Charles Lummis, "To the Women of the United States in Biennial Convention Assembled," June 6, 1924, reel 9, Collier Papers; and John Collier, "Official Persecution of American Indian Religions: The Facts and the Reasons," *Churchman* (September 25, 1926): 9–13.

68. Collier, *From Every Zenith*, 136–37.

69. Alice Corbin Henderson, "The Dance-Rituals of the Pueblo Indians," *Theatre Arts Magazine* 7 (April 1923): 109–14.

70. Hewett, "My Neighbors, the Pueblo Indians," 123–34.

71. Estabrook, "Those Indian Dances."

72. Otto Lomavitu, "Hopi Indian Says Snake Dances Should Stop," *Coconino Sun*, July 28, 1923.

73. Charles Burke to Herbert Welsh, August 27, 1923, reel 39, IRA Papers; Herbert Welsh to I.R.A. Members, September 25, 1923, reel 39, IRA Papers; "Hopi Indian Snake Dance August 24 May Conclude Noted Ceremonials; Investigators Class Dance a Fraud," *El Paso Herald*, August 18, 1923.

74. Roberts Walker to Charles Burke, June 11, 1923, box 317, folder 5, AAIA Papers; Roberts Walker to James Gregg, June 4, 1923, box 317, folder 4, AAIA Papers; Roberts Walker to Mary Reynolds, October 26, 1923, box 317, folder 5, AAIA Papers.

75. Roberts Walker to Doctor Julien E. Benjamin, September 18, 1923, box 317, folder 5, AAIA Papers; Roberts Walker to Denis Riordan, March 30, 1923, box 317, folder 4,

AAIA Papers; Roberts Walker to James Gregg, June 4, 1923, box 317, folder 4, AAIA Papers; Roberts Walker to Mary Reynolds, October 26, 1923, box 317, folder 5, AAIA Papers.

76. Roberts Walker to James Gregg, June 4, 1923, box 317, folder 4, AAIA Papers; Eastern Association on Indian Affairs, "Bulletin Number Three: Concerning Indian Dances," January 1924, AAIA Papers, 4, 10, 12–14.

77. Stansbury Hagar to Herbert Welsh, August 25, 1923, reel 39, IRA Papers; Arthur Aldis to Herbert Welsh, October 1, 1923, reel 39, IRA Papers.

78. R. Newberne, "Report Regarding Letters of H. C. Fleming, F. W. Hodge, and Andrew Dasburg on Zuni," April 14, 1924, file 063, NARA-Zuni Records; Barnabas Meyer, "Pueblo," *Indian Sentinel* 2, no. 8 (October 1921): 377–80; John G. Worth to Herbert Welsh, November 22, 1924, reel 41, IRA Papers.

79. "Secretary Work Asks Citizens Aid with Counsel in the Solving of the Indian Problem," *Santa Fe New Mexican*, May 18, 1923; Matthew Sniffen, "Minutes of the Advisory Council on Indian Affairs," December 12, 1923, reel 39, IRA Papers; Warren Moorehead to Matthew Sniffen, June 20, 1923, reel 39, IRA Papers.

80. Pablo Abeita to Rev. William Hughes, June 11, 1923, reel 113, BCIM Records.

81. "Yellowtail, Robert," and "Cloud, Henry Roe," in *Encyclopedia of North American Indians*, ed. Frederick Hoxie (Boston: Houghton-Mifflin, 1996), 705–6, 125–27, <http://www.netlibrary.com>, consulted May 1, 2007.

82. Warren Moorehead to Matthew Sniffen, June 20, 1923, reel 39, IRA Papers; Matthew Sniffen to S. M. Brosius, April 7, 1923, reel 87, IRA Papers.

83. Eastern Association on American Indian Affairs, "Joint Meeting to Decide on a Tentative Program of Indian Policy," June 8, 1923, box 317, folder 5, AAIA Papers.

84. "Draft New Policy on Indian Welfare," *New York Times*, June 10, 1923; Matthew Sniffen, "Minutes of the Advisory Council on Indian Affairs," December 12, 1923, reel 39, IRA Papers.

85. Sniffen, "Minutes of the Advisory Council on Indian Affairs," December 12, 1923; Indian Rights Association, "Forty-first Annual Report," 1923, reel 104, IRA Papers; Elizabeth Shepley Sergeant, "The Red Man's Burden," *New Republic* 34 (January 16, 1924): 199–201.

86. Herbert Welsh to I.R.A. Members, September 25, 1923, reel 39, IRA Papers.

87. Matthew Sniffen to Mrs. J. Herbert Sawyer, October 4, 1923, reel 39, IRA Papers.

88. Herbert Welsh, "Indian Rights Association Monthly Bulletin No. 125," January 1, 1924, IRA Papers; Flora Seymour, "The Delusion of the Sentimentalists," *Forum*, March 1924, 273–80; Mary Austin, "The Folly of the Officials," *Forum*, March 1924, 281–88; Matthew Sniffen, "Pueblo Indians at the Union League," *Indian Truth* 1, no. 1 (February 1924): 4; Matthew Sniffen, "The Seymour-Austin Debate," *Indian Truth* 1, no. 2 (March 1924): 3–4.

89. Matthew Sniffen, "The Eastern Association Brochure," *Indian Truth* 1, no. 3 (April

1924): 3–4; Matthew Sniffen, "Dr. Hodge and We-Wha," *Indian Truth* 2, no. 2 (February 1925): 2–3; Mary Dissette to Miss Willard, March 3, 1924, reel 40, IRA Papers.

90. Hubert Work to the Council of the Tewa Tribe, San Ildefonso, February 20, 1924, reel 40, IRA Papers; Memorandum for the Press, February 23, 1924, reel 9, Collier Papers.

91. Hubert Work to the Council of the Tewa Tribe, San Ildefonso, February 20, 1924, reel 40, IRA Papers; Mary Dissette to Miss Willard, March 3, 1924, reel 40, IRA Papers.

92. Herbert Welsh, "Immorality under the Guise of Religion," *Living Church*, April 25, 1925, 865; Hubert Work, "Our American Indians," *Saturday Evening Post* 196, no. 48 (May 31, 1924): 27, 92–98.

93. Herbert Welsh to Hon. George Wharton Pepper, March 31, 1923, reel 87, IRA Papers.

94. Edith Dabb, "Indian Dances Degrading, Says Y.W.C.A. Leader," *New York Tribune*, November 25, 1923; Edith Dabb, "Evils of Tribal Dances," *New York Times*, December 2, 1923.

95. Pueblo Day Schools Superintendent to the Commissioner of Indian Affairs, March 3, 1914, file 802, NARA-SPC; Leo Crane to the Mother Superior, Sisters of Loretto, December 14, 1921, file 806.3, NARA-SPC; J. D. DeHuff to C. J. Crandall, May 31, 1923, file 297, NARA-SFIS; Charles Burke to C. J. Crandall, June 23, 1923, file 297, NARA-SFIS; C. J. Crandall to J. D. DeHuff, May 19, 1923, file 297, NARA-SFIS.

96. Dabb, "Evils of Tribal Dances," IX:8.

97. Mary Dissette to Miss Willard, March 3, 1924, reel 40, IRA Papers.

98. C. J. Crandall to Emory Marks, December 24, 1923, file 314, NARA-NPLB, Emory Marks to C. J. Crandall, December 5, 1923, file 314, NARA-NPLB; C. J. Crandall to Emory Marks, February 21, 1924, file 314, NARA-NPLB.

99. C. J. Crandall to J. D. DeHuff, May 19, 1923, file 297, NARA-SFIS.

100. Frederick B. Howden to Herbert Welsh, March 12, 1925, reel 41, IRA Papers.

101. Herbert Welsh to Ralph Miller, June 13, 1923, reel 39, IRA Papers; Indian Rights Association, "Forty-first Annual Report," 1923; W. E Johnson, "Those Sacred Indian Ceremonials," 176.

102. Dabb, "Evils of Tribal Dances"; Edith Dabb to Matthew Sniffen, January 24, 1924, reel 40, IRA Papers; Matthew Sniffen to Mrs. Robert E. Speer, January 26, 1924, reel 87, IRA Papers.

103. S. M. Brosius to Herbert Welsh, August 8, 1923, reel 39, IRA Papers.

104. Clara True to Matthew Sniffen, July 1, 1924, reel 41, IRA Papers.

105. Parsons, *Pueblo Mothers and Children*, 90–93, 103–4.

106. Elsie Clews Parsons in Eastern Association on Indian Affairs, *Bulletin Number Three*, January 1924, 8–10. On Parsons's views of Indian sexuality and gender roles, see Jacobs, *Engendered Encounters*, 61, 69, 72, 77, 118–19.

107. Luhan, *Edge of Taos Desert*, 179.

108. Mabel Dodge Luhan to Elizabeth Shepley Sergeant, June 10, 1925, reel 5, Collier Papers; see Jacobs, *Engendered Encounters*, 77–78.

109. Collier, "Indian Dances Defended."

110. Eastern Association on Indian Affairs, "Bulletin Number Three: Concerning Indian Dances," January 1924, AAIA Papers. Hodge's contribution was first published as F. W. Hodge, "Indian Dances Defended," *New York Times*, December 20, 1923, 16.

111. Selden, "Women Saved the Pueblos," 18–19, 128.

112. Stella Atwood to Elizabeth Shepley Sargeant, July 21, 1923, reel 5, Collier Papers; "General Federation Backs Mrs. Atwood and Collier; Mrs. Parker among 'Noes,'" *Santa Fe New Mexican*, May 24, 1923.

Chapter 5

1. Progressive Pueblo Council, "Resolutions of the All-Pueblo Progressive Indian Council," May 27, 1924, file 049, Hewett-ALA.

2. A majority of Native Americans had become citizens before 1924 through such means as military service, marriage, or land allotments. Still, the Indian Citizenship Act had enormous significance in an era of nativism and xenophobia as part of a symbolic redefinition of citizenship as something innate rather than acquired; it could not override inborn racial differences and did not imply equality between the races. Michaels, *Our America*, 32.

3. John Collier to Robert J. Bauman, January 1924, reel 4, Collier Papers; C. V. Safford, "Record of a Meeting with Zuni Caciques," February 29, 1924, file 018, Cassidy Collection.

4. Ruth Bunzel to Franz Boas, August 15, 1924, Boas Papers. Lorenzo Chaves to Amelia Elizabeth White, December 18, 1923, Indian Correspondence, folder 109, SWAIA Records. Amelia Elizabeth White to Mr. Harris, March 4, 1924, reel 117, BCIM Records, repeated these charges to the sole Catholic board member of the Eastern Association on Indian Affairs. Father Kroger responded by accusing the "Protestant" Zunis of working with the Christian Reformed missionary to unfairly malign his mission. Rev. Anthony Kroger to Rev. William Hughes, March 20, 1924, reel 117, BCIM Records.

5. John Collier to Elizabeth Shepley Sergeant, January 1924, reel 4, Collier Papers; John Collier to Robert J. Bauman, January 1924, reel 4, Collier Papers; John Collier to Hon. Hubert Work, February 13, 1924, reel 4, Collier Papers.

6. C. V. Safford, "Records of Meetings with Zuni Officials and Caciques," February 1924, file 018, Cassidy Collection.

7. John Collier, "Brief Report Concerning Religious Liberty Etc. Issue in New Mexico," May 15, 1924, reel 9, Collier Papers.

8. Safford, "Record of a Meeting with Zuni Caciques," February 29, 1924.

9. Ibid.

10. Taos Pueblo to Commissioner Charles Burke, January 16, 1924, file 816, NARA-NP Records. Marks had previously agreed to recommend that the boys "be excused for a year." Emory Marks to C. J. Crandall, November 21, 1923, file 314, NARA-NPLB.

11. A. B. Renehan to Charles Burke, June 7, 1924, box 318, folder 4, AAIA Papers.

12. Statement of Emory Marks, May 14, 1924, reel 38, IRA Papers.

13. C. J. Crandall to Charles Burke, August 13, 1924, file 816, NARA-NP Records.

14. Charles Burke to Antonio Romero and Other Officials, February 12, 1924, reel 5, Collier Papers.

15. C. J. Crandall to H. B. Peairs, April 24, 1924, file 806.1, NARA-NPCa.

16. H. B. Peairs to C. J. Crandall, April 26, 1924, file 806.1, NARA-NPCa; Charles Burke to C. J. Crandall, April 29, 1924, file 121, NARA-NPCa.

17. Taos Pueblo Governor and Council to Charles Burke, May 7, 1924, box 318, folder 4, AAIA Papers; Statement of Antonio Romero, May 15, 1924, reel 40, IRA Papers.

18. Council of All the New Mexico Pueblos, "Declaration to All Indians and to the People of the United States," May 5, 1924, reel 40, IRA Papers.

19. Statement of Antonio Romero, May 15, 1924.

20. Charles Burke to Antonio Romero, May 20, 1924, box 318, folder 4, AAIA Papers; Charles Burke to A. B. Renehan, June 13, 1924, file 816, NARA-NP Records.

21. Council of All the New Mexico Pueblos, "Declaration to All Indians and to the People of the United States," May 5, 1924.

22. John Collier, "Statement to Pueblo Indian Council on Religious Freedom," May 5, 1924, reel 40, IRA Papers, citing Safford, "Record of a Meeting with Zuni Caciques," February 29, 1924. The BIA's earlier refusals are noted in Parsons, "Notes on Zuni," 246.

23. Collier, "Statement to Pueblo Indian Council on Religious Freedom," May 5, 1924.

24. John Collier to Mrs. John D. Sherman, September 16, 1924, reel 9, Collier Papers; John Collier, "Official Persecution of American Indian Religions: The Facts and the Reasons," *Churchman*, September 25, 1926, 9–13.

25. "Government at Washington Still Lives Despite Two Small School Boys of the Pueblo of Taos," *Santa Fe New Mexican*, May 19, 1924.

26. Cash Asher to Elizabeth S. Sergeant, May 29, 1924, reel 5, Collier Papers; Cash Asher to Elizabeth S. Sergeant, June 3, 1924, reel 5, Collier Papers; Cash Asher, "Pueblo Indians Fear for Their Religion," *New York Times*, July 13, 1924.

27. A. A. Berle to Ina Sizer Cassidy, April 29, 1924, file 012, Cassidy Collection.

28. Francis Wilson to Roberts Walker, May 19, 1924, box 318, folder 4, AAIA Papers; Roberts Walker to Nicholas Roosevelt, May 31, 1924, box 318, folder 4, AAIA Papers; Roberts Walker to Francis Wilson, May 15, 1924, box 318, folder 4, AAIA Papers; Roberts Walker to Mrs. H. K. Estabrook, June 2, 1924, box 318, folder 4, AAIA Papers.

29. Herbert Welsh to Hubert Work, May 15, 1924, reel 87, IRA Papers.

30. Matthew Sniffen, "Notes on Sexual Scandal at Taos and Other Pueblos," May 6, 1924, reel 40, IRA Papers.

31. Adelina Otero-Warren to the Commissioner of Indian Affairs, May 20, 1924, file 816, NARA-NP Records.

32. Matthew Sniffen, "Delays and Defiance at Taos," *Indian Truth* 1, no. 5 (June 1924): 2.

33. "Memorandum on Pueblo matters to the Commissioner," May 14, 1924, file 816, NARA-NP Records; Charles Burke to Hubert Work, May 26, 1924, file 816, NARA-NP Records; Charles Burke to Amelia White, May 29, 1924, box 318, folder 4, AAIA Papers; C. J. Crandall to Charles Burke, August 13, 1924, file 816, NARA-NP Records.

34. Charles Burke to Antonio Romero, May 20, 1924, box 318, folder 4, AAIA Papers; Department of the Interior, "Press Release," June 2, 1924, reel 120, IRA Papers.

35. Nathan Bibo, "Old Men among Indians Blocking Education, Says Nathan Bibo, an Old Timer," *Santa Fe New Mexican*, October 5, 1923; Nathan Bibo, "Pioneer Settler Says Old Clique Governs Indians," *Albuquerque Morning Journal*, November 5, 1923. For more on the Bibos, see Fierman, *The Impact of the Frontier on a Jewish Family*.

36. Mary Bryan to S. M. Brosius, March 11, 1924, reel 40, IRA Papers; Mary Bryan to Herbert Welsh, April 5, 1924, reel 40, IRA Papers.

37. Ralph Twitchell, "Investigation into the Hunt Case," April 10, 1924, microfilm reel 2, frame 616, NARA-SA; Statement of Solomon Bibo, May 8, 1924, reel 40, IRA Papers; Nabokov, *A Forest of Time*, 192–94.

38. Edward Hunt to R. E. Twitchell, November 17, 1923, reel 2, frame 609, NARA-SA.

39. Ralph Twitchell, "Investigation into the Melchor Case," April 11, 1924, reel 2, frame 616, NARA-SA.

40. C. J. Crandall to Mr. Joseph Montoya Melchor, March 10, 1924, reel 40, IRA Papers; Ambroso Martinez et al., "Statement of All-Pueblo Council," June 1924, Indian Correspondence, folder 110, SWAIA Records.

41. Digest of the Discussions at the Council of Progressive Pueblo Indians Held at Santa Ana, May 1–3, 1924, file 150, NARA-NP Records.

42. Statement of John Dixon, April 23, 1924, reel 40, IRA Papers.

43. Twitchell, "Investigation into the Hunt Case," April 10, 1924; C. V. Safford, "Report on Cochiti Pueblo," December 17, 1924, reel 41, IRA Papers.

44. Twitchell, "Investigation into the Hunt Case," April 10, 1924.

45. Statement of Antonio Romero, May 15, 1924, reel 40, IRA Papers.

46. Twitchell, "Investigation into the Hunt Case," April 10, 1924.

47. Digest of the Discussions at the Council of Progressive Pueblo Indians Held at Santa Ana, May 1–3, 1924.

48. Ibid.; Progressive Pueblo Council, "Report of Resolutions Committee," May 2, 1924, reel 40, IRA Papers.

49. Joseph Montoya, "San Juan Indian Has Reply to Cacique," *Santa Fe New Mexican*, July 7, 1924; Joseph Montoya to John Collier, August 17, 1924, reel 119, BCIM Records.

50. Statements of John Dixon and Edward Hunt, May 3, 1924, reel 40, IRA Papers.

51. Ibid., Statement of Joe Lejon and Manuel Mondragon, May 15, 1924, reel 40, IRA Papers.

52. Laguna Pueblo Governor and Council to Charles Burke, January 29, 1927, reel 5, Collier Papers.

53. Vidal Gutierrez to Rev. William Ketcham, December 22, 1920, reel 97, BCIM Records.

54. Santa Clara Pueblo to the Honorable Chairman of the Subcommittee and His Committeemen and the Officials of the Indian Service, n.d. (1927?), reel 1, Collier Papers; Ortiz, *The Tewa World*, 62–65, 72–73, 82–84.

55. Ina Sizer Cassidy to Judge Richard Hanna, March 2, 1925, file 013, Cassidy Collection; Progressive Pueblos of Santa Clara to Superintendent C. J. Crandall, December 4, 1924, reel 41, IRA Papers.

56. Ina Sizer Cassidy to John Collier, March 2, 1925, file 005, Cassidy Collection.

57. Martinez et al., "Statement of All-Pueblo Council," June 1924.

58. Ibid.; Charles de Y. Elkus to Ina Sizer Cassidy, December 31, 1924, file 012, Cassidy Collection; Council of All the New Mexico Pueblos, "Minutes," July 17, 1924, file 046, Hewett-ALA.

59. Espanola Chamber of Commerce Settlers Committee and A. B. Renehan, "The Pueblo Indians and Their Land Grants," 1923, reel 128, IRA Papers; U.S. House, *Hearings on H.R. 13452 and H.R. 13674*.

60. John Collier to Acoma Governor James Miller, June 12, 1924, file 005, Cassidy Collection.

61. Council of All the New Mexico Pueblos, "Minutes," July 17, 1924.

62. Council of All the New Mexico Pueblos, "Declaration to All Indians and to the People of the United States," May 5, 1924.

63. Chester Faris to the Commissioner of Indian Affairs, October 4, 1926, file 816.2, NARA-SP Records.

64. "All Lies, Declare Governors of Pueblos, and Village Officials," *Santa Fe New Mexican*, July 2, 1924.

65. This letter was reprinted and distributed by Indian Defense Association of Central and Northern California: "The Pueblo Indians and Constitutional Government," August 1924, Indian Correspondence, folder 110, SWAIA Records.

66. Indian Rights Association, "Thirty-ninth Annual Report," 1921, reel 104, IRA Papers; Matthew Sniffen to Leo Crane, February 2, 1922, reel 86, IRA Papers.

67. Clara True to Herbert Welsh, April 19, 1922, reel 37, IRA Papers.

68. Matthew Sniffen to S. M. Brosius, March 17, 1924, reel 87, IRA Papers.

69. Matthew Sniffen, "Progress or Retrogression," *Indian Truth* 1, no. 3 (April 1924): 4.

70. Adelina Otero-Warren to the Commissioner of Indian Affairs, May 20, 1924, file 816, NARA-NP Records; R. E. Twitchell to Hon. Charles Burke, November 19, 1923, reel 2, frame 609, NARA-SA.

71. C. J. Crandall to Mr. Joseph Montoya Melchor, March 10, 1924, reel 40, IRA Papers.

72. C. J. Crandall to Charles Burke, August 13, 1924, file 816, NARA-NP Records; Digest of the Discussions at the Council of Progressive Pueblo Indians Held at Santa Ana, May 1–3.

73. S. M. Brosius to Mary Bryan, March 26, 1924, reel 40, IRA Papers.

74. Herbert Welsh to Mrs. Horace Berry, April 12, 1924, reel 87, IRA Papers.

75. Herbert Welsh to Hon. George Wharton Pepper, March 27, 1924, reel 87, IRA Papers; Herbert Welsh to Hon. Henry C. Lodge, March 27, 1924, reel 87, IRA Papers.

76. Matthew Sniffen to Hubert Work, April 11, 1924, reel 40, IRA Papers.

77. S. M. Brosius to Matthew Sniffen, March 15, 1924, reel 40, IRA Papers.

78. Matthew Sniffen, "Religious Liberty and the Pueblo Councils," *Indian Truth* 1, no. 4 (May 1924): 2–3; Matthew Sniffen to Mr. F. A. Marshall, June 4, 1925, reel 88, IRA Papers; Matthew Sniffen, "Religious Liberty," *Indian Truth* 2, no. 5 (May 1925): 2–3.

79. Useful discussion of these themes appears in Shaw, "Religious Experience and the Formation of the Early Enlightenment Self," 61–71; and Hundert, "The European Enlightenment and the History of the Self," 72–83.

80. Sniffen, "Religious Liberty," 2–3.

81. Sniffen, "Progress or Retrogression," 4.

82. See also Mazur, *The Americanization of Religious Minorities*, 118–21.

83. Amelia Elizabeth White to Herbert Welsh, April 2, 1924, reel 40, IRA Papers.

84. Matthew Sniffen, "Collier's Sunset Magazine Article," *Indian Truth* 1, no. 7 (August–September 1924): 3–4.

85. John Collier to Herbert Welsh, November 6, 1924, reel 41, IRA Papers; John Collier to Herbert Welsh, November 7, 1924, reel 41, IRA Papers.

86. Matthew Sniffen to S. M. Brosius, March 17, 1924, reel 87, IRA Papers.

87. Matthew Sniffen to Edith Dabb, April 14, 1924, reel 87, IRA Papers; Matthew Sniffen to Mrs. Clarence Hyde, June 10, 1924, reel 88, IRA Papers.

88. Matthew Sniffen to Edith Dabb, April 14, 1924, reel 87, IRA Papers; Matthew Sniffen to Herbert Welsh, April 30, 1924, reel 40, IRA Papers.

89. R. E. Twitchell to Hon. Charles Burke, November 19, 1923, reel 2, frame 609, NARA-SA.

90. Father Albert Daeger, O.F.M., to Rev. William Ketcham, December 7, 1920, reel 97, BCIM Records; Rev. Fridolin Schuster to Rev. William Hughes, April 4, 1923, reel 113, BCIM Records; Rev. Fridolin Schuster to Rev. William Hughes, March 12, 1924, reel 119, BCIM Records.

91. Rev. Fridolin Schuster to Charles Lusk, May 22, 1924, reel 119, BCIM Records.

92. Rev. John Woods to Rev. William Hughes, May 5, 1924, reel 119, BCIM Records.

93. Matthew Sniffen to Herbert Welsh, April 29, 1924, reel 40, IRA Papers; Matthew Sniffen, "Clara True," *Indian Truth* 1, no. 5 (June 1924): 2; Matthew Sniffen to Clara True, May 23, 1924, reel 88, IRA Papers; Matthew Sniffen to Clara True, May 24, 1924, reel 88, IRA Papers.

94. Progressive Pueblo Council, "Progressive Pueblo Council Meeting Minutes," May 27, 1924, file 150, NARA-NP Records.

95. "Lays Ban on Indians' Religion," *Los Angeles Times*, June 8, 1924; "Indians Called Virtual Slaves," *Los Angeles Times*, June 10, 1924; "Indians' Status Discussed," *Los Angeles Times*, June 11, 1924.

96. Charles Lummis, "To the Women of the United States in Biennial Convention Assembled," June 6, 1924, reel 9, Collier Papers; John Collier to Ina Sizer Cassidy, June 1924, file 005, Cassidy Collection.

97. Clara True to Matthew Sniffen, July 1, 1924, reel 41, IRA Papers; "Editorial— Father Woods Aids Pueblo," *Indian Sentinel* 4, no. 3 (July 1924): 115; "Christian Indians Protest Persecution," *Tidings*, July 4, 1924.

98. Clara True to Matthew Sniffen, July 1, 1924, reel 41, IRA Papers; "Pueblo Indians and Publicity," *Indian Sentinel* 4, no. 3 (July 1924): 103–4.

99. Matthew Sniffen to Herbert Welsh, August 13, 1924, reel 41, IRA Papers.

100. Dr. Hewett to the Secretary of the Interior, August 10, 1924, file 046, Hewett-ALA; Francis Wilson to Roberts Walker, May 19, 1924, box 318, folder 4, AAIA Papers.

101. Clara True to Matthew Sniffen, July 1, 1924, reel 41, IRA Papers; Grace Baer to Mrs. John W. Sherman, August 6, 1924, box 10, Hewett-CHL; Grace Baer et al. to Officers of the General Federation of Women's Clubs, August 30, 1924, reel 41, IRA Papers.

102. John Collier to Mr. Rosenberg, November 3, 1924, file 005, Cassidy Collection; Ina Sizer Cassidy to Mrs. Atwood, August 3, 1924, file 012, Cassidy Collection; Ina Sizer Cassidy to Mrs. John D. Sherman, August 25, 1924, file 003, Cassidy Collection.

103. Amelia Elizabeth White to Stella Atwood, n.d., 1926, reel 5, Collier Papers; Stella Atwood to John Collier, June 17, 1926, reel 1, Collier Papers; Kelly, *Assault on Assimilation*, 318–20; Frankiel, "Natural Sympathies: Anglo Women and Native American Culture," 76–77.

104. Leo Crane to Matthew Sniffen, April 2, 1924, reel 40, IRA Papers; Crane, *Indians of the Enchanted Desert*, 167.

105. Crane, *Indians of the Enchanted Desert*, 255, 259.

106. Achebe, "An Image of Africa: Racism in Conrad's *Heart of Darkness*," 251–62. For an opposing view, see Firchow, *Envisioning Africa*.

107. Edith Dabb, "Evils of Tribal Dances," *New York Times*, December 2, 1923.

108. Harvey Watts to Robert Catherwood, June 9, 1925, reel 42, IRA Papers.

109. The relevant literature includes Prakash, *After Colonialism*; Rajan, *Under Western Eyes*; Trivedi, *Colonial Transactions*. See also Booker, *Colonial Power, Colonial Texts*; Singh,

Colonial Narratives/Cultural Dialogues; Moore-Gilbert, *Kipling and "Orientalism"*; and Morey, *Fictions of India*.

110. William E. Johnson, "Those Sacred Indian Ceremonials," *Native American* 24, no. 13 (September 20, 1924): 173–77.

111. Crane, *Indians of the Enchanted Desert*, 258.

112. Richard Payne Knight, *Discourse on the Worship of Priapus*, in Knight and Wright, *A History of Phallic Worship*; see Verter, "Dark Star Rising: The Emergence of Modern Occultism, 1800–1950," 71–87.

113. Mary Austin, "Cults of the Pueblos: An Interpretation of Some Native Ceremonials," *Century Magazine*, November 1924, 32.

114. Parsons, "Notes on Zuni," 236–37.

115. Johnson, "Those Sacred Indian Ceremonials," 173–77; John Collier to Mrs. John D. Sherman, September 16, 1924, reel 9, Collier Papers.

116. Herbert Welsh to Charles C. Connell, December 6, 1924, reel 88, IRA Papers.

117. Herbert Welsh to IRA Members, November 19, 1924, box 317, folder 5, AAIA Papers; Herbert Welsh to John Finley, October 25, 1924, reel 88, IRA Papers.

118. Herbert Welsh to Charles C. Connell, Esq., December 6, 1924, reel 88, IRA Papers; Herbert Welsh to John Finley, October 25, 1924, reel 88, IRA Papers; W. Smith, *Dictionary of the Bible*, 1:912, 75.

119. Herbert Welsh to Rt. Rev. Frederick F. Reese, D.D., February 2, 1925, reel 41, IRA Papers; see Tyson, *The Progressive Revelation of the Bible*.

120. Jordan, *The Invention of Sodomy in Christian Theology*, traces the development of "sodomy" as a category of condemnation that gained traction in the eleventh century. Medieval theologians in various times and places applied this charge to a shifting array of behaviors in order to advance their own ideological agendas. The same is true in the Pueblo controversy.

121. Clara True to S. M. Brosius, May 26, 1925, reel 42, IRA Papers.

122. Matthew Sniffen, "Religious Liberty for Indians," *Christian Century* 42, no. 22 (May 28, 1925): 705–6.

123. Herbert Welsh to Hon. Scott Leavitt, January 16, 1925, reel 88, IRA Papers.

124. Matthew Sniffen and Clara True, "Dutch Reformed Church Resolution on Religious Liberty for the Pueblos," 1925, reel 41, IRA Papers.

125. Matthew Sniffen to Frederic Morehouse, March 13, 1925, reel 41, IRA Papers.

126. Board of National Missions of the PCUSA, "At Work among the American Indians," 1925, box 5, folder 35, PCUSA.

127. Matthew Sniffen, "Government Doesn't Force Religion on Indians," *Indian Truth* 2, no. 5 (May 1925): 1.

128. C. E. Faris to Charles Burke, September 16, 1924, file 070, NARA-SPC.

129. Santo Domingo Pueblo to the American Red Cross, November 1925, box 3B, White Papers; Ina Sizer Cassidy to John Collier, July 18, 1925, reel 1, Collier Papers.

130. John Collier to the Gentlemen of the House Indian Affairs Committee, April 15, 1926, reel 2, Collier Papers; John Collier to Matthew Sniffen, n.d., 1930?, reel 3, Collier Papers.

131. John Collier, letter to the editor, *Christian Century*, March 29, 1928, reel 1, Collier Papers.

132. Matthew Sniffen, "The American Indian Defense Association Appeal," *Indian Truth* 1, no. 9 (November 1924): 2.

133. C. J. Crandall to Charles Burke, August 13, 1924, file 816, NARA-NP Records; Emory Marks to C. J. Crandall, July 27, 1924, reel 41, IRA Papers.

134. John Collier, "Religious Persecution of Indians Charged by Defense League Official," *Sacramento Bee*, August 23, 1924; John Collier to Mrs. John D. Sherman, September 16, 1924, reel 9, Collier Papers.

135. Matthew Sniffen to Herbert Welsh, August 13, 1924, reel 41, IRA Papers.

136. H. B. Peairs to Charles Burke, January 23, 1925, file 816, NARA-NP Records.

137. Council of all the New Mexico Pueblos, "To the President of the U.S., the Congress, and Our Friends the American People," August 31, 1925, file 064, NARA-NPCb.

138. C. J. Crandall to Emory Marks, August 15, 1925, file 828, NARA-NPCb.

139. Council of all the New Mexico Pueblos, "To the President of the U.S., the Congress, and Our Friends the American People," August 31, 1925.

140. Santa Clara Pueblo Progressives to Adelina Otero-Warren, April 2, 1924, Pueblo Collection. MacLachlan, "Indian Law and Puebloan Tribal Law," 345, notes a conservative takeover of Santa Clara's government in 1894.

141. Progressive Pueblo Council, "Resolutions of the All-Pueblo Progressive Indian Council," May 27, 1924, file 049, Hewett-ALA; Progressive Pueblos of Santa Clara to Superintendent C. J. Crandall, December 4, 1924, reel 41, IRA Papers.

142. C. J. Crandall to Santa Clara Pueblo, December 19, 1924, file 064, NARA-NPCa.

143. Santa Clara Pueblo to C. J. Crandall, December 24, 1924, file 012, Cassidy Collection.

144. Charles Fahy to John Collier, January 28, 1928, reel 1, Collier Papers. According to Fahy, an AIDA lawyer in Santa Fe, Santa Clara's progressives did not dispute the conservative plan's fairness. Instead, they complained that it had never worked because the conservatives had not informed them of meetings or honored the individual's right to abstain from the ceremonies.

145. Clara True to Herbert Welsh, January 4, 1925, reel 41, IRA Papers.

146. Charles de Y. Elkus to Ina Sizer Cassidy, December 31, 1924, file 012, Cassidy Collection.

147. Victoriano Sisneros to C. J. Crandall, January 2, 1925, file 019, Cassidy Collection.

148. C. J. Crandall to Charles Burke, January 19, 1925, file 150, NARA-NP Records.

149. Charles Burke to C. J. Crandall, January 14, 1925, file 150, NARA-NP Records.

150. Charles Fahy to John Collier, January 28, 1928, reel 1, Collier Papers.

151. E. B. Meritt, "Agreement of Progressive and Conservative Parties of the Santa Clara Pueblo," October 22, 1927, file 064, NARA-NPCa; Ina Sizer Cassidy to John Collier, February 18, 1933, file 005, Cassidy Collection.

152. Santa Clara Pueblo to the Honorable Chairman of the Subcommittee and His Committeemen and the Officials of the Indian Service, n.d. (1927?).

153. Chester Faris to the Commissioner of Indian Affairs, December 24, 1929, file 155, NARA-NP Records.

154. Sando, *Pueblo Nations*, 249, 14–15; MacLachlan, "Indian Law and Puebloan Tribal Law," 345–46; and Ortiz, "The Dynamics of Pueblo Cultural Survival," 301.

155. Herbert Welsh to IRA Board of Directors, February 16, 1925, reel 41, IRA Papers; Matthew Sniffen, "Minutes of IRA Board Meeting," February 20, 1925, reel 41, IRA Papers. See also Kelly, *Assault on Assimilation*, 334–39.

156. Clara True to Father Schuster, May 4, 1925, reel 42, IRA Papers.

157. Herbert Welsh to T. F. McCormick, April 1, 1929, file 094, NARA-NPCb.

158. Collier, "Amerindians: Problems in Psychic and Physical Adjustments to a Dominant Civilization," 117, 119; John Collier, "Status of the Red Man in America Today," December 10, 1930, reel 2, Collier Papers.

159. Chester Faris to the Commissioner of Indian Affairs, October 4, 1926, file 816.2, NARA-SP Records; Daily, *Battle for the BIA*.

160. Philp, *John Collier's Crusade*, 90.

161. Charles de Y. Elkus to Lewis Meriam, November 5, 1931, reel 5, Collier Papers.

162. Lewis Meriam to Charles de Y. Elkus, November 19, 1931, reel 5, Collier Papers.

163. Acoma Pueblo to the House Committee on Indian Affairs and John Collier, March 21, 1926, reel 4, Collier Papers; Governor and Council of Picuris Pueblo to House Committee on Indian Affairs and to John Collier, March 26, 1926, reel 4, Collier Papers.

164. Videl Sanchez to John Collier, March 19, 1926, reel 4, Collier Papers.

165. Council of All the New Mexico Pueblos to the House Indian Affairs Committee, April 10, 1926, reel 2, Collier Papers; American Indian Defense Association, "Report on Indian Affairs," June 9, 1926, file 005, Cassidy Collection; "Law and Order for Pueblos Waits Statute," *New Mexico State Tribune*, December 13, 1926.

166. "Those Indians Again," *Santa Fe New Mexican*, July 7, 1924; "Indians of the Progressive Bunch Want Peace and Seek Agreement," *Santa Fe New Mexican*, July 21, 1924.

167. Margaret McKittrick, "Law and Order in the Pueblos," February 1930, box 2A, White Papers; Margaret McKittrick to Amelia White, February 19, 1930, box 2A, White Papers.

168. Walter Cochrane to Margaret McKittrick, November 26, 1929, box 1A, White Papers; Walter Cochrane, "Law and Order in the Pueblos," n.d., 1930, box 1A, White Papers; Walter Cochrane to Margaret McKittrick, April 16, 1930, box 1A, White Papers.

169. Roberts Walker to Alice Corbin Henderson, January 30, 1924, box 318, folder 1,

AAIA Papers; Roberts Walker to Flora Seymour, February 25, 1924, box 318, folder 2, AAIA Papers. Similar perspectives are expressed in Amelia E. White to Hubert Work, April 10, 1926, file 730, NARA-Zuni Records; Corinna Lindon Smith to Hon. H. M. Lord, September 4, 1928, reel 5, Collier Papers.

170. Alice Corbin Henderson to Roberts Walker, July 14, 1924, box 318, folder 4, AAIA Papers.

171. Press Release, "Declares Simms Bill a Threat to Pueblo Indian Life," June 8, 1930, reel 9, Collier Papers.

Chapter 6

1. Stewart, *Peyote Religion*, 68–127; Long, *Religious Freedom and Indian Rights*, 4–21.

2. Testimony along these lines from John Collier, and from anthropologists including Franz Boas and Alfred Kroeber, can be found in U.S. House of Representatives, Special Investigating Committee of the Committee on Indian Affairs, *Hearing to Investigate Indian Conditions in the United States*, 310–17, 322–31.

3. Rhodes, "An American Tradition," 39; Stewart, *Peyote Religion*, 128–47, 213–38; David Sikkink, "From Christian Civilization to Individual Civil Liberties: Framing Religion in the Legal Field, 1880–1949," in C. Smith, *The Secular Revolution*, 310–54.

4. Wood, *Taos Pueblo*, 33–34; Stewart, *Peyote Religion*, 202–8, 31–38.

5. Crow Dog and Erdoes, *Crow Dog*; Deloria, *God Is Red*; Kidwell, Noley, and Tinker, *A Native American Theology*.

6. Stewart, *Peyote Religion*, 308–10, 19–38.

7. Deloria, "Secularism, Civil Religion, and the Religious Freedom of American Indians," 9–20; Moore, "Reflections on the Elusive Promise of Religious Freedom for the Native American Church," 42–50; Lawson and Morris, "The Native American Church and the New Court," 79–91; Pavlik, "The U.S. Supreme Court Decision on Peyote," 30–39; Sharon O'Brien, "A Legal Analysis of the American Indian Religious Freedom Act," in Vecsey, *Handbook of American Indian Religious Freedom*, 27–43; Long, *Religious Freedom and Indian Rights*.

8. Greenawalt, *Religion and the Constitution*, 68–85.

9. See, for example, McNally, *Ojibwe Singers*.

10. Archdiocese of Santa Fe Press Release, August 16, 2003.

11. Hyer, *One House, One Voice, One Heart*.

12. Ellis, *A Dancing People*.

13. Deloria, *God Is Red*; Treat, "Intertribal Traditionalism and the Religious Roots of Red Power," 270–94; and Treat, *Around the Sacred Fire*.

14. Sweet, "'Let 'Em Loose,'" 59–74.

15. Aldred, "Plastic Shamans and Astroturf Sun Dances," 329–52; Hernandez-Avila,

"Mediations of the Spirit," 329–52; A. Smith, "For All Those Who Were Indian in a Former Life," 70–71; Tinker, *Spirit and Resistance*, 52–53.

16. Vine Deloria, conclusion to Biolsi and Zimmerman, *Indians and Anthropologists*, 221.

17. Bellah et al., *Habits of the Heart*. Philip Deloria develops a similar point in Deloria, *Playing Indian*, 154–80.

18. Jenkins, *Dream Catchers*, 245–55.

19. Gulliford, *Sacred Objects and Sacred Places*, 13–24.

20. Blair, "Indian Rights," 125–54; Gulliford, *Sacred Objects and Sacred Places*, 43–44.

21. Gulliford, *Sacred Objects and Sacred Places*, 24–25. The full text of the act, along with the details of its history and implementation, are available at U.S. Department of the Interior, National Park Service, "National NAGPRA."

22. Ferguson, Anyon, and Ladd, "Repatriation at the Pueblo of Zuni," 251–73; Gulliford, *Sacred Objects and Sacred Places*, 45–53; LaDuke, *Recovering the Sacred*, 79–81, 106–8.

23. Zuni Tribal Council resolution No. M70-78-991, reprinted in Blair, "Indian Rights," appendix A, 148–49.

24. Sen. Daniel Inouye, Opening Statement, Testimony, "Oversight Hearing."

25. Rosita Worl, Interim Executive Director, Sealaska Heritage Foundation, Juneau, Alaska, "Oversight Hearing."

26. Minthorn, "Human Remains Should Be Reburied."

27. The full text of these scientific investigations is available online at U.S. Department of the Interior, National Park Service, "Kennewick Man."

28. Don Sampson, former board of trustees chairman for the Confederated Tribes of the Umatilla Indian Reservation, "Tribal Chair Questions Scientists' Motives and Credibility"; and Confederated Tribes of the Umatilla Indian Reservation, "Press Statement Following Federal Court Hearing." For the perspective of the scientists who filed suit to study Kennewick Man, see Benedict, *No Bone Unturned*.

29. Confederated Tribes of the Umatilla Indian Reservation, "Press Statement: Reaction to Court's Denial of Stay in Ancient One Case."

30. Confederated Tribes of the Umatilla Indian Reservation, "Press Statement: CTUIR Will Not Pursue Case in the US Supreme Court."

31. Friends of America's Past, "NAGPRA."

32. Vine Deloria makes this comment in the film *In the Light of Reverence*, produced by the Earth Island Institute, available through the Sacred Lands Film Project Web site at <http://www.sacredland.org/index.html>, consulted October 8, 2007.

33. Vine Deloria, "Reflection and Revelation: Knowing Land, Places and Ourselves," in Deloria and Treat, *For This Land*, 256.

34. Keegan, *The Taos Pueblo and Its Sacred Blue Lake*, 52; Frank Waters, introduction

to Gordon-McCutchan, *The Taos Indians and the Battle for Blue Lake*, ix–xii; Graybill, "'Strong on the Merits and Powerfully Symbolic,'" 125–60.

35. *Sequoyah v. Tennessee Valley Authority*, 620 F.2d 1159 (6th Cir. 1980); B. Brown, "Native American Religions," 22–25; B. Brown, *Religion, Law, and the Land*, 9–38, quote on 14; Rhodes, "An American Tradition," 53–54; Tapahe, "After the Religious Freedom Restoration Act," 339.

36. *Badoni v. Higginson*, 455 F. Supp. 641 (C.D. Utah 1977); B. Brown, "Native American Religions," 19–44; B. Brown, *Religion, Law, and the Land*, 39–60.

37. B. Brown, *Religion, Law, and the Land*, 61–91.

38. B. Brown, "Native American Religions," 28–32; B. Brown, *Religion, Law, and the Land*, 93–118.

39. B. Brown, *Religion, Law, and the Land*, 119–32; Dorothea Theodoratus, Joseph Chartkoff, and Kerry Chartkoff, "Cultural Resources of the Chimney Rock Section, Gasquet-Orleans Road, Six Rivers National Forest," cited in ibid., 127, 130.

40. Ibid., 132–49; *Northwest Indian Cemetery Protective Association v. Peterson*, 565 F. Supp. 586 (1983), cited in ibid., 132–33, 135; *Northwest Indian Cemetery Protective Association v. Peterson*, 795 F.2d 688 (9th Cir. 1986), cited in ibid., 147–49.

41. Ibid., 149–72; *Lyng v. Northwest Cemetery Protective Association*, 485 U.S. 439 (1988), cited in ibid., 150, 162, 163, 164. See also Echo-Hawk, "Native American Religious Liberty: Five Hundred Years after Columbus," 33–52.

42. Parker and King, "National Register Bulletin: Guidelines for Evaluating and Documenting Traditional Cultural Properties."

43. *Apache Survival Coalition v. United States*, 21 F.3d 895 (9th Cir. 1994); Gulliford, *Sacred Objects and Sacred Places*, 133–34.

44. *Bear Lodge Multiple Use Association v. Babbitt*, 175 F.3d 814 (10th Cir. 1999).

45. *National Arch and Bridge Society v. Alston*, 98 Fed. Appx. 711 (10th Cir. 2004).

46. Sacred Land Film Project, "Cave Rock"; see also the Pluralism Project at Harvard University, "Research Report: Cave Rock, NV."

47. *The Access Fund v. United States Department of Agriculture*, 691 F.2d 1242 (9th Cir. 2007).

48. Sacred Land Film Project, "Cave Rock"; see also the Pluralism Project at Harvard University, "Research Report: Cave Rock, NV."

49. John Young, "New Age Assault on Bear Butte Decried," *Indian Country Today*, June 29, 1994, A1; "New Age Rites at Sacred Place Draw Indian Protests," *New York Times*, June 24, 1994.

50. *Navajo Nation v. U.S. Forest Service*, nos. 06-15371, 06-15436, 06-15455 (9th Cir. Aug. 8, 2008).

51. The National Congress of American Indians, Resolution #ANC-07-020, "Support of the Current Language and Tribal Recommendations to the 2007 Draft Bill of the

'Native American Sacred Lands Act'"; U.S. House of Representatives, "Native American Sacred Lands Act," H.R. 2419, 108th Congress, 1st Session, June 11, 2003.

52. Sacred Land Film Project, "Declaration on the Rights of Indigenous Peoples Passes after Thirty Years of Struggle"; United Nations, "Declaration on the Rights of Indigenous Peoples."

53. Lassiter, "Southwestern Oklahoma, the Gourd Dance, and 'Charlie Brown,'" 161–62.

54. Sacred Land Film Project, "Is Nothing Sacred? Corporate Responsibility for the Protection of Native American Sacred Sites," 57.

BIBLIOGRAPHY

Published Primary Sources

For archival sources consulted, see the list of abbreviations at the beginning of the notes.

Archdiocese of Santa Fe. Press Release, August 16, 2003. <http://www.archdiocesesantafe .org/Offices/Communications/Archived%20Press%20Releases/03.08.13.Kateri Tekak witha.html>, consulted January 18, 2005.

Austin, Mary. *The American Rhythm*. New York: Harcourt, Brace, 1923.

———. *Earth Horizon: Autobiography*. New York: Houghton Mifflin, 1932.

———. *Taos Pueblo, Photographed by Ansel Easton Adams and Described by Mary Austin*. San Francisco: Grabhorn Press, 1930.

Austin, Mary, and T. M. Pearce. *Literary America, 1903–1934: The Mary Austin Letters*. Westport, Conn.: Greenwood Press, 1979.

Baird, Robert. *Religion in America; or, An account of the origin, progress, relation to the state, and present condition of the evangelical churches in the United States: with notices of the unevangelical denominations*. New York: Harper and Brothers, 1845.

Bandelier, Adolph Francis Alphonse. *The Delight Makers*. New York: Dodd, Mead, 1918.

Benedict, Ruth. *Patterns of Culture*. Boston: Houghton Mifflin, 1989.

Board of Indian Commissioners. *Annual Report of the Board of Indian Commissioners*. Washington, D.C.: Government Printing Office, 1896.

Boas, Franz. *The Ethnography of Franz Boas: Letters and Diaries of Franz Boas Written on the Northwest Coast from 1886 to 1931*. Edited by Ronald Rohner. Chicago: University of Chicago Press, 1969.

———. *The Mind of Primitive Man*. New York: Macmillan, 1911.

Bourke, John Gregory. *The Snake-Dance of the Moquis of Arizona*. New York: C. Scribner's Sons, 1884.

Brown, J. Newton, and B. B. Edwards. *Encyclopedia of Religious Knowledge; or, Dictionary of the Bible, Theology, Religious Biography, All Religions, Ecclesiastical History, and Missions*. Brattleboro, Vt.: Brattleboro' Typographic Company, 1842.

Burlin, Natalie Curtis. *The Indians' Book*. New York: Harper and Brothers, 1923.

Cather, Willa. *Death Comes for the Archbishop*. 1927; Lincoln: University of Nebraska Press, 1999.

Collier, John. "Amerindians: Problems in Psychic and Physical Adjustments to a Dominant Civilization." *Pacific Affairs: Journal of the Institute of Pacific Relations* 3 (March 1929): 116–21.

———. *From Every Zenith: A Memoir; and Some Essays on Life and Thought*. Denver: Sage Books, 1963.

———. *Patterns and Ceremonials of the Indians of the Southwest*. New York: Dutton, 1949.

Confederated Tribes of the Umatilla Indian Reservation. "Press Statement: CTUIR Will Not Pursue Case in the US Supreme Court," July 19, 2004. <http://www.umatilla.nsn.us/kman14.html>, consulted September 19, 2007.

———. "Press Statement Following Federal Court Hearing," June 21, 2001. <http://www.umatilla.nsn.us/kman7.html>, consulted September 19, 2007.

———. "Press Statement: Reaction to Court's Denial of Stay in Ancient One Case," January 9, 2003. <http://www.umatilla.nsn.us/kman11.html>, consulted September 19, 2007.

Crane, Leo. *Indians of the Enchanted Desert*. Boston: Little Brown, 1925.

Crow Dog, Leonard, and Richard Erdoes. *Crow Dog: Four Generations of Sioux Medicine Men*. New York: HarperCollins, 1995.

Cushing, Frank Hamilton, and Jesse Green. *Cushing at Zuni: The Correspondence and Journals of Frank Hamilton Cushing, 1879–1884*. Albuquerque: University of New Mexico Press, 1990.

DeWitt, Miriam Hapgood. *Taos: A Memory*. Albuquerque: University of New Mexico Press, 1992.

Dorchester, Daniel. *Christianity in the United States from the First Settlement down to the Present Time*. New York: Hunt & Eaton, 1888.

———. *Romanism vs. the Public School System*. New York: Phillips and Hunt, 1888.

Ellis, Havelock. *The Dance of Life*. Boston: Houghton Mifflin, 1923.

Fergusson, Erna. "Justice for the Pueblo Indians." *Science* 56 (December 8, 1922): 665.

Friends of America's Past. "NAGPRA." <http://www.friendsofpast.org/nagpra/news.html>, consulted September 19, 2007.

Henri, Robert. *The Art Spirit*. New York: J. B. Lippincott, 1939.

Herzog, J. J., Philip Schaff, and Samuel Macauley Jackson. *A Religious Encyclopaedia; or, Dictionary of Biblical, Historical, Doctrinal, and Practical Theology. Based on the Real-Encyklopädie of Herzog, Plitt, and Hauck*. Rev. ed. New York: Christian Literature Company, 1889.

Hodge, F. W., ed. *Handbook of American Indians North of Mexico*. Bulletin, Smithsonian Institution Bureau of American Ethnology, no. 30, 2 vols. Washington, D.C.: Government Printing Office, 1907–10.

Inouye, Sen. Daniel. Opening Statement. Testimony, "Oversight Hearing before the Senate Committee on Indian Affairs on the Native American Graves Protection and

Repatriation Act," April 20, 1999. <http://indian.senate.gov/1999hrgs/nagpra4.20/
nag—wit.htm>, consulted September 13, 2007.

Jung, C. G. "The Pueblo Indians." In *The Spell of New Mexico*, edited by Tony Hillerman,
37–43. Albuquerque: University of New Mexico Press, 1976.

Knight, Richard Payne, and Thomas Wright. *A History of Phallic Worship*. New York:
Dorcet Press, 1992.

Kroeber, Alfred L. *Anthropology*. New York: Harcourt, Brace, 1923.

———. *Zuñi Kin and Clan*. Anthropological Papers of the American Museum of Natural
History, vol. 18, part 2. 1917; New York: Brookhaven Press, 2003.

———. *Zuni potsherds*. Anthropological Papers of the American Museum of Natural
History, vol. 18, part 1. New York: The Trustees, 1916.

Lawrence, D. H. "New Mexico." In *The Spell of New Mexico*, edited by Tony Hillerman,
29–36. Albuquerque: University of New Mexico Press, 1976.

———. *The Selected Letters of D. H. Lawrence*. Edited by Diana Trilling. New York: Farrar
Straus and Cudahy, 1958.

Lindquist, Gustavus Elmer Emanuel. *The Red Man in the United States*. New York:
George H. Doran, 1923.

Luhan, Mabel Dodge. *Edge of Taos Desert: An Escape to Reality*. Vol. 4 of *Intimate
Memories*. New York: Harcourt, Brace, 1937.

———. *Intimate Memories: The Autobiography of Mabel Dodge Luhan*. Edited by Lois Palken
Rudnick. Albuquerque: University of New Mexico Press, 1999.

———. *Movers and Shakers*. Vol. 3 of *Intimate Memories*. 1936; New York: Harcourt, Brace,
1971.

———. *Winter in Taos*. New York: Harcourt Brace, 1935.

Lummis, Charles F. *Land of Poco Tiempo*. 1893; Charles Scribner's Sons, 1928.

———. *Letters from the Southwest*. Edited by James W. Byrkit. Tucson: University of
Arizona Press, 1989.

———. *Mesa, Cañon and Pueblo*. 1925; New York: Century Company, 1938.

———. *Some Strange Corners of Our Country: The Wonderland of the Southwest*. 1891;
Tucson: University of Arizona Press, 1989.

———. *A Tramp across the Continent*. 1892; Albuquerque: Calvin Horn Publisher, 1969.

Lummis, Charles Fletcher, Robert Olney Easton, and Donald Mackenzie Brown.
Bullying the Moqui. 1903; Prescott, Ariz.: Prescott College Press, 1968.

Minthorn, Armand. "Human Remains Should Be Reburied." September 1996 position
paper, <http://www.umatilla.nsn.us/kman1.html>, consulted September 19, 2007.

Moorehead, Warren K. *American Indian in the United States*. Andover, Mass.: Andover
Press, 1914.

Morgan, Lewis Henry. *Ancient Society*. Tucson: University of Arizona Press, 1985.

National Congress of American Indians. Resolution #ANC-07-020, "Support of the
Current Language and Tribal Recommendations to the 2007 Draft Bill of the 'Native

American Sacred Lands Act.'" <http://www.ncai.org/ncai/resolutions/doc/020_Lummi_Sacred_Land_Act_w_sigs.pdf>, consulted October 8, 2007.

Parker, Patricia, and Thomas King. "National Register Bulletin: Guidelines for Evaluating and Documenting Traditional Cultural Properties." 1990; rev. 1992, 1998. U.S. Department of the Interior, National Park Service. <http://www.nps.gov/history/nr/publications/bulletins/nrb38/>, consulted October 4, 2007.

Parsons, Elsie Clews. *Fear and Conventionality*. 1914; Chicago: University of Chicago Press, 1997.

——. *Hopi and Zuñi Ceremonialism*. Menasha, Wis.: American Anthropological Association, 1933.

——. "Notes on Zuni." *Memoirs of the American Anthropological Association* 4 (1917): 151–327.

——. *The Old-Fashioned Woman: Primitive Fancies about the Sex*. New York: G. P. Putnam's, 1913.

——. *Pueblo Indian Religion*. Vols. 1 and 2. 1939; Lincoln: University of Nebraska Press, 1996.

——. *Pueblo Mothers and Children: Essays*. Edited by Barbara Babcock. Santa Fe, N.M.: Ancient City Press, 1991.

——. *The Pueblo of Jemez*. New Haven: Yale University Press, 1925.

——. *Taos Pueblo*. Menasha, Wis.: George Banta Publishing, 1936.

Pluralism Project at Harvard University. "Research Report: Cave Rock, NV." <http://www.pluralism.org/research/profiles/display.php?profile=74332>, consulted October 4, 2007.

Sacred Land Film Project. "Cave Rock." <http://www.sacredland.org/historical_sites_pages/caverock.html>, consulted October 4, 2007.

——. "Declaration on the Rights of Indigenous Peoples Passes after Thirty Years of Struggle," September 13, 2007. <http://www.sacredland.org/new.html>, consulted October 7, 2007.

——. "Is Nothing Sacred? Corporate Responsibility for the Protection of Native American Sacred Sites." <http://www.sacredland.org/PDFs/csr_dl.pdf>, consulted October 7, 2007.

Sampson, Don, former board of trustees chairman for the Confederated Tribes of the Umatilla Indian Reservation. "Tribal Chair Questions Scientists' Motives and Credibility," November 21, 1997. <http://www.umatilla.nsn.us/kman2.html>, consulted September 19, 2007.

Smith, William. *Dictionary of the Bible*. Hartford: S. S. Scranton, 1896.

Smith, William, and Samuel Cheetham. *Dictionary of Christian Antiquities*. London: John Murray, 1893.

Stevenson, Matilda Coxe. *The Zuni Indians: Their Mythology, Esoteric Fraternities, and*

Ceremonies. *Twenty-third Annual Report of the Bureau of American Ethnology, 1901– 1902*. Washington, D.C.: Government Printing Office, 1904.

———. "Zuni Religion." *Science* 11, no. 268 (1888): 136–37.

Talayesva, Don C., and Leo W. Simmons. *Sun Chief: The Autobiography of a Hopi Indian*. 1942; New Haven: Yale University Press, 1963.

Tylor, Edward Burnett. *Primitive Culture: Researches into the Development of Mythology, Philosophy, Religion, Language, Art and Custom*. 3rd American, from the 2nd English ed. New York: H. Holt, 1889.

Tyson, Stuart L. *The Progressive Revelation of the Bible*. New York: n.p., 1922.

United Nations. "Declaration on the Rights of Indigenous Peoples." <http://daccessdds .un.org/doc/UNDOC/LTD/N07/498/30/PDF/N0749830.pdf?OpenElement>, consulted October 7, 2007.

U.S. Congress. House of Representatives. *Hearings on H.R. 13452 and H.R. 13674*, 67th Cong., 4th sess., February 1–15 1923.

———. "Native American Sacred Lands Act," H.R. 2419, 108th Cong., 1st sess., June 11 2003. <http://www.sacredland.org/legal_pages/NA_SLA_HR_. html>, consulted October 8, 2007.

———. Special Investigating Committee of the Committee on Indian Affairs. *Hearing to Investigate Indian Conditions in the United States*. December 13 1944.

U.S. Congress. Senate. *Hearings on S. Res. 79 and 308 (70th Cong.), and S. Res. 263 and 416: Survey of Conditions of the Indians in the United States*, 71st Cong., 2nd sess., May 1931.

———. Subcommittee on Public Lands and Surveys. *Hearings on S. 3865 and S. 4223, Bills Relative to the Pueblo Indian Lands*, 67th Cong., 4th sess., January 1923.

U.S. Department of the Interior. National Park Service. "Kennewick Man." <http:// www.nps.gov/archeology/kennewick/index.htm>, consulted September 19, 2007.

———. "National NAGPRA." <http://www.nps.gov/history/nagpra/index.htm>, consulted September 13, 2007.

U.S. Office of Indian Affairs. *Annual Report of the Commissioner of Indian Affairs to the Secretary of the Interior for the Year 1871*. Washington, D.C.: Government Printing Office, 1872.

———. *Annual Report of the Commissioner of Indian Affairs to the Secretary of the Interior for the Year 1872*. Washington, D.C.: Government Printing Office, 1873.

———. *Annual Report of the Commissioner of Indian Affairs to the Secretary of the Interior for the Year 1873*. Washington, D.C.: Government Printing Office, 1874.

———. *Annual Report of the Commissioner of Indian Affairs to the Secretary of the Interior for the Year 1881*. Washington, D.C.: Government Printing Office, 1881.

———. *Annual Report of the Commissioner of Indian Affairs to the Secretary of the Interior for the Year 1882*. Washington, D.C.: Government Printing Office, 1882.

——. *Annual Report of the Commissioner of Indian Affairs to the Secretary of the Interior for the year 1885*. Washington, D.C.: Government Printing Office, 1885.

——. *Annual Report of the Commissioner of Indian Affairs to the Secretary of the Interior for the Year 1887*. Washington, D.C.: Government Printing Office, 1887.

——. *Report of the Commissioner of Indian Affairs*. Washington, D.C.: Government Printing Office, 1898.

——. *Report of the Commissioner of Indian Affairs*. Washington, D.C.: Government Printing Office, 1903.

——. *Report of the Commissioner of Indian Affairs*. Washington, D.C.: Government Printing Office, 1909.

——. *Report of the Commissioner of Indian Affairs*. Washington, D.C.: Government Printing Office, 1921.

——. *Sixty-first Annual Report of the Commissioner of Indian Affairs to the Secretary of the Interior*. Washington, D.C.: Government Printing Office, 1892.

Welsh, Herbert. *Report of a Visit to the Great Sioux Reserve, Dakota, Made during the Months of May and June, 1883, in Behalf of the Indian Rights Association*. Philadelphia: Printed by order of the Executive Committee, 1883.

——. *Report of a Visit to the Navajo, Pueblo, and Hualapais Indians of New Mexico and Arizona*. Philadelphia: Indian Rights Association, 1885.

Worl, Rosita. Interim Executive Director, Sealaska Heritage Foundation, Juneau, Alaska. Testimony, "Oversight Hearing before the Senate Committee on Indian Affairs on the Native American Graves Protection and Repatriation Act," April 20, 1999. <http://indian.senate.gov/1999hrgs/nagpra4.20/nag_wit.htm>, consulted September 13, 2007.

Wyaco, Virgil, J. A. Jones, and Carroll L. Riley. *A Zuni Life: A Pueblo Indian in Two Worlds*. Albuquerque: University of New Mexico Press, 1998.

Selected Court Cases

The Access Fund v. United States Department of Agriculture, 691 F.2d 1242 (9th Cir. 2007).

Apache Survival Coalition v. United States, 21 F.3d 895 (9th Cir. 1994).

Badoni v. Higginson, 455 F. Supp. 641 (C.D. Utah 1977).

Bear Lodge Multiple Use Association v. Babbitt, 175 F.3d 814 (10th Cir. 1999).

Lyng v. Northwest Cemetery Protective Association, 485 U.S. 439 (1988).

National Arch and Bridge Society v. Alston, 98 Fed. Appx. 711 (10th Cir. 2004).

Navajo Nation v. U.S. Forest Service, nos. 06-15371, 06-15436, 06-15455 (9th Cir. Aug. 8, 2008).

Northwest Indian Cemetery Protective Association v. Peterson, 795 F.2d 688 (9th Cir. 1986).

Sequoyah v. Tennessee Valley Authority, 620 F.2d 1159 (6th Cir. 1980).

Newspapers and Periodicals

Albuquerque Herald
Albuquerque Morning
    Journal
Boston Herald
Century Magazine
Christian Century
Churchman
Coconino Sun
Current Opinion
El Palacio (Santa Fe,
    New Mexico)
El Paso Herald
Forum
Home Missions Monthly
Indian Country Today

Indian Sentinel
Indian Truth, Indian
    Rights Association,
    Philadelphia,
    Pennsylvania
Ladies' Home Journal
Living Church
Los Angeles Times
Nation
Native American
New Mexico State Tribune
New Republic
New York Times
New York Tribune
New York World

Outlook
Rocky Mountain
    Presbyterian
Sacramento Bee
Santa Fe New Mexican
Saturday Evening Post
Science
Searchlight
Southern Workman
Sunset Magazine
Survey and Survey Graphic
Theatre Arts Magazine
Tidings (Los Angeles)

Secondary Sources

Achebe, Chinua. "An Image of Africa: Racism in Conrad's *Heart of Darkness*." In *Heart of Darkness: An Authoritative Text, Backgrounds and Sources, Criticism*, edited by Robert Kimbrough, 251–62. New York: Norton, 1988.

Adams, David Wallace. *Education for Extinction: American Indians and the Boarding School Experience, 1875–1928*. Lawrence: University Press of Kansas, 1995.

Aldred, Lisa. "Plastic Shamans and Astroturf Sun Dances: New Age Commercialization of Native American Spirituality." *American Indian Quarterly* 24, no. 3 (Summer 2000): 329–52.

Asad, Talal. *Formations of the Secular: Christianity, Islam, Modernity*. Stanford, Calif.: Stanford University Press, 2003.

———. *Genealogies of Religion: Discipline and Reasons of Power in Christianity and Islam*. Baltimore: Johns Hopkins University Press, 1993.

Babcock, Barbara. "Arrange Me into Disorder: Fragments and Reflections on Ritual Clowning." In *Rite, Drama, Festival, Spectacle: Rehearsals toward a Theory of Cultural Performance*, edited by John MacAloon, 102–28. Philadelphia: Institute for the Study of Human Issues, 1984.

———. "Mudwomen and Whitemen: A Meditation on Pueblo Potteries and the Politics of Representation." In *Discovered Country: Tourism and Survival in the American West*, edited by Scott Norris, 180–95. Albuquerque: Stone Ladder Press, 1994.

Balagangadhara, S. N. *"The Heathen in His Blindness—": Asia, the West, and the Dynamic of Religion*. Leiden: E. J. Brill, 1994.

Bederman, Gail. *Manliness and Civilization: A Cultural History of Gender and Race in the United States, 1880–1917*. Chicago: University of Chicago Press, 1995.

———. "'The Women Have Had Charge of the Church Work Long Enough': The Men and Religion Forward Movement of 1911–1912 and the Masculinization of Middle-Class Protestantism." *American Quarterly* 41, no. 3 (1989): 432–65.

Bellah, Robert, Richard Madsen, William M. Sullivan, Ann Swidler, and Steven M. Tipton. *Habits of the Heart: Individualism and Commitment in American Life*. New York: Harper and Row, 1985.

Benedict, Jeff. *No Bone Unturned: The Adventures of a Top Smithsonian Forensic Scientist and the Legal Battle for America's Oldest Skeletons*. New York: HarperCollins, 2003.

Biolsi, Thomas, and Larry J. Zimmerman, eds. *Indians and Anthropologists: Vine Deloria, Jr., and the Critique of Anthropology*. Tucson: University of Arizona Press, 1997.

Blair, Bowen. "Indian Rights: Native Americans versus American Museums—A Battle for Artifacts." *American Indian Law Review* 7 (1979): 125–54.

Bodine, John. "The Taos Blue Lake Ceremony." *American Indian Quarterly* 12, no. 2 (Spring 1988): 91–105.

———. "Taos Pueblo." In *Southwest*, edited by Alfonso Ortiz, 255–67. Handbook of North American Indians, edited by William C. Sturtevant, vol. 9. Washington, D.C.: Smithsonian Institution, 1979.

Booker, M. Keith. *Colonial Power, Colonial Texts: India in the Modern British Novel*. Ann Arbor: University of Michigan Press, 1997.

Brandt, Elizabeth. "On Secrecy and the Control of Knowledge: Taos Pueblo." In *Secrecy, a Cross-Cultural Perspective*, edited by Stanton K. Tefft, 123–46. New York: Human Sciences Press, 1980.

Brooks, James. *Captives and Cousins: Slavery, Kinship and Community in the Southwest Borderlands*. Chapel Hill: University of North Carolina Press, 2002.

Brooks, Van Wyck. *John Sloan: A Painter's Life*. New York: E. P. Dutton, 1955.

Brown, Brian Edward. "Native American Religions, the First Amendment, and the Judicial Interpretation of Public Land." *Environmental History Review* 15, no. 4 (Winter 1991): 19–44.

———. *Religion, Law, and the Land: Native Americans and the Judicial Interpretation of Sacred Land*. Contributions in Legal Studies, no. 94. Westport, Conn.: Greenwood Press, 1999.

Burke, Flannery. "Finding What They Came For: The Mabel Dodge Luhan Circle and the Making of a Modern Place." Ph.D. diss., University of Wisconsin at Madison, 2002.

Burris, John P. *Exhibiting Religion: Colonialism and Spectacle at International Expositions, 1851–1893*. Charlottesville: University Press of Virginia, 2001.

Carr, Helen. *Inventing the American Primitive: Politics, Gender, and the Representation of Native American Literary Traditions*. Cork, Ireland: Cork University Press, 1996.

Castro, Michael. *Interpreting the Indian: Twentieth-Century Poets and the Native American*. Norman: University of Oklahoma Press, 1991.

Chauvenet, Beatrice. *Hewett and Friends: A Biography of Santa Fe's Vibrant Era*. Santa Fe: Museum of New Mexico Press, 1983.

Chidester, David. *Savage Systems: Colonialism and Comparative Religion in Southern Africa*. Charlottesville: University Press of Virginia, 1996.

Clifford, James. *The Predicament of Culture: Twentieth-Century Ethnography, Literature and Art*. Cambridge, Mass.: Harvard University Press, 1988.

Coleman, Michael C. *American Indian Children at School, 1850–1930*. Jackson: University Press of Mississippi, 1993.

Curtis, Susan. *A Consuming Faith: The Social Gospel and Modern American Culture*. Baltimore: Johns Hopkins University Press, 1991.

Daily, David W. *Battle for the BIA: G. E. E. Lindquist and the Missionary Crusade against John Collier*. Tucson: University of Arizona Press, 2004.

Daly, Ann. *Done into Dance: Isadora Duncan in America*. Bloomington: Indiana University Press, 1995.

Deacon, Desley. *Elsie Clews Parsons: Inventing Modern Life*. Chicago: University of Chicago Press, 1997.

DeBerg, Betty A. *Ungodly Women: Gender and the First Wave of American Fundamentalism*. Minneapolis: Fortress Press, 1990.

Deloria, Philip Joseph. *Playing Indian*. New Haven: Yale University Press, 1998.

Deloria, Vine, Jr. *God Is Red: A Native View of Religion*. 2nd ed. Golden, Colo.: North American Press, 1992.

———. "Secularism, Civil Religion, and the Religious Freedom of American Indians." *American Indian Culture and Research Journal* 16, no. 2 (1992): 9–20.

Deloria, Vine, Jr., and James Treat. *For This Land: Writings on Religion in America*. New York: Routledge, 1999.

D'Emilio, John, and Estelle B. Freedman. *Intimate Matters: A History of Sexuality in America*. 2nd ed. Chicago: University of Chicago Press, 1997.

De Mille, Agnes. *Martha: The Life and Work of Martha Graham*. New York: Random House, 1991.

Dilworth, Leah. *Imagining Indians in the Southwest: Persistent Visions of a Primitive Past*. Washington, D.C.: Smithsonian Institution Press, 1996.

Dippie, Brian W. *The Vanishing American: White Attitudes and U.S. Indian Policy*. 1982; Lawrence: University Press of Kansas, 1991.

Dockstader, Frederick J. *The Kachina and the White Man: The Influences of White Culture on the Hopi Kachina Cult*. 1954; Albuquerque: University of New Mexico Press, 1985.

Dolan, Jay P. *The American Catholic Experience: A History from Colonial Times to the Present*. Garden City, N.Y.: Doubleday, 1985.

Dolan, Jay P., and Gilberto Miguel Hinojosa, eds. *Mexican Americans and the Catholic Church, 1900–1965*. Notre Dame, Ind.: University of Notre Dame Press, 1994.

Echo-Hawk, Walter. "Native American Religious Liberty: Five Hundred Years after Columbus." *American Indian Culture and Research Journal* 17, no. 3 (1993): 33–52.

Ellis, Clyde. *A Dancing People: Powwow Culture on the Southern Plains*. Lawrence: University Press of Kansas, 2003.

Epstein, Barbara Leslie. *The Politics of Domesticity: Women, Evangelism, and Temperance in Nineteenth-Century America*. Middletown, Conn.: Wesleyan University Press, 1981.

Ferguson, T. J., Roger Anyon, and Edmund J. Ladd. "Repatriation at the Pueblo of Zuni: Diverse Solutions to Complex Problems." *American Indian Quarterly* 20, no. 2 (1996): 251–73.

Ferris, David S. *Silent Urns: Romanticism, Hellenism, Modernity*. Stanford, Calif.: Stanford University Press, 2000.

Fessenden, Tracy. *Culture and Redemption: Religion, the Secular, and American Literature*. Princeton, N.J.: Princeton University Press, 2007.

Fierman, Floyd. *The Impact of the Frontier on a Jewish Family: The Bibos*. Tucson: Bloom Southwest Jewish Archives, University of Arizona, 1988.

Filene, Peter G. *Him/Her/Self: Sex Roles in Modern America*. 2nd ed. Baltimore: Johns Hopkins University Press, 1986.

Firchow, Peter Edgerly. *Envisioning Africa: Racism and Imperialism in Conrad's Heart of Darkness*. Lexington: University Press of Kentucky, 2000.

Fiske, Turbesé Lummis, and Keith Lummis. *Charles F. Lummis: The Man and His West*. Norman: University of Oklahoma Press, 1975.

Fitzgerald, Timothy. *The Ideology of Religious Studies*. New York: Oxford University Press, 2000.

Forrest, Suzanne. *The Preservation of the Village: New Mexico's Hispanics and the New Deal*. Albuquerque: University of New Mexico, 1998.

Fowler, Don. *A Laboratory for Anthropology: Science and Romanticism in the American Southwest, 1846–1930*. Albuquerque: University of New Mexico Press, 2000.

Franchot, Jenny. *Roads to Rome: The Antebellum Protestant Encounter with Catholicism*. Berkeley: University of California Press, 1994.

Frankiel, Tamar. "Natural Sympathies: Anglo Women and Native American Culture in California and the Southwest, 1890–1925." Unpublished manuscript, University of California, Riverside, 2001.

Gibson, Arrell Morgan. *The Santa Fe and Taos Colonies: Age of the Muses, 1900–1942*. Norman: University of Oklahoma Press, 1983.

Gordon-McCutchan, R. C. *The Taos Indians and the Battle for Blue Lake*. Santa Fe, N.M.: Red Crane Books, 1991.

Grant, Blanche C. *Taos Today*. Taos, N.M.: B. C. Grant, 1925.

Graybill, Andrew. " 'Strong on the Merits and Powerfully Symbolic': The Return of Blue Lake to Taos Pueblo." *New Mexico Historical Review* 76, no. 2 (2001): 125–60.

Greenawalt, Kent. *Religion and the Constitution*. Vol. 1. Princeton, N.J.: Princeton University Press, 2006.

Greene, William Chase. *The Achievement of Greece: A Chapter in Human Experience*. Cambridge, Mass.: Harvard University Press, 1924.

Gulliford, Andrew. *Sacred objects and Sacred Places: Preserving Tribal Traditions*. Boulder: University Press of Colorado, 2000.

Gutierrez, Ramón A. *When Jesus Came, the Corn Mothers Went Away: Marriage, Sexuality, and Power in New Mexico, 1500–1846*. Stanford, Calif.: Stanford University Press, 1991.

Hagan, William Thomas. *The Indian Rights Association: The Herbert Welsh Years, 1882–1904*. Tucson: University of Arizona Press, 1985.

Hamburger, Philip. *Separation of Church and State*. Cambridge, Mass.: Harvard University Press, 2002.

Handler, Richard. "Ruth Benedict and the Modernist Sensibility." In *Modernist Anthropology: From Fieldwork to Text*, edited by Marc Manganaro, 164–78. Princeton, N.J.: Princeton University Press, 1990.

Handy, Robert T. *A Christian America: Protestant Hopes and Historical Realities*. 2nd, rev. and enl. ed. Oxford: Oxford University Press, 1984.

Hanks, Nancy. "Lamy's Legacy: Catholic Institutions of New Mexico Territory." In *Seeds of Struggle/Harvest of Faith: The Papers of the Archdiocese of Santa Fe Catholic Cuatro Centennial Conference*, edited by Thomas J. Steele, Paul Rhetts, and Barbe Awalt, 385–414. Albuquerque: LPD Press, 1998.

Hernandez-Avila, Ines. "Mediations of the Spirit: Native American Religious Traditions and the Ethics of Representation." *American Indian Quarterly* 20, nos. 3–4 (Summer–Fall 1996): 329–52.

Hieb, Louis. "Meaning and Mismeaning: Toward an Understanding of the Ritual Clown." In *New Perspectives on the Pueblos*, edited by Alfonso Ortiz, 163–96. Albuquerque: University of New Mexico Press, 1972.

Hill, Patricia Ruth. *The World Their Household: The American Woman's Foreign Mission Movement and Cultural Transformation, 1870–1920*. Ann Arbor: University of Michigan Press, 1985.

Hinsley, Curtis M. "Zunis and Brahmins: Cultural Ambivalence in the Gilded Age." In *Romantic Motives: Essays on Anthropological Sensibility*, edited by George W. Stocking, 169–207. Madison: University of Wisconsin Press, 1989.

———. *The Smithsonian and the American Indian: Making a Moral Anthropology in Victorian America*. Washington, D.C.: Smithsonian Institution Press, 1994.

Hittman, Michael, and Don Lynch. *Wovoka and the Ghost Dance*. Expanded ed. Lincoln: University of Nebraska Press, 1997.

Hollinger, David. *Science, Jews, and Secular Culture: Studies in Mid-Twentieth-Century American Intellectual History*. Princeton, N.J.: Princeton University Press, 1996.

Holm, Tom. *The Great Confusion in Indian Affairs*. Austin: University of Texas Press, 2005.

Hoxie, Frederick E. *A Final Promise: The Campaign to Assimilate the Indians, 1880–1920*. Cambridge: Cambridge University Press, 1989.

Huhndorf, Shari. *Going Native: Indians in the American Cultural Imagination*. Ithaca: Cornell University Press, 2001.

Hultkrantz, Åke. *The Religions of the American Indians*. Berkeley: University of California Press, 1979.

Hundert, E. J. "The European Enlightenment and the History of the Self." In *Rewriting the Self: Histories from the Renaissance to the Present*, edited by Roy Porter, 72–83. London: Routledge, 1997.

Hunter, Jane. *The Gospel of Gentility: American Women Missionaries in Turn-of-the-Century China*. New Haven: Yale University Press, 1984.

Hyer, Sally. *One House, One Voice, One Heart: Native American Education at the Santa Fe Indian School*. Santa Fe: Museum of New Mexico Press, 1990.

Jacobs, Margaret D. *Engendered Encounters: Feminism and Pueblo Cultures, 1879–1934*. Lincoln: University of Nebraska Press, 1999.

Jenkins, Philip. *Dream Catchers: How Mainstream America Discovered Native Spirituality*. Oxford: Oxford University Press, 2004.

Johnson, Greg. "Ancestors before Us: Manifestations of Tradition in a Hawaiian Dispute." *Journal of the American Academy of Religion* 71, no. 2 (June 2003): 327–46.

Jordan, Mark D. *The Invention of Sodomy in Christian Theology*. Chicago: University of Chicago Press, 1997.

Keegan, Marcia. *The Taos Pueblo and Its Sacred Blue Lake*. Santa Fe, N.M.: Clear Light Publishers, 1991.

Keller, Robert H. *American Protestantism and United States Indian Policy, 1869–82*. Lincoln: University of Nebraska Press, 1983.

Kelly, Lawrence C. *The Assault on Assimilation: John Collier and the Origins of Indian Policy Reform*. Albuquerque: University of New Mexico Press, 1983.

Kendall, Elizabeth. *Where She Danced*. New York: Knopf, 1979.

Kessell, John L. *The Missions of New Mexico since 1776*. Albuquerque: University of New Mexico Press, 1980.

Kidwell, Clara Sue, Homer Noley, and George E. Tinker. *A Native American Theology*. Maryknoll, N.Y.: Orbis Books, 2001.

King, Richard. *Orientalism and Religion: Postcolonial Theory, India and "The Mystic East."* London: Routledge, 1999.

Kroeber, Theodora. *Alfred Kroeber: A Personal Configuration*. Berkeley: University of California Press, 1970.

Kuper, Adam. *The Invention of Primitive Society: Transformations of an Illusion.* New York: Routledge, 1988.

Kvasnicka, Robert M., and Herman J. Viola, eds. *The Commissioners of Indian Affairs, 1824–1977.* Lincoln: University of Nebraska Press, 1979.

LaDuke, Winona. *Recovering the Sacred: The Power of Naming and Claiming.* Cambridge, Mass.: South End Press, 2005.

Lamadrid, Enrique. *Hermanitos Comanchitos: Indo-Hispano Rituals of Captivity and Redemption.* Albuquerque: University of New Mexico Press, 2003.

Lash, Nicholas. *The Beginning and the End of "Religion."* New York: Cambridge University Press, 1996.

Lassiter, Luke. "Southwestern Oklahoma, the Gourd Dance, and 'Charlie Brown.'" In *Contemporary Native American Cultural Issues,* edited by Duane Champagne, 145–66. Walnut Creek, Calif.: AltaMira Press, 1999.

Lawson, Paul E., and C. Patrick Morris. "The Native American Church and the New Court: The Smith Case and Indian Religious Freedoms." *American Indian Culture and Research Journal* 15, no. 1 (1991): 79–91.

Lears, T. J. Jackson. *No Place of Grace: Antimodernism and the Transformation of American Culture, 1880–1920.* Chicago: University of Chicago Press, 1994.

Leontis, Artemis. *Topographies of Hellenism: Mapping the Homeland.* Ithaca: Cornell University Press, 1995.

Lincoln, Bruce. *Holy Terrors: Thinking about Religion after September 11.* Chicago: University of Chicago Press, 2003.

Linnekin, Jocelyn. "Cultural Invention and the Dilemma of Authenticity." *American Anthropologist* 93, no. 2 (June 1991): 446–49.

Lint Sagarena, Roberto. "Re-Forming the Church: Preservation, Renewal, and Restoration in American Christian Architecture in California." In *Practicing Protestants: Histories of Christian Life in America, 1630–1965,* edited by Laurie Maffly-Kipp, Leigh Eric Schmidt, and Mark Valeri, 118–34. Baltimore: Johns Hopkins University Press, 2006.

Long, Carolyn Nestor. *Religious Freedom and Indian Rights: The Case of Oregon v. Smith.* Lawrence: University Press of Kansas, 2000.

Loughery, John. *John Sloan: Painter and Rebel.* New York: Henry Holt, 1995.

MacLachlan, Bruce. "Indian Law and Puebloan Tribal Law." In *North American Indian Anthropology: Essays on Society and Culture,* edited by Raymond J. DeMallie and Alfonso Ortiz, 345–46. Norman: University of Oklahoma Press, 1994.

Manganaro, Marc, ed. *Modernist Anthropology: From Fieldwork to Text.* Princeton, N.J.: Princeton University Press, 1990.

Martin, Joel W. *The Land Looks after Us: A History of Native American Religion.* Oxford: Oxford University Press, 2001.

Martin, Ronald E. *The Languages of Difference: American Writers and Anthropologists Reconfigure the Primitive, 1878–1940.* Newark: University of Delaware Press, 2005.

Masuzawa, Tomoko. *In Search of Dreamtime: The Quest for the Origin of Religion.* Chicago: University of Chicago Press, 1993.

——. *The Invention of World Religions; or, How European Universalism Was Preserved in the Language of Pluralism.* Chicago: University of Chicago Press, 2005.

May, Elaine Tyler. *Great Expectations: Marriage and Divorce in Post-Victorian America.* Chicago: University of Chicago Press, 1980.

Mazur, Eric Michael. *The Americanization of Religious Minorities: Confronting the Constitutional Order.* Baltimore: Johns Hopkins University Press, 1999.

McCloud, Sean. *Making the American Religious Fringe: Exotics, Subversives, and Journalists, 1955–1993.* Chapel Hill: University of North Carolina Press, 2004.

McFeely, Eliza. "Palimpsest of American Identity: Zuni, Anthropology, and American Identity at the Turn of the Century." Ph.D. diss., New York University, 1996.

——. *Zuni and the American Imagination.* New York: Hill and Wang, 2001.

McGreevy, John T. *Catholicism and American Freedom: A History.* New York: W. W. Norton, 2003.

McKenzie, F. A. *"Pussyfoot" Johnson: Crusader—Reformer—A Man among Men.* New York: Fleming H. Revell Company, 1920.

McKinney, Lillie G. "History of the Albuquerque Indian School." *New Mexico Historical Review* 20, no. 2 (1945): 109–38.

McNally, Michael David. *Ojibwe Singers: Hymns, Grief, and a Native Culture in Motion.* Oxford: Oxford University Press, 2000.

Michaels, Walter Benn. *Our America: Nativism, Modernism, and Pluralism.* Durham: Duke University Press, 1995.

Mooney, James. *The Ghost-Dance Religion and the Sioux Outbreak of 1890.* 1896; Lincoln: University of Nebraska Press, 1991.

Moore, Steven C. "Reflections on the Elusive Promise of Religious Freedom for the Native American Church." *Wicazo Sa Review* 7, no. 1 (1991): 42–50.

Moore-Gilbert, B. J. *Kipling and "Orientalism."* London: Croom Helm, 1986.

Morey, Peter. *Fictions of India: Narrative and Power.* Edinburgh: Edinburgh University Press, 2000.

Morrill, Claire. *A Taos Mosaic: Portrait of a New Mexico Village.* Albuquerque: University of New Mexico Press, 1973.

Morrison, Kenneth M. *The Solidarity of Kin: Ethnohistory, Religious Studies, and the Algonkian-French Religious Encounter.* Albany: State University of New York Press, 2002.

Moses, L. G. *The Indian Man: A Biography of James Mooney.* Bison Books ed. Lincoln: University of Nebraska Press, 2002.

Murray, David. "Object Lessons: Fetishism and the Hierarchies of Race and Religion." In

Conversion: Old Worlds and New, edited by Kenneth Mills and Anthony Grafton, 199–
217. Rochester, N.Y.: University of Rochester Press, 2003.

Nabokov, Peter. *A Forest of Time: American Indian Ways of History*. Cambridge:
Cambridge University Press, 2002.

Olson, James Stuart, and Raymond Wilson. *Native Americans in the Twentieth Century*.
Provo, Utah: Brigham Young University Press, 1984.

Ortiz, Alfonso. "The Dynamics of Pueblo Cultural Survival." In *North American Indian
Anthropology: Essays on Society and Culture*, edited by Raymond J. DeMallie and
Alfonso Ortiz, 301. Norman: University of Oklahoma Press, 1994.

———. "Ritual Drama and the Pueblo World View." In *New Perspectives on the Pueblos*,
edited by Alfonso Ortiz, 135–62. Albuquerque: University of New Mexico Press,
1972.

———. *The Tewa World: Space, Time, Being, and Becoming in a Pueblo Society*. Chicago:
University of Chicago Press, 1969.

Pandey, Triloki Nath. "Factionalism in a Southwestern Pueblo." Ph.D. diss., University
of Chicago, 1967.

Parezo, Nancy J. "Matilda Coxe Stevenson: Pioneer Ethnologist." In *Hidden Scholars:
Women Anthropologists and the Native American Southwest*, edited by Nancy J. Parezo,
38–62. Albuquerque: University of New Mexico Press, 1993.

Pavlik, Steve. "The U.S. Supreme Court Decision on Peyote in *Employment Division v.
Smith*: A Case Study in the Suppression of Native American Religious Freedom."
Wicazo Sa Review 8, no. 2 (1992): 30–39.

Peterson, Derek R., and Darren R. Walhof. *The Invention of Religion: Rethinking Belief in
Politics and History*. New Brunswick, N.J.: Rutgers University Press, 2002.

Pfister, Joel. *Individuality Incorporated: Indians and the Multicultural Modern*. Durham
N.C.: Duke University Press, 2004.

Philp, Kenneth. *John Collier's Crusade for Indian Reform, 1920–1954*. Tucson: University
of Arizona Press, 1977.

Pietz, William. "The Problem of the Fetish, IIIa: Bosman's Guinea and the
Enlightenment Theory of Fetishism." *Res* 16 (Autumn 1988): 105–23.

Porter, Joseph C. *Paper Medicine Man: John Gregory Bourke and His American West*.
Norman: University of Oklahoma Press, 1986.

Prakash, Gyan, ed. *After Colonialism: Imperial Histories and Postcolonial Displacements*.
Princeton, N.J.: Princeton University Press, 1995.

Prucha, Francis Paul. *American Indian Policy in Crisis: Christian Reformers and the Indian,
1865–1900*. Norman: University of Oklahoma Press, 1976.

———. *The Churches and the Indian Schools, 1888–1912*. Lincoln: University of Nebraska
Press, 1979.

———. *The Great Father: The United States Government and the American Indians*. 2 vols.
Lincoln: University of Nebraska Press, 1984.

Pulido, Alberto L. *The Sacred World of the Penitentes*. Washington, D.C.: Smithsonian Institution Press, 2000.

Rajan, Balachandra. *Under Western Eyes: India from Milton to Macaulay*. Durham, N.C.: Duke University Press, 1999.

Rhodes, John. "An American Tradition: The Religious Persecution of Native Americans." *Montana Law Review* 52 (1991): 13–72.

Robert, Dana Lee. *American Women in Mission: A Social History of Their Thought and Practice*. Macon, Ga.: Mercer University Press, 1996.

Rodriguez, Sylvia. "Art, Tourism, and Race Relations in Taos: Toward a Sociology of the Art Colony." In *Discovered Country: Tourism and Survival in the American West*, edited by Scott Norris, 144–60. Albuquerque: Stone Ladder Press, 1994.

Rudnick, Lois Palken. *Mabel Dodge Luhan: New Woman, New Worlds*. Albuquerque: University of New Mexico Press, 1984.

Sando, Joe S. *Pueblo Nations: Eight Centuries of Pueblo Indian History*. Santa Fe, N.M.: Clear Light, 1992.

———. *Pueblo Profiles: Cultural Identity through Centuries of Change*. Santa Fe, N.M.: Clear Light Publishers, 1998.

Satter, Beryl. *Each Mind a Kingdom: American Women, Sexual Purity, and the New Thought Movement, 1875–1920*. Berkeley: University of California Press, 1999.

Schilbrack, Kevin. "Religion, Models of, and Reality: Are We through with Geertz?" *Journal of the American Academy of Religion* 73, no. 2 (June 2005): 429–52.

Schmidt, Leigh Eric. *Hearing Things: Religion, Illusion, and the American Enlightenment*. Cambridge, Mass.: Harvard University Press, 2000.

Schultze, Robin. "Harriet Monroe's Pioneer Modernism: Nature, National Identity, and Poetry, A Magazine of Verse." *Legacy* 21, no. 1 (2004): 50–67.

Scott, Anne Firor. *Natural Allies: Women's Associations in American History*. Urbana: University of Illinois Press, 1991.

Shaw, Jane. "Religious Experience and the Formation of the Early Enlightenment Self." In *Rewriting the Self: Histories from the Renaissance to the Present*, edited by Roy Porter, 61–71. London: Routledge, 1997.

Shelton, Suzanne. *Ruth St. Denis: A Biography of the Divine Dancer*. Austin: University of Texas Press, 1990.

Silverman, Sydel. *Totems and Teachers: Key Figures in the History of Anthropology*. 2nd ed. 1981; Walnut Creek, Calif.: AltaMira Press, 2004.

Singh, Jyotsna G. *Colonial Narratives/Cultural Dialogues: "Discoveries" of India in the Language of Colonialism*. London: Routledge, 1996.

Smith, Andy. "For All Those Who Were Indian in a Former Life." *Cultural Survival Quarterly* 17, no. 4 (1994): 70–71.

Smith, Christian. *The Secular Revolution: Power, Interests, and Conflict in the Secularization of American Public Life*. Berkeley: University of California Press, 2003.

Smith, Jonathan Z. *Relating Religion: Essays in the Study of Religion*. Chicago: University of Chicago Press, 2004.

———. "Religion, Religions, Religious." In *Relating Religion: Essays in the Study of Religion*, 179–96. Chicago: University of Chicago Press, 2004.

Smith, Sherry Lynn. *Reimagining Indians: Native Americans through Anglo Eyes, 1880–1940*. Oxford: Oxford University Press, 2000.

Smith, Wilfred Cantwell. *The Meaning and End of Religion: A New Approach to the Religious Traditions of Mankind*. 1963; Minneapolis: Fortress Press, 1991.

Smith-Rosenberg, Carroll. *Disorderly Conduct: Visions of Gender in Victorian America*. New York: Alfred A. Knopf, 1985.

Spence, Mark David. *Dispossessing the Wilderness: Indian Removal and the Making of the National Parks*. New York: Oxford University Press, 1999.

Spicer, Edward Holland. *Cycles of Conquest: The Impact of Spain, Mexico, and the United States on the Indians of the Southwest, 1533–1960*. Tucson: University of Arizona Press, 1967.

Stansell, Christine. *American Moderns: Bohemian New York and the Creation of a New Century*. New York: Metropolitan Books, 2000.

Stanton, Phyllis Deery. "Processing the Native American through Western Consciousness: D. H. Lawrence and the Red Indians of the Americas." *Wicazo Sa Review* 12, no. 2 (1997): 59–84.

Stewart, Omer Call. *Peyote Religion: A History*. Norman: University of Oklahoma Press, 1987.

Stocking, George W. "The Ethnographic Sensibility of the 1920s and the Dualism of the Anthropological Tradition." In *Romantic Motives: Essays on Anthropological Sensibility*, edited by George W. Stocking, 208–70. Madison: University of Wisconsin Press, 1989.

———. *Race, Culture, and Evolution: Essays in the History of Anthropology*. 1968; Chicago: University of Chicago Press, 1982.

Strenski, Ivan. "On 'Religion' and Its Despisers." In *What Is Religion? Origins, Definitions, and Explanations*, edited by Thomas A. Idinopulos and Brian C. Wilson, 113–32. Leiden: Brill, 1998.

Styers, Randall. *Making Magic: Religion, Magic, and Science in the Modern World*. New York: Oxford University Press, 2004.

Sweet, Jill D. *Dances of the Tewa Pueblo Indians: Expressions of New Life*. Santa Fe, N.M.: School of American Research Press, 1985.

———. "'Let 'em Loose': Pueblo Indian Management of Tourism." *American Indian Culture and Research Journal* 15, no. 4 (1991): 59–74.

Tapahe, Luralene. "After the Religious Freedom Restoration Act: Still No Equal Protection for First American Worshipers." *New Mexico Law Review* 24 (Spring 1994): 331–63.

Taves, Ann. "Feminization Revisited: Protestantism and Gender at the Turn of the Century." In *Women and Twentieth-Century Protestantism*, edited by Margaret Lamberts Bendroth and Virginia Lieson Brereton, 304–24. Urbana: University of Illinois Press, 2002.

Tedlock, Barbara. "Zuni Sacred Theatre." *American Indian Quarterly* 7, no. 3 (1983): 93–110.

Thomas, George, Lisa Peck, and Channin De Haan. "Reforming Education, Transforming Religion, 1876–1931." In *The Secular Revolution: Power, Interests, and Conflict in the Secularization of American Public Life*, edited by Christian Smith, 355–94. Berkeley: University of California Press, 2003.

Thompson, Mark. *American Character: The Curious Life of Charles Fletcher Lummis and the Rediscovery of the Southwest*. New York: Arcade Publishing, 2001.

Tinker, George. *Spirit and Resistance: Political Theology and American Indian Liberation*. Minneapolis: Fortress Press, 2004.

Torgovnick, Marianna. *Gone Primitive: Savage Intellects, Modern Lives*. Chicago: University of Chicago Press, 1990.

Treat, James. *Around the Sacred Fire: A Native Religious Activism in the Red Power Era*. New York: Palgrave Macmillan, 2003.

———. "Intertribal Traditionalism and the Religious Roots of Red Power." In *Native American Spirituality: A Critical Reader*, edited by Lee Irwin, 270–94. Lincoln: University of Nebraska Press, 2000.

Trivedi, Harish. *Colonial Transactions: English Literature and India*. New York: Manchester University Press, 1996.

Tweed, Thomas A. *Crossing and Dwelling: A Theory of Religion*. Cambridge, Mass.: Harvard University Press, 2006.

Van Hook, Larue. *Greek Life and Thought: A Portrayal of Greek Civilization*. New York: Columbia University Press, 1923.

Vecsey, Christopher. *On the Padres' Trail*. Notre Dame, Ind.: University of Notre Dame Press, 1996.

———, ed. *Handbook of American Indian Religious Freedom*. New York: Crossroad, 1991.

Verter, Bradford J. M. "Dark Star Rising: The Emergence of Modern Occultism, 1800–1950." Ph.D. diss., Princeton University, 1998.

Weigle, Marta, and Barbara Babcock, eds. *The Great Southwest of the Fred Harvey Company and the Santa Fe Railway*. Phoenix: Heard Museum, 1996.

Weigle, Marta, and Kyle Fiore. *Santa Fe and Taos: the Writer's Era, 1916–1941*. Santa Fe, N.M.: Ancient City Press, 1982.

Wenger, Tisa. "Land, Culture, and Sovereignty in the Pueblo Dance Controversy." *Journal of the Southwest* 16, no. 2 (Fall 2004): 381–412.

———. "Modernists, Pueblo Indians, and the Politics of Primitivism." In *Race, Religion,*

Region: Landscapes of Encounter in the American West, edited by Fay Botham and
  Sarah Patterson, 101–14. Tucson: University of Arizona Press, 2006.

———. "'We Are Guaranteed Freedom': Pueblo Indians and the Category of Religion in
  the 1920s." *History of Religions* 45, no. 2 (2005): 89–113.

White, Richard. "Using the Past: History and Native American Studies." In *Studying
  Native America: Problems and Prospects*, edited by Russell Thornton, 217–305.
  Madison: University of Wisconsin Press, 1998.

Whiteley, Peter M. "Burning Culture: Auto-Da-Fe at Oraibi." *History and Anthropology*
  (Great Britain) 6, no. 1 (1992): 46–85.

———. *Deliberate Acts: Changing Hopi Culture through the Oraibi Split.* Tucson: University
  of Arizona Press, 1988.

———. "Reconnoitering 'Pueblo' Ethnicity: The 1852 Tesuque Delegation to Washington."
  Journal of the Southwest 45, no. 3 (Autumn 2003): 437–518.

Wilken, Robert L. *Anselm Weber, O.F.M., Missionary to the Navaho, 1898–1921.*
  Milwaukee: Bruce Publishing, 1955.

Woloshuk, Nicholas. *E. Irving Couse, 1866–1936.* Santa Fe, N.M.: Santa Fe Village Art
  Museum, 1976.

Wood, Nancy C. *Taos Pueblo.* New York: Knopf, 1989.

Worster, Donald. *A River Running West: The Life of John Wesley Powell.* New York: Oxford
  University Press, 2001.

Wright, Robert. "How Many Are 'A Few'? Catholic Clergy in Central and Northern New
  Mexico, 1780–1851." In *Seeds of Struggle/Harvest of Faith: The Papers of the
  Archdiocese of Santa Fe Catholic Cuatro Centennial Conference*, edited by Thomas J.
  Steele, Paul Rhetts, and Barbe Awalt, 219–62. Albuquerque: LPD Press, 1998.

Yohn, Susan M. *A Contest of Faiths: Missionary Women and Pluralism in the American
  Southwest.* Ithaca: Cornell University Press, 1995.

Zumwalt, Rosemary Lévy. *Wealth and Rebellion: Elsie Clews Parsons, Anthropologist and
  Folklorist.* Urbana: University of Illinois Press, 1992.

INDEX

Abeita, Pablo (Isleta Pueblo), 104 (ill.); biography, 102–3; on Bursum Bill, 105, 106, 112, 115–17; criticizes reformers, 103–5, 122, 169; on dance circular, 146–47

Acoma Pueblo, 21–24, 197, 206

Advisory Council on Indian Affairs. *See* Committee of One Hundred

Albuquerque Indian School, 55, 66

Allegations of immorality: made by assimilationists, 44–45, 135–43, 151–54, 164–65; rejected by Pueblo Indians, 135–36, 190–91, 203–4; as reflection of cultural disputes, 142–43, 154–55; rejected by reformers, 157–60, 165–68

All-Pueblo Council. *See* Council of All the New Mexico Pueblos

American Indian Defense Association: founding and priorities of, 113, 126, 128, 169; and Pueblo land disputes, 133, 206; on Indian tradition and religious freedom, 192–93, 195, 225, 228, 232–34, 236; on Indian health care, 222. *See also* Collier, John; Modernists

American Indian Movement (AIM), 240. *See also* Red Power movement

American Indian Religious Freedom Act, 242, 247, 257

Anthropologists: define Indian religion, 4, 41–43, 54–55, 63–64, 239, 256, 258, 265–66; involvement in Indian affairs, 7, 112–13, 169–70; and primitivism, 8, 125, 149; mistrusted by Indians, 27, 187; and civilizing programs, 42–43, 64, 137; defend Pueblo traditions, 136, 141, 157, 159, 162, 167, 179–80, 186; and cultural artifacts, 246–49, 250–52. *See also* Benedict, Ruth; Boas,

Franz; Cushing, Frank Hamilton; Hewett, Edgar Lee; Hodge, Frederick Webb; Kroeber, Alfred; Mooney, James; Morgan, Lewis Henry; Parsons, Elsie Clews; Social evolutionary theory; Stevenson, Matilda Coxe

Anti-Catholicism, 29–30, 32–34, 50–51, 62, 144, 160

Apache Indians, 31, 258–59

Artists and writers: depict Pueblos and Pueblo religion, 1–2, 4, 59–61, 90–92, 125–26; involvement in Indian affairs, 7, 112–13, 137–38, 211; and primitivism, 8, 71–73, 122–24, 148–49, 156, 160–61, 191, 216–17; secularism among, 64, 70, 89–90, 92; in Taos and Santa Fe art colonies, 70–71, 81–82; and Indian arts, 93–94; criticized by Indians and assimilationists, 103–4, 171, 172–73, 196, 202–3, 208, 212; defend Pueblo traditions, 118, 136, 159. *See also* Austin, Mary; Couse, E. Irving; Lawrence, D. H.; Luhan, Mabel Dodge; Lummis, Charles Fletcher; Modernists; Sloan, John

Assimilation: ideology of, 7–8, 30, 35–36; policies attacked, 117–18, 123–25, 148–50, 159–60, 179–80; debated among moderate and modernist reformers, 125–28, 157. *See also* Bureau of Indian Affairs; U.S. Indian policy

Assimilationist reformers: allied with Pueblo progressives, 9–10, 100, 201–4, 205–6, 208; link Christianity and civilization, 29–30, 35–36, 41–42, 45, 47, 220; reform priorities of, 38–39, 43–47, 137–40; justify colonialist policies, 40–41, 216–20, 222; on Indian ceremonies, 43–45, 135–37, 143–45, 151–55, 168, 217–20; and Pueblo land disputes, 114, 130–31, 147; influence of, in Indian affairs, 37–38, 155–56, 164–66, 168–75, 184–85, 211–12, 231–33; and religious freedom, 171, 175, 195–96, 208–11, 215; criticize modernists, 172–74, 195–96, 212, 215–16; on morality, 173–76; on women's rights, 175–78. *See also* Bibo, Nathan; Brosius, S. M.; Bryan, Mary; Bureau of Catholic Indian Missions; Crane, Leo; Dabb, Edith; Dissette, Mary; Indian Rights Association; Johnson, William E. "Pussyfoot;" Sniffen, Matthew; Welsh, Herbert

Atwood, Stella: and Pueblo land disputes, 111–12, 130, 131; on Pueblo traditions, 124, 168, 180, 213, 214–16. *See also* General Federation of Women's Clubs

Austin, Mary, 91, 93, 112, 160, 161, 172, 218

Aztecs, 76; compared to Pueblos, 30–31, 119, 125

Benedict, Ruth, 80

Bibo, Nathan, 195–96, 197, 208, 219–20

Board of Indian Commissioners, 32, 37, 47, 137, 157

Boas, Franz, 73–75

Brosius, S. M., 153, 209

Bryan, Mary, 196–97

Bureau of Catholic Indian Missions (BCIM): in Indian affairs, 48–49, 55–56, 152, 168; on Indian ceremonies, 53–54, 152; and Pueblo land disputes, 105–6; and Pueblo progressives, 204–5, 213, 215. *See also* Catholic Church; Hughes, William; Schuster, Fridolin

Bureau of Indian Affairs (BIA): suppressing Indian traditions, 29–30, 39–40, 43–45; and Protestant-Catholic conflicts, 31, 33, 34–35, 55–58; charges of corruption in, 31, 38, 46, 131, 138, 139, 222; civilizing policies of, 31, 95, 138–40, 188–89, 208–9, 212, 216, 232–33; and Indian education, 32, 34–35, 44–45, 48–51, 55–58, 188–89, 195,

220; and Pueblo land disputes, 97, 102, 114, 133, 147; and tribal governance, 98–99, 100–101, 185–87, 197, 224–31, 233–34; and Pueblo ceremonies, 98–99, 101–2, 145–48, 184–85; and Indian dances, 140, 143–45, 151, 152–53, 168; in conflicts at Taos Pueblo, 187–91, 195, 222–26; and Pueblo cultural changes, 220–22, 224, 229–31; and Indian religious freedom, 100–102, 222–29, 233. *See also* Burke, Charles; Crandall, C. J.; Crane, Leo; Dorchester, Daniel; Faris, Chester E.; Marble, H. P.; Meritt, Edgar B.; Morgan, Thomas Jefferson; Otero-Warren, Adelina; Safford, C. V.; Schools, Indian; Sweet, Evander; Twitchell, Ralph E.; U.S. Indian policy; Work, Hubert

Burke, Charles (commissioner of Indian affairs): and dance circular, 7, 137, 143, 145, 155, 165; and Pueblo land disputes, 102, 105, 106, 130; and Indian education, 187–91, 195; and Pueblo progressives, 209; and religious freedom, 222–23, 228. *See also* Bureau of Indian Affairs

Bursum Bill. *See* Pueblo land disputes

Carlisle Indian School, 66, 99, 143, 202

Catholic Church: influence of in Indian affairs, 8, 20, 55–58, 105–6, 152, 214; missions under Spain and Mexico, 19, 21–29; missions under United States, 29, 52–55, 57, 185–86, 213; conflicts with Protestants, 32, 34–35, 47–57, 144, 212–13; civilizing efforts of, 52–54, 57, 177–78; views of Indian traditions, 53–54, 139–40, 151–52, 177–78, 243; missions refused by Zunis, 54–55. *See also* Anti-Catholicism; Bureau of Catholic Indian Missions; Catholicism; Hughes, William; St. Catherine's Indian School; Schools, Indian; Schuster, Fridolin; Weber, Anselm

Catholicism: modernist views of, 1–2, 72, 84–85, 90, 108–9, 120–21, 150, 163, 166; as

Pueblo Indian religion, 5, 19, 28, 48, 51–52, 105, 114–15, 146, 207; distinguished from Pueblo religion, 19, 192–93, 200–201, 207; as practiced by Pueblos, 25–28, 54, 168, 200, 243

Cave Rock, 259–61

Cherokee Indians, 253–54

Christian establishment, 4, 7–8, 57–58, 239; undermined, 61, 184, 193, 233. *See also* Missionary establishment; Protestant establishment

Christianity: viewed by secularists, 69–70; as basis for morality and civilization, 155, 174–75, 188–89, 220. *See also* Catholicism; Protestantism

Christian missions. *See* Catholic Church: missions under Spain and Mexico; Catholic Church: missions under United States; Protestant missions

Church and state, separation of, 31–32, 49–50. *See also* First Amendment; Religious freedom

Circular No. 1665: Indian Dancing. *See* Dance circular

Cochiti Pueblo, 99–102, 146, 196, 197–99. *See also* Dixon, John; Melchor, Joseph; Montoya, Alcario

Collier, John, 108 (ill.); as commissioner of Indian affairs, 5, 58, 185, 230, 240; and Pueblo land disputes, 96, 111–13, 128–29, 131–33; biography, 107–10; on Pueblo ceremonies, 110–11, 157–58, 214–15; defining Pueblo religion, 117–22, 161, 163; criticizes assimilationists and BIA, 120, 157–58, 222, 223, 232; colonialist attitudes of, 121–22, 124, 127–28, 179; attacked by moderates and assimilationists, 129–30, 215–16; on religious freedom, 185–86, 191–93, 210–11

Colonialism: and concepts of religion and civilization, 9, 11–12, 14, 35, 40, 42; Spanish, 21–28, 73, 96, 230; and primitivism, 87–88, 120–21, 127–28, 179; and U.S. Indian policy, 189, 216–17. *See also* Assimilationist

reformers: justify colonialist policies; Collier, John: colonialist attitudes of

Committee of One Hundred, 168–71, 175

Council of All the New Mexico Pueblos: history, 24–25; on land disputes, 95–96, 106, 117, 131; on tribal sovereignty, 98, 100–101, 224–25, 233–34; on Pueblo ceremonies and religious freedom, 100–101, 135–36, 147, 190–91, 205–7, 224–25. *See also* Pueblo leaders

Council of Progressive Pueblo Indians: formation and concerns of, 183, 201–5; and assimilationists, 203–5, 213–14, 215; criticized, 205–7. *See also* Pueblo progressives

Couse, E. Irving, 71–73

Crandall, C. J.: accused of corruption, 46–47, 138–39; on schools and education, 55, 176, 188–89, 195; on Pueblo traditions, 176, 221; on Pueblo progressives and tribal authority, 208–9, 226, 228; on religious freedom, 223–25

Crane, Leo, 43–44, 101, 197, 208, 216–18

Cultural hybridity, 29, 80

Cultural relativism, 66, 79–80, 158–60

Cushing, Frank Hamilton, 41, 60, 65

Dabb, Edith, 175, 179, 211, 217

Dance: modern, 92–93; popular, compared to Pueblo ceremonies, 154–55, 158, 162, 168; as origin for religion, 161

Dance circular, 7, 136–37; drafting and contents of, 143, 145; debated, 145–56; criticized, 148–49;

Dawes Allotment Act, 46

Deloria, Vine, Jr., 240–41, 245, 252

Department of the Interior. *See* Bureau of Indian Affairs

Dissette, Mary, 44–45, 135, 136, 172–74, 175–76

Dixon, John (Cochiti Pueblo), 99–100, 101, 198–99, 202, 203–4, 206, 212, 214

Dorchester, Daniel, 29–30, 33, 40–41, 42, 50, 66–67, 70

Morgan, Lewis Henry, 35, 62–63

Morgan, Thomas Jefferson (commissioner of Indian affairs), 50–51, 66–67

National Historic Places Act, 257–61

National Register of Historic Places, 257–61

Native American Church, 139, 239–42. *See also* Peyote religion

Native American Graves Protection and Repatriation Act (NAGPRA), 247–52

Native Americans. *See* Apache Indians; Cherokee Indians; Hopi Indians; Lakota Indians; Navajo Indians; Pueblo Indians

Native American Sacred Lands Act, proposed, 264

Navajo Indians, 31, 254–55, 262–63

New Age movement, 244–46, 261–62, 265

New Mexico Association on Indian Affairs, 113, 128, 131, 148–49, 169, 193–94, 215–16, 234–36. *See also* Henderson, Alice Corbin; Wilson, Francis

Noble savage. *See* Primitivism

Oñate, Juan de, 21

Orientalism, 9, 121

Ortiz, Sotero (San Juan Pueblo), 106, 148

Otero-Warren, Adelina (BIA inspector), 151, 194, 198, 201, 202, 208–9, 212–13, 215

Paganism, Christian views of, 19–20, 29–30, 40–41, 137, 212, 217–19. *See also* Idolatry, Christian views of

Parsons, Elsie Clews, 78 (ill.); biography, 77; on religion, 77–81; on ceremonial secrecy, 98; as controversial figure, 136, 142; defends Pueblo ceremonies, 141, 167, 178

Peace Policy of 1869, 31, 32, 34, 48–49

Penitentes, 29, 53, 84

Pentecostalism, 162

Peyote religion, 138–40, 153–54, 162–63, 238–42

Phallic religion, 217–18

Powell, John Wesley, 63

Presbyterian missions, 32, 34–35, 48, 56–57. *See also* Jackson, Sheldon

Primitivism: defined, 8–9; linked to commercialism, 59, 149; history of, 60–61; political impact of, 61–62, 72, 87–88, 93–94; among modernists, 67–69, 71–72, 84–86, 87–89, 121–25. *See also* Artists and writers; Modernists

Progressive Pueblo Council. *See* Council of Progressive Pueblo Indians

Progressive Pueblos. *See* Pueblo progressives

Protestant establishment, 32–33, 37–38; challenged by Catholics and Indians, 47–58; attacked by modernists, 150; defended, 211–12. *See also* Christian establishment; Missionary establishment

Protestantism: seen as most advanced or only true religion, 19–20, 30, 41, 47

Protestant missions: views of Indian religion, 19–20, 40–41; used as civilizing tool, 31–32, 34–35, 45; and women's rights, 44–45; rebuffed by Pueblo Indians, 207. *See also* Catholic Church: conflicts with Protestants; Home Missions Council; Missionary establishment; Presbyterian missions; Protestant establishment

Psychoanalysis, 83, 84

Pueblo ceremonies: secrecy in, 2–3, 27, 98, 185–87; allegations of immorality in, 2–3, 135–36, 140–43, 164–65, 173, 194, 217–18; defined as customs, 28; Catholic missionary views of, 52–53; defined as art, 59, 90–91; defined as religion, 59–60, 117–22, 162–64, 189–93, 200–201; and tribal sovereignty, 98; as community work, 100; and Pueblo land disputes, 113–14; as part of Catholic religion, 115; defended, 135–36, 141, 145–46, 148–51, 157–64, 165–68, 176, 178–80, 214; fertility symbolism in, 140–42, 159–60; compared to popular dancing, 154–55, 158, 162, 168; newly individualistic norms in, 184, 224, 229–30. *See also* Zuni Pueblo: Shalako ceremony

Pueblo Indians: origins and history, 20–29, 30, 32; Catholic identity of, 25–28, 51–52; romanticized, 68–72, 83–86, 87–89, 90–94, 110–11, 117–28; factional conflicts, 99–102, 131, 204–5, 209, 226–30; and health care, 222, 235; and intertribal ceremonials, 244. *See also* Acoma Pueblo; Catholicism; Cochiti Pueblo; Isleta Pueblo; Jemez Pueblo; Laguna Pueblo; Pueblo ceremonies; Pueblo leaders; Pueblo progressives; San Ildefonso Pueblo; San Juan Pueblo; Santa Ana Pueblo; Santa Clara Pueblo; Santo Domingo Pueblo; Taos Pueblo; Tribal sovereignty; Zia Pueblo; Zuni Pueblo

Pueblo land disputes, 95–97, 102, 105–6, 111–17, 128–33; and Pueblo traditions, 98–102, 113–17; and dance controversy, 147, 148, 205–6

Pueblo Lands Act, 128–29, 133, 147

Pueblo Lands Board, 205–6

Pueblo leaders: and cultural change, 9–10, 220–21; respond to dance circular, 145–47; define traditions as religion, 185–87, 189–91, 206–7, 230–31; and ceremonial participation, 199–201, 224; defend traditional governance, 226–30; criticize Pueblo progressives, 205–7; apply religious freedom to sovereignty, 233–34. *See also* Abeita, Pablo; Council of all the New Mexico Pueblos; Ortiz, Sotero; Pueblo progressives; Romero, Antonio; Vigil, Martin

Pueblo progressives, 9–10, 99; and religious freedom, 6, 183, 195–99, 202, 215, 223; praised by assimilationists, 46–47, 209, 215, 219–20; and ceremonial participation, 100, 201–2, 204–5; and dance circular, 164–65; criticize modernists, 202–3; refute allegations of immorality, 203–4; and tribal governance, 226–30; and individual rights, 234–35. *See also* Abeita, Pablo; Assimilationist reformers: allied with Pueblo progressives; Council of Pro-

gressive Pueblo Indians; Dixon, John; Hunt, Edward; Mondragon, Manuel; Montoya, Joseph; Santa Clara Pueblo: factional conflicts

Pueblo traditions: compared to Quakers, 69, 118; compared to medieval Europe, 119; compared to ancient Greece, 119–20; debates on survival of, 122–28; compared to Christianity, 192–93; defined as custom, 207; religion separated from politics and health care in, 233–36, 248–49. *See also* Pueblo ceremonies; Tradition, adaptations of

Quakers, 31, 69, 118

Racism, 8, 46, 60, 74, 124–25

Red Power movement, 244

Religion, concept of: provides constitutional protection, 4; and indigenous traditions, 5, 6, 57–58, 101, 207, 230–31, 237–38, 264–65; as individual conscience, 6, 101, 210, 229–30, 245; separated from politics and health care, 6, 233–36, 248–49; history, 11–12; and modernity, 12–13; in academy, 13–14; redefined by non-westerners, 14–15; seen as primitive artifact, 74–79; origins of, theorized, 160–61; as commodity, 245; and repatriation debates, 246–52; legal formulations of, 253–57, 261; reinterpreted by Indians, 265–66. *See also* Pueblo ceremonies: defined as religion; World religions

Religious Crimes Code of 1883, 39, 43, 143

Religious freedom: as ongoing struggle, xiii, 232, 237; claimed by Pueblos, 6, 147–48, 190–91; promised by BIA, 47–48; and tribal governance, 100–101, 224–30, 233–34; applied to Pueblo ceremonies, 120, 149–51, 160, 185–90, 195–99, 224, 232–33; seen as inapplicable to Pueblo dances, 153–54; and Pueblo progressives, 183; as individual right, 208–11; favors New Age religion, 246, 261–62; in repatriation cases, 247–52; in sacred land disputes, 253–57. *See also* First Amendment

Religious Freedom Restoration Act, 242

Renehan, A. B., 131, 147, 188, 198–99, 202, 205, 212

Repatriation debates, 246–52

Romero, Antonio (Taos Pueblo), 187, 190, 200

Roosevelt, Franklin Delano, 5, 105

Roosevelt, Theodore, 253

Sacred, concept of, xiv, 249

Sacred land: history and significance of, 252–53; in courts, 253–64; and National Historic Preservation Act, 257–61. *See also* New Age movement; Pueblo land disputes; Taos Pueblo: Blue Lake

Safford, C. V. (BIA inspector), 186–87, 199

St. Catherine's Indian School, 50, 54, 114, 197

Salvage ethnography, 42

Sandoval case (*United States v. Sandoval*, 1913), 97, 102, 129

San Ildefonso Pueblo, 114, 131, 146, 173; Corn dance, 23 (ill.); Deer dance, 26 (ill.)

San Juan Pueblo, 97. *See also* Montoya, Joseph; Ortiz, Sotero

Santa Ana Pueblo, 196–97, 199–201

Santa Clara Pueblo, 46–47, 97, 138–39; factional conflicts, 131, 204–5, 209, 226–30; tribal council, 227 (ill.)

Santa Fe Indian School, 100, 126–27, 243–44

Santo Domingo Pueblo, 54, 141, 221–22

Schools, Indian: Catholic, 29, 48–52, 54, 55–57; and Protestant-Catholic conflicts, 33, 48–51, 55–58; Protestant, 34–35; and U.S. civilizing efforts, 34–35, 38, 44–45, 57, 65–67, 95, 99; enforced enrollment in, 44, 66–67, 69, 188–89. *See also* Albuquerque Indian School; Carlisle Indian School; St. Catherine's Indian School; Santa Fe Indian School

Schuster, Fridolin: on Pueblo ceremonies, 52–53, 137; and Protestants, 56, 144; and

Pueblo land disputes, 105–6, 112, 129; and dance circular, 147, 151–52; and Pueblo progressives, 202, 212–13

Secrecy. *See* Pueblo ceremonies: secrecy in

Secret dance file, 152–53

Secularism: cultural bias of, 15, 175, 185; and anthropological theory, 62–64, 74–79; among artists and writers, 70, 89–90, 123

Secularization: defined, 15; of Indian affairs, 57–58, 184–85, 231–36

Sergeant, Elizabeth Shepley, 125–26, 161, 170–71

Sexual mores: in American culture, 136, 141, 142–43, 154–55, 168, 174–75; among Pueblos, as viewed by reformers, 176, 178–79

Sexual symbolism: in Hopi and Pueblo ceremonies, 135, 140–41; praised by modernists, 159–61, 178–79; theorized as origins of religion, 160

Sloan, John, 61, 89, 92

Sniffen, Matthew, 154 (ill.); on Pueblo progressives, 46–47, 208–10, 212–13, 219, 224; allegations of, against Pueblo traditions, 153–55, 194–95, 203, 220; on morality, 155–56; as voice of moderation, 169–70, 171–73; on religious freedom, 171, 202, 208–10, 211; condemns modernists, 222, 223

Social evolutionary theory, 35–36, 41, 62–64, 73–81, 173

Spanish colonial rule, 21–28; land grants, 96–97

Stevenson, Matilda Coxe, 42–43, 55, 60–61, 63–64, 172

Sun dance, 39

Sweet, Evander (BIA inspector), 140–41

Talayesva, Don (Hopi), 141

Taos Pueblo: appeal of, to artists and writers, 1–2, 71, 110; allegations of immorality at, 2, 194; and Blue Lake, 2–3, 253; and peyote, 139–40, 239–40; initiation ceremonies at, 187–88, 200, 223; and religious freedom, 187–90, 223–26. *See also* Lujan, Tony; Mondragon, Manuel; Romero, Antonio

Tesuque Pueblo, 114, 168; Eagle dance, 116
(ill.). See also Vigil, Martin
Tradition, adaptations of, 10, 238. See also
Pueblo traditions
Treaty of Guadalupe Hidalgo, 30, 96, 190
Tribal governance, separated from religion,
233–36. See also Tribal sovereignty
Tribal initiations: at Taos Pueblo, 3, 187–88,
200, 223; at Zuni Pueblo, 191
Tribal sovereignty: and religious freedom, 6–7,
100–101, 224–31; restricted by BIA, 95,
98–99; threatened by legislation and
reform, 113–14, 127–28, 184, 233–36; and
ceremonial participation, 199–201. See also
Pueblo leaders
True, Clara, 132 (ill.); and Pueblo land disputes, 130–31, 205; and Pueblo progressives, 138–39, 201–2, 208, 209, 212–13,
215–16, 219–20, 228, 231–32; and
women's rights, 177, 215
Twitchell, Ralph E., 102, 105, 114, 147, 197,
208, 212

U.S. Indian policy: secularization of, 4–5, 184–
85, 193, 231, 232–36; on Indian ceremonies, 7, 39–40, 137–40, 143–45, 170–
71, 193; nineteenth-century, 7–8, 19–20,
30–32, 34–40, 43–47, 50, 55–58;
twentieth-century, 20, 95, 96–98, 102, 114,
128–29, 133, 168–70, 184, 220, 230–36.
See also Bureau of Indian Affairs
United States v. Sandoval. See Sandoval case

Vigil, Martin (Tesuque Pueblo), 114–15, 115
(ill.)

Walker, Roberts, 123–24, 129, 147, 160, 162,
165–67, 194, 235, 259–61
Weber, Anselm, 37, 53, 55
Welsh, Herbert: biography and concerns of, 36,
37 (ill.), 38, 46–47, 49, 155–56; condemns
Pueblo ceremonies, 174, 177, 218–19; on
religious freedom for Pueblo progressives,
208–10, 231–32. See also Indian Rights
Association
Wilson, Francis, 125, 128–29, 131, 194
Women's rights: as argument against Indian
dances, 2, 44–45, 135–36, 175–78, 213, 215,
217, 219; and modernist feminists, 77–79,
136; in defense of Pueblo ceremonies, 178–
79, 180
Work, Hubert (secretary of the interior), 150,
156, 168–69, 173, 189, 191
World religions, 11–12, 167
Wovoka. See Ghost Dance
Writers. See Artists and writers
Wyaco, Virgil (Zuni Pueblo), 19, 141

Zia Pueblo, 146
Zuni Pueblo: Shalako ceremony, 17, 18 (ill.),
19, 185–86; traditions defined as distinct
religion, 19, 54–55; under Spanish rule,
20–21, 27; Catholic and Protestant missions to, 27, 32, 34–35, 44–45, 54–55, 186;
and anthropologists, 41–43, 63–64, 65, 76,
81, 141, 172, 178, 180, 186–87, 218; allegations of immorality at, 44–45, 135, 168,
175–76; and ceremonial clowning, 141; factional conflicts, 185–87; and religious freedom, 191–92; and repatriation of cultural
artifacts, 247, 248–49